THE   HEGEL   MYTHS   AND   LEGENDS

Northwestern University
Studies in Phenomenology
and
Existential Philosophy

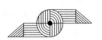

THE
HEGEL
MYTHS AND
LEGENDS

Edited by Jon Stewart

Northwestern University Press
Evanston, Illinois

Northwestern University Press
625 Colfax Street
Evanston, Illinois 60208-4210

Library of Congress Cataloging-in-Publication Data

The Hegel myths and legends / edited by Jon Stewart.
     p.   cm.—(Northwestern University studies in phenomenology
and existential philosophy)
   Includes bibliographical references.
   ISBN 0-8101-1300-7 (hard).—ISBN 0-8101-1301-5 (pbk.)
   1. Hegel, Georg Wilhelm Friedrich, 1770–1831.   I. Stewart, Jon
Bartley. II. Series: Northwestern University studies in
phenomenology & existential.
B2948.H335   1996
193—dc20   95-53189
                                                                      CIP

Contents

Acknowledgments

This collection would not have been able to be realized if it were not for the help and cooperation of a number of individuals and institutions. I would like to thank the following journals and publishing houses for their generosity in granting the reprint rights for the essays included here: *Bulletin de l'Academie Royale de Belgique*, *Bulletin of the Hegel Society of Great Britain*, Cambridge University Press, *History of Political Thought*, Humanities Press International, *International Studies in Philosophy*, *Iyyun*, *Journal of the History of Ideas*, *Journal of the History of Philosophy*, Karl Alber Verlag, *Mind*, *The Owl of Minerva*, *Philosophical Review*, *Philosophisches Jahrbuch*, *Philosophy*, *Review of Metaphysics*, *Review of Politics*, *Revue Philosophique de Louvain*, The Royal Institute of Philosophy, Vittorio Klostermann Verlag, and *Zeitschrift für Politik*.

The present anthology would likewise not have been possible, were it not for the invaluable assistance of several individuals. I would like to thank Greg Bucher for his help in locating some of the materials necessary for this collection. I am also deeply indebted to Louie Matz and Loy Stewart for their helpful corrections and suggestions on early drafts of the introduction and translations. In addition, I would like to express my sincerest gratitude to Dr. Jürgen-Gerhard Blühdorn and Professor Robert B. Pippin for their encouragement and support of the project from its earliest stages. Finally, I am grateful to the contributors for their willing participation and assistance with the various aspects of this collection.

The essays from Franz Grégoire ("Is the Hegelian State Totalitarian?" and "A Semi-Legend: The 'Divinity' of the State in Hegel") and the contributions of Reinhart Klemens Maurer ("Hegel and the End of History") and Henning Ottmann ("Hegel and Political Trends: A Criticism of the Political Hegel Legends") were translated from their respective French and German texts by the editor of the present collection. The translations were done when possible in consultation with the original author. The citations of Hegel which appear in these texts either in the original German or in the French translation, I have, unless otherwise noted, translated myself instead of relying on the standard English translations of Hegel's works. Quotations from secondary literature in languages other than English have also been translated.

The original sources for the essays included here are as follows:

M. W. Jackson, "Hegel, the Real and the Rational," *International Studies in Philosophy* 19 (1987), 11–19.

Yirmiahu Yovel, "Hegel's Dictum that the Rational is Actual and the Actual is Rational," in *Konzepte der Dialektik*, ed. Werner Becker and Wilhelm K. Essler (Frankfurt: Vittorio Klostermann, 1981), 111–27. Original, unabridged version, "Hegel on Reason, Actuality, and Philosophical Discourse," *Iyyun* 26 (1975), 59–115.

Emil L. Fackenheim, "On the Actuality of the Rational and the Rationality of the Actual," *Review of Metaphysics* 89 (1969), 690–98. © 1985 by Emil L. Fackenheim.

Henning Ottmann, "Hegel und die Politik: Zur Kritik der politischen Hegellegenden," *Zeitschrift für Politik* 26 (1979), 235–53.

T. M. Knox, "Hegel and Prussianism," *Philosophy* 15 (1940), 51–63. Reprinted by permission of The Royal Institute of Philosophy and Cambridge University Press.

Walter A. Kaufmann, "The Hegel Myth and its Method," *Philosophical Review* 60 (1951), 459–86.

Franz Grégoire, "L'État hégélien est-t-il totalitaire?" *Revue Philosophique de Louvain* 60 (1962), 244–53.

Shlomo Avineri, "Hegel and Nationalism," *Review of Politics* 24 (1962), 461–84. Also in *Hegel's Political Philosophy*, ed. Walter Kaufmann (New York: Atherton Press, 1970), 109–36.

Shlomo Avineri, "The Problem of War in Hegel's Thought," *Journal of the History of Ideas* 2 (1961), 463–74.

D. P. Verene, "Hegel's Account of War," in *Hegel's Political Philosophy: Problems and Perspectives*, ed. Z. A. Pelcynski (Cambridge: Cambridge University Press, 1971), 168–80. Reprinted by permission of Cambridge University Press.

Errol E. Harris, "Hegel's Theory of Sovereignty, International Relations, and War," in *Hegel's Social and Political Thought*, ed. Donald Phillip Verene (Atlantic Highlands: Humanities Press, 1980), 137–150.

Steven Walt, "Hegel on War: Another Look," *History of Political Thought* 10 (1989), 113–24.

Philip T. Grier, "The End of History and the Return of History," *The Owl of Minerva* 21 (1990), 131–44.

Reinhart Klemens Maurer, "Teleologische Aspekte der Hegelschen Philosophie," in his *Hegel und das Ende der Geschichte*, 2d ed. (Freiburg: Karl Alber, 1980), 173–207. Earlier version, "Endgeschichtliche Aspekte der Hegelschen Philosophie," *Philosophisches Jahrbuch* 76 (1968), 88–122.

Abridged French version, "Hegel et la fin de l'histoire," *Archives de Philosophie* 30 (1967), 483–518.

H. S. Harris, "The End of History in Hegel," *Bulletin of the Hegel Society of Great Britain* 23–24 (1991), 1–14.

Robert Pippin, "Hegel's Metaphysics and the Problem of Contradiction," *Journal of the History of Philosophy* 16 (1978), 301–12.

Robert Hanna, "From an Ontological Point of View: Hegel's Critique of the Common Logic," *Review of Metaphysics* 40 (1986), 305–38.

Bertrand Beaumont, "Hegel and the Seven Planets," *Mind* 63 (1954), 246–48. Reprinted by permission of Oxford University Press.

Franz Grégoire, "Une semi-légende. La divinité de l'État chez Hegel," *Bulletin de L'Academie Royale de Belgique* 41 (1955), 315–29.

Gustav Mueller, "The Hegel Legend of 'Thesis-Antithesis-Synthesis,' " *Journal of the History of Ideas* 19 (1958), 411–14.

Jon Stewart, "Hegel and the Myth of Reason," *The Owl of Minerva* 26 (1995), 187–200.

Introduction

Jon Stewart

When one looks up the entry for "Hegel" in a standard reference work, it is not unlikely that one will find something like the following characterization: "the triadic process from thesis through antithesis to synthesis . . . proves to be essential to Hegel's philosophy."[1] Likewise, we are told not infrequently by such reference works or introductory texts that, according to Hegel, "in history everything happens according to reason."[2] These formulas are often reinforced in introductory classes where the usual time constraints and the level of difficulty of Hegel's texts make it all but impossible to treat his thought carefully or responsibly. The result is that a handful of key concepts or slogans have come to be associated with Hegel and his philosophy in a way that, for instance, the famous phrase "I think, therefore I am" has come to be seen as representative of the spirit of the entirety of Descartes's thought.

This sort of sloganizing is not necessarily pernicious in itself. Such phrases or catchwords can be found for virtually every famous philosopher, and it may even be argued that they serve some sort of rudimentary pedagogical function. However, in Hegel's case the slogans or anecdotes are much more plentiful and usually much more malicious than in the case of other philosophers. Indeed, the reputation of no other major philosopher has suffered such universal opprobrium on such a broad spectrum of issues as Hegel's has. For instance, with respect to Hegel's political philosophy, the following view is far from atypical in nonspecialized reference works: "By taking the Prussian State of the Restoration period, in which he lived, as the model for his rational analysis, he seemed more

1

and more inclined to idealize the Prussian monarchy. What he said of the state in general, as a manifestation of the divine will, seemed to apply to this particular state."[3] Negative misconceptions such as this serve only to prejudice the student toward Hegel's philosophy before he or she has ever embarked on a serious study of it. Even arguably neutral or benign slogans such as the thesis-antithesis-synthesis triad have an adverse effect on the proper understanding of Hegel's ideas. These slogans have developed into what specialists have called the "Hegel myths" or "legends." Under these headings fall the various misconceptions or misrepresentations, popular or otherwise, concerning Hegel's philosophy.

The problem represented by these misconceptions is made more acute by the extremely difficult nature of Hegel's own texts. His complex philosophical system, couched in a stilted, abstract, and idiosyncratic language, has certainly been one of the major causes for the disparity of opinion. Where some see profundity and originality in the obscurity, others see simply gibberish and nonsense. The result of Hegel's opaque writing style and neologistic vocabulary is that his works remain largely inaccessible to the nonspecialist. Consequently, the primary text is rarely consulted in order to confirm or refute the legitimacy of a given legend, and when the text is consulted, it does not seem in all cases to yield an unambiguous response. Hence, the myths live on and regenerate themselves in the absence of an accessible standard of adjudication.

The cleft between the popular understanding of Hegel's philosophy, prejudiced as it often is by the various myths and legends, and the professional philosopher's specialized understanding creates a difficult situation in the classroom. Students come to Hegel, as to few other philosophers, full of misconceptions and prejudices. The Hegel instructor, on the other hand, invariably has his or her own pedagogical agenda to execute in accordance with the goals of the class at hand. The problem is that the sort of student questions that issue from the various myths tend to depart from the goals and subject matter of most courses. The present collection aims at, among other things, ameliorating difficulties of this kind. It seeks to serve primarily the negative function of disabusing the student and general reader of these various Hegel myths in a way that will clear the ground for a serious study of his philosophy. It also seeks to make the unwary attentive to the trouble spots in Hegel's texts that still constitute points of contention among Hegel experts. Thus, the objective of this anthology is not merely to set the historical record straight and to clear Hegel's name of unjust charges, but also to be an aid to the already difficult task of teaching Hegel.

In an extremely useful essay on Hegel pedagogy, Robert Solomon suggests that one begin a course on Hegel by purging the students of whatever misconceptions they might have heard about him and his philosophy.[4] This is also the strategy of a number of books on Hegel which dedicate an introduction or first chapter to just this task.[5] This job of disabusing the student of the general prejudices toward Hegel can be accomplished effectively with the present collection. Simply cataloging the various Hegel myths for students and telling them that they are nothing more than myths will do little to change the rooted misconceptions at hand. However, in the essays collected here, in addition to accurate expositions of Hegel's own thought, the student will find detailed accounts of the origin and development of these misconceptions. Once their beginnings have been laid bare, the various myths immediately lose their credibility. These essays provide historical accounts of the reception of Hegel's philosophy and of the proliferation of the various misnomers. It is hoped that the essays will serve as useful pedagogical tools and will save the instructor a number of unfortunate detours in the classroom.

As is evinced by the contents of this collection, modern scholars of German idealism, in contrast to the popular understanding, have achieved an unusual measure of consensus with respect to most of these familiar misconstruals of Hegel's work. Those who have made a study of Hegel their specialization have unanimously rejected the various Hegel myths such that they have, in most cases, ceased to be points of genuine academic debate. Most of these exotic beliefs, referred to by Croce as "half comical and half disgusting,"[6] have no reasonable basis whatsoever in Hegel's texts themselves. Although there are a number of egregious Hegel myths to which no respectable scholar would give credence, there are other misconceptions that gradually shade over into the realm of legitimate dispute. For instance, in the area of Hegel's political philosophy and his views on war, there are still live interpretive issues surrounding significant Hegel legends. The goal of the present collection is twofold: first, to expose and correct the most flagrant of the Hegel myths once and for all; and second, when the issue is less clear, to separate the mythical version from the sphere of justifiable disagreement in the realm of legitimate Hegel interpretation.

The Problematic Reception of Hegel's Philosophy

Hegel's philosophy has been the source bitter debate ever since its inception. In his own time, Hegel had already become such a controversial figure that his reputation reached both extremes of the spectrum. On the one hand, he was deeply revered by his students and considered the genius of his day by many. He was, for example, hailed as "the modern Aristotle"[7] by his British admirer J. H. Stirling. On the other hand, he was openly ridiculed as a sophist and a charlatan by some of his rivals and colleagues, such as Schopenhauer and the later Schelling. Since those days, Hegel has firmly established himself as one of the most important figures in the history of European letters. His philosophy, which marks the crossroads in the modern intellectual tradition, has given birth to virtually all of the major schools of contemporary thought: phenomenology, existentialism, Marxism, critical theory, structuralism, pragmatism, hermeneutics, and so on. However, until very recently his influence has been limited almost exclusively to circles of continental philosophy. One reason for this has been the various myths and legends surrounding his philosophy that still continue to enjoy wide currency above all in the English-speaking world. In order to understand the development and proliferation of these misconceptions, we must take a brief look at the historical reception of Hegel's philosophy.

There is a surprisingly long tradition of Hegelianism in the United States[8] that began with two main centers in St. Louis[9] and Cincinnati.[10] The most important members of the St. Louis school included Henry Conrad Brokmeyer (1826–1906) and William Torrey Harris (1835–1909). The latter was the editor of the celebrated *Journal of Speculative Philosophy*, which served as the principal organ for the dissemination of classical Greek and German philosophy in America at the time. The Cincinnati group, which included August Willich (1810–78), John Bernard Stallo (1823–1900), and Mocure D. Conway (1832–1907), represented the Hegelian left on the American continent. This alignment can be seen, for instance, in the socialist political views of Willich, or in the unorthodox religious convictions of Conway. This American tradition of Hegelianism, although significant for many aspects of Hegel studies and American cultural life, was, however, less important for the development of the Hegel myths and legends in the English-speaking world than was the history of Hegel research in Great Britain.

The reception of Hegel in British philosophy has been particularly complicated and problematic, since it was there that Hegel found some of his most fervent allies as well as his most hostile critics. The first important expositors of Hegelian philosophy in Great Britain were T. H. Green (1836–82) and Edward Caird (1835–1908). Green employed idealist arguments against some of the classics of British philosophy, such as the empiricism of Locke and Hume. His main work, the *Prolegomena to Ethics*,[11] was left unfinished at his death. By contrast, Edward Caird, a more systematic thinker and dynamic expositor than his longtime friend Green, produced a vast philosophical corpus in his lifetime. His early writings include *A Critical Account of the Philosophy of Kant*[12] and *Hegel*.[13] His other two significant works, *The Evolution of Religion*[14] and *The Evolution of Theology in the Greek Philosophers*,[15] strongly reflect Hegelian methodology in their attempt to trace the conceptual movement of theological ideas through their manifold historical forms. He, like Hegel, sought to unite long-standing pairs of opposites from the philosophical tradition, such as freedom and necessity, subject and object, and reason and passion.

The second generation of Hegel scholars in Great Britain was constituted by, among others, F. H. Bradley (1846–1924) and Bernard Bosanquet (1848–1923). Bradley's influential investigation, *Ethical Studies*,[16] shows the marked influence of Hegel's moral theory. In that work he examines different aspects of Hegel's conception of *Sittlichkeit* or ethical life. He then uses this account of the situatedness of moral principles in historical communities to criticize the abstract individualism of utilitarianism and classical liberalism. On the other hand, Bosanquet's influential essay, "Logic as the Science of Knowledge" (1883), betrays the influence of Hegel's logical and metaphysical theory. There Bosanquet criticizes the hard distinction between judgment and inference as well as between deduction and induction. In addition, he tries in a Hegelian spirit to show the systematic unity of various logical propositions. From this generation of Hegel scholars came the teachers of the eventual founders of analytic philosophy such as Russell, Moore, and others.

J. M. E. McTaggart (1866–1925) developed, along Hegelian lines, his own theory of idealism, which served as a ready target for the incipient analytic philosophy. After his early exegetical works on Hegel, such as *Studies in the Hegelian Dialectic* (1896), *Studies in Hegelian Cosmology* (1901), and *A Commentary on Hegel's Logic* (1911), McTaggart applied Hegelian methodology to construct his own philosophical system in his magnum opus, *The Nature of Existence* (vol. 1, 1921; vol. 2, 1927).[17] There he developed a theory of ultimate spiritual reality, which he conceived as a reified aggregate of individual minds. McTaggart's extravagant metaphysical form of Hegelianism made him a preferred object of criticism of the early analytic philosophers, and it was his view that for many came to be synonymous with that of Hegel himself.

The birth of logical positivism and British analytic philosophy at the turn of the century has been analyzed largely by intellectual historians as a result of a rejection of the generation of British Hegel scholars, which included Bradley and McTaggart, in favor of a more "rigorous" philosophical method favoring analysis and more in line with mathematics or linguistics.[18] Both Russell and Moore were convinced idealists in their early years, and this conviction of youth, as often happens, became the target of the most impassioned criticism in maturity. This intellectual transition is marked by the publication of Moore's essay "Refutation of Idealism" in 1903. As analytic philosophy grew and came into its own, distinctions hardened between, on the one hand, the various schools of continental philosophy, which traced their origins back to Hegel, and, on the other hand, the new analytic philosophy, which rejected Hegel and his followers categorically.

In addition to reasons of philosophical import such as these, there were later a number of historical, and perhaps less rational, reasons involved in the rejection of Hegelian philosophy in England and America. During the World Wars, Hegel's popularity, like that of many German thinkers, was at low ebb in the English-speaking world. First in L. T. Hobhouse's antipathetic *The Metaphysical Theory of the State*,[19] Hegel's "wicked doctrine" was made responsible for the ills of the First World War. Later, Karl Popper picked up where Hobhouse left off and performed the same function of saddling Hegel with the atrocities of World War II. He galvanized the already negative sentiment against Hegel and spread it beyond all previous dimensions with his well-known book *The Open Society and Its Enemies*.[20] In the second tome of that work, Popper, in a rather untempered tone, argues that Hegel's political philosophy amounts to nothing less than a straightforward totalitarianism that has certain affinities with Nazi Germany. Thus, Hegel, like Nietzsche, suffered the fate of being branded as a forerunner of German national socialism, and this unfortunate association had a profound impact at the particular historical moment. This justly criticized reading was, despite its scholarly shortcomings, taken up uncritically by a number of scholars on both sides of the Atlantic.

The freeze between analytic and Continental philosophy gradually began to thaw, thanks largely but unintentionally to the work of P. F. Strawson. With his book, *The Bounds of Sense*,[21] he rendered the service of making a small part of European philosophy reputable in the English-speaking world. In this book, Strawson analyzed Kant's classic, the *Critique of Pure Reason*, and showed how Kant was in fact engaged in a number of epistemological issues that were relevant to the research program of the analytic philosophy of the day. Since Strawson himself had already established a solid reputation in the analytic camp, his name helped to propel Kant's work into the mainstream discussion of the analytic tradition. Kant became a philosophically legitimate topic in America and England, and a second, independent body of Kant research in English came into being alongside the already existing body of German literature. While Kant enjoyed this comeback of sorts in circles of analytic philosophy, Hegel remained in the shadows. No established analytic philosopher wrote on his philosophy or tried to bring him into the analytic fold. During this time the prejudices against him continued to grow, and he was rarely represented in the classroom or in the professional journals.

Although Hegel's reputation has suffered most markedly in the English-speaking world, nevertheless, his work, with respect to some issues, has hardly received a fairer hearing on the continent itself. In Germany, the publication of Rudolf Haym's *Hegel und seine Zeit* in 1827 was perhaps the most important event in the reception of Hegel's philosophy for several years afterwards. Haym, a virulent critic of Hegel, inveighed primarily against the philosopher's political theory and philosophy of history, arguing that Hegel had written his theory of the state in order to justify and legitimate the oppressive Prussian political order of his day.[22] According to Haym, Hegel's claim that the actual was the rational amounted to no less than a straightforward apologia for the reactionary Prussian status quo.[23] On this view, Hegel, enjoying a distinguished and comfortable professorship in Berlin after an arduous career with humble beginnings, simply sacrificed his philosophical integrity and placed his intellectual abilities in the service of the Prussian authorities during the ticklish period of political agitation that followed the Congress of Vienna. Although Haym's thesis has been often and decidedly refuted by more exacting philosophical and historical analyses, nevertheless the view of Hegel as the official philosopher of the Prussian state enjoyed a wide following in Germany before it became famous in the English-speaking world. The view that Hegel was a political reactionary continues to this day to find adherents in the German academic world.[24]

After Haym's work, Schelling's Berlin lectures in the 1840s must be seen as one of the most decisive negative influences on the reception of Hegel's philosophy in Germany. Although Hegel and Schelling were friends of youth, boarding together as theology students at Tübingen and later collaborating on the *Critical Journal of Philosophy* as colleagues in Jena, with time they gradually became estranged, and their mutual criticisms became less and less veiled. In 1841, ten years after Hegel's death, Schelling, the one time child-prodigy who had witnessed his own influence decisively wane as that of Hegel waxed, received a distinguished professorship in Berlin. In his Berlin lectures, which were attended by, among others, Marx and Kierkegaard, Schelling mercilessly criticized and caricatured various aspects of Hegel's thought. Many Hegel myths that originated in Schelling's bitterness quickly spread through the influence of his famous pupils. As one writer puts it, "Through Kierkegaard legions of twentieth-century readers who barely know Schelling's name have come to take for granted as historically accurate his spiteful caricature of Hegel."[25]

In France the lectures at the Sorbonne in the 1930s delivered by the Russian emigré Alexandre Kojève represent without a doubt the key event in French Hegel studies.[26] Kojève's provocative, yet at times fully misguided, interpretation was the main source of information about Hegel's philosophy for the entire postwar generation of French intellectuals. The key figures of French phenomenology, existentialism, and Marxism, such as Raymond Aron, Maurice Merleau-Ponty, Georges Bataille, and Jacques Lacan,[27] were all present at Kojève's lectures and later developed the interpretation of Hegel that they received there in various directions in accordance with their own research programs. These lectures, which were subsequently collected and published by Raymond Queneau in 1947,[28] remained influential for future generations of French scholars long after Kojève's death. The interpretation offered by Kojève was not hostile to Hegel in the way Haym, Schopenhauer, and the later Schelling were, but it was rather idiosyncratic and contained a philosophical agenda foreign to Hegel's own. Kojève's reading focused almost entirely on the *Phenomenology* and on the "Lordship-Bondage" dialectic found there, thus doing much to render famous both this text and this chapter. Kojève seems to have borrowed heavily from the work of his fellow émigré, Alexandre Koyré, primarily with respect to the latter's emphasis on Hegel's purported claims about the end of history.[29] These claims found clear affinities in the teleology of Marxist theory, where Kojève was most at home. The view that Hegel saw the end of history in his own time or with his own philosophical system has had its most widespread acceptance in France due to the influence of these two men. Although in the literature these problematic views have long since been corrected and revised by more thorough French Hegel scholars such as Hyppolite[30] and Labarriére,[31] nonetheless in the popular mind they are still quite pervasive.

The Hegel Myths and Legends

As a result of some of the historical factors and influential caricatures and misinterpretations I have discussed, a number of the so-called myths or legends about Hegel's philosophy arose and found fertile ground to take root and flourish. In the course of time, these have developed into a sort of common lore among students and nonspecialists. I cannot here pretend to be able to recount exhaustively all of the regrettable misconceptions that have plagued the reception of Hegel's philosophy; however, in what follows, by way of introducing the essays included in this collection, I catalog the caricatures of Hegel and his philosophy that have been most widespread.

The Myth of the Rational and the Actual

It is often maintained that Hegel, carrying on in the spirit of Leibniz, was the ultimate optimist or a sort of German Candide, believing that everything that exists is good. This myth is usually traced back to Hegel's claim in the preface to the *Philosophy of Right* and in the Introduction to the *Encyclopedia* that the rational is the actual and the actual the rational. This disputed phrase, which was controversial even in Hegel's own time, overlaps with a number of other Hegel legends, in particular in the area of his political philosophy. The problematic passage concerning the actual and the rational is directly addressed and interpreted by three different commentators in the present collection.

First, M. J. Jackson's article, while providing an extremely useful overview of the literature and the various positions taken with respect to this issue, offers an interpretation and defense of Hegel's statement in its political context. Jackson aims at refuting above all the erroneous interpretations offered by Popper and others in the Anglo-American philosophical tradition. His essay thus serves as a useful and accessible introduction to this issue and foreshadows the next section of this collection, which is dedicated to the major myths and legends concerning Hegel's political philosophy.

Yirmiahu Yovel, the author of a number of works on Kant and Hegel,[32] interprets Hegel's idiom in an ontological fashion. Yovel, insisting on Hegel's own hierarchy, which places philosophical knowing above religious knowing, tries to make sense of the disputed dictum by means of an interpretation of the meaning of the categories from Hegel's *Logic*, such as *Sein, Dasein, Existenz, Wirklichkeit*, and so on. This article nicely complements the final contribution to this section by Emil Fackenheim, in that it represents a working out of what might be called a secular version of some of Fackenheim's conclusions.

Fackenheim, the author of the influential study *The Religious Dimension in Hegel's Thought*,[33] interprets the famous dictum in a religious context. According to his view, the rational becomes the actual, for Hegel, in the course of history with the rise and spread of Christianity. What is still required is the secular philosophical understanding of this world-historical event. Thus, for Fackenheim, the correct interpretation of Hegel's statement is one that grasps both its religious and its philosophical meanings.

The Myth of Hegel as Totalitarian Theorist or Prussian Apologist

Of all the aspects of Hegel's many-sided thought, it is probably his political theory that has drawn the most venomous criticism. His political philosophy, as indicated above, has been reproached for its purported accommodation with the Prussian authorities, for its implicit German or Prussian nationalism, and for its role as a forerunner of modern totalitarianism or fascism. There are a handful of articles included here, each devoted to refuting one or more of the myths concerning Hegel's political philosophy.

The German scholar Henning Ottmann, known for his ambitious interpretive studies on Hegel,[34] traces the history of the reception of Hegel's political philosophy through the ages. He instructively shows how every generation and every new political movement has attempted to portray Hegel as an ally of its particular creed. The result has been the unjustified association of Hegel's name with a number of unsavory political causes, many of which he himself had never heard of. Ottmann's account forms an extremely useful overview of the variety of legends about Hegel's political thought.

As we have seen above, due largely to the influence of Haym's interpretation, Hegel has been seen as the official court philosopher of the Prussian state, who not merely countenanced its reactionary and repressive regime, but served as its philosophical ideologue. T. M. Knox, known for his excellent English translation of the *Philosophy of Right*,[35] addresses the question of Hegel's accommodation with the Prussian authorities, on the one hand, by setting the development of Hegel's political philosophy in its proper historical context and, on the other hand, by carefully analyzing a number of disputed passages in Hegel's text. His essay is intended largely as a response to E. F. Carritt's bitter condemnation of Hegel in *Morals and Politics*.[36] Knox convincingly shows that the rational state that Hegel sketches in the *Philosophy of Right* has little to do with the Prussian political order of the day.

Karl Popper's caustic treatment of Hegel, as was discussed above, has done much to tarnish the philosopher's reputation in the Anglo-American world. The most powerful and sustained response to Popper's Hegel interpretation comes from Walter Kaufmann. Aside from his well-known work on Nietzsche, Kaufmann was also the author of an influential and highly readable book on Hegel.[37] Although that study cannot be compared with more recent work in point of scholarly rigor, it did, however, do much to make Hegel respectable in the Anglo-American world at a time when analytic philosophy was at its zenith. In the essay selected here, Kaufmann directly addresses and conclusively refutes Popper's abusive contribution to the political legends by eloquently exposing Popper's distortions of Hegel's views.

According to one apocryphal view, Hegel's theory of the state amounts to a simple totalitarianism in which individuals are crushed and have no meaning in themselves. Franz Grégoire, the author of *Études hégéliennes,*[38] was an important yet little-known expositor of Hegel's philosophy in the French-speaking world. In his first contribution to this collection, he responds to the claim of the Catholic French philosopher Jacques Maritain that Hegel's state amounts to a totalitarianism that recognizes no intrinsic rights or values in the individual, and whose power is absolute and unlimited. Grégoire responds to the first charge by sketching Hegel's conception of the state as an organism in which the individual and the state stand in a reciprocal relationship, with each term being fundamental and necessary for the whole. The second charge is likewise repudiated when Grégoire reminds us that the authority of the Hegelian state is limited in many aspects due to the fact that it is obliged to recognize the subjective freedoms of its citizens.

Despite an immense body of biographical evidence to the contrary, it has often been claimed that Hegel was a forerunner of German nationalism. This view is, of course, only a short step away from the interpretations that see Hegel either as a Prussian apologist or as a forerunner of Nazi Germany. This legend is addressed by Shlomo Avineri, who has been recognized as the leading authority in the field of Hegel's political philosophy in the English-speaking world ever since the publication of his now standard study, *Hegel's Theory of the Modern State.*[39] His article effectively responds to the myth that Hegel was a nationalist by carefully tracing and exposing the development of this myth from its origin. Together these articles represent the best responses to the central political myths that have surrounded Hegel's philosophy.

The Myth that Hegel Glorified War

One of the more subtle issues relevant to Hegel's political thought involves the philosopher's genuinely ambiguous views on war. Those who would see Hegel as a totalitarian theorist or fascist ideologue claim that his views were fundamentally militaristic and that he glorified war as a human achievement. Although this caricature has been universally rejected, there is still much room for legitimate debate on the interpretive issue of exactly where Hegel stands on the issue of war and international relations. Due to the subtlety of the issue and the seriousness of the charge, a separate section in this collection has been devoted to responding to this question. There is a wide body of literature on this issue, and in this collection four of the best articles have been selected, all of which treat the key passages in the *Philosophy of Right* where Hegel provides a philosophical analysis of the phenomenon of war. The authors carefully demarcate the myth from the realm of credible interpretation, and within the sphere of the latter a handful of different views are put forth and argued for.

Avineri's lucid contribution to this issue nicely complements his first essay in the collection. Here he develops further his interpretation of the Hegelian state, arguing that it is in its basic principles consistent with liberal democracy. His conclusion with respect to the issue at hand is that Hegel's views on war cannot be rightfully construed as militaristic or as providing an ideological support for an expansionist or imperialist foreign policy. In fact, since Hegel is concerned with the concept of war itself and not with any particular war, his views cannot be justly called into the service of particular political causes such as nationalism. Avineri shows how Hegel, in contrast to many of his contemporaries, rejected the distinction between just and unjust wars, and thus eliminated the very concept of the former.

D. P. Verene, known for among other things his investigation on the *Phenomenology*[40] and his collection on Hegel's political theory,[41] claims that one must go beyond an account of Hegel's political philosophy to Hegel's overall system and general methodology in order to make sense of the philosopher's statements on war, which when taken on their own prove to be inconclusive. He tries to avoid traditional lines of interpretation and their concomitant polemics by understanding Hegel's methodology as taking up a third way, avoiding both a merely prescriptive and a merely descriptive account of war.

In his remarkably concise and straightforward essay, Errol E. Harris traces Hegel's views on war back to the account of the sovereignty of states that Hegel gives in the *Philosophy of Right*. Harris's analysis begins by convincingly refuting Popper's acrimonious interpretation, according to which Hegel identified national sovereignty with the person of the monarch and thus advocated a simple despotism. He goes on to show how Hegel's view of the sovereignty of states leads to a sober view of international relations and war. Far from glorifying war, Hegel, on Harris's view, gave a disabused philosophical account of it which, far from being outmoded, still in large measure accurately mirrors many of the unfortunate political realities of our day.

The characteristic feature of Steven Walt's account of Hegel's treatment of war is its attempt to carve out a middle position between, on the one hand, expressly negative views such as Popper's, according to which war is for Hegel a good in itself, and, on the other hand, what he sees as unqualified positive views such as Avineri's that claim that Hegel in fact condemned war. Walt argues that, although never glorifying or exalting war as Popper asserts, Hegel does nevertheless see it as something that is necessary and that follows directly from his account of the relation of individuals to the state and from his views of the sovereignty of individual states.

The Myth of the End of History

Due to the influence of Kojève and Koyré, there is, particularly in French Hegel studies, a widespread belief that Hegel believed that time would stop and history would come to an end, or that he saw the end of history in his own philosophical system. A further contributing factor to this Hegel legend was a quip by Nietzsche to the effect that Hegel, in a bout of vanity, thought that history reached its end point at the moment when he obtained the long desired professorship in Berlin.[42] Recently, Fukuyama's surprisingly popular new book has brought this Hegel myth once again into the public eye, by attempting to defend Hegel's claim about the end of history in light of the political revolutions in Europe of 1989 and what he sees as the attainment of perfection of the liberal democratic state.[43] In the present collection, the end of history myth is addressed by three different articles from established Hegel scholars.

Philip T. Grier's contribution addresses the popular misconceptions of the end of history that were disseminated recently by Fukuyama's work. He shows how Fukuyama uncritically takes the idiosyncratic interpretation offered by Kojève as an accurate account of Hegel's views on history. In his refutation of Fukuyama, Grier provides us with an excellent overview of this tradition of Hegel *mis*interpretation that begins with Koyré and Kojève.

The distinguished German Hegel scholar Reinhart Klemens Maurer has dedicated much of his philosophical career to just this issue. The thorough essay included here is perhaps the most concise statement of Maurer's conclusions, which receive their full treatment in his book *Hegel und das Ende der Geschichte*.[44] In his essay, Maurer carefully isolates the various meanings of the concept "the end of history" that have been in circulation, and then attempts to determine whether any of these meanings can be correctly ascribed to Hegel.

Finally, the well-known Hegel scholar H. S. Harris, celebrated for his rigorous and detailed studies of Hegel's philosophy leading up to the *Phenomenology*,[45] offers another perspective on this issue. Harris begins by showing that much of Hegel's philosophy of history can be seen as a development of Kant's notion of universal history. By putting Hegel's conception of the end of history in a Kantian context, Harris's essay serves as a useful supplement to the two preceding studies. Like Grier, Harris also takes issue with Fukuyama's slanted Hegel interpretation. He effectively demonstrates the poverty of Fukuyama's account, and shows that what Hegel means by "the end of history" is in no way consonant with Fukuyama's unqualified encomium of Western liberal democracy. Harris's essay is particularly readable and provocative due to its integration of current political events and issues in his analysis of Hegel's theory.

The Myth that Hegel Denied the Law of Contradiction

It is often claimed in the Anglo-American tradition, which prides itself on its methodological rigor and deference to formal logic, that Hegel foolishly denied the law of contradiction. Some analytic philosophers, such as Bertrand Russell, have been led to this conclusion by a mistaken interpretation of Hegel's dialectical method, which they claim resolves all dualisms and oppositions by simply not recognizing the contradiction involved in simple statements such as "*P* and not *P.*" The implication is that Hegel would have miserably failed a course on introductory logic. This Hegel legend is addressed by two different essays in this collection.

Robert Pippin, acclaimed for among other things his seminal study, *Hegel's Idealism: The Satisfactions of Self-Consciousness*,[46] recounts this myth and focuses on the notion of contradiction as a logical category in Hegel's *Logic*. In his analysis of the *Wesenslogik* where Hegel's disputed doctrine makes its appearance, Pippin tries to unpack some of Hegel's most obscure philosophical terminology, such as "determinate negation" and "*Aufhebung.*" On the basis of this he offers a corrective interpretation of the notion of contradiction according to Hegel's dialectical view.

In his essay, Robert Hanna complements Pippin's analysis of Hegel's doctrine of contradiction. Hanna indicates the different conceptual levels of logic according to Hegel, which allows him to make sense of Hegel's criticism of the logic of his predecessors. Far from denying any logical principles per se, Hegel's critique amounts to reinterpreting them from a higher standpoint. Hanna analyzes carefully Hegel's account of judgment, syllogism, and contradiction, and lays to rest the view that Hegel rejected the law of contradiction.

Miscellaneous Myths

Aside from the hitherto discussed Hegel myths and legends, which lend themselves to some measure of categorization, there are a number of misconceptions about Hegel's philosophy that stand on their own and need to be addressed individually. The final section of this collection is dedicated to these miscellaneous Hegel myths.

The general ignorance concerning Hegel's natural philosophy in the inaugural dissertation, *De Orbitis Planetarum*,[47] and in the second book of the *Encyclopedia of the Philosophical Sciences* has given rise to some influential misinterpretations. His theory of the natural sciences has particularly been in disrepute because of its alleged attempt to demonstrate *a priori* that there were only seven planets, which proved to be particularly embarrassing given the discovery of Uranus in 1781, of which Hegel was apparently unaware. Thus, in a paradigm case of rationalism gone wild, Hegel, working with a purely nonempirical method, is thought to have wrongly deduced the necessity of the number of planets in the solar system. This myth is concisely treated by Bertrand Beaumont, who demonstrates that it has no foundation whatsoever in Hegel's texts.

One legend that touches at once on Hegel's political theory, his metaphysics, and his philosophy of religion is the view that Hegel deified the state and saw in it God on earth. This myth, like some of the ones discussed above, seems to ascribe to Hegel a form of political totalitarianism. Franz Grégoire's second essay offers a two-pronged attack on this myth of the divinity of the state. First, using what he calls the "philological method," Grégoire analyzes Hegel's difficult language and concludes that what Hegel means by "divine" in the context in question has little to do with the standard usage. Instead, "divine" is for Hegel a term applied to anything at all that evinces some form of rationality, such as human beings, history, nature, and so forth. Second, Grégoire discusses the Hegelian system as a whole, and isolates in it Hegel's theory of the state and his account of religion. By determining the roles played by the various members of the system, Grégoire concludes here, as in his first essay, that the individual and the state stand in a reciprocal organic relation to one another, and thus that the individual has a necessary and fundamental value which stands on equal terms with that of the state.

It is further asserted, even by some enthusiastic supporters of Hegel such as McTaggart[48] and Stace,[49] that Hegel's dialectical method of argumentation takes the form of the thesis-antithesis-synthesis triad. This is among the most famous of all the Hegel myths and, as we have already seen, can still be readily found in encyclopedias and handbooks of philosophy. If students "know" one thing about Hegel, this is usually it. In his essay, Gustav Mueller, the author of a number of works on Hegel,[50] irrefutably exposes this legend for what it is, by tracing the regrettable dissemination of this view back to Marx, who inherited it from a certain Heinrich Moritz Chalybäus, a long since forgotten expositor of the philosophy of Kant and Hegel.

Lastly, there exists the widespread belief that Hegel was an arch-rationalist. According to this misinterpretation, he is seen as the last gasp of rationalism before the onset of the so-called irrationalists such as Schopenhauer, Freud, and existentialists such as Kierkegaard and Nietzsche. According to this view, Hegel is regarded as a naive product of the Enlightenment, who believed that reason could conquer all and that everything in history is ultimately rational. This in turn gives rise to the misnomer that, as one writer puts it, "Hegel is the antipodes of existentialism."[51] "The Myth of Reason in Hegel" tries to eradicate this Hegel legend by indicating certain continuities between Hegel and the irrationalist or existentialist tradition, which demonstrate Hegel's disabused awareness of the negative and destructive side of reason.

In the last few decades there has been an outpouring of literature on Hegel in the world of Anglo-American philosophy. The so-called Hegel renaissance is indeed in full swing, particularly in America.[52] However, in the face of the resurgence of interest in Hegel, a number of the same intransigent prejudices still persist. The new Hegel commentators are faced with a reading audience that knows little about Hegel and still suffers from the numerous misconceptions stemming from the various myths and legends. The time is ripe to correct these long-standing prejudices once and for all, and at present the means are happily at our disposal for doing so.

PART   1

THE MYTH OF
THE RATIONAL AND
THE ACTUAL

1

Hegel: The Real and the Rational

M. W. Jackson

Outside the classroom even an educated person's knowledge of political theory is a few pithy sentences, each putatively encapsulating the essence of a great mind's thought. Publicly, the history of political theory is a history of sentences such as Aristotle's "all actions aim at some good," Hobbes's "life is nasty, brutish, and short," and Marx's "philosophers have hitherto only understood the world but the point is to change it."

Even when correctly quoted, at best these sentences conceal as much as they reveal of each writer's thought, and at worst they distort the complexity of that thought. Nonetheless, such sentences comprise the public knowledge of political theory.

No political theorist has suffered more distortion because of a single sentence than Hegel. Any reader of Hegel has encountered many people in person or in print with decided views on Hegel, uniformly negative, who have obviously neither read nor understood anything by Hegel. Their views are based entirely on secondary sources such as the Karls, Marx and Popper. This is the price Hegel has paid for what he himself referred to as "the severe style" (*der strenge Stil*) that makes no concession to the reader (1975a, 616).

Any discussion of Hegel inevitably arrives at the sentence in which he asserted a relationship between rationality and reality. That sentence occurs in the Preface to the *Philosophy of Right* of 1821. Within one generation of his death critics had fastened onto this sentence among thousands of published words. Rudolf Haym interpreted this sentence to mean that existing reality was rational and so immune from criticism (1857, 357). For Haym that sentence was proof of Hegel's perfidy. Though

Haym's book has not been translated into English or French and has been out of print in German most of the time, his interpretation is well known. It was scattered broadcast inadvertently in 1888 when Engels quoted Hegel from memory—as having written "all that is real is rational" (266).[1] Since then MackIntosh (1903, 211), Sturt (1906, 207), Hobhouse (1918, 17), Gooch (1920, 300–301), MacIver (1926, 451), Hocking (1926, 86), Laski (1935, 29, 94), Sabine (1937, 632), Russell (1945, 731), Weldon (1946, 95), Elliot and MacDonald (1950, 273), Catlin (1962, 360), Sartori (1962, 45), Popper (1966, 27), Voegelin (1968, 40–44), Holborn (1969, 512), Hook (1970, 87), Nelson (1982, 306), and Goodwin and Taylor (1982, 178), to name a few, have subscribed to variations of the Engels quotation and the Haym interpretation. The most unsparing critic to do so is, of course, Sir Karl Popper. Despite Walter Kaufmann's devastating rejoinder, Popper and his admirers remain unrepentant (Popper 1976, 113–20, Quinton 1976, 155, Magee 1979, 74–86, and Champion 1985, 11) and unredeemed.

Naturally such a disparate group of writers is not homogeneous in its interpretation, but all are a party to the Haym interpretation to considerable degree. Sabine offers no bombast, unlike most of the others, but simply misquotes Hegel, following Engels. Russell clearly knew more than his simplistic conclusion contained.

Lest it be thought that the Haym interpretation was inevitable, please note that there have always been scholars who have avoided it. Among them are Muirhead (1915, 37–39), Vaughan (1925, 142–83), Mead (1936, 144–45), Pfannestill (1936, 88), Neumann (1942, 78), Ruggiero (1959, 234), and Copleston (1963, 255–58).

For Hegel's numerous critics the implications of the Haym interpretation are monumental, leading to a quiescent authoritarian politics or worse. Hapless citizens are condemned not only to obey any dictate of the state, but also to acknowledge those dictates and the state as rational because they are real. Those who have argued along these lines include Russell (1947, 16–17), Joll (1960, 495), d'Entrèves (1967, 167), Kohn (1967, 147), Paterman (1979, 113), Gordon (1980, 127), and Kolakowski (1981, 75). From this argument it is only a short step to the conclusion that Hegel was an absolutist—e.g., Coker (1932, 89), Kierkegaard (1941, 450n), Barker (1951, 20, 34), Fisk (1980, 83), and Miewald (1984, 24). Others have concluded that Hegel was the official philosopher of Prussianism in the worst sense—e.g., Barker (1914, 4), Artz (1934, 78), Aris (1936, 17), Simon (1953/54, 313), Kaminsky (1962, vii), Findlay (1962, 323–24), Lichtheim (1967, 166), Watkins (1967, 199–203), and Gottfried (1978, 177). A direct connection has been asserted between Hegel's ostensible absolutism and Hitler's fascism by Cole (1934, 29), Joad (1938,

504), Heiden (1944, 216–17), Ryle (1947, 170, 172), Ebenstein (1956, 595), Maritain (1960, 159), Shirer (1961, 98–99), Bullock (1962, 384), Viereck (1965, 38, 286), and Peters (1966, 140).

The Haym interpretation together with the unpleasant political implications drawn from it have made Hegel a particular *bête noir* of English writers. Though these ideas can be found in other languages, they have never been dominant in French (Fleischmann 1964), Spanish (Pavon 1971), Italian (Bruno 1969), and German (Riedel 1984) for some reason. If an increased knowledge of Hegel in the recent past has decreased the tendency to cast aspersions on him, those already cast constitute a sizeable library of works all too likely to be encountered by the general reader or introductory student.

What does that infamous sentence say? In the preface to the *Philosophy of Right* it is "Was vernünftig ist, das ist wirklich; und was wirklich ist, das ist vernünftig" (Hegel 1955, 14). Curiously enough, this controversial sentence did not appear in the earliest English renderings of Hegel. Morris (1887) deletes it from his exposition, while Sandars leaves it in the German (1855, 213).

Because it comes first, the emphasis in this sentence is on "*die Vernunft*" which is the rational. Sterrett (Hegel 1893) and Dyde (Hegel 1896b), the first English translators, rended "*die Wirklichkeit*" as reality. Knox, in the current translation, termed it as "actuality." Knox made this change to distinguish reality which encompasses all that exists in the palpable disorder of the world from the portion of that reality which is true (because it is rational). The rational part of reality is the actual in Hegel's system. The actual is not the unchanging truth of the forms as it was for Plato, but something that develops in history as Hegel explained in the *Phänomenologie des Geistes* (1977). A philosopher like Hegel himself does not create either rationality or reality, but the philosopher discovers and explains actuality as the archaeologist and zoologist does. Ordinary speech recognizes the same distinction between the ephemeral which is nonetheless real and the actual which is rational. For example, it is perfectly intelligible for me to say that "Margaret Thatcher is not a real Prime Minister." No one chancing to hear that remark would suppose me to be calling in question the existence of the person named or to be denying that she holds the office of Prime Minister. Rather that remark would be easily understood to imply certain criteria to judge whether a particular token (the individual) was a good or bad instance of the type (Prime Minister). We often do affirm the rationality of a concept like the office of Prime Minister while denying the rationality of a particular specimen, though that is not how we think of it while we do it. Maintaining that the office of Prime Minister has rational value in our political system does not imply that any and all existing Prime Ministers must therefore be regarded as rational. Quite the contrary. The elaboration of the criteria according to which the office of Prime Minister has rational value equips us to evaluate each and every incumbent to that office.

As for Prime Ministers so for states in Hegel's political theory. His avowal that the (concept of the) state is rational does not mean that the existing state(s) is rational. A major purpose of his political theory is to establish the criteria by which to evaluate the existing state, as he wrote in his *Encyclopedia* (1975, secs. 6, 198).

It is characteristic of Hegel's optimism that he came to conclude not only that rationality could be brought into existence gradually, but also that there was (some) rationality existing in reality. More often than not that rationality was unintended—"the cunning of reason"—as he put it elsewhere (1955, 105). An example would be the Napoleonic conquest and occupation of Germany. It was violent and repressive, but it also reduced the number of self-governing entities from more than three hundred to about thirty. This reduction promised, Hegel thought, a more rational economic, social, and political life for Germans, ending the economically inefficient, socially feudal, and politically parochial remnants of the middle ages that had been Germany. We might say the same today, if we were optimistic, of the short-sighted, self-interested contest of government and opposition. Regardless of motivations of the participants, it has a rational value for the common good. For his part Hegel concluded deep within the *Philosophy of Right* that a "bad state is one which exists; a sick body exists too, but has no genuine reality" (270A).[2] Genuine reality is actuality.

That the "rational is actual" is a *speculative proposition* in terms of Hegel's system. Elsewhere in the Preface he wrote of speculative knowledge (1952, 2; 1977, 38–40). To read a proposition speculatively is to give a double reading, at once positive and negative. An ordinary proposition asserts an identity between subject and predicate. A speculative proposition both affirms and denies the identity it asserts (Rose 1981, 49).

Why does Hegel use such an unusual device as the speculative proposition? He does so because he wishes to avoid the abstraction that he found in Kant's ethical teaching (1896a, 460). In Kant's theory normative statements were necessarily separated from empirical reality. Normative statements could only be rational if they were empirically empty in Kant's system. Now the *Philosophy of Right* is Hegel's ethics and could easily have been so titled (Reyburn 1921; Hegel 1893). Though it is common to stress the differences between Hegel's and Kant's ethics as I have just done, it is well to remember how similar they are, too (Knox 1957/1958; Kelly 1978). The abstract statement of normative principles in the Kantian manner, according to Hegel, would simply make manifest the fact that we do not live in accord with such principles, an observation that students are quick to make in courses on moral philosophy. In the abstract, ethics is an ideal. Ideals do not exist on earth and so are not real. For Hegel an ideal is not justified precisely because it is not implicit in reality. To avoid Kant's abstraction, Hegel concentrates on the ethical life that does exist. By concentrating on normative principles, Kantian ethics is concentrated on the ethical life that does not exist. The archaeologist, the zoologist, and the philosopher like Hegel need not concentrate on the disorder and corruption of reality that all can see, but must concentrate on explicating the hidden order in reality, the actuality within reality that escapes all but the most patient and insightful observers. Speculative propositions and the books in which they are explored are Hegel's attempt to unify theory and practice, and not the clumsy attempt to justify the political status quo that so many critics have been pleased to see in it. All too often the speculative proposition that the rational is the real has been read as if it equated the natural law of reason with the existing positive law of the state. In fact, the proposition summarizes Hegel's critique of Kant's abstract natural law. *Vernünftig* (rational) means *both* "intelligible" and "as it ought to be" for Hegel (Inwood 1983, 497).

If there is any excuse for the persistent misinterpretation of Hegel's sentence, aside from his severe style, it is the history of the *Philosophy of Right*. Like nearly all books written by university men at the time, it was a textbook for the author's course (Hegel 1952, 7). Hegel lectured on the *Philosophy of Right* in the German academic years 1818–19, 1822–23, 1824–25, and 1831 when he died in November. Students' lecture notes for all of those years exist, and some of them were used when Hegel's son, another Karl, edited the book. Selections from these notes appear as the additions to the Knox translation following Karl Hegel's edition. They are otherwise unavailable to the English reader.

The textbook manuscript was finished before October 1819. In that month there was a great deal of nationalistic agitation by students, ending with the murder of the poet August Kotzebue, who was suspected of being a Russian agent. The Carlsbad Decrees were promulgated at the behest of Metternich to end the post-Napoleonic period of Prussian reform. Among other things these decrees curtailed press and academic freedom, which had been quite liberal. Hegel withheld the *Philosophy of Right* from publication for more than a year in these confused times (d'Hondt 1968, 56). Karl-Heinz Ilting has concluded in his masterful study of all students' notes on Hegel's lectures on the *Philosophy of Right* that Hegel revised the preface in that year in the hope of escaping the notice of the censor and university curator (Hegel 1974, vol. 1, 43–69). That revision is apparent when we compare the published preface with the oral prefaces in the lecture notes. In the notes the divide between natural law and positive law that only gradually emerges within the published text is made plain from the start (Brudner 1978, 41–48).

In 1818–19, before the publication of the *Philosophy of Right*, Hegel's prefatory remarks, which would have been made before the Kotzebue murder, contain the assertion that historical rational justifications for constitutional arrangements must be distinguished (Hegel 1974, vol. 1, 230). He added that criticism in particular and philosophy in general are essential (1974, vol. 1, 231).

In 1822–23, after the publication of the textbook and the relaxation of the Carlsbad Decrees, Hegel acknowledged, according to the lecture notes, that a citizen may dissent from the positive law because it is deficient. In his words, "conflict is possible between what is and what ought to be" (Hegel 1974, vol. 3, 93), a very Kantian formulation. In 1824–25 he noted that a law may be "irrational, unjust, completely arbitrary." The bare fact that such a laws exists, he concluded, is not indication of its worth (Hegel 1975, vol. 4, 82). All of this is consistent with the teaching of the *Philosophy of Right* for those who care to read it. The tension between what is and what ought to be is clearly felt within the book, the only question is why it is not apparent in the preface. In the book Hegel wrote that "in considering the idea of the state, we must not have our eyes on particular states" (258A).

The charge that Hegel was an apologist for the absolutism of the Prussia of his day that usually follows from misinterpreting the speculative proposition of rationality and reality is wrong on all counts. It is historically wrong: the Prussian regime during Hegel's tenure at Berlin was liberal and reformist, marked by the leadership of men like vom Stein, von Altenstein, and von Hardenburg (Seeley 1878; d'Hondt 1968). When this period ended and the Prussian reaction set in, Hegel was dead. His teachings were so widely associated with the political leaders named above and the reformist movement that his successor in the Berlin chair of philosophy was charged personally by the king with combatting the influence of Hegel's liberal teaching. Far from being the official philosopher of the Prussian state, Hegel enjoyed the patronage of one minister with many enemies who were opponents of all reforms (Treitschke 1916, vol. 2, 509). Hegel himself was never invited to join the royal society, one of the few professors at Berlin not to be accorded this recognition. Hegel has been made an enemy by xenophobic nationalists such as Treitschke (1916, vol. 1, 225, 292) and was largely ignored by Nazi writers (Grégoire 1955, 1962). He was the personal friend of the professional agitator Victor Cousin (1866, 612).

It is politically wrong because in the *Philosophy of Right* Hegel argued that certain political arrangements were the necessary means to freedom. Among these arrangements were trial by jury in public proceedings (219), the equality of citizens before the law (219), a division of the functions of government into a balance à la Montesquieu (275),[3] freedom of the press (316–19), popular participation in assemblies (275), and assent to taxation (275). Moreover, he acknowledged conscientious objection to military service (270N). He also wrote of conscience as "a sanctuary which it would be a sacrilege to violate" (137R). Not a single one of these conditions yet existed in Hegel's Prussia, despite the great reforms following the defeat of Napoleon, and there are many places in the world today where they still do not exist. Yet one G. A. Wells has claimed that Hegel had nothing to offer the reform movement of his day (1959, 151). Others assert that as a good conservative Hegel was uncritical of the existing political reality of Prussia (Catt 1962, 370).

Most important of all, the charge of Hegel's Prussianism is philosophically wrong because his identification of the rational and the actual/real encourages rational action by showing where and how rationality already exists and can be built up, and it implies a program of further rational action by showing where and how rationality does not already exist. This speculative proposition is a program of action, not the advocacy of acquiescence. And it was taken in that way by his patron Altenstein (Hoffmeister 1963, 251), the opponent of serfdom, advocate of economic liberty, enemy of ecclesiastical privilege, and outlawer of child labor (d'Hondt 1968, 71). "The driving force of history" is not "something metaphysical" as some people seem to think it is for Hegel (Tucker 1980, 42), nor is it simple historical determinism (Miliband 1977, 9). It is human freedom (Berki 1968). Only insofar as the rational is the actual is it in fact rational. Only insofar as the real is rational is it in fact actual.

2

Hegel's Dictum that the Rational is Actual and the Actual is Rational: Its Ontological Content and Its Function in Discourse

Yirmiahu Yovel

W hy return to this rather overtrodden dictum?[1] First, I think it worthwhile to undermine its authority as a supposed clue and shortcut to Hegel's thought. Secondly, doing so may lead to more positive results, such as bringing out the elements of Hegel's theory of rational discourse (within which this saying, too, must find its proper function), or reexamining the ontological, rather than political background that gives this saying its primary meaning.

Perhaps naturally we are, alas, much too attracted to succinct sayings and oblique formulas, severing them from their functional context[2] and taking them either as self-sustained units of discourse or, worse, as bits of revealed wisdom, instilled with their authors' overriding authority and laden with countless layers of implicit meanings, which a devout exegesis will lay bare or on which a tendentious reading will capitalize. Improper in itself, this approach is particularly inadequate to Hegel's philosophy, whose depth does not lie in ambiguous blazes of oracular insight but in the rationally articulated, if very complex, interrelation between its rich and diverse components. Hegel's system allows of no easy shortcuts. It requires, as Hegel insists, "the arduous labor of the Concept," implying a rational and systematic process of explication, as well as a solid preparation in philosophy and a confrontation with its cardinal issues, as they have given rise to partial solutions, leading to collapses and new *Aufhebungen*. How can a formula, bright as it may be, capture this process even remotely or serve as a substitute for it?

If Hegel himself, either by natural temptation or, as in our case, by deliberation, sometimes chose to utter a slogan or pronounce a Heraclitean-sounding dictum, he did so with a nonsystematic intent and mostly in nonsystematic texts, such as prefaces and *Zusätze*. The role of such sayings was rhetorical and didactic; they were not meant as genuine philosophy but as "mere talk" *about* philosophy, which had, however, its proper function: it was to serve the aims of preparation, initiation, or—less frequently—of summing up, as code words for memory, of a whole systematic issue that had already been worked out and mastered by the individual philosopher.

Before turning to a more positive analysis, let me summarize the criticism that current tendencies in reading Hegel's dictum seem to invite.

1. Above all, we should not try to learn of Hegel's systematic views from oblique dicta. The order should rather be reversed: only on the basis of our knowledge of Hegel's systematic doctrine can we assess the meaning and role of his occasional dicta.

2. I think it is wrong to read this dictum directly and primarily in a political vein. Hegel insists, on the contrary, that its primary context is *ontological*, having to do with such categories, or modes of being as *Sein, Dasein, Existenz,* and so on. And obviously, the key concepts in our dictum, "actuality" and "rationality," cannot be grasped without their original context, that of Hegel's *Logic*, or more broadly, his theory of the dynamic degrees of being and of rational discourse.

The political bias in reading this dictum is common among scholars and social thinkers who, either because of Marxian antecedents, or due to their own emphasis on the primacy of politics (which Hegel does not share), or, simply, because they lack philosophical training, approach Hegel in general from the narrow standpoint of politics. This does little justice to Hegel as philosopher; it also misses a crucial dimension of the *Rechtsphilosophie*, itself, and blurs the secondary and subservient (if indispensable) position that politics holds vis-à-vis speculation in the Hegelian scheme of realizing rationality.

Even within the purely political reading of the dictum, failure to draw the basic ontological distinctions has led to classic fallacies:

3. Left-wing Hegelians, stressing the first part of the famous equivalence (*was vernünftig ist, das ist wirklich*), tended to make the "rational" a kind of a priori ought, a desirable state of affairs in view of which

the actual world should be reformed. They have thereby confused the Hegelian *Vernunft* with *Verstand*, leading Hegel, even if unwittingly, back in the direction of Kant.

4. Right-wing Hegelians—and also their adversaries, Hegel's liberal critics—tend to stress the second part of the equivalence (*was wirklich ist, das ist vernünftig*). But in their eagerness to make Hegel an arch-conservative, who sanctifies as rational any state of affairs that simply happens to exist, they confuse, sometimes deliberately, the crucial onto-logical distinction between *Wirklichkeit* and *Existenz*.

5. Both left- and right-wing Hegelians share the "oracular bias," supposing, or acting as if they did, that Hegel's dictum contains per se a deep and authoritative truth, to be laid bare by exegesis.

6. Trying to exonerate Hegel from the charge of conservatism, a new scholarly trend, which I may call "historical apologetics," directs attention away from the systematic implications of Hegel's work to his life, personality, circumstances and actual decisions. This school has greatly enriched our understanding of the real situation in which the Hegelian philosophy took shape; but to understand it as *philosophy*, we must focus on its systematic and logical implications, not on extraneous historical material. With all its interest, the hermeneutic import of this material is limited.

7. The ineffectiveness of historical apologetics is demonstrated in a recent example. K.-H. Ilting's new publications of material on Hegel's *Rechtsphilosophie* included an unknown reference by Hegel to his famous dictum, made as late as 1831, shortly before he died. The discovery gave rise to claims that Hegel before his death "corrected" his dictum away from its conservative overtones. But Hegel had nothing to correct: if read adequately—that is, according to its ontological context—the original dictum already contains the alleged correction.[3]

8. Emil Fackenheim avoided both the political and the oracular biases, and offered what seems to me the most fruitful line to date, stress-ing that the dictum should be read primarily in a metaphysical vein. But instead of interpreting actuality and rationality in straight philosophical terms, Fackenheim prefers the theological idiom (God, Providence, etc.). However, in the Hegelian system, the universe of discourse of theology is inferior to that of philosophy, relating to it as an image to a concept, or metaphorically. Why prefer *Vorstellung* to *Begriff*, the world of theological metaphor to straight ontological language? This must again compress the Hegelian system to a restricted and inferior aspect of itself. Fackenheim was right in stressing "the theological dimension in Hegel's thought," lost on so many readers, but not in stopping short at it. Trying to read the dictum in its primary context, that of Hegel's *Logic* and general

philosophy, I shall first examine the dictum's *form of discourse* (section I), and then discuss its *ontological message* (section II). On this basis I shall proceed, in section III, to make a suggestion about the precise function the dictum is supposed to fulfill within the Hegelian discourse and with respect to its intended and unintended audience.[4]

1. The Dictum's Form of Discourse

Hegel's logic should, of course, apply to his own discourse. Given the dialectical form Hegel ascribes to philosophy, it is obvious that our dictum, being an isolated proposition, cannot express the content it purports to transmit. On Hegel's theory, all single statements or generalizations are doomed to miss their object and distort the message they seem to contain. Philosophical claims become meaningful—and can be verified—only within their full dynamic context, which involves the system as a whole. Detached from its explication in the system, any generalization, such as ours, must count as an "abstract universal," lacking (1) truth, (2) meaning, and (3) subjective intelligibility.

Even the statement that summarizes this view—*das Wahre ist das Ganze*—is similarly an empty universal, whose form contradicts its content. Metaphilosophical statements are bound by the same condition as substantive statements: to be true, to gain meaning, and to become intelligible to the subjective mind, they must already be embodied and explicated within a system that has actually accomplished the ideal of organic coherence.

It should be noted that the systematic whole is both the verification-context and the *meaning*-context of any philosophical idea. It is by its explication, which includes dialectical transformations, that a philosophical principle or idea first attains meaning. The inter-implication of the various components of the system also imparts their specific distinction to its individual members.

It may be noted that, for Hegel, this is not simply a coherence theory of truth (and of meaning), but equally an ontology. If philosophy must have an organic feature, it is because reality itself assumes this feature, as it actualizes itself according to its idea, that is, in dialectical relation to the rational categories that make up its essential aspect. Unless this inherent link existed between actuality and rational discourse, the "coherence" conditions could not in themselves ensure the truth of the system, but might, on the contrary, establish an arbitrary universe of discourse, a "flying castle" closed upon itself, beautifully constructed but abstract and severed from all reality. However, Hegel does not recognize an independent, self-sustained methodological theory, that lays down a priori the model for philosophy. The form of philosophy and its methodological constraints (including its "coherence" conditions) are said to derive from the nature of its subject matter, actuality, whose dynamic structure they are supposed to reflect. (This is a major speculative point, without which no faithful interpretation of Hegel is possible.)

Subjective Intelligibility and Learning

In addition to truth and meaning, detached statements also lack subjective intelligibility. Subjective intelligibility is not the same as objective meaningfulness. Take two persons, a novice and one whose mind has already undergone—and developed with—all the transformations and *Aufhebungen* of the Hegelian system. Present them now with a generalized statement, such as "what is rational, is actual" (or "the true is the whole," etc.). Although, on Hegel's theory, the statement is objectively meaningless, it will have different subjective results. For the novice, the statement will be hollow, unintelligible, and very possibly misleading. For the other person, however, it will be subjectively intelligible, not because it transmits to him any meaningful content in itself, but because it serves him as a shorthand code word to invoke a whole process he had already interiorized and mastered.

Obviously, the distinction between objective meaningfulness and subjective intelligibility is not specific to Hegel. It is current anywhere in ordinary, nondialectical discourse, where a statement may well be considered meaningful itself, yet requiring a long didactic process to make the subjective mind understand it. Hegel departs from this common view in two major respects. First, as we saw, he denies that in *philosophy* (that is, in rational discourse proper, that of *Vernunft*, to be distinguished from *Verstand* and the sciences based up it, such as mathematics and empirical knowledge), a single generalized statement can be meaningful in itself; and secondly, he does not recognize a possible separation between the order in which a philosophical idea is systematically unfolded and the process by which alone it can be grasped. Subjective intelligibility depends, in philosophy, on the same systematic unfolding that gives the idea meaning and truth.

One major reason for this is that the mind is no passive receiver in the process of philosophizing, but undergoes the same changes and transformations indicated by the successive moments of the system; the mind thus *develops* and is *formed* by its own philosophizing. But there is another, more speculative reason as well: the constitutive role Hegel ascribes to the rational subject in the formation of his object. The moment of subjective thinking is considered by Hegel not as mirroring a ready-made truth but as participating in its very constitution. Without entering into this issue per se, I should only like to indicate its methodological and educational implications; namely, that the mind develops dialectically alongside its content, and that the didactic procedure for learning and grasping philosophy is bound to be the same as the logical procedure in which the system unfolds, no shortcuts or alternative approaches being possible.

The Predicative Bias of Propositions

The failure of single dicta to express a philosophical truth is also due to *their predicative* form. The structure of ordinary language reflects an inadequate theory of predication—itself the offshoot of an inadequate ontology. It takes the logical subject as fixed, ready-made, and self-identical at the outset, whereas the predicates "hinge" or depend upon this subject unilaterally. This is the logical view of the "understanding." Dialectical reason, however, grasps the subject and predicates as mutually dependent. The subject is *constituted qua subject* only by the process of its explication and transformation in the dialectical system of predicates. The actual subject is therefore a result, not a starting point. It is not a single privileged item, as in the traditional view, but the overall interconnectedness of all the predicates, i.e., their dialectical *totality*. In the actual subject there is therefore no residual content over and above the system of predicates in which it was explicated; and what undergoes change and actualization are not the properties of a fixed entity but the very status of being-subject.

Let me mention again that all these logical views are grounded in Hegel's ontology. Whatever constraints the forms of philosophical discourse are derived from, the structure of being is its process of self-actualization. Thus, Hegel's rejection of the fixed logical subject is equivalent to his refusal to view reality in terms of a fixed substance; and Hegel's claim that truth abides only in a systematic whole is more than a simple "coherence theory of truth"; for the coherence requirements themselves derive from the ontological view of reality as a self-actualizing totality, and of truth as a mode of being, not just as an epistemic property of statements and theories.

The Antinomy of Language

Hegel's problem with the predicative language is that he can have no alternative to it. (The oblique mention of a "speculative proposition" is hardly helpful.) He cannot offer a specially formed, "artificial," language for philosophy since, according to his dialectic of culture and spirit, philosophical knowledge must emerge from within the development of actual knowledge and cultural forms, and not as an artificial imposition upon them. This gives rise to an "antinomy of language" within Hegel's theory; and his solution is rather pragmatic: instead of replacing the ordinary language, he chooses to *manipulate* it (sometimes, as we know, rather violently), using as his basic unit of discourse not the sentence but the paragraph, and sometimes the whole chapter. This unit allows him to go back on his initial statements, point out the contradictions and transformations they involve, and proceed in a progressive-regressive way that constantly closes given loops of discourse while opening new ones. This explains in part the impossible style of Hegel's systematic works and the fact that very frequently there is no clear meaning to a sentence or a group of sentences in themselves. They must be understood from the "contextual movement" of whole bodies of discussion.

In short, the dictum's form makes it incapable of expressing a philosophical truth. It must belong to that category of discourse Hegel calls mere *Konversation,* which includes all prefaces, generalizations, and so on, about philosophy. However, we should note that Hegel distinguished a subcategory of conversation, that serves as a prephilosophical initiation to philosophy; in other words, its function is propaedeutic, preparing the untrained mind, in a nondialectical way, to the mode of thinking implied in the dialectic.

If Hegel cannot get around his antinomy of language by syntactic means, he does—and may without contradiction—use a semantic device, creating a new philosophical glossary by exploiting existing ambiguities and connotations of ordinary language. In declaring this program (e.g., in *Wissenschaft der Logik* II, 375; cf. I, 10), Hegel specifically proposes to make systematic distinctions between terms that are usually considered to be synonyms, especially the set: *Existenz, Dasein, Wirklichkeit,* and so on. This leads us directly to the developmental ontology behind Hegel's dictum.

2. The Dictum's Ontological Content

> Wenn aber ich von Wirklichkeit gesprochen habe, so wäre von selbst daran zu denken, in welchem Sinne ich diesen Ausdruck gebrauche, da ich in einer ausführlichen *Logik* auch die Wirklichkeit abgehandelt, und sie . . . von Dasein, Existenz und anderen Bestimmungen unterschieden habe. (*Enz.* sec. 6)

To understand Hegel's concept of actuality, we must view it in relation to the rest of Hegel's ontological categories, denoted by terms that, in ordinary language, are close if not synonymous, but which stand for different ontological moments within Hegel's theory of the dynamic degrees of being. This "ontological glossary" of Hegel contains the terms *Sein, Dasein, Realität, Existenz, Wirklichkeit,* and *Objektivität.* In the space of this summary I shall not be able to discuss them all but will focus especially on the distinction between *Existenz* and *Wirklichkeit.* A special problem is raised by the fact that *Wirklichkeit* is the final category of the "Objective Logic" but not of the whole system, and we find *Objektivität* in the "Subjective Logic" as apparently superior to *Wirklichkeit.* However, it can be shown that, implicitly, the distinction *Existenz-Wirklichkeit* recurs on a higher level in the "Subjective Logic" as that of *Begriff* and *Idee.* Thus Hegel uses *Wirklichkeit* both in a narrow sense, referring to the category discussed explicitly in the *Logic,* and in a broader sense, indicating the supreme actualization of the idea.

Sein and *Dasein* do not yet indicate a depth-dimension in reality; empirical being is seen as a quantified aggregate of self-sufficient particulars. *Existenz,* however, is empirical being taken as the externalization of a supersensible essence or ground; it thus involves the duality of "inner" and "outer." The relation between the inner ground and its externalization is not reciprocal but one-sided; the essential element is considered self-sufficient, whereas empirical existence presupposes it and depends upon it. The relation is one-sided also in that existence, although it depends on the hidden essence, does not express it in a genuine and adequate manner. It is rather an externalization that distorts the original, causing it to lose status and content, and thus it serves as an alienating rather than as an actualizing factor. For this reason, existence, ontologically speaking, is considered a "phenomenon" and not "actuality." Actuality, on the contrary, is a system in which the essential and the empirical moments mediate each other such that the empirical externalization is an authentic manifestation of the essential ground. Rather than decreasing the content and value of the ground, it gives it actuality and elevates it to the status of rationality. Here the empirical manifestation exhausts the content of the essential principle and stands in a relation of realization and enrichment to it. It follows that in the stage of actuality there is no room left for hidden, ineffable interiorities. Beyond empirical existence there are no independent intelligible entities; the depth-dimension of reality is fully expressed in its surface-dimension, and only thereby does it reconstitute itself as truly in-depth dimension. In other words, we are entitled to speak of the rationality of the world only through its empirical self-manifestation.

Hegel's concept of actuality thus rejects the rationalist metaphysics that maintains the actuality of separate entities of the understanding, located beyond the world and possessing a pure "interiority" that is not manifested empirically. But Hegel's concept of actuality equally rejects the positivist metaphysics that identifies the totality of being with its surface (events, facts, sense data, etc.), and that regards these abstractions as actual and self-sufficient individuals. It certainly follows from Hegel's position that whatever is actual has empirical existence, but the empirical side of actuality does not exhaust it. The empirical side must be grasped as a moment in a dialectical synthesis, i.e., as manifesting and realizing a logical principle. In this way—by its empirical realization—the logical ground of the world is elevated from the status of mere *Verstand* to that of *Vernunft* and becomes genuinely rational. What is rational is only that universal ground which has been actualized in the empirical world and has gained thereby an actualizing self-manifestation. But as long as it has not been so actualized—as long as it is only a notion, an ideal, an unrealized essence, retaining a hidden interiority with regard to the empirical particulars—it is not rational either.

The theological equivalent (or, metaphor) of this concept of actuality is pantheism. In pantheist theology, the world does not represent something inferior to a transcendent creator but the full self-realization of God. In Hegel, however, we have a historical form of pantheism, where the self-realization of God is itself mediated by human history; and equally, the category of actuality does not attain its genuine expression in the realm of natural entities, but in history. Hence the historical dimension of rationality (and actuality), and the fact that, as long as history has not fully realized its essence (freedom), no man can be truly rational, and— Kierkegaard not withstanding—no particular man can be an *actual individual* either. Expounding now the ontological content our dictum is supposed (partly in vain) to convey, we must start with the fact that "rational" and "actual" stand in Hegel in opposition to "merely of the understanding" and "merely existing," respectively. Therefore, the way these terms are used in the dictum confronts the ordinary user with a challenge and a provocation. Hegel wants to say that "rational" and "actual" are not what ordinary understanding and the traditional language of philosophy take them to be; and thus he assigns a primarily negative task to his dictum. The first part of the dictum ("what is rational, is actual") sets out to reject the current opinion that whatever is rational is, as such, something airy and abstract, hovering over reality and only, at best, reflecting it from the outside or dictating to it the desirable direction in which it ought to develop.

On this point, Hegel's ontology represents the philosophical *Aufhebung* of Kant. Reason, Hegel suggests, is a principle that determines reality from within. Hegel agrees with Kant that subjective reason is constitutive of reality; yet not because reason imposes its forms externally upon an alien being facing it, but insofar as reason is immanent in being itself—as the principle of its development and actualization. Therefore—and this is again against Kant, and against most dualists since Plato—reason is not a different and foreign element, isolated from the empirical variety of the world, and neither is it alien to such factors as imagination, sensation, passion, and utilitarian interests. On the contrary, reason is a principle that abides in them all and can attain its own development and self-explication only by their mediation. Whoever says that the rational is actual is therefore saying that, inter alia, reason is the dialectical principle of all the *other* forms of culture and spirit, and whatever Kant and the dualist tradition held to be inferior, foreign elements that only oppose reason, is here understood as a dialectical duality within itself.

The same applies to the second part of the dictum: "what is actual, is rational." Ordinary philosophy tends to believe that what is actual is, as such, an inert and opaque being, existing in itself, while reason is only a subjective representation of this being from without, a representation which, at best, can be "adequate" to the represented being. Alternatively, the philosophy of the understanding maintains that what is actual is a merely empirical existence which, as such, does not express any rational principle or content (although subsequently it might be subordinated to such a principle). Against the common view Hegel suggests that actuality, as distinguished from simple existence or *Dasein*, has to be grasped as rational *within itself*, because it is being realized as the dialectical identity of the structure of the empirical object and the structure of the rational subject. Therefore, the self-actualization of reason as rational involves its reaching a rational *consciousness* of itself (by means of human knowledge).

There is in Hegel, to be sure, also the so-called "substantive" form of rationality, embedded in nature and history in the still incomplete form of "existence" and lacking systematic explication and self-consciousness. But precisely because of this lack, the forms of life, praxis, and culture that are only substantively rational are neither actual in the full ontological sense, nor genuinely rational. (At most, they are to be considered a form of self-alienated rationality.)

It is clear that Hegel puts here the principle of speculative theoretical comprehension on a higher level than life and action. The climax in realizing rationality lies not in the domain of substantive life, not even in the domain of praxis and the state, but in pure speculative knowledge. In contrast to Kant before him and to Marx after him, who had given priority to praxis, Hegel adheres to the Aristotelian idea of the priority of speculation, even though he makes historical praxis a necessary prerequisite for attaining the speculative goal. Actuality in the complete sense is to be sought in the systematic self-understanding of the totality in its actualization—not in any specific form of nature, society, or the state. It is true that attaining the supreme speculative goal is made possible only insofar as the principle of freedom is also realized in the practical and historical domain; but it is not here that absolute rationality or actuality are to be found. Actuality is the supreme goal having been realized; but realizing the goal lies in the field of speculation, not of action, even though the latter is a mediating condition of the former.

3. The Dictum as an Amphibolic Epigram

In the last section I should like to unite the results of the former two sections in order to understand the role of Hegel's dictum, while taking into consideration both its form of discourse (section I), and what is supposed to be its ontological message (section II).

We saw it is impossible for this dictum to express a philosophical truth. The reasons are that it has a predicative form and that it is detached from the complete systematic context in which alone it can gain truth, meaning, and subjective intelligibility. Therefore, this saying must have *another* function within the Hegelian discourse. I would like to suggest that the saying is supposed to function as a noncognitive aphorism or epigram and the context designed for it is not philosophical but prephilosophical. To appreciate the role of this aphorism we should not lose sight of either the ordinary use of "actuality" and "reason" or of their inner-systematic use in Hegel. Rather, the fact that the saying hints at both— and at the same time misses them both, creating an amphibolic play of meaning between them—is here, I think, the crucial fact, upon which the effect of the aphorism is built.

However, this play of meanings is effective only with respect to a novice who does not yet know Hegel's ontology. For the dialectical thinker, acquainted with Hegel's ontology, on the contrary, it is a simple systematic tautology, carrying neither provocation nor novelty.

The Dictum as Systematic Tautology

As to this, let me sum up the ontological theory behind Hegel's dictum. We have see that rational for Hegel is that conceptual content which has been fully actualized in the empirical world and attained systematic self-consciousness. Its being actualized closes a dialectical circle, and its empirical externalization serves as an exhaustive and realizing manifestation of itself—not as a phenomenal cover that hides or alienates its essence. As such, actualizing the concept sets up a totality: it is the dialectical unity of subject and object, of universality and particularity, unity and plurality, identity and otherness, temporality and eternity, necessity and contingency, a conceptual content and its empirical (phenomenal) manifestation. This totality is not given beforehand, but results from a process of self-realization; and its emergence indicates that self-identity has been constituted and that true individuation has been attained. Moreover, the appearance of this totality also means that the principle of freedom, or autonomy, had gained an exhaustive manifestation according to its concept; for now, the system exists in the form of "in-itself and for-itself," that is, its identity is constituted by its own means, and each of its aspects regains itself and is able to identify itself within the "other" that grounds it.

On the basis of this Hegelian theory, one could extend the dictum about the rational and the actual and present a richer scheme, from which many other dicta could be engendered at will—to the benefit of lazy readers who look for shortcuts into Hegel's philosophy and to the entertainment of the general public. Let us consider the following scheme:[5]

what is rational (and not merely of the "understanding")	is ↔	*what is actual* (and not merely "existing")	is ↔	* a concrete individual * a dialectical totality * a free entity * a fully realized end * etc.

↓ is * an entity with empirical dimensions * the result of a process in time * etc.	↓ is * the externalization of a conceptual content * endowed with self-consciousness * etc.

This is a lazy-man's schematic representation of Hegel's position. It includes the essential elements—but in a frozen, nondialectical form. As such, however, the scheme above is an adequate explication of the dictum about rationality and actuality—in the dictum's own form of discourse; for the dictum, too, like this formal scheme, must miss its implied philosophical content.

Keeping for awhile to this nondialectical form of discourse, one could go on engendering new dicta from this scheme—some rather surprising. For instance:

* What is rational is an entity with empirical dimensions.
* A concrete individual is endowed with self-consciousness.
* A free entity is the result of a process in time.
* A fully realized end is a dialectical totality.

And also:

* Not every entity with empirical dimensions is actual.
* Not everything endowed with self-consciousness is rational.

and so forth. This pastime, although quite barren in a fundamental sense, may have some instructive value as *Konversation*. At times it can even spotlight some hidden corners in Hegel's system. But it is clear that all dicta produced in this way are systematic tautologies. They are engendered from the basic scheme which was based on our acquaintance with the internal use of the terms within the Hegelian ontology.

This applies to our original dictum as well. Saying that what is rational is actual and vice versa is also a tautology in terms of the system. Whoever has understood the meaning of "actuality" in Hegel (as distinguished from mere "existence") will hear in it "rationality" as well, and vice versa. And to the same extent he will understand *from the very meaning of the terms used*, that not every existing state of affairs is rational and not everything belonging to the understanding is actual. Moreover, this person already knows the issue according to its true form—namely, by means of its complete theoretical context; therefore, using the dictum for him is not only redundant but also a possible source of falsification. At best he might smile at the expense of the Prussian censor, whom this dictum is supposed to mislead; he may also attribute some pragmatic value to the dictum, as a concise code by which one could conduct a "mere conversation" between two philosophical savants or between a savant and himself. But he will not draw from this dictum anything new, will not be surprised at it, and will not be urged on its account to reexamine any of his previous ideas and positions. For him, substantively, the dictum is a simple pleonasm.

But then, this person is not the addressee of Hegel's dictum. The dictum is meant for an audience that has already had preparation and gained some competence in the philosophy of the understanding, but has not yet undergone the dialectical reversal produced by speculative reason; the dictum is supposed to hint at this reversal and suggest it externally. For such an audience, therefore, the dictum does involve an element of novelty, indeed of provocation, for it suggests a complete reversal of the ordinary modes of thought along with the traditional concept of rationality. The fact that a philosopher in his right mind could maintain a position in which the identity of the actual and the rational is considered tautological is not at all tautological for the target audience of the dictum. On the contrary it must come as a surprising novelty, provoking curiosity, building up expectation, and thus serving as external preparation for what is still to come. It may even happen that the reader will be so shocked, that he will decide the whole idea is a meaningless absurdity. But if he endeavors to make some sense of it—and this is a basic rule of the game—he will find himself drawn to the threshold of a new universe of thought—that which Hegel's dictum is indeed designed to invoke in a *non*dialectical way.

It should be emphasized, however, that the novel element that the dictum has with regard to its target audience does not lie in that it provides the audience with any new information. Rather, it provokes the audience and prepares it for the possible change of its cognitive dispositions; and so, the innovation in the dictum concerns the audience's *state of mind* but not its *state of knowledge.* As yet, the audience does not know anything new, either about the universe or even about Hegel's philosophy. In point of fact it cannot properly understand the dictum, since the dictum cannot in itself contain or convey its true philosophical meaning, and since the audience has not arrived at the discovery of this meaning by way of a systematic dialectical explication.

The Dictum as Amphibolic Aphorism: The Play of Meanings

We have now reached a clarification of the status and functions of our dictum within the Hegelian discourse. The dictum belongs to that form of discourse we called "mere conversation"—but of the second, *propaedeutic* kind mentioned earlier; and it functions as an amphibolic epigram, or aphorism, designed to serve the needs of *initiation.* As such, the dictum has two different tasks. For the reader who already knows Hegel's system from within, it is, as we said, a systematic tautology. While the censor might be glad to discover that Herr Professor Hegel sanctifies everything that exists with the halo of reason, the philosophical savant will easily comprehend that not everything that exists is rational by its mere existence—since it is not yet actual. Yet the wish to mislead the censor, if it existed at all, is secondary. For the philosophical reader who has not yet been prepared in dialectics, the aphorism must serve as a stimulus and a surprise. It is not used to make a statement or to convey information, but to change a state of mind—and that in a basically negative mode, which neither instructs nor proves anything, but plants doubts, raises curiosity, or serves as a promise and invitation for something yet to come.

For this purpose Hegel makes use of the dual sense—the ordinary and the systematic—of the two key concepts that figure in the aphorism. In other words, he exploits the pseudodialectical tension between the systematic and the nonsystematic senses of "rational" and "actual" respectively, in order to create an initiating game of hints. This play consists in that the reader tends to use "actual" in its commonsense meaning and is thus driven to reform his concept of "rationality" and vice versa.

For instance, in the first part of the sentence, "what is rational is actual," the reader takes "rational" as figuring in Hegel's systematic sense but understands "actual" in the ordinary sense. The sentence would then hint to him that what is truly rational has empirical existence, is a real being and not only an abstract principle, a subjective concept, or an absent ideal. Thereby the reader would be introduced (even if externally and in a vague way) to the universe of discourse determined by the dialectic and would be invited to revise his ordinary concept of reason, distinguishing it from the merely formal forms of thought that deserve being considered under a different concept, namely "understanding." The sentence is expected to strike the reader at first as surprising, because he is used to identifying reason with understanding and to regarding them both as merely ideal and subjective. However, if he does not suppose that a madman is speaking to him, then hearing Hegel declare that the rational is actual—and this in the ordinary sense of actuality, to which the listener himself is accustomed—he would find himself driven to seek a new sense of "rational," different from the one he was using initially; thus the dictum would suggest to him the need to revise what is usually considered as reason, and in particular to grasp the empirical and actually realized feature of that which truly deserves to be called "rational." Of course, this will not constitute a proof and is not even a dialectical explanation of the matter, but it is certainly not a tautology, and it involves stimulus and preparation.

In the second part of the sentence, "what is actual is rational," we shall read the first term in the ordinary and the second term in the systematic sense. The reader now understands "actual" in the usual sense of an empirical, factual, and external entity—and to his surprise he finds that Hegel says of this entity that it is rational. This stands in direct contradiction to the philosophy of the understanding, which establishes a radical and unbridgeable hiatus between the universe of empirical fact and the universe of rational truths, between synthetic and analytic, and so forth. Therefore the reader is driven to realize that Hegel is using "rational" in a new and different sense, which is compatible with the domain of empirical reality, even in the way in which the philosopher of the understanding is used to think of it. Thereby the reader has already been exposed to the conception that rejects the exclusive rule of formal thinking and regards reason itself as an ontic factor, determining reality "from within." In this way he would be invited to revise his concept of reason (or thinking) and distinguish between actual rationality and those forms of thought that are only formal and external—that which Hegel calls "the understanding." Moreover, in this way he would again be exposed to the suggestion that even the concept of actuality, and not only that of rationality, must undergo a philosophical revision—which brings him back to the first part of the aphorism.

In summary, the epigrammatic effect of the saying and its play of meanings are meant to arouse, to initiate, to suggest a new philosophical horizon in a *non*philosophical way. But they cannot express or contain the idea they aim at. The philosopher who already knows the Hegelian system by its unfolding will find little use in this dictum. He will see that, judged by the inner criteria of the system itself, the dictum must be found inadequate in its form and tautologous in its content. Its only use is rhetorical—and it certainly cannot serve as a short-cut to Hegel's system or as a clue to his system.[6]

3

On the Actuality of the Rational and the Rationality of the Actual

Emil L. Fackenheim

I

In the preface to his *Philosophy of Right* Hegel writes: "*Was vernünftig ist, das ist wirklich; und was wirklich ist, das ist vernünftig*"—"What is rational is actual, and what is actual is rational." In paragraph 6 of the third edition of his *Encyclopedia of Philosophical Sciences* he repeats this statement verbatim, calling it "simple." Few interpreters, however, have ever found it so. Even friendly critics are baffled; hostile ones dismiss it as either scandalous or senseless. Two centuries after Hegel's birth there is thus still room for a modest exposition of the meaning of this famous (or infamous) Hegelian statement, much more so for one of its "simplicity." Both tasks, however—and in particular the second, seemingly hopeless one—should be undertaken in full awareness of two conditions which the *Encyclopedia* passage considers evident but which can be taken as such no longer. One is possession of (or at least respect for) "religion." The other is the kind of philosophical "culture" which includes "knowledge" of "God."

II

The charge "scandalous or senseless" was popularized if not originated by Rudolph Haym's influential *Hegel und seine Zeit.*[1] Little troubled by any possible difficulties concerning the meaning of Hegelian "rationality" (to which he correctly ascribes moral as well as logical significance) Haym concentrates his critical attention on Hegelian "actuality." Does this latter term signify any and all existing facts? But then the Hegelian statement is scandalous and "the theories of the divine right of kings and of absolute obedience are innocent and harmless compared to the terrifying doctrine which sanctifies the existing as such" (367–68). Or does it signify only such existing facts as are in accord with Hegelian notions of logic and morality? But then the statement is indeed harmless but also an "empty tautology" (368). Haym is not unaware of Hegel's effort to distinguish between "existence" and "actuality." Yet he asserts that the whole Hegelian "system, as it stands, results *exclusively* from a continuous, veritably unholy, *confusion* of two concepts of actuality" (368; italics added). We are thus told that Hegel's statement—indeed, his whole system—suffers shipwreck on a basic dilemma; and the view expressed by Haym has been shared to this day by countless critics, not all of them hostile or superficial. Thus, recently Sidney Hook has written: "One interpretation of the distinction between the actual and the existent gives us a sheer tautology; the other, a scandalous absurdity."[2]

III

But is it plausible that Hegel's statement (not to speak of his system in its entirety) is destroyed by an, after all, extremely obvious and elementary dilemma when it is formulated with obvious care, put in a prominent place, and repeated and defended in another, hardly less prominent place? Or could it be that preconceptions on our part preclude an understanding? No less than three such preconceptions are brought to light in a brilliant passage in Franz Rosenzweig's *Hegel und der Staat*[3]—an extraordinary, never fully appreciated work. The passage merely mentions these in passing; we must first of all fully expose them and explicitly set them aside. Rosenzweig writes:

> "What is rational is actual": immediately from . . . [a] discussion of the world-historical significance of the Platonic states leaps forth, as if shot from the pistol, this famous (or infamous) dictum. It has by no means been valid . . . from all eternity but only since, through Christianity, the Idea of the divine Kingdom on earth has become a moral demand and thus the standard by which all human institutions are to be judged. Since then, however, it has been *actually* valid. And because for the agent the task of making Reason actual is fixed, cognition has—since

then!—the task of examining Actuality—*become* actual since then!—with a view to discovering how Reason has been actual in it. *Only* because the Rational has become actual—principle of action!—is the Actual rational—principle of cognition! The second half of the dictum, which in contradiction to Hegel's own usage has always been adduced as the kernel of the thought—"Hegel's assertion of the rationality of the Actual"—is thus in fact merely the consequence of the thought, revolutionary in its core, of the actuality of the Rational—a thought expressed in the first half. (Vol. 2, 79)

Some critics have considered the order of Hegel's two-part statement insignificant. Others, as Rosenzweig states, have seen its essence in the second part. Still others have actually reversed its order, thereby misquoting Hegel.[4] Each case reflects mistaken, however seemingly natural, preconceptions, serious enough to make an understanding impossible. A reversal of Hegel's own order may seem to complement him in that it attributes to him a "modern" critical view for which "ontological" assertions about history must be justified by prior "epistemological" assertions about human knowledge. Yet Hegelian "rationality" is not primordially a standard *in us* (logical, moral, or both), nor is his "actuality" exclusively "the world *without* us." Hegelian "rationalism" is far closer to Plantonic idealism (a closeness hinted at by Rosenzweig) than to modern—Kantian-moral, not to speak of epistemological—subjectivism. And if, like Haym and others, one investigates Hegelian "actuality" while paying little attention to his "rationality" one risks projecting upon Hegel non-Hegelian conceptions—and then charging him with either senselessness or scandalousness.

It may seem proper to suppose that Hegel's statement is valid either "universally" or not at all. Not so according to Rosenzweig. Hook asks what shamans and medicine men would assert of their own cannibalistic societies if they were Hegelian philosophers (53). On Hegel's own view (and Rosenzweig's correct interpretation) such societies could not produce Hegelian philosophers; indeed, even Greek society could produce only Platonic and Aristotelian, but not Hegelian, idealism. For Hegel the actuality of the rational is a *specific historical condition*; and only if and when that condition exists is the recognition of the rational in the actual a philosophical possibility. This assertion, to be sure, leaves Hegel with two questions which may permit no easy answer. One concerns the *origin* of the specific historical condition in question and the possibility of a philosophical comprehension of that origin. The other is whether— and if so with what philosophical consequences—that altogether crucial historical condition may *pass away*.[5]

Once having identified the actuality of the rational as a specific historical achievement, we are predisposed to look for exclusively human achievements—moral, cultural, political, technological. Once again Rosenzweig warns us. At least in its own self-understanding the decisive Christian event is a divine-human event, not a human event only. And since the "principle of action" precedes the "principle of cognition," the former must first of all be taken in its own terms before it can be taken in philosophical terms. To be sure, *both* parts of Hegel's statement are philosophical; yet *neither* part would be possible without a *pre*philosophical form of historical existence which, if not entirely religious, has in any case an indispensable religious dimension. Hegel's statement is a translation and transfiguration of a (partly) religious into a philosophical affirmation. In attempting to fathom the meaning of the second, we are well advised first of all to retranslate it from its philosophical into the appropriate religious terms, with a view to discovering what meaning, if any, is yielded by them.

IV

In Hegel's own view it is "unnecessary to cite religion" in defense of his statement, and he confines himself to a passing reference to divine providence.[6] Today such citing, while no longer unnecessary, may be altogether brief if its sole purpose is to dispose of Haym's dilemma. Consider the following Christian (it is Christianity which Hegel's "religion" refers to) affirmation: "God's Providence governs the world, and the world is the place where His Providence may be recognized." Some Christian theologians may have their doubts about divine "providence," preferring instead "grace" or revelation" or "redemption." All will have vast and intricate difficulties with the distinction between worldly events in which God's providence (or grace or revelation or redemption) is, and is not, manifest. None of this matters to establish one fundamental point: unless on other, here irrelevant, grounds all theological statements are dismissed as senseless, *the statement in question is neither tautologous nor scandalous.* Not the first, for one may affirm a God who remains indifferent to the world or, indeed, a *deus absconditus*; not the second because, with the possible exception of certain "heretics," no Christian theologian affirms a divine providence (or grace or revelation or redemption) which has an *indiscriminate* worldly presence. The vast and intricate difficulties bound up with the distinction between such worldly events as do, and such as do not, manifest a divine presence, concern the correct conception of the distinction, and even more the correct identification of instances: they do not concern the fact and necessity of a distinction as such. This remains assured if only (except, as has been said, for certain "heretics") because the world is not identified with or dissipated into God, even though God is its creator and redeemer.

Thus, at least if retranslated into its prephilosophical form (or rather into its religious aspect), Hegel's statement, while possibly causing difficulties, causes none of Haym's difficulties. There is no tautology. There is no obviously scandalous absurdity. There is no "confusion" between "the actual" ("worldly events manifesting God") and the "merely existing" ("worldly events not manifesting God"). Indeed, for those "possessing religion" the statement is "simple."

V

But then, the Hegelian statement is not a Christian theological one but rather gives the Christian "true content" its "true [i.e., philosophical] form." This feat is not external to the content, as may be the case when a philosophy attempts to prove an affirmation which in religion is accepted on faith—and the affirmation itself remains unaltered. The philosophical form alters the religious content in that it transfigures the externality which remains between its terms. To express Hegel's purpose in the simplest (i.e., historical) terms, the rational cannot be *exclusively* a God *external* to man and world if Hegel is any kind of Kantian; and the actual cannot be *exclusively* a natural and/or human world (or a divine manifestation in that world) if Hegel is any sort of Spinozist. Religious representation, though expressing a form of spiritual life in which all things are inwardly related, is nevertheless forced to resort to a symbolism in which God, man, and world have the form of mere side-by-sideness. The form of Hegel's philosophical thought transfigures this side-by-sideness (and thus religious life itself) into a single, self-explicating, spiritual self-activity. And the question arises as to whether in this process the significant differences that remain between God and world vanish when these religious terms become, respectively, the rational and the actual— with the dire consequences asserted from Haym's days to our own.

A brief comment on a single Hegel passage will suffice to answer this question for the modest purposes of this article. Hegel writes:

> I am to make myself fit for the indwelling of the Spirit. . . . This is
> my labor, the labor of man; but the same is also the labor of God,

regarded from His side. He moves toward man and is in man through the act of raising him. What seems my act is thus God's and, conversely, what seems His is mine. This, to be sure, runs counter to the merely moral standpoint of Kant and Fichte; there the Good always remains something yet to be produced . . . , something that ought to be, as if it were not already essentially there. A world outside me remains, God-forsaken, waiting for me to bring purpose and goodness into it. But the sphere of moral action is limited. In religion the Good and reconciliation are absolutely complete and existing on their own account.[7]

We comment:

1. The "moral standpoint" of Kant and Fichte is valid in its own "sphere," and for it "the highest is infinite process."[8] In this sphere the rational is infinite but at the price of being an ideal *in us* only, the world being "God-forsaken" except insofar as we already *have done* what we ought to do and can do.

2. This standpoint is *both* valid in its own "sphere" *and* limited, i.e., superseded by a religious sphere. Infinite process is not *absolutely* highest, for in "religion" the highest is *already* accomplished. Yet this must leave—albeit limited—room for the persistent validity of a human action for which "the highest" is forever *yet to be* accomplished. As for philosophical thought, it must explicate a "reconciliation" that is already implicit in religion itself.

3. Some religions (and their philosophical transfigurations) do not make possible such a reconciliation. Thus the Spinozistic "divine Substance" (according to Hegel, the philosophical transfiguration of Judaism) dissolves the world (and thus human freedom), being itself "acosmic." Christianity (and the Hegelian philosophical "Subject" which is its transfiguration) possesses the "indwelling of the Spirit" by virtue of whose activity "what seems my act . . . is God's, and . . . what seems His is mine." A dialectic of divine giving and human receiving, it "raises" human freedom instead of dissolving it.

4. The freedom thus achieved, however, would still dissolve *moral* freedom (and thus be acosmic in an Hegelian if not a Spinozistic sense) unless, rather than self-sufficient as "religious" (i.e., cultic), it preserved and indeed demanded for its own completion a "secular" (i.e., moral and political) counterpart, in which what "religiously" is *already* divinely achieved is "secularly" forever *yet to be* achieved, by an action that is human. As for the Hegelian philosophical comprehension of this relation between the "religious" and the "secular," it must so internalize it as to preserve rather than dissipate the difference.

VI

The famous (or infamous) Hegelian statement that is the subject of this essay may thus be expounded as follows. Since the rise of Christianity the rational has become actual; but whereas Christian faith has from the start grasped the religious aspect of this event (that through the indwelling of Spirit all is accomplished) it has been left to secular reality, often indifferent or even hostile to the Christian faith, to grasp its secular aspect (that through human action much, if not everything, is forever yet to be accomplished). Only the existence of these two aspects makes the philosophical (instead of merely the theological) formula true. And only the existence of this truth renders possible the Hegelian philosophy—the recognition of the rationality in the actual.

In the *Encyclopedia* passage in which he repeats his controversial statement first made in the preface to the *Philosophy of Right*, Hegel remarks that philosophical "culture" is necessary for its comprehension. Of this culture he tells us that it must know "not only that God is actual, the most actual, indeed, alone truly actual, but also . . . that existence in general is partly appearance and only partly actual." He does not tell us, but rather takes for granted, that the philosophically cultured recognize that appearance is not unreality or illusion but brute, existent fact— that for this philosophical "thought" the distinction between existence and actuality remains as vital and indispensable as the corresponding distinction in "religious representation."

VII

Four major omissions will have been noticed in the above account. All are due to the modesty of the task claimed in the initial paragraph. First, all references to the *Logic* have been avoided: we have sought to show that Hegel *seeks* to distinguish between existence and actuality, not whether or how he succeeds. Second, all references to the *Philosophy of Right* have been avoided, and this despite the fact that the controversial statement that has been under discussion occurs in the preface of that work: we have sought to show that Hegel *can* and *does* distinguish between "actual" and "merely existing" states, not that his criteria of distinction are sound or even defensible—much less that soundness or defensibility attaches to his political judgments. Third, we have refrained from inquiring into the *origin* of what Rosenzweig refers to as Hegel's "principle of action" (see above, sec. III). This is no insignificant question. For Christian faith the divine incursion into history may drop from heaven; Hegel's actuality of the rational cannot. Moreover, the question does not lose its significance when Hegelianism takes an atheistic, left-wing turn: Marx projects the actuality of the rational into the postrevolutionary future; unless there are present origins of this future, this projection reduces itself to a groundless hope and an empty conceit.

The fourth omission is most serious, and it concerns the question most of all in need of contemporary examination. Can the historical conditions producing the actuality of the rational (and hence the rationality of the actual) pass away? (see above, sec. III). The religious incursion into the world of God in Christ may or may not leave room for subsequent eruptions of demonic evil in the world, which produce genocidal industries with by-products including human skin made into lamp-shades, human hair used for pillows, human bones for fertilizer. Hegel's actuality of the rational leaves room only for world-historically insignificant evils to be disposed of as relapses into tribalism or barbarism. In their post-Enlightenment optimism all but a few modern philosophers have ignored or denied the demonic. Hegel's philosophy—which unites Christian religious with modern secular optimism—is the most radical and hence most serious expression of this modern tendency. This modest essay has inquired only into the meaning of Hegel's philosophy. Any inquiry into its truth must confront its claims with the gas chambers of Auschwitz.

PART   2

THE MYTH OF HEGEL
AS TOTALITARIAN
THEORIST OR PRUSSIAN
APOLOGIST

4

Hegel and Political Trends: A Criticism of the Political Hegel Legends

Henning Ottmann
Translated by Jon Stewart

T he effects of Kant's political philosophy and ethical theory on the liberalism of East Prussia and Southwest Germany during the first part of the nineteenth century and on the socialism of the second part of that century correspond to an expectation in the observer which has not really met with all too great disappointment even given different political orientations.[1] One can recognize the advocate of the constitutional state and perhaps even the father of some ethical socialists in the dress that a later age and a later political program have tried to put on this great master. The issue becomes more difficult for the student of Fichte who tries to discern his Fichte behind the masks that have been held before his face: the mask of the socialist, of the nationalist, of the national socialist, of the totalitarian, and of the democrat.[2] And finally the situation seems almost hopeless for the fans of Hegel who try to protect their philosopher from false friends and needless enemies. Every political trend, whether liberalism, socialism, communism, conservatism, nationalism, or national socialism, has tried to bring him over to its side, and when he seemed to reject any such affiliation, every trend has wanted to attack and dismiss him. In any case, it was impossible to avoid him altogether.

In view of this situation, the question about the relationship between Hegel's philosophy and his politics can be neither easily posed nor answered. As is shown at first glance, the omnipresent Hegel seems always to be there. But this omnipresence at first invites the suspicion that Hegel did not have "something to offer everyone," but rather too little for everyone, since instead of offering a lot he offered only something that could be used in various ways. This suggests *prima facie* that one can attack Hegel's dialectic as an "empty formula" which can be applied to any arbitrary ideology and which, so the argument goes, lends itself everywhere, since its pronouncements have complete latitude (and are therefore empirically empty), fit with everything, and cannot be refuted by anything at all.[3] According to this view, any political movement is free to put Hegel's philosophy and its dialectic into its arsenal as a sort of all-purpose weapon. And who would want to deny that the history of the effect of Hegelianism sometimes gives the impression that one saw in Hegel's philosophy nothing but an arms depot where one would go when one needed weapons for any sort of political maneuvers and disputes?

But the images of the "arsenal" and the "empty formula" suggest ideas which, in the case of Hegelianism, do not help us to understand the labyrinthine issues involved in any careful account of the relevant political movements and notions. Ideas are not forged independently of previously existing political trends in order then to be stored in distant arsenals and kept ready for future deployment. They are not blank banners which can be adorned with every emblem and which can be borne by every political movement. They do not belong exclusively to any one age or political trend. And if one should ask what they have to give to a time period or a political movement, one must at the same time ask the other question, what that time period and that given political movement have taken from them. In this way, Hegel's philosophy in the course of its history has been hoisted aloft as the flag of every political movement. But this philosophy (this is the appropriate image) has also changed color in accordance with whether one tried to enrol it in the service of the red, black-white and red, brown, or black-red and gold flags.

Many misunderstandings and Hegel legends are not so much a result of the effect of Hegel's philosophy but rather a consequence of mistaken interpretations of that effect. They largely rest on the fact that the contemporary "colorings" of Hegel's ideas have not been attributed to the various decades of the historical reception, but rather have been presented as the true colors of Hegel's own philosophy. Thus arise the pictures of a Hegel unambiguously ascribed to a certain age: as the official philosopher of the Prussian state, the advocate of Bismarck's totalitarian state, the national socialist, the father of the left Hegelians, or the liberal proponent of the constitutional state. From this results the strange idealistic denunciation of Hegel, which sees his ideas alone (and not competing ideas or the power of concrete conditions) as the moving force behind almost all of German or European history. Whether by classical or leftist liberals, Hegel is charged with the resiliency of the Prussian policy of Restoration, and regardless of whether Hegel is made responsible for the power politics of the Bismarck Era[4] and the founding of the Reich,[5] whether he is to blame for national socialism[6] or is taken as a relative to his capitalist or Marxist sons, in any case without Hegel nothing seems to have been possible. Hegel is always required to pay the debts that others have incurred. To be sure, his political philosophy had an effect like virtually no other. But interpreters of Hegel and the historians of Hegelianism, more so than either Kant or Fichte researchers, are continually thrown back to the point of departure that compels them to separate the effects of the misunderstandings from the misunderstanding of the effects.

The history of the political effects of the misunderstandings and contemporary prejudices begins with the birth of the thesis of Hegel as the philosopher of the *Prussian Restoration and of the policy of accommodation.* This thesis was already introduced into currency by the first reviewers of the *Philosophy of Right,*[7] and, despite its year of birth (1821), it still today enjoys a robust health (even if the circle of friends, which have kept it alive for different reasons, has often changed). In the 1820s and 1830s, one spoke everywhere of the servile Hegel, who accommodated himself to the Prussian policy of Restoration.[8] With this, the first countercaricature seemd to be triggered in 1829 in the form of Schubarth's attacks, where he tried to point out the incommensurability of the Hegelian doctrine of "constitutional" monarchy with the "highest principle of life and development of the Prussian state," (for Schubarth, the "absolute monarchy in the form of the Hohenzollerns' 'family spirit' ").[9] At first one still saw most Hegelians such as Gans, Koeppen, Förster, Elsner, and Varnhagen van Ense busy defending the "modern" spirit of Hegel's political doctrine and of the Prussian state against the double equivocation (by someone, moreover, philosophically incompetent).[10] But being insufficiently and superficially grounded, Schubarth's denunciation was not adequate to effect the consternation which would have been necessary to make questionable the clichés about the philosopher of the Restoration which were already familiar to the public. Instead, in the transition from the 1830s to the 1840s that influential process took place, to which the thesis of accommodation ultimately owes its enormous success.

In those years, those students of Hegel, who (often educated in the fraternities) hoped to realize their more or less liberal ideals in the protestant, reformable Prussian state,[11] became the familiar and well-known group of oppositionists and left Hegelians, who wanted to put the republic and democracy in the place of the constitutional monarchy, the revolution in the place of reform, and an atheistic policy of emancipation in the place of a protestant policy of reform. Among the members of this group, the thesis about Hegel's accommodation spread quickly after 1840, since it offered a form in which the political and private disappointments of these Hegelians who had wandered to the left could be digested. They were disappointed with the romantic and conservative policy of Friedrich Wilhelm IV, in whom they had placed such high hopes.[12] They were disappointed with the expulsions from the universities and the editing rooms, disappointed with the favor with Eichhorn, the Minister of Culture, which was enjoyed at the time by Schelling, the orthodoxy, pietists, romantics and followers of the historical school of law.[13] Now the strange spectacle took place that those who originally celebrated the modern Prussian state and Hegel's doctrine in a single breath now tried to put the change in Prussian policy after 1840 in a line with the policy of the Restoration of the early 1820s, and tried to project the origin of their misfortune back onto Hegel. Indeed, for many the evening mood [*abendliche Stimmung*] of a philosophy, which wanted to await the flight of the owl of Minerva at dusk, had yielded to the cock's crow of a new day of world history, which a philosophy of "deed" [*Philosophie der Tat*] would help to bring about.[14] What one first thought to accomplish with an alliance of Hegel with Prussia was now to be carried through by means of an opposition of Hegel against Prussia. Hegel's philosophy was from now on to be understood only in its independence from the Restoration, which Hegel was thought to have indicated when he discussed the contingent "historical existences" of the Prussian state as "metaphysical" determinations.[15] Hegel's philosophy was "commensurable" with the Prussian state, but only with the "absolutistic" state, which knew how to honor the lack of theory and the "Olympian calm" of this system. Ruge, who was successful in this masterpiece of repression and switching of positions, was able to compare the effect of his criticism of accommodation with the effect which Strauß's *Leben Jesu* had had on the theological Hegel discussion.[16] From now on, for left Hegelians the political front against Hegel was firmly marked out, even if the meaning of the reproach gradually spread to a criticism of Hegel as one who accommodated himself to "bourgeois society." Moreover, Feuerbach's criticism of religion and of Hegel's theological system helped to found an opposition on grounds of principle between the philosophy of emancipation, which was critical of religion, and the "reactionary" philosophy of origin [*Ursprungsphilosophie*]. There probably remained the uneasy feeling that, as Engels once put it, "one cannot write off a fellow like Hegel with the simple word 'Prussian',"[17] but for this purpose, the widespread criticism of accommodation and the opposition against the philosophy of origin in general were at one's disposal in the period that followed. For Marx the accommodation meant the "lie" of the idealistic "system" and "principle" which tried to bridge the contradictions of reality in the idea, and which must be led back, in a manner like that of Feuerbach, from the heaven of politics to the ground of society; Hegel, so it was argued, did not succeed in the mediation of the *bourgeois* with the *citoyen*, and instead he made the state fit with society, attributed the title "*homme*" to the private citizen, and changed the citizen of the state into its servant.[18] Engels tried to distinguish between the conservative "system" and the revolutionary "method," and from here comes the formula of the Hegel interpretation which Marxism up until the present is supposed to employ.[19] Even if in the meantime the dogma of the division between system and method is no longer undisputed and Hegel's philosophy must prove its living power against the tendencies toward torpidity of orthodox Marxism, in principle the image of Hegel which remains the representation customary for left Hegelianism is that of a Janus, of a philosopher of the system and of the origin, partly revolutionary and a partly reactionary, who accommodated himself with Prussia or bourgeois society.[20]

The left Hegelian "philosophy of deed" began to get help from other workshops of thought. Just as Cieszkowski did before, so also Koeppen, Ruge, Bruno Bauer, and Moses Heß recalled Fichte's pathos for freedom.[21] For liberalism, on the other side, the course was already just as much set with the success of the critique of accommodation as it was for the further history of left Hegelianism. Certainly, for the liberals, Kant had been the preferred ally anyway, whose spirit gave wings to the constitutional aspirations in East Prussia, to the policy of Theodor von Schön, to Jacoby's demands, and to the editorials in the *Königsberger Zeitung*.[22] But the slide of the Hegelians to the left began to destroy the bridges between Hegelianism and liberalism which might otherwise have been able to be maintained.[23] Indeed, in East Prussia Rosenkranz provides an excellent example of the possible alliance of Hegelianism with liberalism, since he was in agreement on many things with the liberals inspired by Kant. But the history of the group called "the Free" [*"Freien"*] (to whom Engels, Buhl, Stirner, Nauwerk, Koeppen, and the Bauer brothers all belonged) shows in an exemplary fashion with the behavior of Edgar and Bruno Bauer how the general worsening of the political climate began to dissolve the alliance between Hegelianism and liberalism. In 1841 Bruno Bauer, on the occasion of a celebration for the Southwest German liberal Welcker, proposed a toast in which he did not neglect to say that Hegel's doctrine by far surpassed the Southwest German views "of the state in point of boldness, liberality and determination."[24] Indeed, he had already made clear his intention to open up a "terrible and powerful bombardment" against these "proponents of constitutionalism."[25] Then Edgar Bauer also brought out the heavy artillery, when in 1843 he published his critique of the liberal movements in East Prussia and Southwest Germany.[26] Ruge, in one of the last editions of the *Deutsche Jahrbücher*, calls for a dissolution of liberalism into democratism.[27] The movement then set in toward ever more radical positions to the left of the middle, e.g., movements toward socialism (Moses Heß), communism (Engels, Marx) and anarchism (Stirner).[28] For the Southwest German liberals around Rotteck and Welcker the prejudice could only be confirmed that this Hegelianism must lie just as far to the left as Hegel's "Restoration philosophy" to the right. As Scheidler wrote in the *Staatslexikon*, the standard work of "*Vormärz*" liberalism, Hegel's philosophy "consistently leads to servility and to an unnatural *political quietism*, which is diametrically opposed to the principle of *reform* or *political progress* which the *Staatslexikon* confesses."[29] It had been diametrically opposed to liberalism for a long time now. In the resigned climate of the years following 1848, the liberal Rudolf Haym in 1857 brought the opposition to a head in a formulation which stuck with the public for a long time, according to which Hegel's philosophy was that "Restoration system" which reserved a "place" for the spirit of the Restoration in all its parts, and which pronounced "the classical word of the spirit of the Restoration . . . of political conservatism, quietism and optimism" in its motto about the identification of reason and reality.[30] For Haym the time had passed beyond this system, which in 1857 lay just as far away as the classical age of poetry and art in Germany. The field of history was supposed to enter into the heritage of classicism and of systematic philosophy and, in the dawning age of natural science and technology, was supposed to preserve critically the spirit of Weimar and Berlin.[31]

Clearly, Hegel was not a man of the *conservatives* as one would expect in view of the criticism of accommodation issued by the left and the liberals. To the high estimation which he enjoyed as an academic teacher, there corresponded an amazingly small resonance of his doctrine of the state among influential conservative theoreticians and groups, amazingly small if Hegel's philosophy is supposed to have been "the" theory of the Restoration. Moreover, a large number of his students (Carové, Ulrich, von Henning, Förster, Asverus, Cousin) became victims of the persecution of the "demagogues,"[32] and, indeed, his well-wishers and friends such as Hardenberg, Altenstein, Schulze, and Niethammer cannot easily be placed in the conservative camp.[33] The crown prince and later Friedrich Wilhelm IV, the court camarilla, the Gerlach brothers, and Radowitz were political enemies of Hegel and Hegelianism, just as were

Hengstenberg and Leo and the true ideologues of absolute monarchy and the legitimacy, such as Haller and Stahl.[34] The political orientation of the "Christian state" was furnished by, among others, pietistic, orthodox, Schellingian and other sources, and not by the "Restoration philosophy" of Hegel. It is one of the oddities of the history of the reception of Hegel's philosophy that a genuinely conservative Hegel reception only came about when the age of the Prussian Restoration and reaction had already past. And it is also an oddity that just as at first it was the slide to the left of many Hegelians which produced so many legends, so also here once again changed political conditions produced the climate in which the picture of the former philosopher of the Restoration could be superimposed on a new legend, on the picture of the Hegel who anticipated Bismarck.

In fact, only in the 1850s did the conservative Hegel trend set in, which led to the picture of *the conservative Hegel*, of *the philosopher of Bismarck's totalitarian state* [*Machtstaat*] and of *the German nationalist*. At first it was only Erdmann—and he is probably someone whom one can call the "state philosopher of Prussia" with more justice than Hegel— who thundered against the "professors' politics" of the Frankfurt National Assembly. He opposed to the liberal demands a doctrine of the "organic," "ethical," commonwealth, which decidedly contrasted the state with society, and wanted to advocate more patriotism, conservatism, and Christianity than he saw in the liberals of his day.[35] In the course of time the mutable liberalism began to associate itself with this sort of "stock Prussianism," a liberalism which in 1848 had documented its impotence and now in part went over into conservative national liberalism. For these liberals the question about the philosopher of the Prussian state and his relevance for the Bismarck Era soon appeared in a new light. If it had been Erdmann alone who had first raved about Hegel's "philosophy of the Prussian state and court" and had recalled the alliance once ratified in heaven between Prussia and philosophy,[36] then there was soon to be heard another tone from those who, like Ruge and Haym, had to be held responsible for the enormous effect of the critique of accommodation. Under the impression of the events of 1866, Ruge made his peace with Prussia and Bismarck, who in 1877 bequeathed an honorary stipend on him.[37] Haym could say in 1870 that Hegel had possessed "the instinct for power as the first, indispensable condition for civil life."[38] Just as the like-minded national liberal Rümelin,[39] Haym also asserts that Hegel, as a "southern German"—which now apparently seems to be attributed to him as a sign of merit—had "found the way to the recognition of . . . the north German state, which was destined to become the *cornerstone* of German freedom and unity."[40] In 1870 one can think of the philosopher with "full honors who more recklessly and more unconditionally than any other adopted the Prussian state a half a century earlier."[41]

In this way, the judgment of the interpreters changed with the political trends of the times, and one legend intertwined with another to form a chain in which one weak link was connected with the next. The time had come for the Bismarck Hegelians, Constantin Rößler and Adolph Lasson, who unburdened by a liberal past, as were Ruge and Haym, consciously set about the synthesis of Hegel's philosophy with the age of blood and iron. Rößler, the very prototype of the Bismarck Hegelian,[42] in his grandiose doctrine of the state made Hegel appear as the great grandfather of the philosophy of the totalitarian state, who had already just as much surpassed the revolutionary theories (of Montesquieu and Rousseau with their effects on the philosophy of Kant and Fichte as well as on liberalism) as the theories of counterrevolution (of Burke, via the romantics to de Maistre, de Bonald, Haller, and up to the historical school of law).[43] For Rößler, the course of history after Hegel's death could only confirm how right Hegel had been to seek a path between revolution and Restoration. The liberals' state, the constitutional state with the hidden goal of material utility, had already been outdated by the chaotic development of civil society and by the partially justified demands of socialism; conservative attempts to weaken the centralization of power that had become necessary, and to construct a policy on the basis of a single personality or (and on this score Rößler recognizes the commonality between liberalism and reaction) still to believe in a self-producing harmony of the different parts of the state, had all been the dangerous illusions of a political orientation that had turned reactionary. Hegel's doctrine of the state, on the contrary, and on this point Rößler and Adolf Lasson were in agreement,[44] offered the contemporary solution, since it, in contrast to liberalism, promised to preserve against civil society the motifs of the traditional good life, and since it made power comprehensible in the state beyond the illusions of the reaction, power which civil society would be able to overcome. Finally, Hegel's doctrine was relevant to the age since it made it possible to replace the Kantian "empty" ideals of perpetual peace, international rights, and humanity with ideas about war and nations asserting themselves in battle, which were more appropriate to the epoch; first of all war and not mere treaties was supposed to be inserted into world history as the judge, which would award one nation its title of ruler.[45] The philosopher of the Prussian state had now become the philosopher of the totalitarian state and the forerunner of a nation, which only came into existence forty years after his death. Once again the prejudices against Hegel were turned into their opposite. Just as he had once been blamed from the liberal side for his

reverence toward Napoleon and his (partial) opposition to the fraternities, and had been rebuked as "the fellow without a fatherland,"[46] so also
now he was the philosopher of the Reich, whom even liberals such as
Rosenkranz at least verbally wanted to dub "the national philosopher,"[47]
or whom even left liberals such as Michelet in 1870 saw as an ally to
the unsavory cause.[48] Hegel was introduced into the Reich, which at the
beginning of the World War he was called upon to supply with the "ideas
of 1914."[49]

Hegel was thus forced into the service of power politics and nationalism. Soon he would have to serve even worse masters. Out of the
philosopher of the totalitarian state and the nationalist, he became *the
national socialist Hegel,* who for most juristic neo-Hegelians (such as Binder,
Busse, Dulckeit, Larenz, Schmidt, Schönfeld, Spann, Bülow, and Häring)
had anticipated what was necessary to establish for the new age. His
critique of individualistic natural right and of modern contract theory,
his doctrine of classes, his subordination of abstract right and morality
to ethical life (understood as the subordination of society to the state),
his conception of an "organic" state, his notion of a spirit of a people,
and his philosophy of history all seemed to offer what was necessary: the
sublation of the legal person into the comrade in a social class or a people,
the dissolution of the notion of the constitutional state to the advantage
of the doctrine of a community of a people and of a total people's state,
and the replacement of the ideals of international rights and peace with
a philosophy of nationalism and war which provided the spirit of the
Germanic people and the world historical personality of the Führer with
a special mission.[50] It was a time of simple replacements, in which one
wanted to replace Hegel's monarch with the Führer, his concept of a
spirit of the people (which covered both natural and mental aspects) with
race, his Aristotelian, modern ethical life with unreflected custom, and
his philosophy of history with providence.[51] Certainly, it was also the age
of rather ambitious philosophical interpretations, which argued often
with traces of brilliant sophism not merely against other theories and
methods of the grounding of right,[52] but also against competing views of
Hegel. Thus, one could not charge Hegel with being a state philosopher
of Prussia, since neither the "homeless liberalism" of a Ruge nor the
Prussian conservatism of Erdmann was able to be applied to the Hegel
who had pointed out the people [*Volk*] ahead of time.[53] Thus, the entire
question of liberal Hegel interpretation and Hegel criticism was wrong for
the national socialist right Hegelians, since Hegel's question was never
how the objective ethical life of the state could be grounded starting
with the individual. Hegel's universalism, as it was put by the formula
of demarcation from liberalism, Marxism, anarchism, and a grab bag of

other political trends, had from the beginning stood by the priorities of the community, after which right and morality had to be logically ordered.[54]

One of the most regrettable developments in the reception of Hegel's philosophy is that his opponents have until the present day confused Hegel himself with these legends, which have only received their force on the basis of German history after Hegel. The liberal Hegel criticism and also Hegel research abroad for almost a hundred years have not granted Hegel the courtesy of a fair hearing, since the pictures of Hegel held responsible by the critics for the ideology of the Prussian state, for the Bismarck Hegelians and national socialists have merged to such a degree with the ideas of German history that there no longer remains any room for a Hegel who does not fit into these schemes. The misunderstandings now go into a second dimension, so to speak, since onto a thesis which is already too widespread once again another oversubscribed criticism is placed. In France one reacts to the Germany of Bismarck, since Hegel is declared responsible for the German policy of the totalitarian state (Caro, Beaussire, Vermeil, Andler, Delbos).[55] In the Anglo-Saxon countries Hegel is regarded as the bewildering illiberal outgrowth of power politics, who is only acknowledged with a sigh and a shaking of the head (Dewey, Hobhouse, Vaughan, Sabine, Hook, Carrit, Plamenatz).[56] In Germany itself the impression becomes solidified among important historians and jurists that Hegel was responsible for the collapse and transformation of the nation of culture into the nation of the totalitarian state, since he, as Meinecke once put it, had let fall an "apologetic light" on the "dark side of the reason of the state."[57] Heller, who was inspired by Meinecke to work out this thesis, traced Hegel's influence on the history of national totalitarian thought and so successfully confused Hegel with the Bismarck Hegelians as well as the historians and jurists of the nineteenth century that it seemed impossible to separate Hegel from the Bismarck Era forever after.[58] The Hegelianism of national socialism closed the chain of misunderstandings and the legends (which were by now intertwined three times). Now there was no longer even a distinction made between the philosopher of the Prussian state, the Hegel of Bismarck, and the national socialist, but rather Hegel was all of them rolled into one: Prussian, German nationalist, national socialist, as the stages of the German collapse leading to the catastrophe are now wont to be designated (McGovern, Popper, Topitsch, Cassier, Apelt, von Martin, Kiesewetter).[59] The fact that neither the theoreticians of the Prussian Restoration nor Bismarck himself nor the leading ideologues of the Third Reich could find no use for Hegel did nothing to change the situation.[60] The legends by accretion gained such force that they could no longer be stopped. Anyone who, like the German historians of the nineteenth century, tended toward the thought of the totalitarian state, or who justified the First World War or tried to legitimate national socialism with a quotation from Hegel, was considered a Hegelian.[61] Hegel alone was saddled with the theoretical blame for the German fate, since other theories or even real factors apparently played no role in these matters. To point out the simple fact that Prussia had not been the Bismarck Reich and that the latter in its turn had not been the state of the national socialists was already regarded as the sin of historical hair-splitting. The fact that a Prussian conservative of the type of an Erdmann cannot be confused with the Bismarck Hegelians and that the latter cannot be confused with the national socialist appropriators of Hegel was not able to hold out against the seductive association of German history and right Hegelianism.[62] Left Hegelians had to point out that their reactionary philosopher of the system had nevertheless lived in the classical epoch of the German spirit and humanism, which was worlds away from the barbarism of national socialism.[63] But Hegel and Hegelianism were caught in the mill of those commentators of German history who from 1840 until today have tried to carry out the conquest of the past by loading it onto Hegel's back.

Although there are a number of historiographies on right and left Hegelianism, there is today still no similarly extensive and detailed history of middle Hegelianism and of its Hegel, of the proponent of the constitutional monarchy and the modern constitutional state. Not only were the students of the first generation (who defended Hegel against Schubarth) liberal at least for a time, but also important Hegelians such as Rosenkranz, Hinrichs, and Michelet testify to a liberal Hegelianism in the nineteenth century, which tried to resist the trend of German history and the self-perpetuating Hegel legends. It was above all Rosenkranz who, as the "academic herald of liberalism,"[64] wanted to make Hegel's doctrine of the constitutional monarchy and of the constitutional state comprehensible in its contemporary context, which was continually being clouded by the Hegel legends. Just as the earlier Hegel students did against Schubarth, so also Rosenkranz pointed out against Haym the differences between Hegel's philosophical state and the Prussia of the Restoration. He began by making clear the continuity in Hegel's thought between the Jena and Berlin periods, which could not come into view with a perspective limited only to Prussia.[65] He recalled Hegel's distinction between "actuality" and "existence,"[66] as well as the separation between "absolute" and "objective" Spirit, which indicate the complicated relations of the different parts of Hegel's doctrine of spirit vis-à-vis the simplistic charge of a philosophical or religious deification of the state.[67] Rosenkranz wrote, setting forth a list, which in the later history of Hegelianism would be constantly supplemented, of the institutions featured in Hegel's state that outstripped those of the Prussian state: "Prussia at the time was not a constitutional state; it possessed no room for public opinion, no consent in questions of the administration of justice, no freedom of the press, no equality of citizens before the law, no participation of the people in the legislation of laws or allocation of taxes—and Hegel taught that all of that was philosophically necessary."[68] His doctrine of the state, as Rosenkranz highlighted thereby pointing the way for future research, "could not satisfy the parties, between whose battle lines it appeared."[69] Hegel sketched the "idea" of the modern state, which historically had only just begun to come about.[70]

There was an Hegelian liberalism in the nineteenth century; Rosenkranz, Hinrichs, Michelet are some of its representatives, who, as Lübbe has shown, tried to preserve Hegelian liberalism in the changing times.[71] Partly, as in the case of Rosenkranz, by becoming politically active, but in any case by an extensive political writing campaign, these Hegelians of 1848 and later tried to bring the liberal elements of Hegel's philosophy into the politics of the times. That after 1848 it happened that this liberalism "became bourgeois," and that the progress of technology had to be made a joke as the stopgap for the snail's pace of the political world reason, that one invested America or even the uprising of the Czechs with the old hopes, and that one bet like Michelet with prophetic optimism on the "end of war in Europe," on "the constitutional state as the state of the future" and on Christianity as the unifying power of mankind,[72] in short that this liberalism in the second half of the nineteenth century became untimely and withdrew into a dream world is not so much the "fault" as the consequence of German history whose climate allowed other ideas to prosper. Nevertheless, these Hegelians—and this can still be followed in the discussions of the "Philosophy Club" in Berlin and in the history of the journal *Der Gedanke*—even in the age of blood and iron did not allow Hegel to become either a state philosopher of Prussia or a national socialist.[73]

Middle Hegelianism has today corrected some hyperbolic versions of the Hegel legends. Even during the war a rehabilitation of Hegel began in the Anglo-Saxon countries through the work of Knox. This work has been carried on by Findlay, Kaufmann, Pelczynski, Avineri, and Taylor.[74] In France after the war in Eric Weil's heritage, Fleischmann, Grégoire, and Jacques d'Hondt have put aright what had grown out of proportion. Only in ignorance of these researchers, can one still simply charge Hegel with the Prussian Restoration, the Bismarck Era, and national socialism. In Germany as early as the first half of the twentieth century, Rosenzweig had set the standard for an interpretation which provided further arguments for the distinction of Hegel's theory of the state from the Prussia of the Restoration and, by expanded proofs, made good the continuity in Hegel's thought between the Jena and Berlin periods. This account of the historical development, which explodes the legends, has been a postulate of the first order for Hegel research.[75] After the war the ground was already prepared for Joachim Ritter's Hegel interpretation. Ritter revived Hegel in his own right against his left- and right-wing students and saw him not only as mediating (politically) between the Restoration and revolution but also as reconciling (metaphysically and theoretically) classical theory and the knowledge of the age. Hegel in his theory incorporated the French Revolution and civil society just as much as he did romanticism and the Restoration; he had understood them as the poles of a "split" [*Entzweiung*], which had to be endured and which, being both utopian as well as reactionary, could be closed only at the price of an already accomplished freedom and reason.[76] Recognized once again as a politics in the classical tradition of Aristotelian natural right, Hegel's theory of the state was withdrawn from oversimplified politicizing. In his theory of natural right, the presence of the tradition of an Aristotelian practical philosophy and ethical politics and also of revolution (e.g., the separation of the *oikos* in the "family" and in the "national economy," the distinction between "morality" and "ethical life," the emancipation of society from the state) can be conceptually and historically demonstrated.[77] And just as Hegel's philosophy was able to be a seizing of its time in thought and thus was a classical theory, and likewise just as it was able to be a doctrine of civil society and the modern state and yet a doctrine of traditional natural right, so also it now seemed to make possible an understanding of the connection of religion and politics, which had only been clouded over by the left Hegelian criticism of the reactionary philosophy of the origin. Moreover, Hegel's doctrine unified the traditional and the modern, the emancipation of the state from religion and secularization, and also the freedom of the Christian (without which the modern state would not have been able to come about) and the indirect political effects of religion, which prepares (by its ethical element) the private citizen of the ideologically neutral state for the political universality, which (by its suprapolitical horizon) hinders extremism just as much as the totalization of politics in general.[78] Today, we can sum up the picture of Hegel presented by the middle Hegelianism by saying that Hegel's philosophy as a whole belongs in the tradition of modern political theory of the West, which helped to ground the constitutional state in which we now live.

Hegel, thus seen as one of the fathers of the modern constitutional state, who belongs in the genealogy of Locke and Mill and can be unconditionally reintegrated into the "main stream of Western political theory,"[79] is a picture which although doubtless trims down to size the legends of the state philosopher of Prussia, the ideologue of the authoritarian state and the national socialist, nevertheless today almost threatens to become a legend itself.[80] Opposing the complete integration of Hegel into the spirit of Western liberal democracies (as with other political movements as well) is the fact that they belong to a time that is no longer Hegel's own. Although today it can be asserted that the interpretations from Rosenkranz to Ritter which mediated the left and the right come the closest to Hegel's universal attempts at mediation, nevertheless, Hegel's doctrine is not exhausted by these interpretations. Just as his philosophy of the constitutional state and of division comes down neither on the side of the revolution nor the Restoration and cannot be reduced to the common denominator of the Prussian Restoration, the politics of the totalitarian state, or the people's state, so also it did and does offer liberalism some cumbersome and problematic doctrines as building blocks.

In Hegel's account, contract theory is rejected, and the contract is pushed aside in abstract right, so to speak, in private law. There, the state of nature is rejected as a model for legitimation and is assigned to the "apparent beginning of states," which are supposed to have their "substantial principle" only in ethical life[81] (which once again is reached in "right" in the clever overlapping of nature and freedom beyond the facticity of external nature, and in "morality" in the becoming ethical of the inner nature only as the "second" nature having become the "present world"). This dialectic of nature and spirit which is fundamentally different from contract theory rejects any prepolitical rights of citizen or man, when it founds these as rights of man transpolitically and in the historical context of the French Revolution and civil society. To be sure, Hegel's doctrine was one of a constitutional monarchy, but the legitimation of the monarch is supposed to be speculatively demonstrated from the "nature" of the succession (if it is indeed not already supposed to mirror even at the conceptual level the synthesis of natural particularity and spiritual universality, which Hegel otherwise reserves for the comprehension of the becoming human of Christ).[82] The necessity of a constitution is for Hegel beyond question, and yet he emphasizes constantly that a constitution is not merely "made" (but rather is the product of a world Spirit cunningly making use of individuals and peoples).[83] The separation of powers was not established for the sake of their function as control, (and in general Hegel's whole way of thinking cannot be compared to the liberal construal of checks and balances), but rather is comparable to an integrative way of thinking oriented toward a concept of organism. To be sure, the emancipation of society was incorporated into the foundation of his account, but there remains the acceptance of primogeniture and the binding of the individual to the classes and corporations, and Hegel denies to the private citizen as such the right to vote on or associate with these classes or corporations simply as one pleases.[84] The formal legal state, with its legality and its opposition between private and public, is surpassed by the organic state composed of classes and by the ethical commonwealth. The state of nature, which the doctrine of the state had to spiritualize by means of right, morality, and ethical life, comes up again at the end in the opposition of the states in "international law." The Hegelian state internally, in spite of the organism of the classes and a form of legitimation that is incongruous with the tradition of modern contract theory, leaves externally the traces of the later totalitarian state when it dissolves Kant's ideal of international law and peace in favor of "ethical" war and the conception of world history as a new state of nature.

Is Hegel's political theory, therefore, merely an empty formula? Or is it as the young Marx with a view to Hegel once put it: "I say everything to you, since I have said nothing!"[85] The opposite seems to be the case. The fact that Hegel cannot be incorporated into the group of philosophers of the modern constitutional state proves only that this thinker was too big to be able to be reduced to individual political movements or to his own political dimension. In this we find not the uselessness or arbitrary application of his theory but rather its greatness and its historical power. From the history of the political effect of Hegel's philosophy, the conclusion can be drawn that Hegel had something to say to a particular time period precisely because he viewed neither the problems of politics from the perspective of a given party nor politics itself from a purely political standpoint. Left Hegelianism, as understandable as its demands for a philosophy of deed seemed in view of the teleological historicality of the Hegelian system and the tone of finality found there, and as convincing as it was in its criticism of accommodation to the concrete Prussian state or bourgeois society as well as in its criticism of the philosophy of the origin, is today no longer persuasive, because it not only regards the age in which this system was born as a purely political one, but rather it directly politicizes and reduces Hegel himself as well as his philosophy, aesthetics, theory of religion and state at a loss to their transpolitical messages. Thus, the chance was passed up to preserve in Hegel the idea of reason enduring through time, either in the form of classical theory of the tradition of natural law or of Christian freedom. Right Hegelianism, as legitimately as it could ground in Hegel the "good life" and some motifs of its early conservatism (clearly no longer its national socialist naturalization and totalization), with completely reversed premises had missed its chance, since it tried to integrate the political side of Hegel completely into its time and thus lost from view that Hegel who had more to offer than just politics alone. The right Hegelians accommodated themselves with Prussia and with the Second and Third Reich in a way that Hegel in his time had not prescribed. Middle Hegelianism, which best preserved and rehabilitated Hegel's adjustment to the left and right and his doctrine of the modern constitutional state, seemed in the climate of the liberal democracies to be in danger of repeating the error of immediately politicizing Hegel. Yet it certainly more so than the other Hegel schools can be called on to help end the age of political Hegel legends. After the immediate political labels of Hegel are recognized as "laughable misinterpretations,"[86] middle Hegelianism today could relativize its own Hegel liberalizing so that it does not forget the conditions for the existence of modern autonomy and the constitutional state (in Hegel) in its own grounding of freedom and right (in Hegel), which both need, but which neither can guarantee by itself alone: e.g., the *ethos* of the family, the ethical life of the citizen, who can be more than merely a wolf among wolves, the concrete-universal of the state itself which—also and precisely with the present overlapping of society and state through parties, alliances, and a technology becoming autonomous—cannot be reduced to lowest common denominator of compromise on particular interests. Moreover, the gaining of distance to the immediate temporal and partisan appropriation of Hegel would succeed, if Hegel would be recognized not merely as the mediator between the political fronts but also once again as a philosopher who did not want to take politics to be the ultimate criterion of human action.

The history of Hegelianism obliges us to learn from it. And it obliges us to do justice just as much to the distorted picture of the Hegel as a political party man as to the picture of the philosopher who wanted to found politics in an overarching synthesis in which the ancient and the modern, Greek natural law and modern autonomy, bourgeois emancipation and ethical life of institutions, religion becoming mundane and freedom of the Christian person are once and for all reconciled in the name of philosophy. This philosophy outstripped just as much the political fronts of its own time as the political one-sidedness of post-Hegelian history. Not least of all it was the indirect connection of religion and politics in this philosophy which hindered the total positing of politics pure and simple, and preserved it from a relapse behind an historically already achieved reason and freedom. As a theory that was practical only indirectly, it was not immediately useful for political ends. Hegel's philosophy had its place at a distance to the interests and factions of the day, a distance which is a necessary precondition for an understanding of reason embodied in time. And if Hegel's philosophy appears to us today also to be in many respects a philosophy of its age, then Hegelianism will have handed down its suprapolitical heritage if it can avoid the mistaken ways of immediate politicizing in the future.

5

Hegel and Prussianism

T. M. Knox

D espite the effort of Bosanquet,[1] Muirhead,[2] Basch,[3] and many others, it is still frequently stated or implied, in both popular and scholarly literature, that Hegel (1) constructed his philosophy of the state with an eye to pleasing the reactionary and conservative rulers of Prussia in his day,[4] and (2) condoned, supported, and through his teaching, became partly responsible for some of the most criticized features in "Prussianism" and even of present-day national socialism.[5] In this article I propose to give reasons for denying that Hegel the man is justly accused of servility to the Prussian government, and that there is any warrant in the text of his *Philosophie des Rechts* for the charge that Hegel the philosopher was an exponent of "Prussianism" and "frightfulness."

I

After occupying a philosophical chair at Heidelberg for two years, Hegel was appointed Professor of Philosophy at Berlin in 1818, and delivered his Inaugural Lecture on October 22nd. During the winter he lectured on "Natural Law and Political Science" (*Naturrecht und Staatswissenschaft*) as well as on his *Encyclopedia*, and at this time or a little later he must have started to write his *Natural Law and Political Science in Outline, or Fundamental Principles of the Philosophy of Law*[6] (*Naturrecht und Staatswissenschaft im Grundrisse—Grundlinien der Philosophie des Rechts*) as a textbook for future courses of lectures on this subject, which really comprised jurisprudence, ethics, and political philosophy. The book was not published until 1821.

The evidence that he started to write it shortly after his arrival in Berlin is contained in a letter from him to Friedrich Creuzer, formerly his colleague in Heidelberg. Creuzer had sent him a copy of the new edition of his work on ancient mythology, and Hegel replies (30 October 1819) that his acknowledgment has been delayed because he had hoped to send as a return—though too poor a return—"some sheets of my sections on the Philosophy of Law." He had been ready to go to press with his book when the Carlsbad Decrees were issued. "Now that we know where we stand with our exemption from censorship, I propose to print at once."[7] Since the *Philosophie des Rechts* is divided into sections, it is plain that it is to this book that Hegel refers. To enable us to understand the rest of his statements, a short excursion into history is required.

The Congress of Vienna, which settled the map of Europe in 1814, was a triumph for conservatism, for diplomats to whom the revolutionary ideas emanating from France were anathema. It was a defeat for Stein, who for years had labored to make the Germans a united people, and who by his reforms had tried to give them civil and political liberty. He retired into private life, but it was his ideas that led in 1815 to the formation of a German Students' Association with "Honour, Liberty and Fatherland" as its motto. Two years later some hundreds of students from all over Germany held a festival on the Wartburg as a demonstration in favor of freedom and German unity. Fries, Hegel's predecessor in his Heidelberg chair, was one of the speakers on this occasion, and his enthusiastic address is the subject of some criticism in the preface to Hegel's *Philosophie des Rechts*.

In 1819 Kotzebue, the writer, was murdered by a student named Sand on suspicion of being a Russian spy whose activities were inimical to the cause of German liberty. This event caused such a sensation that the Governments of the German States felt that they now had an opportunity to take action against revolutionary ideas prevalent in the universities. After a conference at Carlsbad they issued what are known as the "Carlsbad Decrees" on 20 September 1819. These provided for a strict censorship of periodicals and pamphlets, as well as for the suppression of the Students' Association. At the same time Fries was dismissed from his chair at Jena. On 18 October university teachers in Prussia were officially made aware of the decrees, and they were also informed that *all* their publications would be censored; the exemption from censorship that the Prussian universities, together with the Prussian Academy, had enjoyed would now be suspended.

It is clear from what Hegel says to Creuzer that his book on the *Philosophie des Rechts* was completed by 29 September 1819, the date of the Carlsbad Decrees. Between that date and 30 October, the date of

Hegel's letter, he had been officially informed of the position about the exemption from censorship hitherto enjoyed by university professors, i.e., he had been informed that the exemption was suspended. But now that the atmosphere of uncertainty had passed he proposed to go ahead with his book and submit it to censorship in the ordinary course. The manuscript was sent to the publisher, and some of it may even have been printed at this time, because there is a receipt, signed by Hegel and dated 15 December 1819, acknowledging a payment on account of royalties on his forthcoming book on *Naturrecht*.[8] Having second thoughts, however, he must have decided to withhold the book until the excitement arising from Kotzebue's murder had died down, because the date appended to the preface is 25 June 1820, while the date on the title page is 1821.[9]

What emerges from these facts is that despite the title page date, Hegel's book was begun almost as soon as he arrived in Berlin. This might at first sight lend plausibility to the conjecture that, on entering the service of Prussia, he decided to write a book on political philosophy supporting the Prussian status quo. But his interest in the subject was not new in 1818; it had been a dominant one ever since his student days. Nor were the conclusions embodied in his book new in substance. His opinions developed, as one might expect, with advancing years; but there is no radical change. From first to last he is fascinated by what he regarded as the unity of Greek life, and his problem remains the same: how is it possible to combine the individual Greek's complete devotion to his city with the modern emphasis on the paramount importance of individual freedom? There is hardly anything in the *Philosophie des Rechts* to surprise readers of Hegel's earlier writings on political philosophy; in particular, the theory of the state contained in the book published in 1821 is simply a working out in detail of the material already contained in the relevant portion of the *Encyclopedia* of 1817. Hence, there is no ground for supposing that, when Hegel went to Prussia, he began by reconstructing his philosophy of the state to suit the mind and practice of his new masters.

Moreover, the reason why publication was delayed for eighteen months after the book was ready can hardly have been anything except fear of the censor. But if it had been written to gratify the Prussian government, how could he have had such fears? Their very existence implied that his book contained matter which might be unpalatable to the authorities on the score of its liberalism.

How did Hegel overcome any difficulty that might have been expected from the censor?[10] Two courses were open to him. He might have revised his book and accepted Prussian conservatism; or he might have written a preface explaining that, while his ideas were more liberal than those of his government, he shared its opposition to revolutionary ideas and the dangerous excesses to which they might lead their advocates. It was the latter course which he actually chose. The preface, however, has been called "servile" because it (1) denounces Fries, (2) condemns the Wartburg Festival, and (3) by identifying the real with the rational, justifies the status quo.

1. Now it may be admitted that, in writing as he did, Hegel had his eye on the censor; and it was a cruel thing to attack Fries—a former colleague as *Privatdocent* in Jena—when he was in disgrace and suffering personal hardship. But is Hegel using servility, or is he using legitimate explanation of his own independent position in order to satisfy the censor? The latter is the only answer which fits the facts.

His poor opinion of Fries was of long standing. In 1811, on the publication of Fries's *Logic,* he jotted down his impressions of the book: "Superficiality, vague chit-chat—wholly platitudinous—trivial argumentation, like that used to children—empty narrative, devoid of philosophic precision, etc."[11] These unpublished remarks are more sweeping than those in the preface to the *Philosophie des Rechts,* but their content is the same. The criticisms of Fries in this preface were thus not made to order; nor were they the first criticism of Fries that Hegel published. There is a caustic footnote about him in the introduction to the *Science of Logic,*[12] published in 1812.

2. If Hegel's attack on Fries is nothing new, is the condemnation of the Wartburg Festival a departure from his convictions in order to please a censor? At first sight it may seem that it is. At this festival the writings of von Haller were burned, and in the body of the *Philosophie des Rechts* (sec. 258) there is a trenchant criticism of von Haller's book— "this welter of crudity." The Festival was a demonstration in favor of liberty—the leitmotiv of Hegel's book—and German unity, of which he was the prophet in his essay on the German constitution, written in 1802, though not published until 1893. But it is not the objects of the festival to which he raises objections in his preface; it is the methods adopted to obtain them. Feeling and enthusiasm, he holds, are dangerous guides: in this instance they led to the murder of Kotzebue, and murder, however conscientiously committed, is still murder. This is the theme of much of the second part of the *Philosophie des Rechts,* and the condemnation of the Wartburg Festival follows from the argument there; the assumption of adaptability to a conservative regime is not required to account for it. The Festival is specifically condemned in the preface in order to obviate the misunderstanding that the only alternative to von Haller, condemned in the body of the book, is Fries.

3. The statement that "the real (*wirklich*) is the rational" was misunderstood by some of Hegel's contemporaries to imply that what exists (e.g., the Prussia state) is rational, and he inserted some explanatory sentences into the second edition of the *Encyclopedia* in 1827 in order to remove the misapprehension. It should have been clear, however, to readers of the *Philosophie des Rechts* that, whatever Hegel meant by his identification of the real and the rational, he did not mean to justify the status quo, because the rational state described in the third part of his book was not a description of any state actually existing at the time. (It is sometimes said to have been a description of Prussia, but the differences are so striking, as we shall see in part II of this article, that no contemporary of Hegel's could reasonably have made such an assertion.) Hegel doubtless gave a meaning of his own to the word *wirklich*, and he had explained this meaning as early as 1812 in the *Science of Logic*, but it could have been gathered by an attentive reader from the *Philosophie des Rechts* itself (e.g., preface and sec. 1) without knowledge of Hegel's other books.

Against this view that the preface is simply explanatory of Hegel's general position in the body of his book, and not "servile," there is sometimes adduced a sentence which occurs in it as follows: "*Bei uns die Philosophie . . . eine öffentliche, des Publikum berührende Existenz, vornehmlich oder allein im Staatsdienste, hat*" ("with us [i.e. in Prussia as distinct from Greece] philosophy has an existence in the open, an existence in touch with the public, an existence principally or only in the service of the state"). What does Hegel really mean here? Carritt, for instance, interprets the words as an assertion that "the proper exercise of philosophy is in the service of the state,"[13] or that "philosophy is to be the servant of the state."[14] Now since Hegel, in the *Encyclopedia*, ascribes philosophy to the section on Absolute Mind, which transcends Objective Mind, the section in which the state appears, it would be odd if he were to maintain in the *Philosophie des Rechts* that the higher is the servant of the lower. What Carritt's interpretation seems to overlook is the sense in which Hegel normally uses *Existenz*. In speaking of the *Existenz* of philosophy he is speaking of philosophy's existence as an institution, as an organization of the objective world. The difference between Prussia and ancient Greece, so far as philosophy is concerned, is that in the former philosophy is an organized study in the universities, whose professors are ex officio civil servants, i.e., "in the service of the State." Hegel is simply stating an obvious fact about philosophy as an organized study in Prussia; he makes no assertion about the "*proper exercise*" of philosophy or about what philosophy "*is to be*." I can find nothing in the German to justify Carritt's use of the words italicized, and nothing in Hegel's meaning to justify a charge of servility against him on the strength of his use of this phrase.[15] There is no "servility" in holding that, if a civil servant cannot reconcile his philosophy and his political allegiance, he should demit his office, if his office consists in teaching philosophy.

The question whether Hegel was a man of cringing disposition is relevant to a consideration of the charge that he truckled to the Prussian government. To answer such a question a whole biography would be required, but reference may be made here to some of Hegel's actions during his Berlin period (1818–31) when he was at the height of his powers and his fame, and when he was being accused of servility by Fries and others who were jealous of his success. In youth he had been an enthusiast for the French Revolution as the assertion in practice of man's natural right to freedom. In 1826, on the anniversary of the taking of the Bastille, he drank a toast with his students in honor of the event; "he explained its significance and said that a year never passed without his celebrating the anniversary in this way."[16] In youth he had advocated the unification of Germany; in Berlin he remained faithful to this ideal and had not forgotten that he was a south German himself. In 1826, for instance, when he founded his *Jahrbuch für wissenschaftliche Kritik*, he endeavored to secure the cooperation of Bavarian scholars and hoped that the periodical might help the cause of German unity.[17] When he was leaving Heidelberg for Berlin he said in his letter of resignation that he hoped, in going to Prussia, to have administrative as well as teaching responsibilities.[18] Perhaps he hoped to have charge of the Academy or to have some share in the Ministry of Education, but any such hope was vain. If he was so sound a conservative as some have held, whey was he never given such an administrative post?

When his colleague de Wette was dismissed from his chair for writing a letter of sympathy to the mother of Kotzebue's murderer, Hegel was one of the subscribers to a fund to help him in pecuniary difficulty.[19] He brought with him from Heidelberg an assistant, Carové, whose membership in the Students' Association made him suspect to the faculty in the university as well as to the government, and Hegel was forced to dismiss him. In his place he appointed von Henning, but it took him ten weeks to get the appointment confirmed, because von Henning also was suspected of demagogic sympathies. In 1820 he posted bail for a student arrested on suspicion of disaffection.[20] Another Berlin student was for the same reason inhibited from attendance at the university in 1819. He appealed to Hegel for aid and, despite Hegel's continued efforts, his reinstatement could not be secured. When he was eventually reinstated in 1823, it was not Hegel's but another's pleadings which secured this result. Von Wittgenstein, von Kamptz, and other "demagogue-hunters," who might with some fairness be called "servile," attacked Hegel and attributed the "disordered" minds of students in part to the unhealthy "mysticism" and "pantheism" of his philosophy.

It is difficult to fit facts like these—and Dr. Hoffmeister adduces others—into a picture of Hegel as a reactionary conservative, the trusted ally of the Prussian regime. Like other men, he had his faults, but servility was not one of them.

II

So far we have been concerned with Hegel the man and his relations with the Prussian government. We now turn to the *Philosophie des Rechts* in order to discover whether it actually contains adulation of Prussia or approval of those aspects of Prussianism and national socialism which are commonly criticized in this country. If it did contain these things, it would be hard to explain why Hegel's influence in Germany waned so rapidly after his death, or why his works went out of print during the heyday of Prussianism. English readers sometimes forget that when Hegel was being translated into English in the 1890s his philosophy was dead in Germany.

The rational state that he describes in the last part of the *Philosophie des Rechts* is not, he explains, any existing state; political philosophy is not the same as the empirical study of political institutions. Yet he is often said to have identified the rational state with the Prussia of his own day. This is impossible; the differences between what he regarded as "rational" political institutions and those under which he actually lived are too many and too striking. Three of them may be briefly mentioned here:[21] (1) He holds that "subjective freedom" requires trial by jury; questions of fact should be settled by the defendant's peers (secs. 219ff.). In Prussia there were no trials by jury when his book was published. (2) He advocates parliamentary government, and is at some pains to describe in detail the constitution of the two houses and the manner of appointment of their members. Further, he advocates the publicity of their proceedings—all this in the interests once more of "subjective freedom." He is a supporter of monarchy, but only of monarchy of a kind so limited (*constitutionelle Monarchie*) as to be compatible with liberty; i.e., although the monarch is at the head of the state, his functions are restricted; he is one organ of the body politic, the executive and the legislative being the other two (secs. 275–315). Prussia in Hegel's day was an absolute monarchy, and the estates did not meet as a parliament. Stein had proposed to give Prussia a "constitution," but it did not receive one in Hegel's lifetime. (3) He argues for the freedom of the press and allows the expression of public opinion. It is true that he thinks that there are limits to this freedom, but the important point is that he does hold that personal freedom is robbed of its rights if the individual is not at liberty to hold opinions of his own and to utter them (secs. 316–19). We have seen already in this article that such freedom was not enjoyed in the Prussia of his day.[22]

Hegel thought that Plato had described in the *Republic* not a utopia or a castle in the air, but the rational essence (the *ti ēn einai*) of Greek political life, and in more than one place he develops his own views in contrast with Plato's in a way which suggests that he was trying to do for the modern world what he took Plato to have done for Greece. His rational state, then, is a description of the essence of modern political life, exemplified to some extent in existing states, however bad, just as the essence of manhood is exemplified to some extent even in the cripple. Now he holds that in anything finite there may be a discrepancy between what it is implicitly and what it is overtly; e.g., a man is man, as distinct from an animal, in virtue of his rationality, and implicitly or in essence or in principle any particular man is rational; actually, however, he may act in defiance of this rationality, though he does not thereby cease to be man, i.e., he remains rational in essence. If he learned, however, that rationality *was* his essence, and believed this, he would bring his conduct more into line with his genuine manhood, i.e., his rationality. Similarly, a bad state is still a *state* only because the conception or the essence of political life works within it; and if it comes to recognize that its actual institutions or actions clash with the conception or essence that makes it a state, it will proceed to reform itself and bring itself more into accordance with that conception or essence. It is this essence which Hegel describes in the *Philosophie des Rechts*, and his book amounts therefore to an invitation to statesmen to reform their states in accordance with his principles, principles which he professes not to have invented but to have discerned already at work (*wirkend*, i.e., *wirklich*) in varying degrees within existing states, and in virtue of that fact entitling them to be called states. It is, then, a precise reversal of the truth to regard Hegel's book as a justification of the status quo.

But surely, it will be said, even if this interpretation be sound on the whole, still there are detailed passages in Hegel's book where he (1) asserts or implies that might is right, (2) defends the suppression of freedom of conscience, and (3) holds that the individual is a mere means to the state's ends.

1. Carritt, for instance, says that by adopting Schiller's epigram, *Die Weltgeschichte ist das Weltgericht,* Hegel "frankly identifies might with

right."[23] It is true that the epigram might be adopted by a thinker who intended to make this identification, but did Hegel intend to make it? In the *Philosophie des Rechts* (fn. to sec. 258) he distinguishes between von Haller's advocacy of the rule of the might, or the rule of force, and his own doctrine that it is the right which is in the long run mighty. What triumphs in history, he thinks, is the right of God's purpose, the rightness of which is intrinsic to itself, not dependent—as the might is right doctrine implies—on its might. (See, e.g., the closing paragraph of his *Philosophy of History*, where he contends that the true theodicy is the demonstration, provided by the philosophy of history, that the history of the world is the process of the realization of *Spirit*, not force or might.) Hegel's belief that it is possible to discern in history a progressive development—a development of mind—is doubtless open to numerous difficulties, but it is to turn his doctrine upside down to hold that he thinks that the triumph of one "world-historical" nation over another is a triumph of mere brute force (or *Naturgewalt*) when he thinks in fact that it is a triumph of reason. Had he held that might was right because it was mighty, he would surely have advocated despotic government, or absolute monarchy. As it is, when he treats of sovereignty (sec. 278) he clearly distinguishes, like Aristotle, between the sovereignty of a despot who rules by whim, and so by force, not by law—the type of sovereignty that he rejects—and the sovereignty of limited monarchy that implies law and constitution, and so rests on rationality, not whim or force—the type of sovereignty that he advocates. He speaks there of the common misunderstanding that confuses might with right and tries to remove it, but despite his plain words, he seems so far to have failed to convince some readers that he himself distinguished these two conceptions and gave priority to the second.

2. While he repudiates the doctrine that might is right, he does not repudiate freedom of conscience. He specifically allows conscientious objection to service in warfare (second fn. to sec. 270) and speaks of man's conscience as a "sanctuary which it would be sacrilege to violate" (sec. 137). It is true that this is not his whole teaching about conscience; it is not enough, he thinks, that a man should be conscientious; mere conviction does not ensure infallibility. To be justified, a man must be conscientiously convinced of what is inherently right (sec. 141). This, however, is a long way short of advocating the suppression of conscience altogether.

3. But did Hegel not maintain that the individual was a mere means to the ends of the state? Carritt confidently gives an affirmative answer,[24] though it seems to me that Hegel's own answer is negative. Not once only but repeatedly in the *Philosophie des Rechts* (preface, secs. 46, 185, 206, 299) Hegel criticizes Plato, and each time the point of his criticism

is that Plato's republic did not allow enough freedom of choice to the individual. He objects that Plato makes the state everything, the individual nothing (*Zusatz* to sec. 184), that Plato stifles individuality by denying private property and family life to the guardians and by refusing to allow members of the lower classes to choose their own walk in life. Self-subsistent individuality, Hegel continues, was unknown to the Greeks and was introduced into the world by Christianity, and it is to make room for this principle in his state that he advocates, e.g., a parliamentary constitution and facilities for the expression of public opinion. Whether his criticism of Plato is justified or not is not here in question, but the fact that it is directed against Plato's alleged subordination of the individual to the state is surely sufficient reason for refusing to ascribe to Hegel precisely what he asserts is Plato's chief error.[25]

The view here put forward that Hegel rejects the doctrine that might is right, allows freedom of conscience, and does not make the individual a mere means to the ends of the state is supported by his explicit statements in the passages already cited. These statements, moreover, are not merely incidental remarks or casual phrases inconsistent with his main doctrine: on the contrary, they are integral to that doctrine itself. He tries to find a place in the state *both* for individual liberty *and* for strong government, and he holds that it is a sign of the strength and depth of the modern state that its subsistence is compatible with allowing its particular members to develop to "self-subsistent individuality" (sec. 260). His political doctrine of the state and the individual accords with his logical doctrine of the universal and the particular and his metaphysical doctrine of the infinite and the finite. The all-powerful state in which the individual counts for nothing, or which "absorbs into itself the strength of its individual members" (*Zusatz* to sec. 184), would, in his view, be just an analogue of Schelling's absolute—"the night in which all cows are black." In the *Philosophie des Rechts* he attempts to steer a course between the Scylla of individual license, on the one hand, and the Charybdis of despotism, on the other, and hence it is only to be expected that, in some passages taken by themselves, he should seem to founder on one or other of these rocks. Any such passages, however, should surely be interpreted in the light of his main thesis, and while this thesis has perhaps been sufficiently indicated by citations already, it may be worth clinching the matter by quoting Hegel's own summary (sec. 260) of his general view of the state:

> The State is the realization of concrete freedom. But concrete
> freedom consists in this, that personal individuality and its particular
> interests not only attain their complete development and gain explicit

recognition for their rights (in the family and the system of "civil society"), but pass over of their own accord into devotion to universal interests. When that happens they know and will the universal . . . and are active in its pursuit. The result is that the universal does not prevail or attain perfection except along with the interests of individuals and through the cooperation of their knowledge and will. Individuals likewise do not live like private persons for their own ends alone but, in willing them, will the universal at the same time.

How far Hegel succeeded in his endeavor to do justice to the rights of individuals is a matter for philosophic criticism; but any such criticism will misfire which, despite, e.g., the passage just quoted, maintains that in his view the individual is a mere means to the ends of the state.

"Prussianism" is associated not only with the suppression of conscience and individuality and the doctrine that might is right, but also with the glorification of war. Hegel's view on this subject is summarized by Carritt as follows: "War is justified on the grounds that by it domestic discontent and hankering after liberty are quelled and the inconsiderable nature of human happiness demonstrated by 'hussars with shining sabres.' "[26] What Hegel actually says is: "War is not to be regarded as an absolute evil"—the emphasis is on the word "absolute"—

or as a merely external accident resulting it may be from the injustice or the passions of nations or their rulers. . . . It is a matter of necessity that the finite, i.e. life and possessions, should be definitely established as something merely contingent, because the notion of the finite is the contingent. . . . Edifying sermons are preached about the vanity of temporal goods, but war is the state of affairs which makes us take this vanity in earnest. . . . Everyone thinks when he hears such sermons, however much he may be moved by them, that he will be able to preserve his own possessions. But if their insecurity is made a serious matter by hussars with shining sabres, then preaching turns into curses against the invader (sec. 324).

It is true that Hegel goes on to affirm that peoples stagnate if they remain at peace and that war does result in the composing of domestic feuds, but his main point is that war is an unavoidable necessity. "In time of war," he continues, "right has lost its sway; might and chance rule." And yet "combatants regard it as a passing phase which ought not to be, and for this reason, even in war-time envoys are respected and war is not waged against private individuals or family life." "In modern times" (1820!) "war is humanely waged" (sec. 338). In face of these quotations, can it be maintained either that Carritt's summary is fair or that Hegel is an apostle of frightfulness?

Finally, how does the teaching of *Philosophie des Rechts* compare with the practice of fascism and national socialism? So far as these ideologies make the unity of national life an ideal, Hegel is at one with them. In Italy the use of corporations in the organization of industry is strikingly reminiscent of his proposals, and the resemblance is doubtless not accidental. The relation between the *Deutsche Christen* and the German government recalls Hegel's proposed partnership between church and state. But it is only if half its doctrine is ignored that the *Philosophie des Rechts* can be interpreted as an apologia for the most criticized aspects of national socialism. Above all, where in the totalitarian states are his safeguards of "subjective freedom"? Where in his book is there any warrant for a secret police? What would he have thought of the treatment of the Jews? An answer to this question may be inferred from a passage in the *Philosophie des Rechts* itself, where he says that those who would exclude the Jews even from civil rights on the ground of their race forget that the Jews are *men*, with the rights of men, and that in fact experience has shown that thus to exclude them is the worst of follies (second fn. to sec. 270).

6

The Hegel Myth and Its Method

Walter A. Kaufmann

> I only avail myself of the person as of a strong magnifying glass
> with which one can render visible a general but creeping calamity
> which it is otherwise hard to get hold of.
>
> —Nietzsche, *Ecce Homo*

Hegel is known today, at least in the United States, less through his own
works than through secondary sources and a few incriminating slogans
and generalizations. The resulting myth has, however, long lacked any
comprehensive statement. This situation was altered by the publication
in 1945 of Karl Popper's *The Open Society and Its Enemies.* Now this work,
which has already gone through three impressions in England, has been
published in a revised edition in the United States.[1] The book has many
virtues: it represents a passionate attack against totalitarianism, is written
with superb clarity, contains many interesting quotations and—more
important— a great number of extremely suggestive ideas. Yet the book
also has grave faults. Even those, for example, who will welcome a forceful
critique of the view that Plato was really a democrat are not likely to accept
Popper's picture of him. For the *Republic* is still widely read, and even the
Laws is easily within reach. It is therefore altogether less important to take
issue with Popper's interpretation of Plato than with his method. And by
the same token, it seems preferable to use his chapter on Hegel as an
example rather than the ten on Plato; for far fewer readers are likely to
recall crucial passages in the *Philosophy of Right* or to reach for a worn
copy of this work to check Popper's accusations. Moreover, one can deal
more thoroughly with one chapter than with ten.

Popper's Hegel chapter (fifty pages, plus nineteen pages of notes)
demands detailed criticism for at least two reasons. First, it contains

more misconceptions about Hegel than have previously been gathered in so small a space. Secondly, if one agrees with Popper that "intellectual honesty is fundamental for everything we cherish,"[2] one should protest against his method; for although his hatred of totalitarianism is the inspiration and central motif of his work, his method is unfortunately similar to that of totalitarian "scholars"—and it appears to be spreading. I shall begin with some observations about this method, arranged under topical headings, and then proceed to specific interpretations.

1. *Scholarly Background.* Although the mere presence of nineteen pages of notes suggests that the attack on Hegel is based on careful scholarship, the author completely ignores the most important works on his subject. This is doubly serious because he is intent on psychologizing the men he attacks: he deals not only with their arguments, but also— if not altogether more—with their alleged motives. This practice is as dangerous as it is fashionable, but in the case of Plato there is often no outright evidence to the contrary: one can only say that Popper always credits his enemy with the worst possible intentions. In the case of Hegel, however, there is voluminous evidence that Popper simply ignores: beginning with Dilthey's *Jugendgeschichte Hegels* (1906) and Nohl's edition of *Hegels Theologische Jugendschriften* (1907), the development of Hegel's ideas has been made the subject of several scholarly studies, culminating in Haering's monumental *Hegel.*[3] And among the intervening works there is Rosenzweig's two-volume study, *Hegel und der Staat*, which traces the development of the very ideas with which Popper is concerned.

Furthermore, Popper has relied largely on Scribner's *Hegel Selections*: he takes over such a gross mistranslation as that "the State is the march of God through the world,"[4] and he appears to be unaware of crucial passages (if not entire works) which are not included in these *Selections*, e.g., the passage on war in Hegel's first book, which shows that his later conception of war, which is far more moderate, was not adopted to accommodate the king of Prussia.[5]

2. *Composite Quotations.* This is a device that makes for exciting reading and, perhaps for that reason, has not received the criticism it deserves, regardless of the conclusions it is made to yield. Sentences are picked out of various contexts, often out of different books, and arranged so that they seem more or less continuous, i.e., enclosed by a single set of quotation marks, and separated only by three dots which are generally taken to indicate an omission and not a leap to a different book. Plainly, this device can be used to impute to an author views he never held. And even where the interpreter has no such desire whatever, some philosophers are almost bound to be misrepresented in this way. This is especially true of "dialectical" thinkers, such as Plato, Hegel,

and Nietzsche; for many of their statements are admittedly one-sided, designed to formulate one point of view which is then shown to be inadequate and countered by another perspective. Hegel, for example, can be cited both in support of "equality" and against it. Thus one could concoct out of his collected works an impressive composite quotation, consisting of several sentences which criticize "equality." The correct understanding of Hegel would, however, be better served by the citation of only one of these sentences, *in its context*, as a step in an argument that is designed to lead the reader to a better comprehension of equality, and not to enlist his emotions for it or against it. In that sense, Popper's whole approach to Hegel is unsound, quite apart from his occasional use of composite quotations.

Because the use of composite quotations is not restricted to Popper's book, it may be well to consider this device a little more closely. Popper relies far less on Hegel's own books than on his students' lecture notes, including Gans's additions to the posthumous edition of the *Philosophy of Right*—although Gans himself pointed out in his preface that "the choice of words" was sometimes his rather than Hegel's. Just here, therefore, we should not attach too much significance to single phrases or sentences, but take special pains to understand them in terms of their context and overall intentions. Yet Popper's first composite quotation[6] consists of eight such bits of which not a single one was published by Hegel himself. In his notes at the end of the volume, Popper scrupulously marks references to Gans's additions with an "L"; and he invariably gives the sources of his composite quotations: "For the eight quotations in this paragraph, cp., *Selections.* . . ." Even so, the notes are introduced by these "General Remarks": "The text of the book . . . may be read without these Notes. . . . Readers who wish to consult the Notes . . . may find it convenient first to read without interruption through the text of a chapter, and then to turn to the Notes." How many readers, even among those who do read the notes, are likely to recall that "the eight quotations in this paragraph" are nothing else than a long composite quotation which, when "read without interruption," gave every appearance of being a single quotation?

The question here is not one of Popper's—no doubt, good—intentions. The question is where to draw the line. In 1941, Brinton used composite quotations in his *Nietzsche*, and in his *Ideas and Men* (1950) he no longer indicates that his Nietzsche quotations[7] are of this composite nature—although his arrangement radically changes the original meaning of the sentences involved. Surely, it is ironical that a method so characteristic of totalitarian "scholarship" should be used in books devoted to attacks on totalitarianism. Indeed, it is often hard to distinguish between the arguments of the Nazi writers who claimed that they were the rightful heirs of Plato and Nietzsche, and the arguments of some of our most reputable scholars who so eagerly concede these claims.[8]

3. *The Notion of "Influence."* While Brinton half accepted the Nazis' own view of Nietzsche, Popper goes beyond most of their attempts to establish a respectable ancestry, when he alleges that they were influenced by Hegel. His notion of influence is altogether so unscientific that it seems scarcely credible that it should be employed by an authority on logic and scientific method. At best, it is reducible to *post hoc ergo propter hoc.* Thus he speaks of "the Hegelian Bergson"[9] and assumes, without giving the least evidence, that Bergson, Alexander, Smuts, and Whitehead were are interested in Hegel—simply because they were "evolutionists."[10]

Popper is of course much more concerned with Hegel's influence on the Nazis, and his chapter is studded with quotations from contemporary German writers—almost all from Kolnai's *The War against the West.* (Kolnai considers such men as, for example, Friedrich Gundolf, Werner Jaeger, and Max Scheler "representative of Nazism or at least its general trend and atmosphere.")[11] Popper uses quotation after quotation of Kolnai to point out supposed similarities with Hegel, but never stops to ask whether the men in question had read Hegel, or liked him, or where they actually got their ideas. An interesting quotation from Stapel, for example, would seem to have been influenced by Luther rather than Hegel;[12] but the following passage is even more characteristic: the idea of "fame is revived by Hegel,"[13] for Hegel spoke of fame as a "reward" of the men whose deeds are recorded in our history books— "and Stapel, a propagator of the new paganized Christianity, promptly [i.e., one hundred years later] repeats [*sic*]: 'All great deeds were done for the sake of fame or glory.' " This seems rather a different idea, and Popper himself goes on to admit that Stapel "is even more radical than Hegel." Under the circumstances, one may question the relevance of the whole section dealing with Stapel and with any number of other contemporary writers. This is not history of ideas, but rather an attempt to establish guilt by association on the same page—in the hope, it seems, that *semper aliquid haeret.*

Besides, Popper often lacks the knowledge of who influenced whom. Thus he speaks of Heidegger and "his master, Hegel"[14] and asserts that Jaspers was originally a follower "of the essentialist philosophers Husserl and Scheler."[15] More important, he contrasts the vicious Hegel with superior men "such as Schopenhauer or J. F. Fries,"[16] and constantly makes common cause with Schopenhauer against the allegedly protofacist Hegel, whom he blames even for the Nazis' racism—evidently unaware that Fries and Schopenhauer, unlike Hegel, *were* racists. Fries has often been considered a great liberal, and Hegel has as often been condemned for taking a strong stand against Fries, and it is rarely, if ever, mentioned in this context that Fries published a pamphlet in the summer of 1816 in which he called for the "extermination" of Jewry.[17]

Popper is also quite wrong when he says that Hegel "represents the 'missing link,' as it were, between Plato and the modern form of totalitarianism. Most of the modern totalitarians are quite unaware that their ideas can be traced back to Plato. But many know of their indebtedness to Hegel."[18] Seeing that the context indicates a reference to Nazism, and that all the totalitarians cited in this chapter are fascists, not communists, Popper only shows his ignorance of this particular form of totalitariansim. Hegel is rarely cited in Nazi literature and, when he is referred to, it is usually by way of disapproval. The Nazis' official "philosopher," Rosenberg, in *Der Mythus des Zwanzigsten Jahrhunderts*, mentions, and denounces, Hegel twice.[19] (Rosenberg admires Schopenhauer to whom he devotes the whole second chapter of Book 2.) Of Plato, on the other hand, he writes: "What Plato was essentially—namely, an aristocrat, an Olympic fighter, a poet intoxicated with beauty, . . . one who wanted in the end to save his people [*Volk*] on a racial basis, through a forcible constitution, dictatorial in every detail—that was not Socratic, but the last great flower of the spirit-intoxicated Hellenic character [*Hellenentum*]."[20] Plato, unlike Hegel, was widely read in German schools, and special editions were prepared for Greek classes, gathering together allegedly pro-Nazi passages.[21] And Dr. Hans F. K. Günther, from whom the Nazis admittedly received their racial theories, wrote a whole book on Plato—not Hegel.[22]

Whether Hegel actually influenced the Nazis may not be particularly relevant to Popper's central theses—but then most of the book is not. A large mass of interesting ideas are amalgamated with a great deal of unsound intellectual history, and section 5 (eighteen pages) of the Hegel chapter is representative of the latter.

4. *Vituperation and Allegation of Motives.* Although Popper, in his introduction, speaks of "the application of the critical and rational methods of science to the problems of the open society,"[23] he writes about Hegel as if he were a prosecutor addressing a jury. He begins with an attempt to discredit the accused by citing some passages from Hegel's philosophy of nature; he says of Fichte and Hegel, "such clowns are taken seriously";[24] he demands, "I ask whether it is possible to outdo this despicable perversion of everything that is decent";[25] and he denounces "Hegel's hysterical historicism."[26] Hegel certainly has his faults, and his "historicism" (see below) may be one of them, and his unprepossessing style, dry and unemotional in the extreme, may be another.[27] If "hysterical" means (as Webster

says) "wildly emotional," Popper deserves this epithet much more than Hegel. For all of Hegel's shortcomings, it seems wildly emotional indeed to say that "he is supreme only in his outstanding lack of originality" and was not even "talented."[28] And "the critical and rational methods of science" could hardly establish the connection that the philosophy of Jaspers is a "gangster" philosophy.[29] Nor is this proved by a note on "the gangster philosophy" which furnishes us with a composite quotation (see above) from E. von Salomon's *The Outlaws*, which bears no perceivable relation to Jaspers—not to speak of Hegel.

Popper's allegation of motives is scarcely distinguishable from vituperation. Hegel is accused of "a perversion . . . of a sincere belief in God,"[30] but no evidence whatever is given to substantiate this charge. "Hegel's radical collectivism . . . depends on Frederick William III, king of Prussia" and his "one aim" was "to serve his employer, Frederick William of Prussia";[31] and it is hinted that Hegel misused philosophy as a means of financial gain,[32] but Popper ignores the literature on this question.[33]

Hegel, we are told, "wants to stop rational argument, and with it, scientific and intellectual progress,[34] and his dialectics "are very largely designed to pervert the ideas of 1789."[35] And when Hegel explicitly comes out in favor of the things which, according to Popper, he opposed, this is "lip service."[36] Thus the allegation of motives reaches the point where our interpreter (exactly like Bäumler in his Nazistic version of Nietzsche) claims that the man he writes about did not mean what he clearly said. Composite quotations are used to establish a philosopher's views, and his express statements are discounted when they are inconvenient.

In the name of "the critical and rational methods of science," one must also protest against such emotional arguments as that Heidegger's philosophy must be wrong because he became a Nazi,[37] or that "Haeckel can hardly be taken seriously as a philosopher or scientist. He called himself a free thinker, but his thinking was not sufficiently independent to prevent him from demanding in 1914 'the following fruits of victory. . . .' "[38] By the same token, one might seek to discredit Einstein's scientific theories by a reference to his political views.

Popper's occasional references to "the doctrine of the chosen people" (which he associates with totalitarianism) and to Christianity are also quite emotional. Popper is "for" Christianity, but he means by it something that is in express contrast to the teachings of Paul, the Catholic Church, Luther, and Calvin. Hegel's rejection of the adequacy of conscience as a guide in moral questions is countered by Popper's parenthesis, "that is to say, the moralists who refer, for example, to the New Testament"[39]—as if no crimes had ever been committed in the name of the New Testament. Indeed, one of the most important criticisms of Popper's approach could be expressed in terms of Maritain's epigram: "If books were judged by the bad uses man can put them to, what book has been more misused than the Bible?"[40]

5. *Hegel's Metaphysics.* Let us now turn to Hegel's philosophy. His metaphysics is of less interest here than his social philosophy, but it is noteworthy how completely Popper fails to understand the framework of Hegel's thinking. Thus he claims that Hegel taught that "self-evidence is the same as truth,"[41] although Hegel's first book begins with the denial of this view, and Hegel never changed his mind about this. Popper futher claims: "Hegel believes, with Aristotle, that the Ideas or essences are *in* the things in flux; or more precisely (as far as we can treat a Hegel with precision), Hegel teaches that they are identical with the things in flux: 'Everything actual is an Idea,' he says."[42] Yet one need not look farther than Royce's article on Hegel's terminology in Baldwin's *Dictionary of Philosophy and Psychology* to find that "actual" is, with Hegel, a technical term (as its equivalent was with Plato and Aristotle) and that the statement that "everything actual is an Idea" does not mean that the ideas "are identical with the things in flux."

How did Hegel arrive at the doctrine that "what is rational, is actual; and what is actual, is rational"? According to Popper, "merely by a series of equivocations." We are told that Hegel adopted Plato's equation of the ideal and the real, and Kant's conception that the Idea is mental, which can be expressed in terms of an equation of Idea and reason. "Combined, these two equations, or rather equivocations, yield *Real = Reason.*"[43] This derivation, of course, is not documented from Hegel's writings. And that there might be a connection with Leibniz's conception of the best of all possible worlds or with a sincere belief in God is not mentioned. Nor is there any reference to the immediate context of the dictum in the preface to the *Philosophy of Right,* or to Hegel's own later comment in his *Encyclopedia*:

> These simple sentences have seemed striking to some and have
> excited hostility—even from people who would not wish to deny some
> understanding of philosophy, not to speak of religion. . . . When I have
> spoken of actuality, one might have inquired, without being told to
> do so, in what sense I use this expression; for I have, after all, treated
> actuality in an elaborate *Logic* and there distinguished it precisely
> not only from the accidental, which of course has existence, too, but
> also, in great detail, from being there [*Dasein*], existence, and other
> concepts.[44]

It will be noted that all such distinctions are overlooked when Popper says that Hegel maintained that "everything that is real must be reasonable, and . . . everything that is now real or actual . . . must be reasonable as well as good. And particularly good is, as we shall see, the actually existing Prussian state." Hegel's term *wirklich* should be translated as "actual," not as "real"; and it should be kept in mind that he opposed it to "potential" rather than "unreal" in the sense of nonexistent. An acorn, though certainly "real" enough in the usual sense of the word, is not, as Hegel uses the term, *wirklich*.

6. *The State.* Again, we encounter the most elementary and funda-mental mistake imaginable. Popper overlooks the fact that Hegel speaks of "bad states" and thus does not mean every state encountered in expe-rience when he speaks of "the state." To return to Hegel's dictum about the actual and the rational, his own explanation of it in the immediately following paragraph is most relevant here:

> What matters is this: to recognize in the semblance of the temporal
> and transient the substance which is immanent and the eternal which
> is present in it. For the rational (which is synonymous with the Idea),
> in its actuality, also embeds itself in external existence and thus
> manifests itself in an infinite wealth of forms, appearances, and figures,
> shrouding its core in a multicolored rind. Our consciousness first dwells
> on this rind, and only then does philosophical thinking [*der Begriff*]
> penetrate it to detect the inward pulse and to perceive its beat even in
> the external forms. The infinitely varied relations, however, which take
> shape in this externality, . . . this infinite material and its organization
> are not the subject matter of philosophy.

Thus Hegel distinguishes between the Idea of the state, which he has in mind when he speaks of "the state," and the states around us; but the Idea, he claims, does not reside in a Platonic heaven, but is present, distorted more or less, in these states. The philosopher, undeterred by the distortions, should disentangle the rational core from the web of appearance. And Hegel is not, as Popper claims,[45] driven to "juridical positivism" and the approbation of every state with which he might be confronted: he can pass judgment. Hegel makes a sharp distinction be-tween such philosophic judgment and the arbitrary criticisms that reflect idiosyncrasies and emotions. He believes in a rational world order and in his ability to understand it. Sound criticism must rise to a comprehension of this world order. This notion was, in Hegel's mind, rooted in religion (many other deeply religious people share it) and so interpreted as to hold a subtle balance between quietism and revolution, both of which he rejected. Marx severed this notion from its religious context and gave it a revolutionary interpretation. Theoretically, one could uphold an interpretation which would be both religious and revolutionary, or neither.

A few quotations from the *Philosophy of Right* may furnish some concrete illustrations. "One may be able to show how a law is completely founded in, and consistent with, both circumstances and existing legal institutions, and yet is truly [*an und für sich*] illegitimate and irrational."[46] Later, Hegel speaks of the *"unalienable"* rights of the person and condemns, without qualification,

> slavery, serfdom, the disqualification from holding property or the prevention of its use or the like, and the deprivation of intelligent rationality, of morality, ethics, and religion, which is encountered in superstition and the concession to others of the authority and full power to determine and prescribe for me what actions I am to perform . . . or what duties my conscience is to demand from me, or what is to be religious truth for me.[47]

According to Gans's addition, Hegel further remarked that "the slave has an absolute right to liberate himself."[48]

When Hegel asserts, nevertheless, that "the State cannot recognize conscience [*Gewissen*] in its peculiar form, i.e., as subjective knowledge [*Wissen*], just as in science, too, subjective opinion, assurance, and the appeal to subjective opinion have no validity,"[49] he is not at all inconsistent. Conscience, as Hegel insists, is fallible; and, while no government or church has the right to dictate to our conscience, no government can afford to recognize conscience as a legal standard. As several of his interpreters have pointed out, Hegel, when he wrote the *Philosophy of Right*, was concerned about the recent assassination of the poet Kotzebue by a student who was convinced that he was a Russian spy and deserved death.

We are bound to misunderstand Hegel when we construe his remarks about conscience in terms of the Nazi state. It would be better to think of the German democratic state before 1933 and of the conscience of Hitler. For by "the state" Hegel means one that realizes the freedom of its citizens, recognizing that "a human being counts because he is a human being, not because he is a Jew, Catholic, Protestant, German, Italian, or the like"—and this "is of infinite importance."[50] On the other hand, Hegel is not opposed to conscience as such and might well consider rational the conscience of many an opponent of Hitler—say, of one who recognized his own absolute right to make himself free and to reclaim his unalienable rights—but not that of a fanatic impelled by personal motives or perhaps by an equally objectionable ideology.

It is no wonder that the Nazis found small comfort in a book that was based on the conviction that "the hatred of law, of right made determinate by law, is the shibboleth which reveals, and permits us to recognize infallibly, fanaticism, feeblemindedness, and the hypocrisy of good intentions, however they may disguise themselves."[51] In his preface, too, Hegel called the law "the best shibboleth to distinguish the false brother and friends of the so-called people." One may agree with Marcuse (whose valuable book Popper ignores): "There is no concept less compatible with Fascist ideology than that which founds the state on a universal and rational law that safeguards the interests of every individual, whatever the contingencies of his natural and social status."[52]

To summarize: Popper is mistaken when he says that according to Hegel, "the only possible standard of judgment upon the state is the world historical *success* of its actions."[53] Popper constantly confuses "the state" and particular states;[54] he does not see that "success" is not the standard invoked in the *Philosophy of Right* when Hegel speaks of "bad states"; and he fails to recognize that the state is a normative conception and refers not to one of "the things in flux," but to an idea and standard of judgment, to what states would like if they lived up fully to their *raison d'être*. This *raison d'être*, however, is to be found, in part, "in a higher sphere"[55] for which Hegel himself refers the reader to his system as outlined in the *Encyclopedia*. The whole realm of Objective Spirit and human institutions which culminates in the state is but the foundation of a higher realm of Absolute Spirit, i.e, art, religion, and philosophy. And in his *Philosophy of Right*, Hegel opens his discussion of the state with the pronouncement: "The State is the actuality of the ethical idea" which is freedom. By "freedom," however, Hegel does not mean that freedom from all restraints which, at its worst, culminates in anarchy, license, and bestiality, but rather man's freedom to develop and cultivate such distinctively human capacities of the spirit as art, religion, and philosophy. While Hegel considers the state supreme among human institutions, he does so precisely because he would subordinate the whole realm of institutions to the highest spiritual pursuits, and because he believes that these are possible only in the state.

This last belief is certainly questionable, but it does not imply (as Popper claims) that Hegel's state is "totalitarian, that is to say, its might must permeate and control the whole life of the people in all its functions: 'The State is therefore the basis and center of all the concrete elements in the life of a people: of art, law, morals, religion, and science.' "[56] The quotation from Hegel means—and the context from which it is torn (in the preface to the *Philosophy of History*) makes this quite clear—that the state alone makes possible the development of art, law, morals, religion, and science; and, if Hegel had said "society" instead of "the state," his view would be plausible. He was, however, under the spell not only of Plato, but also of Periclean Athens in which art and religion were indeed so closely integrated with the political life of the people that one might have called the city-state their "basis and center." This, of course, is quite different from saying that the state's "might must permeate and control" art and religion. Hegel's position is open to many objections, but to confound it with totalitarianism is a mixture of misunderstanding and name-calling. Far more just is Ernst Cassirer's conclusion, in *The Myth of the State* (1946), a book dealing with much the same theme as Popper's, but much more judiciously, and unfortunately ignored by Popper. Cassirer's Hegel chapter ends: "Hegel could extol and glorify the state, he could even apotheosize it. There is, however, a clear and unmistakable difference between his idealization of the power of the state and that sort of idolization that is the characteristic of our modern totalitarian systems."

7. *History.* Hegel, like Augustine, Lessing, and Kant before him, and Comte, Marx, Spengler, and Toynbee after him, believed that history has a pattern and made bold to reveal it. All these attempts are controversial in detail and questionable in principle; but a sound critique of Hegel should also take into account his remarkable restraint: he did not attempt to play the prophet and was content to comprehend the past.

Popper himself says that his own book could be "described as a collection of marginal notes on the development of certain historicist philosophies";[57] and, as we have seen, he accuses Hegel of "hysterical historicism." Yet in Popper's sense of the term, Hegel was no historicist at all: he was not one of those who "believe that they have discovered laws of history which enable them to prophesy the course of historical events"— and this addiction to predictions is what Popper means by historicism.[58]

We are told that Hegel was guilty of

> historical and evolutionary relativism—in the form of the dangerous
> doctrine that what is believed today is, in fact, true today, and in the
> equally dangerous corollary that what was true yesterday (*true* and
> not merely "believed") may be false tomorrow—a doctrine which,
> surely, is not likely to encourage an appreciation of the significance
> of tradition.[59]

Hegel, of course, excelled in his appreciation of the significance of tradition: he always took for granted its essential rationality, and he condemned as arbitrary any criticism of the past or present which was not accompanied by an appreciation of the significance of tradition. He did not maintain "that what is believed today is, in fact, true today," but insisted that many of his contemporaries, both philosophers and "men in the street," failed to see the truth. And "what was true yesterday . . . may be false tomorrow" is, in a sense, a commonplace—as when we take the statement "it is raining" or "the Americans, while saying that all men are endowed by their Creator with certain unalienable rights, including liberty, hold slaves" or "another war would likely spread the ideals of the French Revolution, without endangering the future of civilization." And the same consideration applies to many a generalization about a nation or about war.

Hegel did not believe that such propositions as "two plus two equals four" were true at one time but not at another; but he thought that the truth comes to light gradually and tried to show this in his lectures on the history of philosophy—lectures from which one might almost date the history of philosophy as a separate discipline. German historians of philosophy in the nineteenth century, such as Zeller, Erdmann, and Fischer, were consciously following Hegel's example and building on his foundations. Hegel emphasized not how utterly wrong his predecessors had been, but how much truth they had seen; yet Plato's truths were not "all of the truth," but were in need of subsequent qualification and amendment. Hegel's approach permits many profound insights that contrast favorably with the often superficial strictures of the crusading critics of the Enlightenment and their epigoni against whom Hegel reacted.

Hegel's approach is not amoral. Although he finds the aim of history in its "result"[60] and considers the history of the world the world's court of justice,[61] he does not idolize success. His attitude depends on his religious faith that freedom will and must triumph: *that* is Hegel's "historicism." He does not believe that things are good because they succeed, but that they succeed because they are good. He finds God's revelation in history.

This point is best illustrated by Hegel's polemic against Von Haller in section 258 of the *Rechtsphilosophie*. Throughout, he tries to avoid the Scylla of that revolutionary lawlessness which he associates with Fries and the Wartburg festival, and the Charybdis of conservative lawlessness which he finds in Von Haller's *Restauration der Staatswissenschaft*. He cites Von Haller (vol. 1, 342ff.): "As in the inorganic world the greater represses the smaller, and the mighty, the weak, etc., thus among the animals, too, and then among human beings, the same law recurs in nobler forms." And Hegel interposes: "Perhaps frequently also in ignoble forms?" He then quotes Von Haller again: "This is thus the eternal, immutable order of God, that the mightier rules, must rule, and always will rule." And Hegel comments: "One sees from this alone, and also from what follows, in what sense might is spoken of here: not the might of the moral and ethical, but the accidental force of nature."

"A people can only die a violent death when it has become naturally dead in itself,"[62] Popper quotes Hegel as saying; and Hegel continues, "as e.g. the German Imperial Cities, the German Imperial Constitution."[63] However true this analysis may be when applied to the events of 1806, the bold generalization invites criticisms; but one should take into account that Hegel is in agreement with a religious tradition that extends from Isaiah to Toynbee.

Popper, intent on dissociating Hegel from the Western religious tradition and associating him with the Nazis, fastens on Hegel's conception of world-historical peoples. According to Hegel, we are told, history records the fights of nations, "and the object of the fight is world domination,"[64] "History is the contest of the various national spirits for world domination."[65] And Hegel's *Encyclopedia*[66] is quoted: "the Spirit of the time[67] invests its will" in "the self-consciousness of a particular nation" which "dominates the world."[68] Hegel goes on to say (though Popper does not quote this) that the Spirit "steps onward" and "delivers it over to its chance and doom." His position depends on his assumption that ultimate reality is spiritual and that the Spirit reveals itself progressively in history. The stages of this revelation are represented by different peoples, but by only one people at any one time.[69] "This people is the *dominant* one in world history for this epoch—*and it can be epoch-making in this sense only once*. Against this absolute right which it has to be the embodiment of the current stage of development of the World Spirit, the Spirits of the other peoples have no right, and they, even as those whose epoch has passed, do not any longer count in world history."[70]

Hegel's conception is dated today: we know more than he did about the history of a great number of civilizations. We can no longer reduce world history to a straight line that leads from the Greeks, via the Romans, to ourselves; nor can we dispose of ancient Asia as "The Oriental Realm" and understand it simply as the background of the Greeks. We are aware, moreover, of a number of ambiguities and dangers in such conceptions as that of a *Volk* or nation; we would hesitate to apply such terms to the carriers of Greek or Roman civilization; and we would be hard put to construct a line of "world-historical" peoples from, say, the end of the Western Roman Empire to our own time. We understand the flowering of medieval philosophy in terms of the cooperation of Jews, Mohammedans, and Christians, against a Greek background, and would not care to say who, in that epoch, was the representative of the World Spirit.

All this, however, does not imply that Hegel's views are wicked or that his errors are due to his alleged nationalism or tribalism. Very similar objections can be urged against modern philosophers of history who, like Toynbee, repudiate nationalism. Toynbee, to be sure, recognizes many contemporary civilizations all of which "count" in world history. Yet his polemics against the nation as a unit of history and his preference for civilizations rest on the claim that nations cannot be studied without reference to other nations, while civilizations can be studied without reference to other civilizations. Again, one could hardly understand scholastic philosophy without reference to Mohammedans, Jews, and Greeks.[71] Surely, with the exception of entirely isolated communities, no unit can be understood completely without reference to others; and any unit whatever, whether it be Western Civilization, Germany, Athens, or the Burlington Railroad, can be made the object of a historical study. In each instance, one will introduce other units as sparingly as possible and only to throw light on the history of the unit under consideration.

In this sense, Hegel's conception of world history is arbitrary and amounts to an attempt to study the development of his own civilization. Moreover, he was not impeded by the recognition that some of the ancestors of this civilization made their epoch-making contributions simultaneously. Homer may have been a contemporary of the earliest prophets; Thales and Jeremiah wrote at the same time; and Stoicism flourished even as Christianity developed out of Judaism. What is called for is a more pluralistic perspective and more respect for individual units. There is no plan to which all of these can be fitted, and Hegel was certainly something of a Procrustes. Popper's attempt to use the conception of "world domination" in an exclusively political, or even military, sense in order to link Hegel with Hitler is, however, quite illegitimate; and it is doubly misleading when one does not emphasize that Hegel was not making predictions or offering suggestions for the future, but scrupulously limiting himself to an understanding of the past. (See also sec. 9 below.)

8. *Great Men and Equality.* Hegel's conception of world-historical peoples goes together with his belief in world-historical personalities. Both notions are justifiable up to a point. Some peoples have had little effect on anybody outside themselves, while the Greeks and the Jews, for example, have affected the history of the world out of all proportion to their numbers. Similarly, Socrates and Caesar might well be called world-historical personalities. It is the rankest emotionalism when Popper writes:

> Glory cannot be acquired by everybody; the religion of glory implies antiequalitarianism—it implies a religion of "Great Men." Modern

racialism accordingly "knows no equality between souls, no equality between men" (Rosenberg). Thus there are no obstacles to adopting the Leader Principles from the arsenal of the perennial revolt against freedom, or as Hegel calls it, the idea of the World-Historical Personality.[72]

Not only the word "religion," which occurs twice in this quotation, but also Popper's use of the conception of equalitarianism are propagandistic. Popper implies that we ought to be "for" equalitarianism, but, if it involves the belief that no man can achieve anything that cannot be achieved by everybody else, it is surely untenable. Equalitarianism in any sense in which it is worthwhile is not at all incompatible with belief in great men.

Here one may also note that, according to Popper:

> Hegel twists equality into inequality: "That the citizens are equal before the law," Hegel admits, "contains a great truth. But expressed in this way, it is only a tautology; it only states in general that a legal status exists, that the laws rule. But to be more concrete, the citizens . . . are equal before the law only in the points in which they are equal *outside the law* also. *Only that equality which they possess in property, age, . . . etc., can deserve equal treatment before the law.* . . .* The laws themselves presuppose unequal conditions. . . . It should be said that it is just the great development and maturity of form in modern states which produces the supreme concrete inequality of individuals in actuality.[73]

The omissions in the Hegel quotation are Popper's, and he himself explains them in the very next sentence:

> In this outline of Hegel's twist of the "great truth" of equalitarianism into its opposite, I have radically abbreviated his argument; and I must warn the reader that I shall have to do the same throughout the chapter; for only in this way is it at all possible to present, in a readable manner, his verbosity and the flight of his thoughts (which, I do not doubt, is pathological).

Can Popper's omissions in this quotation really be accounted for in terms of (Hegel's) pathology? Consider *Encyclopedia*, section 539. Hegel is not "for" or "against" equality but tries to determine in what sense it can be embodied in the modern state.

> With the appearance of the State, inequality enters, namely the difference between governing forces and the governed, authorities,

magistrates, directories, etc. The principle of equality, carried out consistently, would repudiate all differences and thus be at odds with any kind of state.

It is in the following discussion that we find the sentence italicized by Popper, and it seems best to quote it without omissions, and with Hegel's, rather than Popper's, italics:

Only that equality which, in whatever way, *happens to exist independently*, regarding wealth, age, physical strength, talents, aptitude, etc., or also crimes, etc., can and should justify an equal treatment of these before the law—in regard to taxes, liability to military service, admission to public office, etc., or punishment, etc.

Hegel's sentence, taken as a whole, is very carefully constructed and exhibits a crucial parallelism. Only those with equal wealth should be taxed equally; age and physical strength should be taken into account by, let us say, draft boards; talents and aptitudes are relevant qualifications for public service; etc. Or should we have equal punishment for all, regardless of whether they have committed equal crimes? Should we induct women and children into the armed forces and exact equal taxes from the poor and the rich? Is it Hegel who is guilty of a "twist"?

To return to "great men"—Hegel said (according to Gans's addition to sec. 318): "Public opinion contains everything false and everything true, and to find what is true in it is the gift of the great man. Whoever tells his age, and accomplishes, what his age wants and expresses, is the great man of his age."[74] And the passage ends (in Popper's translation): "He who does not understand *how to despise public opinion*, as it makes itself heard here and there, will never accomplish anything great." Popper's italics, as well as his comments (see below), appeal to the reader's prejudice in favor of the supremacy of public opinion, though he previously appealed to the prejudice in favor of the supremacy of conscience. These two standards, however, are very different; and Hegel recognized the fallibility of both because he did not believe—as Popper alleges[75]—that "self-evidence is the same as truth." Hegel argued (in the body of sec. 318) that "to be independent of [public opinion] is the first formal condition of anything great and rational (in actuality as well as in science)"; and he had the faith that public opinion "will eventually accept it, recognize it, and make it one of its own prejudices."

In the above quotation from Gans's addition, Popper finds an "excellent description of the Leader as a publicist"; and, since he has introduced it with a reference to "the Leader principle," one is led to think of the *Führer* and to consider Hegel a proto-Nazi. The quotation, however, is not at odds with a sincere belief in democracy and fits beautifully not only Franklin D. Roosevelt's "interventionism," but also Lincoln's great speeches, e.g., "A house divided against itself cannot stand. I believe this government cannot endure permanently half slave and half free" or "With malice toward none; with charity for all. . . ." And it is true of Lincoln, too, when Hegel says of the world-historical personalities, "They were practical, political men. But at the same time they were thinking men, who had an insight into the requirements of the time—into what was ripe for development."

Hegel found that world-historical individuals are always propelled by some passion ("Nothing great in the world has been accomplished without *passion*") and that their motivation is rarely disinterested. The latter point he expressed in terms of "the cunning of reason." The individual may be motivated not only by profound insights, but also by "private interests" and even "self-seeking designs." Alexander was passionately ambitious; but in the long run his private interests furthered Western civilization. The same consideration applies to Caesar. And while Popper links Hegel with "the fascist appeal to 'human nature' [which] is to our passions" and proposes that we call this appeal the "*cunning of the revolt against reason*,"[76] he himself evidently believes that Napoleon (whose motivation was hardly quite disinterested, and whose methods could scarcely be approved by a devotee of "the open society") was furthering Western civilization to such an extent that the German uprising against him must be labeled "one of these typical tribal reactions against the expansion of a supernational empire."[77]

9. *War*. Without accepting Hegel's view of war, one should distinguish it clearly from the fascists'. Three points may suffice here. First, Hegel looks back, not forward. He is not less interested in "the furthering of civilization" than is Popper,[78] but finds that our civilization was furthered by any number of wars in the past; e.g., the Greeks' war against the Persians, Alexander's wars of conquest, the innumerable wars waged by the Romans, and Charlemagne's conquest of the Saxons. Believing that it is the philosopher's task to comprehend "that which is"[79]—and not to construct utopias—Hegel speaks of war as one of the factors that have actually furthered civilization.

Second, we should not confuse Hegel's estimate of the wars that had occurred up to his own time with a celebration of war as we know it today. Third, Hegel's attitude is not fully comprehensible when considered apart from its religious roots. He considered all that is finite ephemeral. In Gans's addition to section 324,[80] he says: "From the pulpits much is preached concerning the insecurity, vanity, and instability of temporal

things, and yet everyone . . . thinks that he, at least, will manage to hold
on to his possessions." What the preachers fail to get across, "Hussars
with drawn swords" really bring home to us. (Popper writes "glistening
sabres"; and the change, though slight, affects the tone of the passage.)

These three points suffice to show how Popper misrepresents
Hegel's view. "Hegel's theory," we are told, "implies that war is good
in itself. 'There is an ethical element in war,' we read."[81] This is a curious
notion of implication; from Hegel's contention that "there is an ethical element in war, which should not be considered an absolute evil,"[82] Popper
deduces that Hegel considered war "good in itself." Hegel attempted to
solve the problem of evil by demonstrating that even evil serves a positive
function. Popper overlooks the fact that it is of the very essence of Hegel's
dialectical approach to penetrate beyond such assertions as that war is
good or evil to a specification of the respects in which it is good and those
in which it is evil. Today, the evil so far outweighs any conceivable good
that we are impatient with anyone who as much as mentions any good
aspects; but, in a concrete predicament, the majority still considers that
the good outweighs the evil, even if the point be made in terms of "the
lesser evil."

The one passage, finally, in which Hegel does consider the question
of future wars is not well known and is worth quoting here. It is found in
the lectures on aesthetics that he offered as a Berlin professor:

> Suppose that, after having considered the great epics of the past, which
> describe the triumph of the Occident over the Orient, of European
> measure, of individual beauty, and of self-critical reason over Asiatic
> splendor, . . . one now wished to think of great epics which might exist
> in the future: they would only have to represent the victory of the living
> rationality which may develop in America, over the incarceration into
> an infinitely progressing measuring and particularizing. For in Europe
> every people is now limited by another and may not, on its part, begin
> a war against another European people. If one now wants to go beyond
> Europe, it can only be to America.[83]

In his lectures on the philosophy of history, Hegel also hailed the
United States as "the land of the future."[84] Plainly, he did not believe
that world history would culminate in Prussia; and one may recall that
these lectures culminate, not in a prediction, but in the pronouncement:
"To this point consciousness has come." This may also be the clue to
the famous expression of resignation at the end of the preface to the
Philosophy of Right—a passage which, at first glance, seems at odds with
the subsequent demand for trial by jury and for a real parliament with

public proceedings, institutions then still lacking in Prussia. But apparently Hegel, while trusting that Prussia would develop further, did not believe that it had any real future: "When philosophy paints its grey on grey, a form of life has grown old, and with grey on grey it cannot be rejuvenated, but only comprehended. The owl of Minerva begins its flight only at dusk."

10. *Nationalism.* On this point Popper's account is particularly inadequate. "When nationalism was revived a hundred years ago [about 1850?], it was in one of the most mixed of all the thoroughly mixed regions of Europe, in Germany, and especially in Prussia."[85] A page later we hear of "the invasion of German lands by the first national army, the French army under Napoleon." Another three pages and we are told that Fichte's "windbaggery" gave "rise to modern nationalism." (Fichte died in 1814.) Again, we are informed that Wilson's insistence on the self-determination of nations was due to the fact that "he fell a victim to his upbringing in the metaphysical political theories of Plato and of Hegel."[86] Contemptuous of the concept of nationality, Popper maintains that it is a common belief in democracy "which forms, one might say, the uniting factor of multilingual Switzerland."[87] Why, then, have the Swiss not united with one of their democratic neighbors? Popper's opposition to many features of modern nationalism is well taken; but those who are interested in its background and development, or wish to understand it, will do better to turn to Hans Kohn's *The Idea of Nationalism* (1944) and to his chapter "Nationalism and the Open Society" in *The Twentieth Century* (1949).

One of the major themes of Popper's Hegel chapter is that "Hegelianism is the renaissance of tribalism."[88] Popper's use of "tribalism" and "nationalism" is emotional rather than precise, and he accuses Hegel of both. Even so, he must admit that Hegel "sometimes attacked the nationalists."[89] Popper cites Hegel's *Encyclopedia* where the so-called nation is condemned as rabble—

> and with regard to it, it is the one aim of the state that a nation should *not* come into existence, to power and action, as such an aggregate. Such a condition of a nation is a condition of lawlessness, demoralization, brutishness. In it, the nation would only be a shapeless wild blind force, like that of a stormy elemental sea, which however is not self-destructive, as the nation—a spiritual element—would be.

The Nazis concluded quite correctly that Hegel was unalterably opposed to the conception of the *Volk* and that his idea of the state was its very antithesis.[90]

Popper, on the other hand, is so intent on opposing Hegel that he immediately seeks to enlist the reader's sympathies on the nationalist side, when he finds Hegel criticizing it. Thus Popper is not content to point out (quite correctly) that Hegel is alluding "to the liberal nationalists," but he adds, "whom the king hated like the plague." Hegel's attitude, of course, cannot be understood or reasonably evaluated in terms of the emotional impact of such words as "liberal" and "king." What is wanted is a profile of the movement condemned by Hegel:

> There was much talk of freedom and of equality, but it was a freedom that would be the vested privilege of the Teutonic race alone, and an equality that meant general poverty and privation. Culture was looked upon as the holding of the rich and of the alien, made to corrupt and soften the people. Hatred of the French went along with hatred of the Jews, Catholics, and "nobles." The movement cried for a truly "German war," so that Germany might unfold "the abundant wealth of her nationality." It demanded a "savior" to achieve German unity, one to whom "the people will forgive all sins." It burned books and yelled woe to the Jews. It believed itself above the law and the constitution because "there is no law to the just cause." The state was built from "below," through the sheer enthusiasm of the masses, and the "natural" unity of the *Volk* was to supersede the stratified order of state and society. It is not difficult to recognize in these "democratic" slogans the ideology of the Fascist *Volksgemeinschaft*. There is, in point of fact, a much closer relation between the historical role of the *Burschenschaften*, with their racism and anti-rationalism, and National Socialism, than there is between Hegel's position and the latter. Hegel wrote his *Philosophy of Right* as a defense of the state against this pseudodemocratic ideology.[91]

It has already been mentioned that the "liberal" Fries, whom Popper so definitely prefers to Hegel, called for the extermination of Jewry, while Hegel, in the *Philosophy of Right*, denounces the nationalistic clamor against the extension of civil rights to the Jews, pointing out that all such "clamor has overlooked that they are, above all, human beings."[92] Are we to condemn Hegel because he agreed with the king, or praise Fries because he did not?

Finally, Popper claims that "Hegel introduced the *historical theory of the nation*."[93] Surely, there is truth in this, although the suggestion lacks all precision. Hegel conceived of history in terms of nations and spirits of nations; but he also construed history as the story of freedom and believed that nations made their contributions only when they formed states that made possible the growth of art, religion, and philosophy. Even the best of nations is not an end in itself, and its aggrandizement or glory as such means nothing to Hegel; what matters to him is the way in which some nations have advanced the cause of humanity and civilization.

Hegel was not—as Popper would have us believe— a nationalist who for reasons of expediency, to please the king, occasionally denounced nationalism. He was sincerely and strongly opposed to contemporary jingoism, and he was a nationalist only insofar as he considered nations the stepping-stones toward a supranational end.

11. *Racism.* The last claim we shall consider, and in some respects Popper's most preposterous one, is that the Nazis got their racism from Hegel. We shall make two points. First, the Nazis did not get their racism from Hegel. Second, Hegel was not a racist. (See also sec. 3 above.)

Under the first heading, one may remark that the Nazis did find some support for their racism in Schopenhauer and Fries (whom Popper juxtaposes with Hegel on pages 223, 272, and in note 58) and Wagner (who, Popper insinuates, was something of a Hegelian,[94] though he was of course a devoted disciple of Schopenhauer). And when Popper declares that W. Schallmeyer, when he wrote a prize essay in 1900 "thus became the grandfather of racial biology,"[95] one wonders about such non-Germans as, e.g., Gobineau and Chamberlain, and any number of other writers who publicized their views before 1900 and tremendously influenced the Nazis' racism. We have already had occasion to refer to Popper's curious view that the Nazis were unaware of their debt to Plato but knew Hegel; and one may now add that Popper offers us the epigram: "Not 'Hegel + Plato,' but 'Hegel + Haeckel' is the formula of modern racialism."[96] Why Haeckel rather than Bernhard Förster, Julius Langbehn, Hofprediger, Stöcker, Chamberlain, Gobineau, or Wagner? Why not Plato, about whose reflections on breeding the Nazis' greatest race authority, Dr. Hans F. K. Günther, wrote a whole book—and Günther's tracts on race sold hundreds of thousands of copies in Germany and went through several editions even before 1933? And why Hegel?

Decidedly, Hegel was not a racist; nor does Popper adduce any evidence to prove that he was one. Yet Popper says, "The transubstantiation of Hegelianism into racialism or of Spirit into Blood does not greatly alter the main tendency of Hegelianism."[97] Perhaps the transubstantiation of God into the *Führer* does not greatly alter Christianity? One can indeed sympathize with G. R. G. Mure when he says that the increasingly violent and ill-informed attacks on Hegel have reached a point in Popper's Hegel chapter where they become "almost meaninglessly silly."[98] Familiarity with Hegel has, however, waned to the point where Bertrand Russell can hail Popper's attack on Hegel as "deadly"[99] (for Hegel) and where reviewers, while expressing reservations about the treatment of Plato and

Aristotle, have not generally seen fit to protest against the treatment of Hegel. Hence we can no longer dismiss Popper's attack as "silly." Nor is it merely a matter of defending Hegel against irresponsible vituperation. The increasingly popular methods encountered in this latest version of the Hegel myth must for once be shown in their true light.

One recalls Kant's critique of Herder which Popper, who quotes it, would apply to Hegel and his modern followers, though it would seem to fit Popper himself quite well: "A sagacity quick in picking up analogies, and an imagination audacious in the use it makes of them are combined with a capability for enlisting emotions and passions."[100] What is important, however, is not the failing of one particular author but rather—to refer back to the motto of this article—the general calamity. Hence I shall conclude by citing in my own behalf what Popper says to justify his critique of Toynbee:

> I consider this a most remarkable and interesting book. . . . He has much to say that is most stimulating and challenging. . . . I also agree with many of the political tendencies expressed in his work, and most emphatically with his attack upon modern nationalism, and the tribalist and "archaist," i.e., culturally reactionary tendencies, which are connected with it. The reason why, in spite of all this, I single out . . . [this] work in order to charge it with irrationality, is that only when we see the effects of this poison in a work of such merit do we fully appreciate its danger.[101]

7

Is the Hegelian State Totalitarian?

Franz Grégoire

Translated by Jon Stewart

I n his penetrating and lucid work, *Philosophie morale,*[1] which contains a long account of Hegel's moral theory[2] among other historical and critical analyses, Monsieur J. Maritain rejects my interpretation of the relationship between the individual and the state according to Hegel.[3] According to my manner of interpreting the German philosopher, each of these terms is the end of the other in such a way that the one part, the state—the highly preponderant part—is the ultimate end of the individual considered in terms of his or her external advantages, and that the other part—a lesser part—the individual, as man, is the ultimate end of the state.[4] For Maritain, on the contrary, the Hegelian state is "totalitarian," in that, in the first place, it does not recognize any value or right in the individual as man but rather only as a member of the state, the state being thus the final end of the individual without any form of reciprocity, and this means, in the second place, that the moral authority of the state is absolute and unlimited.[5] I cannot share this obviously overly simplistic interpretation of Hegel's thought, and I should like in this paper to maintain and defend the interpretation adopted in my *Études hégéliennes.*

With respect to the first point, that is, that of the value of the rights of the individual in the face of the state, I maintain my original view first of all in consequence of the doctrine in Hegel concerning the value and rights of man as man, the result of which is, I believe, that for Hegel the individual is in part an end in itself for the state. This doctrine, which Maritain mentions only marginally,[6] I have discussed in some detail.[7] Specifically, Maritain, with one exception,[8] does not make reference to any of the numerous places where Hegel expressly indicates the character of man as man as the foundation of "subjective freedoms" (that is, political and civil rights). Maritain is not any more aware of the general structure of Hegel's system according to which, starting from the category of organism, all the elements of the dialectical order—and therefore, for example, the individual and the state—are the ends, the one for the other, with the greater weight being placed on the superior term of the pair.[9]

It is necessary to note here that, for Hegel, in conformity with a general theme in his philosophy, the rights of the individual are actualized and effective only in their being "recognized" by the state as the rights of man, *as man*,[10] and it is in this sense, and only in this sense, that the individual draws all his value from the state with respect to the "subjective freedoms."

We thus come to certain important passages in Hegel that can be elucidated by the idea of a reciprocal completeness between the state and the individual. I treat these passages in my *Études hégéliennes*.[11] Here I will take up again the same analysis given there with some slight modifications for the sake of precision. Maritain, for his part, comments on these passages[12] in a manner different from my account. I leave it to the reader to decide for himself which interpretation he prefers. But, I insist that it is important with respect to these passages to keep in mind the Hegelian doctrine of the value and rights of the individual as man as well as the structure of Hegel's philosophical system in general.

In two of the texts in question, Hegel expressly intends to correct the conception of the state constructed by Plato and Aristotle. Before coming to this, however, I would first like to stop to discuss a passage from the *Philosophy of History* where these philosophers are not at issue.[13] There, after having insisted on the value of the state, Hegel observes that one might be tempted to say that the state is the goal and the citizens the instruments. But, he adds, this idea is entirely inadequate. It unduly separates the state from the citizens. (Hegel has in mind here the extrinsic completeness which characterizes some instruments or, strictly speaking, some means.) The true relation between the state and the individual is that which exists between two members of an organism.[14] This seems to signify, according to the conception of the organism that Hegel inherited from Kant,[15] that the two terms in question find themselves in a relationship of completeness, first, immanent and, second, reciprocal. It is true that in our passage on the individual and the state, Hegel, despite the very systematic character of his way of thinking, considers only the immanent, intrinsic character of the relation of the first term to the second, and not the character of reciprocity. This being the case, we cannot draw any definite conclusions from this text in favor of the interpretation of the state and the individual as reciprocal ends.

In the *History of Philosophy*,[16] Hegel, giving an account of Aristotle's doctrine of the state, cites as follows the well-known passage from the *Politics* I.1.2: "The state is the essence of the individual; the individual is as little on his own and separate from the whole as a part of an organism separated from the whole." He praises Aristotle for having exalted, in contrast to modern theories of natural right, the value of the state. "However," he adds, "the freedom of the citizen is a necessary moment which the ancients did not know. They did not know this perfect independence [*Selbstständigkeit*] of the atomic elements and this greatest independence of all—the highest organic life."[17] What does Hegel mean by this? In the organism, a member does not have independence; apart from the whole, it has neither true existence nor value. "A cut hand is a hand of stone," says Aristotle in a passage which Hegel cites in the same context. On the contrary, in the modern (Hegelian) state, the individuals have a "perfect autonomy,"[18] which seems to imply first an irreducible value on its own terms, and also, as a result, the character of an end in itself. And since the state enjoys "the greatest autonomy," more weight is put on it as the end for the individual than on the individual as an end for the state. Under these conditions, let us think along with Hegel about the idea of the individual purely directed toward the state (the ancient state)—thesis—and the idea of the state purely directed toward the individual (the modern liberal state)[19]—antithesis—which together make the figure of the synthesis the idea of the state and of the individual directed the one to the other with the predominance of the state (the modern Hegelian state). This dialectic of the three forms of the state is equivalent to another dialectic which is closer to the letter of the text and the terms of which are as follows: *the ancient state* (1) where the rights of man are not recognized, and (2) where the individual is directed toward the state as to an end in itself but in an imperfectly motivated way; *the liberal modern state* (1) where the rights of man are recognized, but (2) where the individual is not directed toward the state as to an end in itself; and *the modern Hegelian state* (1) where the rights of man are recognized, and (2) where the individual is directed toward the state, his eminent end, in a rationally motivated and entirely spontaneous manner.[20]

It is in a similar fashion that Hegel corrects, for some commentators rather less precisely, the Platonic conception of the state.[21] By the rejection of individual rights such as the right to property and of the right to choose one's own profession (which are for Hegel just as many "subjective freedoms," i.e., rights of man as such),[22] Plato has misunderstood the principle of personal freedom which a true "moral organism" (*ein sittlicher Organismus*) requires and which Christianity was obliged to inculcate as a result of its doctrine of the individual soul, i.e., "absolute end." What does Hegel understand here by "a moral organism"? It was this that was explained above: "The state, the whole, as singular essence, should penetrate the many. But, moreover, the right which the individual has as his contents, as his principle, should be introduced into the whole." We find here again the idea of a "highest organic life" that we met with above in our allusion to Aristotle.

These diverse texts, in the light of Hegel's numerous and unequivocal statements about the value and rights of man as such[23] and about the dialectical structure of the system, lead one to the conclusion that, for Hegel, the state and the individual, qua man, each has its own value, albeit an unequal one, and that they are each the main end, the one for the other, with a predominance on the side of the state.[24] To be sure, I am not suggesting that we consider this doctrine as valid, but in any case, it precludes us from accusing Hegel of "totalitarianism" pure and simple. Hegel was much too careful to harmonize diverse points of view to fall into such a one-sided conception.[25]

After all, in everything we have discussed here, we were concerned with the individual envisioned only in the practical, ethical order, the order of the will to action (*Sittlichkeit*), prior to the consideration of the next higher sphere of theoretical life which unites art, religion, and philosophy. If one bears in mind that, for Hegel, the character of this sphere is more divine than the character of the sphere of the state,[26] it appears even more obvious that he cannot be accused of rigorously according no value to the individual except in virtue of his belonging to the state. Maritain recognizes that, for Hegel, the theoretical life has this more divine character,[27] and he admits that the person, insofar as he participates in this sphere, possesses a value which transcends that of the state.[28] In this way Maritain makes more exact the totalitarian interpretation which he favors. He holds Hegel for a totalitarian only in the sphere of ethical, which is lower than the sphere of "Absolute Spirit." But this adjustment is still, in my view, insufficient. It is precisely in the sphere of the ethical itself or the sphere of moral conduct and duty that Hegel does not praise a rigorously totalitarian state, a state where the individual has value and rights only as a member of the political whole.

After our account of the first aspect of Hegel's purported totalitarianism concerning the value and the completeness of the individual, we should say a few words about the related second aspect, regarding the authority of the state which, according to Maritain, would be absolute and unlimited. (In this case, one might say more precisely that the authority of the state is limited only by its duty toward itself.)

If this seems to be Hegel's idea, it is necessary to recall that we are concerned with the Hegelian state, the state which should and effectively does recognize, respect and protect the "subjective freedoms" of the citizen, as man, and which, on the other hand, recognizes and protects the religious and philosophical life of individuals.[29] It is within these limits, if one dares to say it, that the authority of the state is unlimited. We are thus concerned with an entirely relative lack of limitation. Here one might quite naturally pose the following question: if the state in fact violates the diverse rights which have just been evoked, what can or should the individual do? Hegel nowhere examines this hypothesis. To judge by the fact that he in a very supportive manner approves of the civil disobedience of Antigone and Socrates, one might be led to believe that he approves of individual rebellion in cases of manifest abuse on the part of the state. But this conclusion is not entirely justified, and it seems that Hegel's position suffers from ambiguity here.[30]

Whatever it may be in the final analysis, for all its incontestable merits,[31] the interpretation of Hegel's doctrine of the relations between the individual and the state that Maritain furnishes oversimplifies and notably complicates the thought of this philosopher.

8

Hegel and Nationalism

Shlomo Avineri

I

Hegel was a resident of Jena when the Battle of Jena, a shattering defeat for Prussia, took place.[1] On 13 October 1806, the day on which the French entered the town and deployed for the engagement fought the next day, Hegel wrote to his friend Niethammer:

> As I wrote to you earlier, all of us here wish the French victory and success. The Prussians are suffering the defeats they deserve. . . . This morning I saw the Emperor Napoleon, that World Soul [*diese Weltseele*], riding through the town to a parade. It's a marvelous feeling to see such a personality dominating the entire world from horseback. . . . He is capable of doing anything. How wonderful he is![2]

Three months later in a letter to another friend, Zelmann, Hegel summed up the historical lesson of the Battle of Jena: "There is no better proof than the events occurring before our eyes, that culture is triumphing over barbarism and the intellect over spirit-less mind."[3]

Hegel was writing this while Fichte was agitating, first in Königsberg and then in Berlin, against the French. What Fichte preached in his *Addresses to the German Nation* in 1807–8, he fulfilled in 1813, when he joined the nationalist university volunteer corps to fight against the French and died in that service. On his part Hegel, who had become headmaster of a Gymnasium in Nuremberg, remained loyal to his pro-French, anti-German orientation. Commenting on Nuremberg's liberation from

French occupation, Hegel wrote, once again to Niethammer, on 2 May 1813: "Several hundred thousand Cossacks, Bashkirs and Prussian patriots have seized the city."[4]

Several days later he alluded to a nightmare his wife had had concerning the "Cossacks, Prussians and other savage troops."[5] In another letter, dated 23 December 1813, he mocked the enthusiasm of the nationalist students over the liberation: "Liberation? Liberation from what? They talk a great deal here about Liberation. If I ever see one *liberated* person with my own eyes, I shall fall to the ground and prostrate myself before him."[6]

When echoes of Napoleon's final defeat reached Nuremberg, Hegel exclaimed: "Our great Napoleon—who would ever have believed that this would be his end?"[7] And when the German romantic nationalistic movement agitated for the establishment of a united Germany subsequent to liberation, Hegel rejoiced at the outcome of the Congress of Vienna, which perpetuated the numerous small states of Germany.[8] In an essay on the constitutional struggle in Württemberg, Hegel wrote (1816): "The vain idea known as the German Reich has disappeared."[9]

When the nationalist students' fraternities (the *Burschenschaften*) stirred up the Wartburg pilgrimage in 1817, and Hegel's colleague and intellectual opponent at Berlin University, Jakob Friedric Fries, delivered his famous speech at the rally, in which he visualized a unified and liberated Germany, Hegel devoted most of the introduction of his *Philosophy of Right* to an attack on the Fries School and its subjectivism. While the extreme *Burschenschaft*, Teutonia, wrote into its statutes the aim of a Pan-German consciousness in place of loyalty to the individual German states, Hegel pointed out that those who sought to establish in Germany political unity beyond and above the existing boundaries understood nothing of politics or history.[10] When student fraternities refused to accept Jewish students as members, Hegel demanded the granting of full equality of political and civic rights to the Jews, since "a man counts as a man in virtue of his manhood alone, not because he is a Jew, Catholic, Protestant, German, Italian, etc."[11]

As a final example of Hegel's criticism of German nationalism, his hostility to the Aryan concept may be cited. F. von Schlegel's book, *The Language and Wisdom of the Indians*, appearing in the 1820s, first expounded the Aryan view in Germany arguing for a national and racial affinity between the Germans and the Indians on the basis of the linguistic relationship between Sanskrit and Old Gothic. Schlegel was the first to coin the phrase, "the Aryan Peoples." In his *Introduction to the Philosophy of History* Hegel ridiculed these assumptions about the existence of an ancient "original" Indo-European *Ur-Volk*. He stated that any attempt to draw political and historical conclusions from linguistic evidence meant the conversion of science into mythology.[12]

II

The obvious question emerging from this survey of Hegel's actual attitudes toward the different political and cultural manifestations of German nationalism is: How did it happen that a thinker who expressed himself in such unequivocal terms against the German movement over a long period of years came to be regarded, as he still is today, as the intellectual and spiritual father of German nationalism? How did it come about that the man who so harshly criticized the first signs of the Aryan racial doctrine should be regarded as the founder of German nationalism and racialism by a scholar like Karl Popper;[13] or that a thinker who opposed every attempt at political unity in Germany should be considered by Hermann Heller to be the first exponent of the modern nationalist state?[14] It is easy to cite a long list of scholars who hold the same view as to the close connection between Hegel and German nationalism and racialist Nazism.[15]

It is of crucial importance to observe that this view of Hegel is a new and fundamentally revolutionary one. The Germans of the nineteenth century, who knew Hegel in the context of the German political reality of his period, saw him as utterly hostile to nationalism. Such, for example, is the view of Rudolf Haym, the nationalist historian of the Frankfurt Assembly of 1848.[16] Writing in 1857, he denounced Hegel as the foe equally of liberalism and of German nationalism. Haym saw Hegel's attachment to Prussia as a proof of his antinationalism as well as of his antiliberalism. In his lectures of 1897, Treitschke also referred to Hegel in a rather condescending manner: Hegel did not, and could not, understand the nationalist connection between the *Volk* and the state.[17]

How did the evaluation of Hegel come to be altered in such a radical way during recent decades? Three complementary answers may be suggested:

1. The Hegelian school in attempting to emerge from its political isolation and to become part of the German national movement of the 1850s drew nearer to nationalism and took to interpreting Hegel in a nationalist spirit. This is rather obvious, for example, in Karl Rosenkranz's expositions of his master's doctrine. Rosenkranz wrote three books on Hegel. The first, *The Life of Hegel* (1844), made no specific mention of his subject's stand on the national question. The second, dating from 1858,

was a rejoinder to Haym's accusations (*Apologie Hegels gegen Dr. R. Haym*). Here Rosenkranz claimed for the first time that Hegel was not alien to German nationalism. The very title of the third book, published in the significant year 1870, revealed how far in assessing his master's doctrines Rosenkranz had been influenced by his own *Zeitgeist*: it was called *Hegel as a German National Philosopher* (*Hegel als deutscher Nationalphilosoph*)—a title completely inconceivable twenty or thirty years earlier.

2. The *volte-face* which occurred in the role of Prussia in German nationalism in the nineteenth century did much to confuse the meaning of Hegel's so-called "Prussianism." Up to Bismarck's time, Prussia's attitude to German unification was extremely hostile, and in 1857 Haym could denounce Hegel for being antiliberal and antinational *on the ground of his Prussian connections*. Bismarck's policy, by directing Prussia to become the instrument of German unification, completely changed the image of Prussia in European thought: while still remaining antiliberal, it became utterly nationalistic in outlook. Thus Hegel's Prussianism was given not only an antiliberal connotation, but also a nationalistic one. This is clearly an anachronism, achieved by projecting the image of the Prussia of 1870 (or, perhaps, even of 1914–18) back upon 1820. This was carried to its extreme by Popper, who looked on Hegel as the "servant" of the Prussian court *and* the prophet of German nationalism at the same time: these are mutually exclusive political orientations in the context of 1820, but Popper had the Bismarckian image of Prussia before him and read backwards from it to the Prussia of the Congress of Vienna.

3. The fragmentary publication of Hegel's manuscript *The Constitution of Germany* (*Die Verfassung Deutschlands*) did much to create a twisted image of Hegel's attitude toward nationalism. Extracts from his unpublished and unknown manuscript, written during 1801–2, were first published by Rosenkranz when, in his controversy with Haym, he was trying to prove Hegel's nationalism. In this essay Hegel offered an explanation of the collapse of the German states before the French onslaught. Hegel attributed the collapse mainly to the feudal structure of the decrepit Holy Roman Empire. He tried to find a way in which the balance of power in Europe could be redressed by establishing a strong central European power within the framework of the *historical* Reich, but only as a political unit, without national or ethnic-linguistic connotations. The essay trailed off on a rather pessimistic note when he expressed the opinion that the attempt would probably not succeed. Even the name given to the essay is not Hegel's, who left it without a title. The essay runs to some 140 pages, and the extracts published by Rosenkranz do not exceed a tenth of the total. This carefully biased fragmentary publication created around 1850 the impression that Hegel

was advocating something like German unification, and readers were unable to verify this impression which would have been exploded had the work been published in its entirety. This fragmentary acquaintance served as a basis for a popular exposition of Hegel's views in the significant year 1870. The work, written by Karl Köstlin of Tübingen, treated Hegel as the philosopher of the national German states.[18] This book was largely responsible for the popular image of Hegel in Wilhelmian Germany, and to prove his point Köstlin relied heavily on the extracts quoted by Rosenkranz—*without ever having seen the full text of the original for himself.*

The full text of *The Constitution of Germany* was published for the first time in 1893 by Georg Mollat. But by that time the public image of Hegel had already been so wholly transformed by the popular expositions of the fragmentary text, that the publication of the full text did not change much in the interpretation of Hegel's position. Scholars and publicists went on quoting the familiar passages and, though their pagination referred to Mollat's edition, they appear not to have looked afresh at the whole essay. The first one who based his interpretation of the essay on the whole text was Franz Rosenzweig, whose study only appeared after the First World War. And he overlooked a key passage because it did not square with the established image of Hegel; it is the passage in which Hegel remarked about the characteristic of the modern states:

> In our times, there is no need for integration or unity in the states
> as far as custom, tradition, culture, and language are concerned. . . .
> The dialects of many provinces of France and England differ from the
> dominant tongue. . . . In Wales and the Hebrides English is not spoken
> at all. . . . The Austrian and Russian monarchs do not even know how
> many languages are spoken in their states—and precisely their states
> are models of the modern state, whose integration arises . . . from the
> spirit and unity of a common political consciousness.[19]

It is not surprising that this passage, and others as well, were simply overlooked by those who tried to find in Hegel the philosopher of nationalism.

Thus Hegel came to be interpreted as a German nationalist by two absolutely opposed political traditions. First, the German national movement of the end of the last century claimed Hegel as part and parcel of the German heritage on nationalist terms; secondly, liberal Anglo-Saxons maintained during the Nazi regime that Hegel's antiliberalism must involve extreme nationalism—and went about tearing Hegel to pieces on those two grounds alike. It is significant that in the nineteenth century none of the English Hegelians ever mentioned any possibility of

a nationalist connotation of Hegel's philosophy, though they were aware
of his political *étatist* tenets.

It is true, of course, that Hegel would never have been interpreted
in a nationalist vein had there not been similarities between some of his
expressions, if not opinions, and those of nationalist thinkers. As for the
affinities of Hegel's terminology with that of nationalism, the main point
of overlapping seems to be Hegel's use of the terms *Volksgeist* and *Volk*,
which held a central position in German nationalism itself. It may, then,
be helpful, to ascertain Hegel's meaning in using those terms, and to
relate it to the common usage of German nationalism, in an effort to
determine whether the meaning of Hegel's term can be interpreted in a
nationalist light.

The inquiry will be conducted on three levels: the concept of
Volksgeist in Hegel's early writings will be presented; a comparison will
be drawn between Hegel's usage of the term and the meaning attributed
to it by Savigny's School of German Historical Jurisprudence; and finally
the meaning of this term in Hegel's *Philosophy of History* will be examined.

III

Hegel's early writings were first published by Hermann Nohl in 1907,
and down to 1948 remained untranslated into any other language. The
fact that they were completely unknown in the nineteenth century and
are still very little known compared with his later writings, has certainly
done a lot to influence the general image of Hegel's thought and its
development.

These writings reveal Hegel's spiritual development while he was
gradually liberating himself from Kantian philosophy and slowly working
out his own conceptual system. Parallel to this, he was also gradually freeing himself from deep Herderian influences, which must be considered
in order to find out the significances of the concept of *Volk* to Hegel.

The first of Hegel's early writings, written in 1796, is called *The Positivity of the Christian Religion* (*Die Positivität der christlichen Religion*). This is
Hegel's sharpest attack on Christianity. In it he combined Kant's outlook
in the realm of ethics with outlooks derived from Herder in the cultural
sphere. He rebuked Christianity for being a "positive" religion, that
is, based on normative, positive, and institutionalized commandments.
These are external to the individual's self-consciousness and constitute
moral coercion, as they prevent him from exercising his autonomous
moral decision.

The essay is a panegyric of the Greek popular religion of paganism (*Volksreligion*), contrasted with Christianity. In strict Herderian terms, Hegel saw religion, as well as morality and art, as a manifestation of the people's spirit (*Volksgeist*). Every people has its own *Volksgeist*, incorporating a unity of life that is peculiar to it. This appears in the spiritual wholeness of the individual, who merges his entire being into the spirit of his people. Following Herder's "Christianity and the National Religions," Hegel stated that every people has its own specific sociocultural institutions corresponding to its national character. This also explains historically, according to Hegel, the appearance of Christ against the background of "the miserable situation of the Jewish nation."[20] This occurred because the divine legislation of Moses, accompanied as it was by numerous and burdensome statutory commandments, converted the Jewish people into a nation of recluses, priding itself on its servile obedience to the law. When a foreign power, Rome, intruded into this closed system, imposing upon the Jews subjection to an *outside political order*, the hermetic character of Jewish religious exclusivism was impaired. Out of this tension there arose the messianic belief—and Hegel was one of the first moderns to interpret the Messiah as an embodiment of the national consciousness of the Jewish people. The Messiah, "girdled with might as Jehova's plenipotentiary, was to rebuild the Jewish state from its foundations."[21]

This *political* interpretation of early Jewish messianism is a consequence of the entire Herderian explanation of the historical background of the appearance of Jesus. It is a consequence of the uniqueness of Judaism: the Mosaic religion cannot coexist with any other link to the external world, Hegel maintained, and as Judaism and foreign rule are irreconcilable, the reconstitution of the Jewish state becomes a necessity arising from the *peculiar* (and rather heavily criticized from Hegel's side) character of Judaism. *This is not a universal demand for political independence as a prerequisite for every people.* Only the Jewish people, because of its peculiar and hermetic religion, requires itself as "a people dwelling unto itself." Political independence, therefore, is not the historical norm but the deviation, which excludes Israel from the generality of the historical process itself.

In another work, dating from the same year, *On the Difference between the Imaginative Religion of the Greeks and Christian Positive Religion* (*Unterschied zwischen griechischer Phantasie und christlicher positiver Religion*), Hegel sought the reason for the triumph of Christianity over paganism. This essay was written in a spirit similar to that of the work just discussed. But the conclusions deducible from it regarding our inquiry are somewhat different. Hegel ascribed the triumph of Christianity not to any rational superiority on its side, but to a certain prior revolution in habits and cultural outlook. His words strike a very typical note in 1796, and the mature Hegel may already be seen between the lines:

> Great revolutions which strike the eye at a glance must have been preceded by a still and secret revolution in the spirit of the age [*Zeitgeist*], a revolution not visible to every eye, especially imperceptible to contemporaries, and as hard to discern as to describe in words. It is lack of acquaintance with this spiritual revolution which makes the resulting changes astonishing.[22]

What was this inner revolution which enabled and preconditioned the spread of Christianity? It was the transition from the free city-state to the Empire. The pagan religion was the religion of free citizens: the gods are the creation of their imagination in the same way as the polis is the creation of their consciousness. The polis is the eternal essence in which every citizen sees the continuation of his life, even after his physical death. Thus pagan Greek religion could be content with gods replete with human failures, because the eternal and transcendental was engraved on the inner soul of each citizen. But the servility imposed by the Empire needed another sort of deity, and Christianity, itself, according to Hegel, as product of servitude, offered itself to a population degraded by fear and terror. The Christian deity was not produced by free will, as the Empire was no longer the voluntary republican polis. Prayer replaced will and this corrupt generation could without difficulty accept a religion based on the moral corruption of mankind, expressed in the Christian doctrine of sin. Sin itself became a religious value, immanent in human nature— and the emperors viewed favorably a religion that would divert men's attention from their actual sociopolitical conditions to a salvation to be found in heaven. The very debasement of life became a sanctified value.

Behind this fierce republican and anti-Christian tirade, a new meaning of the *Volksgeist* can be seen emerging. As in the previous work, religion appears as one of the manifestations of the *Volksgeist*. The concept itself is not primarily spiritual-cultural but turns out to be mainly political in its essence: the measure of political liberty, the methods of political and social institutionalization are no longer mere *phenomena* of a hidden, rather vague *Volksgeist* working from behind the scene—they are its very *essence*. The political sphere becomes dominant in determining the religious experience and the sociocultural attitudes and values. Thus the *Zeitgeist* of the Roman imperial period differed from the republican not because the *Volksgeist* changed: the *Volksgeist* changed because of the transformation of political institutions, arising from a new social class and/or geographical structure. Thus, the "totality" of the Herderian *Volksgeist* became highly politicized, probably under the impact of the French Revolution. Perhaps even more important, the *Volksgeist* became more of a descriptive than a genetic term.

With this in mind, the question of political independence raised once more by Hegel in connection with the Jewish nation (and it is not raised by him in any other connection at that period) may be considered. In a rather long and involved passage, Hegel held:

> Similarly, so long as the Jewish state found spirit and strength enough in itself for the maintenance of its independence, the Jews seldom, or as many hold, never, had recourse to the expectation of a Messiah. Not until they were subjugated by foreign nations, not until they had a sense of their impotence and weakness, do we find them burrowing in their sacred books for a consolation of that kind. Then, when they were offered a Messiah who did not fulfil their political expectations, they thought it worth toiling to insure that their state should still remain a state; a nation to which this is a matter of indifference will soon cease to be a nation. They very soon discarded their ineffective messianic hopes and took up arms. . . . In history and the judgement of nations they would stand alongside the Carthaginians and Saguntines, and above the Greeks and Romans, whose cities outlived their polities, if the sense of what a nation may do for its independence were not too foreign to us.[23]

The impulse for independence on the part of the Jews is no longer here explained by the *unique* character of Jewish religion: it appears as a *universal* need, in that intriguing remark scribbled by Hegel on the margin of the original manuscript: "A nation to which this is a matter of indifference will soon cease to be a nation." Is this really a demand in the spirit of modern nationalism?

Hardly so, if it be read within the context of Hegel's essay. It is not the national independence of modern nations that Hegel is referring to, but the political independence of ancient city-states. In an essay in which political values are dominant, the existence of a *political organization* as such is conceived as absolutely necessary to the existence of intellectual and spiritual life. Thus, the Greek polis lost its spiritual life following its political subjection—*a subjection that was not necessarily a national one.* A unit that is no longer a political unit in the sense of having its own political institutions and of embodying the will of its citizens, is no longer a social unit at all: it becomes part of another unit, which has engulfed it. That Hegel does not mean national units in any modern sense, but the existence of a state as such as a preliminary condition to cultural life, is evident from the examples adduced of Carthage and Saguntum. Being a people means being organized in a political framework—this is the principle by which *Volk* is defined, here as well as in Hegel's later political writings. This is very similar to Rousseau's *peuple*. Later Hegel wrote about a Prussian *Volk* or a Bavarian *Volk*, and so on, because those *states* did exist.

But this is not the last phase of the gradual but significant transformations of Hegel's *Volksgeist*. In the last work belonging to his early period, *The Spirit of Christianity and Its Fate*, written in 1799, the atmosphere is completely different. Under the influence of Hölderlin and possibly also Schlegel, Hegel switched over from rationalistic criticism of Christianity to Christian mysticism, searching for a speculative expression for his religious experiences. As this development is beyond the scope of the present study, it can only be pointed out that thereafter Hegel considered himself a devout Christian, although he never fully agreed with the accepted theological justification of doctrinal terms, and his Lutheranism is certainly open to criticism on theological grounds. In this essay, however, Hegel presented Christianity as a blending of Judaism, with its austere commandments, and of Hellenism, consisting here mainly in the cult of beauty and aesthetic experience. According to Hegel, those two qualities require each other in order to create the synthesis of *psyche* (soul) and *physis* (nature).

This is, of course, an obvious romanticization of Christianity, and consequently the Jewish and Greek *Volksgeister* involved cannot any longer be considered as *historical* entities. What Hegel meant here when he referred to the Greek or Hebrew spirit has nothing to do with the *actual* Greeks or Hebrews: it is an abstraction of a quality, of a philosophical idea, placed rather arbitrarily by Hegel into an historical reality. The references are no longer to concrete manifestations of any historical phenomenon, a people or a culture, but to the realization of metaphysical ideas ("beauty," "morality," etc.). The concept of *Volksgeist* had in effect become void of all content ascribable to it as a tangibly historical entity.

But before Hegel reached this ultimate reconciliation with Christianity, he wrote, apparently while staying in Berne in 1797, a passage sometimes referred to as "Is Judea, then, the Teutons' Fatherland?" (*Ist denn Judäa der Tuiskonen Vaterland?*). Most characteristically, in their fullest form this passage expresses the Herderian ideas of *Volksgeist*—while dialectically refuting them and going beyond them.

Initially Hegel stated that every people possesses its own traditions and fantasies about gods, angels, demons, and heroes; they are transmitted from generation to generation, constituting the sociopolitical and cultural heritage. The ancient Germanic tribes possessed such a tradition—but it was destroyed by Christianity:

> Christianity has emptied Valhalla, felled the sacred groves, extirpated the national imagery as a shameful superstition, as a devilish poison, and given us instead the imagery of a nation whose climate, laws, culture, and interests are stranger to us and whose history has no connection whatever with our own. A David or a Solomon lives in our popular imagination, but our own country's heroes slumber in learned history books.[24]

This looks as if it were a preliminary to a plea on Herderian lines to resuscitate the German *Ur-Mythos*. But dialectically Hegel proceeded to attack what he calls the "phoney Germanic literature," which tried to put new life into old Teutonic traditions. This sort of literature, very much connected with Klopstock's name, is severely criticized by Hegel:

> But this imagery is not that of Germans today. The project of restoring to a nation an imagery once lost was always doomed to failure. . . . The old German imagery has nothing in our day to connect or adapt itself to; it stands as cut off from the whole circle of our ideas, opinions, and beliefs, and is as strange to us as the imagery of Ossian or of India.[25]

Hegel never reversed this verdict on the German national romantic attempt to revive the old mythology. Over thirty years later, when lecturing on aesthetics at Berlin University, he had this to say about Klopstock and his school:

> Very prominent in Klopstock is the consciousness of the fatherland. As a poet he sensed the need for a rooted mythology, whose names and forms should compose in themselves a solid base for fantasy. . . . It may be said that out of national pride Klopstock tried to revive the mythology of Wothan, Herta and the rest. All he succeeded in doing was that the *names* of the Gods took on German instead of Greek forms, and no more. Klopstock attained to no greater influence and objective actuality than a man who endeavors to argue that the Imperial Diet of Regensburg can constitute the ideal of our present national existence. *Those Gods who have sunk into oblivion will always remain hollow and false,* and a good deal of hypocrisy is needed to pretend that this fantasy is reconcilable with intelligence and with the present consciousness of the nation.[26]

To sum up: Hegel used Herder's term *Volksgeist*, but with a connotation which excludes any interpretation that he favored a return to the Germanic *Ur-Volk*. In Hegel's thought the *Volksgeist* underwent a profound process of rationalization; it is not the origin of the historical phenomena, but is really the outcome of them, and thus tautological with it. It cannot be interpreted in the spirit of national and romantic myth. The selfsame myths that acted as a driving force in the development of revived German national consciousness were those later transformed into the racialist and pagan Nazi ideology. Hegel's historiosophical concepts, on the other hand, were not conceived as a means of romanticizing the present in the image of the past. For, as Heraclitus said, one cannot step twice into the same river, and Hegel the dialectician always remained hostile to any attempt to revive the past: this was his point of view when he was a young private tutor in Berne and remained his belief when in his later years he served as Professor of Philosophy in Berlin.

IV

The second level of our investigation is concerned with the respective meanings attached to the term *Volksgeist* in Hegel and in the writing of the German Historical School of Jurisprudence, founded by Savigny and Puchta.

In the usage of the Historical School the concept served as a lever for the German nationalist consciousness to identify itself with what was thought to have been the institutions of ancient German law. This self-identification reached its peak in the attempt to do away with the existing rational European legal system and reconstruct what was conceived to be ancient German-national tribal law, thus replacing "formal" Roman law by "popular primeval" German justice.[27]

The question here posed is whether the term *Volksgeist* had the same meaning in Hegel's writings as the one it received in the Historical School. The various scholars who have engaged in this line of inquiry agree on the fundamental facts relating to the actual use of the term:[28] the concept of *Volksgeist* reached the Historical School through Hegel. Savigny used it only after it had come to him through Puchta who was Hegel's pupil. But this is not yet an answer to the question, whether the meaning of the concept is identical.

In order to examine this, it is necessary to determine what the Historical School meant in using the term, then to ascertain whether the same meaning can be ascribed to the term in Hegel's writings, and finally to examine in what measure Hegel himself actually took issue with Savigny's school.

According to Savigny's *On Our Generation's Legislative Task* (1813), law stands in an organic connection with the nation's character. The nature of law constitutes the inner essence of the nation and stems from its history, for every nation has its own particular laws and customs in accordance with its particular and unique spirit. The reason and origin of the law are found in that layer of national consciousness which also produces language and custom. Law lives in the nation's original (*ursprünglich*) consciousness. It is created by unconscious historical forces, not by the conscious will of the formal legislator. Just as the grammarian never determines the laws of language, but describes them as they exist and function, so the legislator merely describes the prevailing procedures in the life of society. In accordance with German historical legal consciousness, Savigny stated that the legislator merely gives external formalization to contents already inherent in the national character. He is no more than the external representative of the *Volksgeist*, which does its silent and secret work in concealment, in the bosom of the historical process itself.

In Puchta's works the romanticization of the concept of law goes deeper and further into the political sphere; as law is the product of an unconscious and primeval national force, so is the state, which is not the outcome of rational, conscious will, but a product of dormant historical forces. Neither law nor the state is open to rational criticism or argument. Law and the state, according to the Historical School, always are what they should be. Positive legislation and conscious general codification— insofar as they reflect the *Volksgeist* and the existing legal values inherent in the people—are superfluous; insofar as they introduce innovations and impose new conceptions, as the *Code Napoléon* did in areas of western Germany, they emasculate the people's consciousness. The Historical School violently opposed any attempt at codification and rationalization of existing legal customs.

To what extent can these notions be connected with Hegel? In his *Philosophy of Right* Hegel stated that the *Volksgeist* endows the state with its unique character.[29] But beneath the identity of the term, there exists a difference of content and principles. For the jurists, the *Volksgeist* is an essence creating law, morality, religion, and language. It is a mythical quality that takes on various forms and is implicit in the people, working hidden and unknown to all. But for Hegel the *Volksgeist* does not *create* the unique character of each people, but is the *product* of its concrete arrangements in the realms of religion, tradition, and the like.

The Hegelian *Volksgeist* is *identical* with the features it is describing, and does not *create* them, as the jurists and the romantics generally held. For them it is the unconscious creator of law, for Hegel the conscious product aware of itself.[30] The Hegelian concept is descriptive, while that of the jurists is genetic. Furthermore, Hegel's term is a rational one, while that of the jurists is naturalistic, an *Ursache* of all social existence. Marcuse rightly observed[31] that the jurists' conception is a positivist reaction to the rationalism immanent in the Hegelian *Volksgeist*.

The phenomenological similarity between law and language, as proposed by the jurists, is also very remote from Hegel's view. For him, law embodies a rational, universalistic content, while language is an expression of chance attachment and arbitrary external affiliation. For Hegel the content of law embodies rational ethical qualities, while language is morally irrelevant: one legal norm may be said to be morally superior to another; it would be nonsense to say anything like this about languages.

Nor is this all: for Hegel the idea, as an ethical quality realizing and embodying itself, attains realization only through its objectification in the world of phenomena, in its institutionalization. Where law is concerned this process of objectification of the ethical qualities takes place by explicit legislation and promulgation, which posits the law as an objective fact, and not a mere subjective wish.[32]

From this derived Hegel's specific support for such works of codification as that of Justinian, Frederick the Great, and Napoleon.[33] On this issue Hegel specifically criticized the ideas of the Historical School and of Ludwig von Haller. He saw their opposition to an objective statute law as a shibboleth for their subjectivist, relativist, and irrational philosophical premises.[34] As the criterion for the existence of a traditional customary law is subjective (whether it is known or has already been forgotten), it is basically arbitrary and unclear. From this point of view Hegel argued against the anomalies of the unreformed English Common Law of the 1820s.[35]

Hegel was unable to accept the subjective test of law for an additional reason: it effaced the difference between law, which is objective, and personal morality, which is the specific province of subjectivity.[36] By maintaining a difference between the realms of law and private morality, Hegel also maintained the dual existence of state and society, amalgamated into one concept in the jurists' theory and by the whole romantic movement.

Since Hegel's notions of law are rational categories of universal applicability, the positive content of the law cannot be derived from any national characteristics: the law is one and universal.[37] Hence his positive sympathy with the introduction of the rational Napoleonic Code, which swept away so much old dead wood and was viewed by Hegel as a step toward the victory of the universal general norms of law; after all, Hegel's *Philosophy of Right* is an abstraction of those norms, a blueprint for their inevitable institutionalization.

Hegel devoted one whole essay to a controversy concerning the validity of an actual customary traditional law, his long article on the constitutional struggle in Württemberg, in which he attacked the attitude of those who supported the validity of the traditional customary feudal law of that kingdom. Around the banner of the "Good Old Law" had gathered members of the Historical School of Law, the romantic supporters of the national folk-poet Uhland, and the aristocratic circles of Württemberg, whose traditional rights stood to suffer from any rationalization and modernization of the legal system. In the same fierce language in which he had rejected the attempt to revive German tribal mythology, Hegel here rejected the attempt to uphold antiquated traditional law on the ground that it is the "primeval," "original," "old" law. For him, the very reliance on historical rights was utterly baseless, as it proved nothing:

> The question whether what is accepted as an ancient law and an existing right is good or bad cannot be decided solely by the *age* of the legal arrangement concerned. The abolition of human sacrifice and of slavery, putting an end to feudal despotism, and the abolition of an infinite number of other iniquitous institutions, has been invariably the abolition of something which had been valid law in its time. It has been repeatedly stressed that rights do not disappear with time, and that a hundred years of iniquity cannot make injustice into justice.[38]

There exist, therefore, immanent rational criteria for the critique of social arrangements, and reliance on the past possesses no validating powers for the present. Such validation is possible only in the sphere of past events which always symbolize lower stages of consciousness. Whoever desires to remain within the confines of historical arrangements is reversing historical development, Hegel wrote in a passage in which he coupled social progress with a conscious effort at codification:

> The sun and the planets have their laws too, but they do not know them. Savages are governed by impulses, customs, and feelings, but they are unconscious of this. When right is posited as law and is known, every accident of feeling vanishes together with the form of revenge,

sympathy and selfishness, and in this way the right attains for the first time its true determinacy and is given its due honour.[39]

These four characteristics of the Historical School are those that set them off from Hegel: legal positivism, seeing the *Volksgeist* as the unconscious original creator of law, aspiration to arrive at an original *Ur*-German law, and rejection of the value of conscious and explicit codification.

V

Only one aspect of Hegel's philosophy of history can be discussed here: the allegation that his philosophy of history is linked with German nationalism. To support the charge it is argued that Hegel saw historical development in cycles of nations in successive order ruling over the entire world; that he saw the present age being realized among the German peoples; and that, as he conceived the present age to be the supreme stage of historical development, there is here a correspondence with the Nazi idea of German supremacy.

Now, it is true that the formal division of the *Philosophy of History* into oriental, Greek, Roman, and Germanic periods points to the interpretation of epochs characterized each by a different dominant nation. But these stages, though characterized by successive *Volksgeister*, are not characterized by the political domination of any one national state: true, each *Volksgeist* has to create a state, but this is by no means *one, national* state. The Greek polis, *any* Greek polis, was the outcome of the Greek *Volksgeist*, although Greece never achieved political and national unification. Achieving a state means achieving self-consciousness: wherever there exists a body of people who see in some general political arrangements the embodiment of their essential will, there you have a state. How many states will be the outcome of any particular *Volksgeist* is immaterial: in the Greek case it was probably several hundred. Ethnic, linguistic, or racial frontiers have nothing to do with it. The Greek world was declining when it achieved its political unity by an outside agent, and Meinecke saw this as a clear indication that Hegel never considered or valued or preached "national" unity.[40] He had nothing in common with later German historiography, already infected by nationalism, which criticized the Greeks, as Mommsen did, for not achieving unification. But the criticism was really aimed at contemporary Germany. The later German veneration for the Roman Empire cannot be found in Hegel, who had some rather harsh words to say about Roman imperialism, and who unqualifiedly preferred the Greek spirit to the Roman.[41]

But there is a frequently cited famous passage from the *Philosophy of History*, in which Hegel seemed to maintain that every world-historical nation had an absolute right to dominance during its period of hegemony.[42] From this Popper and McGovern, to say nothing of general textbooks of history and political science, conclude that Hegel believed in world domination by one nation, Germany.

This interpretation, however, does not really sustain examination. It is mainly a projection of a twentieth-century situation back into Hegel's time and mind. Hegel never ascribed *political domination* to what he termed world-historical nations. They seemed to possess quite different attributes: "All historical peoples embody power of literary creation, poetry, art, sculpture and painting, science and philosophy."[43] The *absolute right* is not in the realm of international politics, but in the sphere of cultural leadership. Thus, divided classical Greece was the stage at which the Greek spirit was dominant. Hegel was quite explicit that the Greek world never had any *political* meanings, that it was a cultural sphere— Magna Graecia.[44] The time of universal Greek political hegemony, during and after the Macedonian Empire, was, according to Hegel, a period of decadence.

Thus, it may be concluded that Hegel's cycles of history are cycles of the cultural sphere, and not of political domination or military conquest, and this may also explain the meaning of what Hegel termed the Germanic world or period.

Initially, some semantic misunderstanding has to be cleared up. Hegel termed the last phase of historical development *die germanische Welt* (the Germanic world) and not *die deutsche Welt* (the German world). It is significant—and deplorable—that Sibree in his translation of the *Philosophy of History* never distinguished between *germanisch* and *deutsch* and translated both terms as "German."[45] The term "Germanic" is, in the German usage, always used to connote a cultural sphere, and had no political implications, whereas the term "German" aroused in Anglo-Saxon readers of the last half century every possible association with German political world domination.

Hegel, in generally referring to this Germanic period as the *Christian world*, may have revealed his real meaning: the last and present historical epoch has nothing to do with German political domination, which would be completely incompatible with Hegel's own opposition to German unification. Like the former historical periods, this period has to be interpreted in cultural terms, and the only meaning behind the term

"Germanic world" in Hegel implies that Hegel saw in Western civilization the highlight of mankind's spiritual development. The values of the Germanic world are Christian values; in spite of the fact that his new and last historical phase started with the disintegration of the Roman world, Hegel never forgot that the bearers of the new civilization, the Germanic tribes, accepted the Christianity of the Roman culture. The principle dominating Europe, though sometimes called Germanic by Hegel, is the Christian principle, and not an original Germanic contribution to world history: no *Ur-Volk* mythology can be ascribed to Hegel's terming the last phase as a Germanic one, for he explicitly wrote:

> It is extremely important to stress how different is the course of Germanic history from that of the Greeks and Romans. While the latter embodied their own original principles, the impulse to Germanic development was imparted to the Germanics by alien culture. The principles realized by them, their culture and development, their law and religion, were borrowed.[46]

There could be no stronger condemnation of the Germanistic interpretation of history than this: while Herder and the Romantics were basing their national ideology on the "originality" (*Ursprünglichkeit*) of the Germanics, Hegel regarded them as the bearers of a foreign culture and saw in this their main virtue, as their own "original" culture could never have attained any historical importance because of its inherent barbarism:

> Before the Germanics adopted the Christian principles, they had lived in a state of barbarism. Their pagan religion was superficial and lacking essential contents. . . . Germanic law is not true law, for under it murder is not a crime from the point of view of moral values, but merely a private offense compensated by a payment of damages. . . . The Germanic individual is free, but free as the wild animal is free, possessing no value as a moral being. . . . Ever since Tacitus, much has been said of the ancient original liberty of the Germanics. But woe to us were we to confuse this state of savagery and barbarism with a state of liberty, and let us not be induced to follow Rousseau's fallacy, who saw in the wild American Indians the embodiment of liberty.[47]

The Germanic world is not, therefore, an ethnic, racial, or political nation. It is Christian Europe, Western civilization, including according to Hegel, not only Germany, but Spain and France, England and Italy as well—and, perhaps, even Russia.[48] It is not associated with the geographical region inhabited by Germanic tribes, just as it has no connection with the modern political hegemony of Germany. From a political point of view the settlement of 1815, basically antinational, corresponded to the Christian and conservative *Weltanschauung* of Hegel. This *gens Christiana* had no need for the subjectivist nationalist consciousness or for the ethnic-linguistic links, which are accidental and have no rational or moral meaning. Hegel envisaged the modern world as a world containing a multiplicity of political units and powers, in the manner of classical Greece.[49] It is held together not by political power, but by what Hegel metaphysically termed Spirit, realizing in Christian Europe, what Hegel understood, with a strong Lutheran undercurrent, as liberty: the recognition of necessity.

One may beg to differ from this sort of metaphysics, and historically Hegel's analysis seems to be rather naive, though, for a generation torn by a quarter century of wars, this may be understandable. This comes out clearly when one observes that according to Hegel the unifying common spirit was also affecting a humanization of international conduct in his contemporary world:

> The European peoples form a family in accordance with the universal
> principle underlying their legal codes, their customs, and their
> civilization. This principle has accordingly modified their international
> conduct in a state of affairs (i.e., war), otherwise dominated by the
> mutual infliction of evil.[50]

To read here a nationalist meaning twists Hegel's philosophy into meaninglessness. It is understandable how such a peculiar misreading gained currency in a generation that projected its own image of German unity, German nationalism, and finally Nazism upon the entire German philosophy and history of the nineteenth century. The annals of the historiography of Hegel's teaching, to which some allusions were made at the outset of this discussion, are themselves an interesting chapter in the metamorphosis of the modern *Zeitgeist*. But this explanation cannot alter the nature of Hegel's philosophy itself.

One reservation should, perhaps, be made. The development of modern nationalism may be attributed to two main currents: on the one hand, the increased value attributed to the cultural and ethnic association and to romantic communal togetherness; on the other hand, it sprang up from the crystallization of the modern territorial state that constituted the context in which the national claims were realized.

Both are distinct phenomena, caused by different historical and cultural developments. They met in the course of the nineteenth century through the grafting of the national *idea* into the political *structure* of the territorial machinery produced by monarchical absolutism.

The first phenomenon was completely alien to Hegel. But in relation to the second, more "political," or even better, *étatist* aspect, Hegel's thought may stand in some contributory relations. As A. D. Lindsay once remarked,[51] the transition from the dynastic to the national state arose out of the transition from the individual's allegiance first to his ruler, and later to his fellow citizens in the political unit, the mediation for such allegiance being furnished by rational, political, and universalistic-anonymous institutions. Political obligation, so to speak, was refined and institutionalized. To this development Hegel's contribution was undoubtedly large, for in his philosophy the political sphere became the dominant set of interhuman relations. The political sphere, by becoming dominant, makes the modern state strong in comparison with other historical political arrangements, and, though it was not Hegel's intention, this powerful state became an instrument of nationalism—for without a clear-cut idea of a modern, strong and rationally organized state, nationalism could not have laid its claim to primacy.

In *this*, then, may lie Hegel's contribution, albeit an unconscious one, to the crystallization of the modern national state. It is, perhaps, dialectically fascinating to discover that the doctrine of a thinker who rejected any manifestation of nationalism, should be found to have ultimately contributed to this process from an unexpected angle. But, to Hegel, familiar as he was with the "cunning of reason" (*List der Vernunft*), possibly this would not have been surprising.

PART 3

THE MYTH THAT HEGEL GLORIFIED WAR

9

The Problem of War in Hegel's Thought

Shlomo Avineri

One often encounters the assumption that Hegel's political thought paved the way for the crystallization of a theory of state both nationalist and totalitarian. This view has been presented in a particularly forceful manner since the rise to power of the Nazis in Germany, when many efforts were made on the part of enemies of Nazism to find similarities between the philosophical premises of Hegel's thought and the institutional image of the nationalistic state in its extreme manifestations.[1]

This opinion needs reexamination, as is often the case with an hypothesis which has taken root, gained acceptance, and become fixed to such a degree that it seems to require no proof or confirmation. One can, without much difficulty, indicate the historical associations that contributed to the understanding of Hegel's philosophy in a nationalist spirit, just as one can show that this is not the only interpretation applicable to Hegel's thought. Rudolf Haym's *Hegel und seine Zeit* (Berlin, 1857) is a bitter invective against Hegel, accusing him of being blind to the national aspirations of German unity; and Haym's book is only one example.

We shall not undertake here an exhaustive attempt to examine afresh Hegel's connection with German nationalism. The aim of this paper is to trace the meaning of war in Hegel's thought, and try to find out whether this meaning can be assumed to have contributed toward a nationalistic-militaristic ideology culminating in Nazism and fascism.

It would not be difficult to find passages in Hegel which seem to justify prima facie the opinion of those scholars who have found that the Hegelian concept of war resembles, in a way that leaves no room for doubt, the "new totalitarian-étatistic" or fascist ideas.[2] In one of his early works, called "The System of Ethics" (*System der Sittlichkeit*), written about 1801–2, Hegel says: "Morality must display its vitality in something different from itself. . . . This something different is the enemy, and the dissociation from him, which takes shape in relation to one's fellow man as the opposite of survival . . . is the fear of fighting."[3] In another work dating from the same period, "On the Methods of Scientific Treatment of Natural Law" ("Über die wissenschaftlichen Behandlungen des Naturrechts"), these criteria are transferred from the interpersonal to the interstate level: "War is the moral health of peoples in their struggle against petrifaction. . . . Just as the breeze saves the sea from foulness, which is the result of continued complacency, so does war for peoples."[4]

But the most extreme formulation is that which appears in the *Phenomenology of the Mind* (*Phänomenologie des Geistes*), which was completed in 1806—precisely on the eve of the Battle of Jena—and whose outlook is strongly influenced by the charismatic experience of the Napoleonic personality and its historical operation:

> In order not to let [the citizens] get rooted and settled in this isolation and thus break up the whole into fragments and let the common spirit evaporate, government has from time to time to shake them to the very centre by war. By this means it confounds the order that has been established and arranged, and violates their right to independence, while the individuals (who, being absorbed therein, get adrift from the whole, striving after inviolable self-existence [*Fürsichsein*] and personal security) are made, by the tasks thus imposed upon them by government, to feel the power of their lord and master, death.[5]

These formulations, in all their intensity, can be taken as the unmitigated consecration of the force of war, and it might appear from them that there is no distinction between Hegel and the formulations of Treitschke[6] or even those of the fascists.[7] But those quotations should be studied within the context of Hegel's general theory of state, most maturely expressed in his *Philosophy of Right*.

Here we encounter Hegel accepting the challenge of one of the most difficult, and perhaps most thankless, theoretical tasks: namely, the painstaking effort to try to give a meaning, in a general philosophical context, to the phenomenon of war. He was not the only one to do so in his generation; a contemporary of his, Adam Müller, tried to tackle the same problem in a series of lectures, delivered in 1808–9 and later published under the general title of *Elemente der Staatskunst*. But Müller reached quite different conclusions on the moral plane: he recognized the expansionist urge of the state and distinguished between "just" and "unjust" wars—a distinction that is completely alien to Hegel's thought, as will be shown later.[8]

Hegel, on the other hand, attempts to understand war in its human setting, "to recognize the rose in the cross of the present."[9] Hegel realizes that we customarily evaluate war as a deviation from the normal condition of peace; under the influence of various schools of natural law, war is conceived as a reversion, a regression to something prior to the rational sociopolitical order, a reversion to an elemental, barbaric state.[10]

This explanation seems to Hegel insufficient: the moral negation of war does not explain it away. War seems to be the product of some specific human ingredient, and seeing it as a mere accident, a product of sheer arbitrariness, only begs the question as to the motives of this outrageous eruption. Seeing fighting as a departure from the norm of peace means sliding into wishful thinking. This might be lauded from the point of view of personal subjective morality, but it cannot be an adequate philosophical explanation, when philosophy means comprehending *that which is*. Here, as with other social phenomena, Hegel holds that moral indignation cannot suffice.

He does explicitly condemn war: "Hence in war, war itself is characterized as something which ought to pass away . . . implying . . . that the possibility of peace be retained."[11] He does not rest on this but goes further in order to explain the inner necessity of the causes which bring about war as part of the cultural world shaped by man. That our ideas about how this world *should have been* are different from historical reality, is in itself a proof of the human capacity for working out the ideal out of the actual.

First of all, Hegel goes on to explain that war cannot be justified by the utilitarian motive of the defense of life and property. This idea, which Hegel recognizes as one of the commonplace answers to the question of the moral justification of war, would lead to an absurd situation: for it is impossible to demand that men sacrifice, in the act of war, those very things toward the preservation of which it is waged.[12] Every attempt to justify war by reference to needs will necessarily culminate in a dubious code of ethics according to which A will have to pay with his life to preserve B's life or mere property. This amounts, in other words, to an absolute violation of Kant's categorical imperative, which is also the basis of Hegel's personal morality: "Be a person and respect other persons."[13] Where war is defended from the point of view of civil society (i.e., the realm of needs), there necessarily emerges this violation of the basic imperative of morality, since man thus serves as a mere tool and means at the hands of his fellow man.[14]

However strange this may seem prima facie, Hegel's theory of war tries to avoid this difficulty and find an explanation, and justification, for war without infringing on the Kantian imperative. According to Hegel, there lies in war an ethical (*sittlich*) element inasmuch as it exposes the accidental, the arbitrary, and finite in life. It prevents the particular interest from becoming the master of the universe. By demanding everything from all, it places the concrete world of phenomena in its true transitory place, it serves as an ethical *memento mori*:

> The ethical moment in war is implied in this. . . . War is not to be regarded as an absolute evil and as a purely external accident, which itself therefore has some accidental cause, be it injustices, the passions of nations or the holders of power, &c., or in short, something or other which ought not to be. It is to what is by nature accidental that accidents happen, and the fate whereby they happen is thus a necessity. Here as elsewhere, the point of view from which things seem pure accidents vanishes if we look at them in the light of the concept and philosophy, because philosophy knows accident for a show and sees in it its essence, necessity. It is necessary that the finite—property and life—should be definitely established as accidental, because accidentality is the concept of the finite.[15]

Hegel himself sees the affinity of his train of thought with religion, and comments that one often hears sermons of this sort from the pulpit. But, he goes on to remark, every one hearing in church that all the goods of this world are ephemeral, still thinks that on the day of judgment *his* life and property will be spared. But when the day of wrath does come and shows up here, in this world, and not in some remote otherworldly existence, "if this insecurity now comes on the scene in the form of hussars with shining sabres and they actualize in real earnest what the preachers have said, then the moving and edifying discourses which foretold all these events turn into curses against the invader."[16]

According to these paragraphs, war is only the permanent writing on the wall, the embodiment of "unto dust thou shalt return." Thus it is not an outcome of a real will of any concrete human being, nor is it waged with an eye toward the aggrandizement of any particular person or group. It is, in a way, a rod of anger, to use the biblical expression, unrelated by itself to any goal, just as the wars of Nebuchadnezzar were unrelated to any ethical purpose, though in the eyes of the pious they always had, behind the scene, the hidden meaning of providential scorn.

This metaphysical explanation will not receive much approval nowadays and may certainly seem dated if not obscurantist. On the other hand, it would not be welcome by any ideology that might be termed militaristic, as it is completely devoid of the ethos of war itself. It is, however, related only to the *concept* of war, and does not yet refer to any *concrete*, historical war. Hegel distinguishes, on another level, between the concept of the state and the concrete state; the latter belongs ultimately to the realm of the accidental and the arbitrary, and so this distinction serves Hegel here also: "This [concept of war], however, is said to be only a philosophic idea, or, to use another common expression, a 'justification of Providence,' and it is maintained that actual wars require some other justification."[17] Obviously this implies that the philosophical significance of the *concept of war* cannot serve as a justification for *waging any concrete war*. In this regard there was a marked development in Hegel's thought after the *Phenomenology of Mind* had been written; there Hegel had not yet arrived at a clear distinction between the conceptualization of war and its concrete incidence.

What, then, is the essence of concrete wars for Hegel?

Hegel asserts that the essence of a state's existence as a unity, an individuality, lies in its relations with other states.[18] This personality of the state, this "fictitious man," to use Hobbes's language, must be distinguished from other personalities in order to find its identity: "The nation as a state is mind in its substantive rationality and immediate actuality and is therefore the absolute power on earth. It follows that every state is sovereign and autonomous against its neighbors."[19]

This *absolute* power of the state derives from the empirical fact that nations have no praetor to preside over them, as Spinoza once put it, for there is no judicial institution before which nations can litigate;[20] but it should be emphasized that this absolute power is *on earth*, and not to be viewed as eternal, *sub specie aeternitatis*. This is a factual, descriptive statement about the nonexistence of an institutionalized supranational law. That we may want things to be different, Hegel would argue, belongs to the realm of hope, and not to the province of reality.

What makes Hegel's statements sound as if they meant that war could never be avoided (and hence they were viewed as obnoxious) is the fact that he criticizes even the *possibility* of ever achieving lasting peace. To understand the reason for his position, it is necessary to examine carefully the language Hegel uses to explain it: "But the state is an individual, and individuality essentially implies negation. Hence even if a number of states make themselves into a family, this group as an individual must engender an opposite and create an enemy."[21]

A proper understanding of this sentence is possible only in the light of Hegel's epistemology, whereas most of those who have relied upon it have not understood the connection. As the state is seen by Hegel as a person, an "individual writ large," we should turn to Hegel's notion of how a person identifies himself. Put into a nutshell, Hegel's answer is that the individual is a *person* by virtue of his being recognized by others and thus distinguishing himself from them[22]—and this holds true also for the state that has the attribute of a *person*. Its existence is possible only through the objectification of its desires as they come into contact with the world external to it. This contact is possible only by means of opposition and struggle—just as with the individual, who distinguishes himself from his fellow man, sets himself in opposition to him, and in doing so attains to self-identification. To make the point clearer, one may paradoxically say that if *states*, in the plural, cease to exist, there cannot, by definition, remain *a* state in the singular.

But this complication, in which Hegel became enmeshed because of the dialectical nature of his epistemology, is apt to lead to yet another surprising conclusion: if the state exists *because it is recognized as such by other states*,[23] it follows that the state is not independent, "sovereign," a monad enclosed within itself. It seems to be limited in its omnipotence, its sovereignty, as it needs *for its very existence* the coexistence of its fellow states. This is the startling point from which Hegel derives dialectically the need for the existence of international law as of vital importance for the very existence of the states themselves. The negation of the possibility of a *comprehensive and perpetual* international order does not therefore, according to Hegel, constitute the denial of the existence of international law itself.[24]

The dialectical paradox is that Hegel's state is sovereign only insofar as the other states recognize it as such, and the essential need for the existence of a *comitas gentium* arises from just the apparently unlimited sovereignty of the state. To the uninitiated, this may sound a bit over-strained; to Hegel, this would only prove that the infinite must necessarily be limited and restricted by its own dialectical reason. And so Hegel comes to the treatment of international law in that section of the *Philosophy of Right* entitled "Sovereignty vis-à-vis foreign States." Here clearly it is incorrect to assume that Hegel denied the existence of international law. He only denies the existence of an aprioristic international law, which would be based only on abstractions of things-as-they-ought-to-be. Hegel stresses, however, the difference between international and intranational positive law. As international law derives its authority not from its essence but rather from the particular wills of the parties involved, it is more like a contract than law.[25] But its very existence (and Hegel here employs a concept with the intense concrete significance of *Wirklichkeit*) is never denied by him.[26]

Hegel even goes further to prove that the norm of international behavior is inherent in what seems prima facie its very negation:

> Even in war—the state of affairs when rights disappear and force and chance hold sway—a bond wherein each counts to the rest as something absolute always remains. Hence in war, *war itself is characterized as something which ought to pass away*. It implies therefore the proviso of the *jus gentium* that the possibility of peace be retained (and so, for example, that envoys must be respected), and, in general, *that war be not waged against domestic institutions, against the peace of family and private life, or against persons in their private capacity*.[27]

Here the nontotalitarian aspect of Hegelian war is emphatically stressed, and this stands miles apart from the prevailing outlook of that period as characterized by the German romantics, e.g. Adam Müller, who complains that war was still considered in Germany the exclusive business of the standing army; according to him, "the fire of war should penetrate all the families, all the laws and institutions of peacetime life."[28] It is in Müller's expressions that we encounter the roots of the ideology of total war. Hegel's distinction, on the other hand, between state and civil society enables him to safeguard an autonomous region, eminently personal and particular, which should be respected even in war—as war is waged between states, never between individuals. Hegel even comes to the conclusion that modern warfare characterized by the anonymity of battle made possible by the discovery of gunpowder expels personal enmity from the act of fighting itself.[29] This might seem a rather naive appreciation of the horrible possibilities of modern warfare, and it might be that Hegel became himself a victim of that wishful thinking so much obnoxious to him. But this attests to the fact that Hegel *wanted* to see war humanized or minimized in spite of his conviction that it could not be abolished altogether. In any case, the individual must be safeguarded from the emotional horror of warfare.

This cannot be interpreted as the modern concept of a people's nationalist war, which needs the concentration of every human effort in the community. As a consequence Hegel stresses his point that the term *patriotism* should not mean the irrational enthusiastic battlecry, but rather the day-to-day identification with the laws, institutions, and values of the state in *peacetime*.[30]

Moreover, according to Hegel war and victory in war can never suffice to indicate which party was right. A concrete war can never decide matters of justice; the victors are never necessarily the righteous, nor the vanquished the villains in the piece: *might is not right*. Hegel first took this position as to the ethically neutral outcome of war in his essay *The German Constitution* (*Die Verfassung Deutschlands*) in 1802, saying:

> The various possibilities of conflict are so numerous that it is impossible to express them at the outset on the basis of human reason. The more they are explicitly stated and formulated, i.e., the more rights that are set down, the more readily will conflict spring up between these rights. . . . Each side bases its position on the right which it claims as its own and charges the other party with violating this or that right. . . . The public takes sides and each party argues that justice is his, and both sides are right: the difficulty is that these just rights themselves have caused the conflict. . . . Law is the utility of the state as asserted and confirmed in contracts and treatises. But since in these contracts the different interests of the state are stated in a general way, while as rights they are exceptionally many-sided, these interests, and with them the rights themselves, must come to conflict. It depends only on the combination of forces, i.e. on the judgment of politics, whether the interests and rights which are thus endangered will be defended by all available means and force, or not. In such a case it is obvious that this right is also reserved by the other party, as it has the interest opposite to it, as well as the right to this interest. And war, *or any other means,* is what will decide the matter: *not which of the two rights is the more just—for both sides have just rights—but which of the rights will yield to the other.* War must decide this, for just the reason that the two mutually contradictory rights are equally true and just.[31]

The same principles, but in less cumbersome and more mature philosophical garb, Hegel expressed twenty years later in his *Philosophy of Right*:

> A state through its subjects has widespread connections and many-sided interests, and these may be readily and constantly injured: but it remains inherently indeterminable which of these injuries is to be regarded as a specific breach of treaty or an injury to the honor and autonomy of the state. The reason for this is that a state may regard its infinity and honor as at stake in each of its concerns, however minute, and it is all the more inclined to susceptibilities to injury the more its strong individuality is impelled as a result of long domestic peace to seek and create a sphere of activity abroad.[32]

This is a rare insight into the self-righteous attitude every state is apt to adopt toward a real or imagined infringement on what it considers its rights.[33] Thus every war creates the unfortunate situation wherein both sides may have a claim to a certain portion of justice, and as a result war cannot be "justified" from the point of view of *one* party alone. This assumption precluded any possibility of relating the Hegelian concept of war to the idea of a national war, since the national movement, even in its humanitarian phase, e.g., Mazzini, has had recourse to the concept of a "just" war: otherwise it cannot justify a national *levée en masse*, or a people's war against the "national enemy," not to mention wars waged on pretexts of rectifying historical injustices or preventive wars.

According to Hegel, no war can be inherently just, for a concrete war does not take place in a realm which is at all relevant to the concept of justice. Thus the circle has been closed: first the *concept* of war has been understood in the ethical sphere of general philosophical speculation, and then *concrete* war retreats to the realm of the accidental. The philosophical solution, in spite of its dialectical brilliance, may seem unsatisfactory, but if so, the failure derives from Hegel's unwillingness to consecrate the phenomenon of concrete war. The solution adopted by Treitschke, who saw a positive moral ingredient in national wars or wars of conquest, or Carl Schmitt's radical treatment of war as the essence of a human and political creature might be more consistent, though morally abhorrent. For Hegel concrete war is always a conflict between accidental-particular desires which contain nothing necessary,[34] and thus no philosophical justification can be given to that or any other war.[35]

From this Hegel draws some institutional conclusions: as war should not be part and parcel of the life of the community at large, it should be conducted by a standing professional army, and not through a *levée en masse*.[36] Universal conscription should be avoided, as the courage and skill needed in war are themselves individual characteristics and not collective mass-psychology virtues.[37] In harmony with this, the military power should be absolutely under civilian authority, and a military state like the late Roman praetorian Empire is cited by Hegel as the inversion of the normal order of things.[38]

This is unquestionably a radically different conclusion from the prima facie impression one gets from the passages quoted at the beginning of this essay, but the distinction, occurring over and again, between the concept and the concrete phenomenon is essential to the understanding of Hegel's position. Thus Hegel can exalt the concept of war, without identifying himself with any concrete war. This ambivalence might perhaps be compared (on a rather superficial level, of course) to the Christian attitude to sin. The *concept* of sin is the cornerstone of Christian theology, and is *sine qua non* to the concept of grace. Yet every *concrete* sin is a subject for negative moral evaluation.

Thus Hegel concludes the passages on war in a vein which correctly expresses his feeling of crucifixion in face of the fact that war is so much with us; yet in spite of his assertion not to turn to wishful thinking, he sees in Europe of the post-Napoleonic period the possibility of minimizing the incidence of war:

> The European peoples form a family in accordance with the universal principle underlying their legal codes, their customs, and their civilization. This principle has accordingly modified their international conduct in the state of affairs [i.e., war] otherwise dominated by the mutual inflicting of evil.[39]

This universalistic attitude toward the unifying concept of the modern world, of contemporary Europe, Hegel also uses in order to stress the fact that the politico-national boundaries dividing the European states are of secondary importance, since the cultural partnership is dominant. Political unity is secondary to cultural unity, as the realm of the state itself is philosophically subordinated to the realm of the Absolute Spirit. Thus Hegel puts it in his *Philosophy of History*:

> States in the modern world seek independence of one another, and this is their honor. This obstinate tendency toward an absolute position of autonomy they have in common with the Greek city-states. . . . But despite all the differences between the individual states . . . , there also obtains a unity among them, *and therefore we should view even political independence as a merely formal principle.* Today there is not the same absolute chasm between the states of Europe which prevailed between Greece and Persia. When one state is annexed to the territory of the other, it loses, to be sure, its formal independence: but its religion, its laws, the concrete in its life remain intact. The trend of the states is, therefore, towards uniformity. There prevails among them one aim, one tendency, which is the cause of wars, friendships, and the needs of dynasties. But there also prevails among them another uniformity, which parallels the idea of hegemony in Greece, except that now it is the hegemony of Spirit.[40]

Although Hegel does not accept, on what seems to him solid philosophical considerations, the vision of an aprioristic eternal peace scheme such as Kant's or that of the Holy Alliance, his empirical description of contemporary Europe is much in the same vein. If there might be raised objections to it, they are on the ground that he has not rightly sensed the pulse of the time.

For it seems doubtful that Hegel's position about war could, or should, be defended. It might seem hardly praiseworthy to explain the immanence of war in human history by reference to its being a continuous *memento mori*; still, it should be remembered that by this notion Hegel did not try to defend any actual war, only to explain it conceptually. Similarly, it may be questioned whether there really are no "just" wars in the sense that in *any* war both sides have an equal portion of justice. Contemporary history certainly could supply us with ample cases in which Hegel's notion would not stand when tested by his own standards.

Yet, apart from the question whether Hegel has supplied us with an *adequate* philosophical explanation of war, it must be maintained that, on the other hand, he did not supply arguments from which the nationalist case for war could be sustained. The last paragraphs quoted amply suggest that Hegel did not speak the language of nationalism or expansionist militarism. His dream of a relatively tranquil Europe was shattered, like all the other dreams of the Restoration period, in 1830 and later, with greater force, in 1848. At that time a new chord was struck, which enabled men to praise war as morally justified under those circumstances that suited them ideologically. Thus Mazzini, the *humanitarian* nationalist, encouraged his followers in his *Duties of Man*, written in 1844, to be concerned that the blood spilt by them should be *ad magnam patriae gloriam*; Wilhelm Jordan, member of the German Constituent Assembly in Frankfurt, justified the continued occupation of Polish areas by a unified national Germany with the following words: "Our right in Poland is the right of conquest, the right of the stronger . . . , and I am proud of it";[41] and the student fraternities (*Burschenschaften*) which declared "we believe that war puts an end to conditions of degeneration and that it is the first and irrepressible way to the final goal of national unity"[42]—all those various trends of thought do not speak the language of Hegel, and the philosophical lineage of those attitudes cannot be ascribed to him.

10

Hegel's Account of War

D. P. Verene

H egel's account of war, although primarily given in a few statements
in the *Phenomenology of Mind* and the *Philosophy of Right*, has been
the subject of some of the most divergent interpretations of his
thought and has engendered some of the strongest feelings regarding
it. It has been a point on which the interpretation of Hegel's theory
of the state has often turned. Opinion has varied from the view that
Hegel advocates a nationalistic, totalitarian state and regards war as a
fundamental and glorious activity;[1] to the view that Hegel is a conservative, reflecting the political situation of his time and acknowledging
the fact that war plays a role in the actual life of nations;[2] to the view
that Hegel's political philosophy is essentially compatible with the liberal
constitutional model of the state and hence is not an enemy of the pursuit
for peace.[3] These interpretations of Hegel's statements on war involve the
scholarly interest in developing a consistent reading of a major figure but
they have behind them a larger need, dictated by the conditions of our
own time, to understand the problem of war itself.

My intention is: (1) to assess the view that can be taken of Hegel's
statements on war; and (2) to decide what they indicate for the problem
of war in general. Questions concerning Hegel's account of war cannot
be answered apart from an assessment of their place within Hegel's
philosophy as a whole. Hegel's statements on war, if approached primarily
within the context of his political philosophy, can lend themselves to
either a militaristic or nonmilitaristic interpretation. The commentators
have approached Hegel's views on war primarily within this context and
have engendered a dispute that in principle can have no resolution.
Beyond the textual question is the larger question of what Hegel has

shown or not shown about the problem of war itself. Has Hegel shown war to be a necessary part of the relations between nations, or is his view in some way compatible with the concept of permanent peace? The answer to this question depends upon a decision regarding what Hegel's political philosophy is fundamentally about. It is my intention to deal first with the question of the interpretation of Hegel's statement on war and then, using this as a base, to inquire into what Hegel offers for the understanding of the nature of war itself.

Hegel's statements on war range from remarks in his early writings such as *The German Constitution,* written and revised between 1799 and 1802,[4] to the *Philosophy of Right* (1821) and his lectures on philosophy of religion, philosophy of history, and philosophy of fine art during the latter part of his career.[5] Hegel's fullest statements on war are contained in his treatment of the initial stage of spirit (*Der Geist*) in the *Phenomenology of Mind* and his theory of the state in the final section of the *Philosophy of Right.*[6] Hegel's views on war do not appear to have undergone any substantial change from his first to his last writings. In fact, in explaining his view on war in *Philosophy of Right,* Hegel quotes from his essay "On the Methods of Scientific Treatment of Natural Law" ("Über die wissenschaftlichen Behandlungsarten des Naturrechts"), from the same early period as *The German Constitution.*[7] Two themes are evident in Hegel's statements on war: (1) the relevance of war to the relationship of individuals to the state; and (2) the role of war in defining the state as a distinct political entity or a politically organized nation and its relations with other nations. These two themes run side by side throughout Hegel's statements on war and appear as essential parts of his discussion of the state.

Hegel regards war as something to be explained. It is, for him, one of the phenomena of human affairs, having a particular content and structure comprehensible by human reason. Hegel states:

> War is not to be regarded as an absolute evil and as a purely external
> accident, which therefore has some accidental cause, be it
> injustices, the passions of nations or the holders of power, &c., or
> in short, something or other which ought not to be. It is to what is
> by nature accidental that accidents happen, and the fate whereby
> they happen is thus a necessity. Here as elsewhere, the point of view
> from which things seem pure accidents vanishes if we look at them in
> the light of the concept and philosophy, because philosophy knows
> accident for a show and sees in it its essence, necessity.[8]

For Hegel the task of philosophy in general is to explain that which has occurred. Philosophical explanations involve the analysis of particular forms of experience and the showing of how they are interrelated with each other such that experience itself can be viewed as a whole.[9] For Hegel the task of political philosophy is to analyze and relate together those forms of experience through which ethical and political life occurs.[10] War, being one of the forms of political life, must have a place in the philosophical account of the political. War can no more be regarded as accidental to the activity of the state than can peace. War and peace are both modes of activity in the actual life of states and are to be part of the philosophical analysis of the state. The state along with the forms of the family and civil society comprises the general structure of the ethical-political world.

1. Hegel regards war as an important factor in the relation of the individual to the state. War makes the individual citizen realize that his existence is bound up with a larger whole. War, by having within it the possibility of the destruction of the existing social order, forces the individual citizen to realize that his private world of family, marriage, and property ultimately exists because of the public world of the state. Through war or its threat each citizen is made to realize in concrete terms that the future of his private world is inexorably tied to the future of his state. Hegel asserts:

> While, on the one hand, war makes the particular spheres of property
> and personal independence, as well as the personality of the individual
> himself, feel the force of negation and destruction, on the other
> hand this engine of negation and destruction stands out as that which
> preserves the whole in security.[11]

War is the security of the state in that it forces its citizens to experience the state as a particular entity. In order to defend his state the citizen must experience his state as something more than the general context in which he pursues his private goals and holds property. In order to defend his state the citizen must internalize the general character of his state and see it as a particular state set off against other states. War also makes the individual experience himself in a new way. War makes individuals feel the finitude of their own existence; they "feel the power of their lord and master, death."[12] War makes the individual realize not only the nature of his citizenship in the state, it also makes him realize the temporal character of his own existence.[13]

2. Hegel regards war as an important factor also in the relation of state to state. War is an activity that originates in the clash of wills and interests of individual states: "It is as particular entities that states enter into relations with one another."[14] States relate to each other not in terms

of a common context but in terms of their own customs, peculiarities, and passions. Thus the realm of international relations is one of abiding contingency in which war is always in the background, residing as the means for ultimately settling any dispute. War can occur as the result of any incident, for a state may regard its honor and interest at stake in any of its activities no matter how small.[15] War, once resorted to by states, however, does not entail the abandonment of their recognition of each other as states. War is undertaken as a limited action with peace as its end.

> Hence in war [Hegel states], war itself is characterized as something which ought to pass away. It implies therefore the proviso of the *jus gentium* that the possibility of peace be retained (and so, for example, that envoys must be respected), and, in general, that war be not waged against domestic institutions, against the peace of family and private life, or against persons in their private capacity.[16]

War in Hegel's account is not an act of total destruction undertaken by one nation against another. War arises from the fact that politically organized nations act as individuals without a common superior; thus no treaty or agreement is ultimately binding. Any treaty may be broken when it is not in the interest of one of the parties. The relation of each nation to others is contingent on the advancement of its own interests. Thus the world of nation-states is characterized by the cycle of war and peace and the return to war.

How are we to understand Hegel's views on war? The alternatives presented by Hegel's commentators noted at the beginning of this essay— that Hegel can be taken as either a totalitarian, conservative, or liberal— can be viewed as responses to the question of whether Hegel in his statements on war is *prescribing* or *describing*.[17] The totalitarian view takes Hegel's statements as prescriptive. Hegel is regarded as advocating war and nationalism and as providing a theoretical basis for the twentieth-century fascist states. The conservative view takes Hegel's statements as essentially descriptive. Hegel is regarded as reflecting the actual state of affairs between nations; his view is regarded as prescriptive only to the extent that he may have reflected some of the positive attitudes toward war of his own day. It is often said on this view that Hegel's statements on war hold only for a limited or conventional war and would probably not have been made if Hegel could have known of the possibility of a global war or war of total destruction. The liberal view is most frequently cast as a reaction to the view that Hegel is a supporter of totalitarianism. The liberal view finds Hegel's statements on war insufficient to support the claim that Hegel advocates war. Yet it does not hold that his political philosophy contains a plan for peace. The liberal view takes a strong stand on the point that Hegel is not an enemy of the constitutional form of government and the open society, and generally takes no definite stand on the interpretation of Hegel's statements on war.

The difficulties concerning a decision on the meaning of Hegel's statements on war arise from the procedure of approaching them wholly or largely within the confines of Hegel's *political* thought. I contend that no amount of concentration on or dissection of Hegel's statements on war can solve the problem of their meaning. Such an approach seems to result in nothing better than the current antinomy between a prescriptive and a descriptive reading. The zealous tone and strong phraseology of some of Hegel's statements, particularly in regard to the effect of war on the individual's awareness of the finitude of his own existence and the importance of war in solidifying the citizens of the state, give support to the view that Hegel's statements are prescriptive. The somewhat factual and neutrally cast statements Hegel makes concerning the way war functions in relations between states give support to a descriptive interpretation. The traditional way out of this dilemma—to regard Hegel as a conservative, claiming that his views are the result of the political situation of Germany of his time and the international situation of the Napoleonic era—is too superficial to be satisfactory. It is no more satisfactory to explain away Hegel's political views by an appeal to the historical conditions of their formulation than it would be to explain away his epistemological views by such an appeal. Hegel's political views and especially his views on war are integral parts of his philosophy and must be met on their own terms. The solution to the problem of the oscillation between a prescriptive and a descriptive interpretation rests not on a closer reading of the texts but on a placing of Hegel's statements on war in their proper relation to his philosophy in general. In order to solve the problem of what Hegel's statements on war mean we must ask what philosophical statements themselves are for Hegel.

The philosophical proposition, for Hegel, aims at the presentation of actuality (*Wirklichkeit*). Philosophy, Hegel points out in the preface to the *Phenomenology of Mind*, is neither the production of edifying discourses, construction of proofs, nor the formulation of inductive generalizations. Philosophy aims at a dialectical presentation of experience and thus derives its method directly from a reflection on the oppositional process inherent in consciousness's own act of knowing the object.[18] The philosophical proposition is itself internally dialectical as is consciousness. In the proposition the predicate brings forth an aspect of the subject and in so doing alters the subject so as to produce a new subject.

The predicate stands to the subject as one of its determinations.[19] The attaching of subjects to predicates in the philosophical or "speculative proposition" is a formal expression of the way in which philosophy builds its total account of experience. Such an account is morphogenic. It distinguishes the various forms or frameworks in which the mind (*Geist*) apprehends its object and orders these in a developmental scheme from the least determinate to the most determinate. Mind is shown to be an internally systematic process that forms itself in a manner analogous to the relationship internally expressed in the philosophical proposition.[20]

The presentation of actuality, for Hegel, is accomplished neither by prescribing nor by describing. Philosophy neither formulates imperatives, whereby states of affairs may be judged or actions directed, nor does it generalize from facts. The philosophical proposition fits neither of these modes; instead it portrays the frameworks of mind that are to be presupposed in order that prescribing and describing are possible. Philosophy accomplishes this by taking the most general form of human consciousness and analyzing it into further forms until the entire system of experience is before us. This is as much a process of analyzing one form out of another as it is a process of taking all the forms actually before us and ordering them in a development. Hegel's statements have a descriptive element in that they grow from reflection on actual states of affairs. They have a prescriptive element in that they cause us to consider alternatives. Hegel's statements, unlike descriptions, do not form facts but form the frameworks through which facts can be formed; and, unlike prescriptions, they do not form actions but form the frameworks wherein actions can be formed.

In order to solve the problem of the status of Hegel's statements on war, the status of his philosophical statements generally must also be considered in relation to the works in which his views on war occur. The *Philosophy of Right*, the basic work of Hegel's political philosophy, comprises a section of the second part of Hegel's total system of spirit.[21] It is thus part of a continuous construction of thought, traceable back to the *Phenomenology of Mind*. The *Phenomenology* presents mind as a series of stages of consciousness wherein the concept is uncritically or un–self-consciously joined with its content. This series terminates in the state of Absolute Knowledge, or the realization by consciousness of its ability to give itself form wholly in terms of concepts divorced from specific content. The *Science of Logic* retraces the "schema of movement" of the *Phenomenology* from the standpoint of Absolute Knowledge, that is, as a conceptual progression.[22] The result is the Absolute Idea or the concept self-consciously joined with content. When this joining occurs in the way of science the Absolute Idea is formed as nature (*Philosophy of Nature*);

when this joining occurs in the social world the Absolute Idea is formed as culture (*Philosophy of Spirit*).

The fact that Hegel's political philosophy as presented in the *Philosophy of Right* can be assigned a definite place within his system provides an answer to the question of the status of his statements on war. If Hegel's political philosophy is systematically derived from the rest of his system,[23] his statements regarding the state will have a status consistent with those in the earlier part of his system. Hegel's statements about the state and its functions, like the statements in his philosophy generally, can neither be regarded as prescriptive nor descriptive, neither as imperatives nor as empirical generalizations.[24] It would be as much a mistake to take Hegel's views on war stated in his account of the initial stage of spirit[25] in the *Phenomenology* as equivalent to the position of his political philosophy as it would be to take his views on the nature of the thing in the second stage of consciousness as equivalent to his epistemology.[26] In both cases Hegel is portraying a particular form of the mind's relation to its object, and it is a principle of his philosophy that no one form of mind is equivalent to the whole of mind nor to his philosophical position. In like manner Hegel's discussion of the state in the *Philosophy of Right* and its relation to war is a portrayal of how the idea of right, determined in the form of the state, is joined in a particular way with its content. The quandary over the status of Hegel's statements on war in the *Philosophy of Right* arises only if we approach it as a kind of independent work. If we regard Hegel as having first written a metaphysics and a theory of knowledge and then having gone on to write a political philosophy, with only a rather broad connection between them, in short, if we approach Hegel's political thought much in the way we approach that of Locke or Hume, then the question arises about the status of Hegel's statements on war. If, however, we see that Hegel's political philosophy proceeds from his philosophy in general with systematic rigor, the status of his statements on war is not a difficulty as such. The question of their status resolves itself into the question of the status of what Hegel calls the "philosophical" or "speculative proposition." One cannot do justice to Hegel's political thought by approaching it as a relatively independent set of ideas having goals apart from the goals of his system.

The question which was stated as the second concern of this essay remains: what light do Hegel's statements on war throw on the problem of war in general? This question is closely tied to Hegel's comments on Kant's *Perpetual Peace*. Kant and Hegel appear at two ends of a spectrum on the question of war. Kant in *Perpetual Peace* proposes a set of principles whereby war may be overcome and a federation of free states or league of nations established. Hegel, in the *Philosophy of Right*, seems to regard war as something necessarily rooted in human existence. Hegel states that Kant's idea

> presupposes an accord between states; this would rest on moral or religious or other grounds and considerations, but in any case would always depend ultimately on a particular sovereign will and for that reason would remain infected with contingency. It follows that if states disagree and their particular wills cannot be harmonized, the matter can only be settled by war.[27]

Hegel maintains that international law as such "does not go beyond an ought-to-be"[28] and criticizes Kant's statement that perpetual peace is possible because of the working of providence in history.

The difficulty in Kant's theory of peace to which Hegel's criticism points is that Kant fails to face the problem of the reasons for the existence of war. The paradox that is posed for ethics by the existence of war is that men can bring themselves together under law as states but seem unable to extend the process beyond the bounds of states to the creation of genuine international law. The response to this problem from the standpoint of Kant's theory is to regard the failure of men to establish international peace as residing in an inability to conceive properly the principles whereby it could be established. The elimination of war from the Kantian view is essentially a conceptual and organizational problem. War is regarded as an unnatural state of affairs that exists because of man's present inability fully to grasp the means for peace. The fact that mankind—although in possession of the idea of peace—seems not to be ready to institute peace does not worry Kant, who optimistically appeals to providence to solve the difficulty. Kant states:

> The guarantee of perpetual peace is nothing less than that great artist, nature (*natura daedala rerum*). In her mechanical course we see that her aim is to produce a harmony among men, against their will and indeed through their discord. As a necessity working according to laws we do not know, we call it destiny. But, considering its design in world history, we call it "providence," inasmuch as we discern in it the profound wisdom of a higher cause which predetermines the course of nature and directs it to the objective final end of the human race.[29]

On Kant's view war is dealt with in the same way evil is dealt with on the traditional solution to the theodicy problem. War is regarded as nothing in itself, as a privation having no positive content.[30] War becomes a delay in the working of providence rather than a moment of its development in history.

Hegel's criticism of Kant derives from the general principle of his thought affirmed at the beginning of the *Philosophy of Right*, that the rational is actual and in turn the actual is rational.[31] For Hegel: "History is mind clothing itself with the form of events or the immediate actuality of nature."[32] War, being actual, cannot be regarded by philosophical reasoning as an unnatural state of affairs or as mere chaos. War must be understood as a form of the state's activity. Kant's view leaves us with a conception of the principles of peace that ought to be followed by men and a hope that the working of providence will soon be fully manifest in the actualities of history. Hegel's view indicates that the possibility of peace must depend not upon a faith in the ultimate order of history, but upon the analysis of the structure of one of its specific moments—war. War, for Hegel, is a moment in the development of social consciousness and action; war is an activity of the state as an independent nation. "A nation," Hegel asserts, "does not begin by being a state. The transition from a family, a horde, a clan, a multitude, &c., to political conditions is the realization of the Idea in the form of that nation."[33] Hegel, following his dictum that every philosopher is a child of his own time,[34] terminates his account of the state with the conception of the state as a politically sovereign nation. The Idea exists in the form of a world of nations related to each other though the contingencies that surround their cycles of war and peace. Kant offers us directly a theory of peace. Hegel offers us directly a theory of war. Kant's theory, although admirable in design, is underpinned by a view of history that in principle forbids a theory of war. War remains a sojourn in the irrational. Its asks human consciousness to overcome a mode of its activity without understanding the roots in its own structure from which the activity it is to overcome has stemmed.[35] The question now to be faced is whether Hegel's theory of war and the metaphysics of history from which it derives can engender a theory of peace.

From Hegel's position any theory of peace would need to follow from an understanding of the phenomenon upon which war is based. War must be seen as having its roots somewhere in the very structure of human consciousness. Karl Jaspers in *The Future of Mankind* states:

> Fighting—risking one's life so as either to meet force with force or else
> to use force to win power and booty—is a primordial phenomenon
> of human life. The primordial element is the fierce fighting spirit.
> Unleashed, it engenders the self-transcending lust of flinging one's
> life away and the savagery that rates other lives no higher, vents itself

in pillage and rape after victory, and finally abates in the climactic feeling of power: to spare the conquered and let him serve as a slave. This abatement led Hegel to interpret the productive meaning of life-and-death struggles. *The warrior is a human type, but not everyone is a warrior.*[36]

In the full context of this statement Jaspers regards the warrior as a particular way of engaging in the master-slave relationship which Hegel portrays in the *Phenomenology of Mind.*[37] His statement captures the point that follows from Hegel's treatment of war—that war exists not because of man's inability to conceive the principles whereby to organize for peace, but because the warrior is a specific way in which men relate to their own existence. Any solution to the problem of war must rest on a solution to the problem of warriors; and this is particularly difficult since the style of life of the warrior is rooted in one of the basic structures of consciousness, the master-slave.

In his theory of the warrior Jaspers further draws out a point that illuminates Hegel. Jaspers maintains that the warrior depends upon the phenomenon of self-sacrifice.[38] Hegel points to this in his discussion of the military as a class. The military, Hegel maintains, are men who realize the nature of their own freedom through courage, and their courage is manifest in their willingness to sacrifice themselves for the sovereignty of their state. Hegel states: "The work of courage is to actualize this final end, and the means to this end is the sacrifice of personal actuality. This form of experience thus contains the harshness of extreme contradictions: a self-sacrifice which yet is the real existence of one's freedom."[39] It follows from Hegel's view that war exists not because nations reach an impasse in their relations with each other; war exists because armies exist. The military exists because the warrior is a human type, and the warrior is a human type because the act of self-sacrifice, of meeting force with force on behalf of an idea, is one of the ways men apprehend themselves as free agents. The genuine threat to peace is not that diplomatic relations will break down and the technical problems of such negotiations will be taken up in the physical conflict of war. The genuine threat to peace is the fact that the warrior is a type of life. Wars are the result of the frustrations that peace brings to the warrior in his drive to act out the freedom of his being. When such frustrations are sufficiently felt by the warriors of two nations, the actual conditions for war are met and the technical, diplomatic justification will soon be found.[40]

If, in the *Phenomenology of Mind*, Hegel has shown the master-slave to be one of the fundamental ways whereby human consciousness structures itself and realizes its own freedom,[41] and if the *Philosophy of Right* has shown that the warrior is the type upon which the state's ability to make war depends, then an end to war lies in a transformation of the warrior's existence. The realization of freedom that the warrior experiences in his act of self-sacrifice, of risking his life by meeting force with force, must be carried to a new form in which the same goal is reached but the violence of its means is overcome. It is not enough to encourage all men to adopt the slave side of the master-slave relation and advocate the realization of their freedom in their work as does the conquered slave.[42] To advocate the replacement of the evil of war with the good of work, to view work as a moral equivalent of war, is to misconstrue the nature of the warrior and view him simply as an energetic man. The warrior must be taken more seriously. If he were simply an energetic man we could have expected warriors long ago to have turned to organized sports and dangerous occupations. The courage of the warrior is not simply the courage of risk but the courage of risking one's life for the sake of an ethical ideal.[43] Any attempt to transform the warrior must account for this ethical element.

Given the direction in which Hegel's account of war takes us, it is difficult to believe that peace depends upon the institution of a set of principles for the actions of nations. In the realm of practical political affairs it is difficult to believe that the United Nations can ultimately be more than organized good will unless we come to grips with the roots of the activity it is dedicated to overcome. Once it is seen that war is grounded in one of the ways consciousness structures itself, in a type of life, the problem of peace becomes one of the redirecting of warriors. To formulate prescriptions for peace apart from the realization that war is not a lapse in the natural state of affairs but is an integral part of their structure is to foster illusion. Hegel's theory, by focusing on the analysis of war rather than advancing prescriptions for peace, does in no way glorify war. His philosophy, being in largest terms the portrayal of the self-alterations of consciousness, would allow for the warrior to be superseded. The grounds for him to be superseded lie in Hegel's placement of art, religion, and philosophy as forms of mind that lie beyond the state.[44] The state to which the life of the warrior is tied has above it the forms of art, religion, and philosophy which could, like the state, be said to entail types of lives, the task of which is the apprehension of other human types. Thus from the perspective of Hegel's philosophy it is in the activity of artists, religious men, and philosophers that the possibility of comprehending and transforming the warrior lies. It does not lie with politicians. The solution to the problem of peace, which is properly the solution to the problem of warriors, cannot lie with those whose existence is tied to the form of the state.

In conclusion, I have intended to show that Hegel neither endorses war nor simply reflects the fact of its existence. For Hegel, war, as anything else actual, is something to be understood philosophically and cannot be regarded as something accidental. His approach in the *Phenomenology of Mind* is to show the relationship of war to human consciousness and in the *Philosophy of Right* to show its relationship to the state. Hegel's insistence on showing the role war plays in human affairs reveals the difficulty of regarding the elimination of war as a matter of correctly conceiving the principles of peace and organizing around them. War exists not because of the weakness of our conception of peace nor our slowness to adopt international order. Our inability to carry the process of law beyond the perimeters of nations rests on the existence of warriors. The warrior's style of life constitutes a particular orientation toward the problem of human freedom which has its roots in the master-slave relationship wherein consciousness discovers one of the fundamental ways of structuring itself. Hegel's philosophy offers no specific solution to the problem of how the warrior's act of self-risk that lies at the base of war can be overcome. Hegel's analysis, however, if correct, does show that if war is to be eliminated, efforts must be directed to the development of alternative ways of relating to the state than the warrior's.

11

Hegel's Theory of Sovereignty, International Relations, and War

Errol E. Harris

Sovereignty

"*L'état c'est moi*" declared Louis XIV, and on his canon he had inscribed the legend: "*Ultima ratio regum.*" Hegel appears to agree, at any rate prima facie, and to endorse both doctrines. For he writes:

> Sovereignty . . . exists only as subjectivity certain of itself, as the abstract (and to that extent groundless) self-determination of will in which the finality of decision lies. It is this, the individual aspect of the state as such, in which alone it is one. Subjectivity, however, exists in its true form only as subject, personality only as person. . . . This absolute decisive moment of the whole is, therefore, not just individuality in general, but an individual, the Monarch.[1]

Further, Hegel maintains that because the relations between states have as their fundamental principle their respective sovereignties, "they are to that extent opposed to one another in the State of Nature," and "the conflict of states, for that reason, so far as their particular wills find no agreement, can only be settled by war."[2]

But quoting passages in isolation from their contexts is as unscholarly as it is unfruitful, and can result only in misunderstanding and misinterpretation. The bad habit of so doing is outstandingly exemplified by Sir Karl Popper's criticism in *The Open Society and Its Enemies.*[3]

In the first place, any careful reader will be aware that Hegel, despite what is quoted above, does not identify sovereignty with the monarch. Certainly, the monarch personifies the state and embodies its individuality; for Hegel protests that the state is no merely legal or fictitious person, but is a genuine individual, which becomes personal in the monarch. To that extent *l'État c'est le Roi*. But the king (or queen) is not the government, as such; he (or she) is but one moment in the total unity, while, as ever in the sphere of the concept (to which the state corresponds in the dialectic of *Sittlichkeit*) each moment is at the same time the whole. The government or constitution of the state, however, is a system of functions, legislative, executive, and judicial, sublating all the functions and institutions of *die bürgerliche Gesellschaft* and the family, and constituting a whole, the members of which are each and all as integral to it as are the cells and limbs of a living body to the mature organism.[4] Monarchy is thus constitutional monarchy, and is neither despotic nor feudal.[5] To that extent, Louis XIV's assertion is un-Hegelian. He represents, perhaps, the historical transition from the feudal to the modern form of the state, the centralization of power, prior to its liberalization.

How far is Hegel justified in this assertion of the personal character of the sovereign and of the embodiment of its will in the monarch? Those who allege that he is advocating a personal despotism, or tyranny, are, as I shall presently show, profoundly mistaken. Strictly, as has already been maintained, the *Rechtsphilosophie* is not the advocacy of any political form so much as the analysis of political forms in general, or more properly of political order as such. If Lord Bryce's description of Hobbes's *Leviathan* as a gigantic political pamphlet[6] is hardly justified, a similar imputation to Hegel's *Philosophie des Rechts* is even less so. When Hegel insists that the individuality of the state is, and must be, embodied in a person, he is doing nothing more than pointing to the undoubted fact that the representative of the sovereign will is always a particular individual, whom we today would identify as the Head of State, be it Queen Elizabeth, President Bush, or Chairman Mao. But, for Hegel, this is not just an empirical fact (and so merely contingent); it is in principle necessary to the actualization of a politically sovereign will. Every sovereign act must, to be sovereign, bear the seal and signature of the head of state.

The conception of sovereignty is to be understood in relation to the organic unity of the society as a whole, which essentially is the state and its sovereignty. The will of the state, what Rousseau would have identified as the General Will, is not the individual will of any particular magistrate, nor that of any citizen, or body of citizens, nor that of any particular institution or function of government, regarded as independent, but is the expression of the community in which any or all of these are but moments and in which they are all sublated.

A self-differentiating unity, specifying itself in mutually interdependent moments is, for Hegel, as we have seen, a being-for-self, or an ideal unity. This unity is immanent in each and all of the moments, but is actual only as a whole. We already know that the whole is nothing other than the united parts, and their unity is rightly referred to by Hegel as their ideality (it is evident only to a cognizing mind). By that Hegel is far from meaning that the unity is not real. On the contrary, it is the truth and actuality (*Wirklichkeit*) of the moments and of the prior dialectical phases which are sublated in it. Consequently, Hegel says that sovereignty is "in the first instance only the general thought of this ideality."[7] It operates in actual fact in (at least) three forms.

1. First, it operates through the quasi-independent pursuit of individual (or family) concerns in civil society. These concerns, although prima facie they appear separate and independent, at times even conflicting, are in principle facets of a common interest, so far as they are all interests in, and subject to, the organization of activities that constitute the economic and social order. It follows that they all contribute to that order not only, as Hegel puts it, "by way of the unconscious necessity of the matter, in accordance with which their self-seeking is transformed into a contribution to reciprocal support of the whole";[8] but also through their undisputed and presumed interest in the general order that their activity upholds. This could be demonstrated and exemplified in detail, but for our present purpose one or two examples may suffice.

The farmer, the tradesman, the craftsman and the contractor, each following his own vocation and pursuing his own interest in apparent independence of one another, is nevertheless providing goods and services to all the others and is contributing to the supply of common needs. The litigants in a civil suit, each maintaining his or her own interest against the other, are, by taking their case to court, serving the common interest in the legal defense of rights and the orderly settlement of disputes. The common benefit is not consciously or deliberately sought by any of these parties individually, but it is served in consequence of the prevailing system of social order, and necessarily so inasmuch as individual ends are deliberately sought according to customary practice and within the recognized framework of social relations.

2. The second way in which the ideality of sovereignty manifests itself is closely related to the first and is coupled with it in Hegel's exposition. It is the direct control of private professional and business activities by government regulation in those respects required by the public welfare. The common interest, here again, impinges upon and

adjusts individual conduct to conform to the requirements of general unity of purpose.

3. Thirdly, in contrast with the relative individualism of the two preceding manifestations, in times of emergency and crisis, when the safety and independence of the whole community is in peril, personal pursuits are consciously subordinated to national requirements, private interests are sacrificed to common needs, and the diverse pursuits of all citizens are unified in the service of the defense of the realm. Thus, Hegel assures us, the ideality of sovereignty comes to its own proper actuality.

Karl Marx accused Hegel of idealizing sovereignty and then "in a mystical way" infusing it into the person of the monarch. Had he started with real subjects as the basis of the state, Marx avers, he would not have found this mystification necessary.[9] But such criticism is rooted in misunderstanding of Hegel's use of the term "ideality" and the exegesis given above is sufficienet to lay bare Marx's profound misconception. For, as we have seen, Hegel is not (as both Marx and Popper[10] imagine) identifying sovereignty with the monarch absolutely, nor is he "idealizing" it in any sense that involves denying its substantial actualization whether in the persons of citizens or magistrates, or in the functions of government and the head of state.

Still more gross is the distortion of Hegel's meaning which represents his theory as approving despotism and providing theoretical grounds for totalitarianism. The former he explicitly repudiates, and he does so in a passage that reveals beyond doubt his conception of the state as a system of rights and liberties:

> Thus oriental despotism may, on account of its similarity in that the will of one individual stands at the head of the State, be included under the vague name of monarchy, as also feudal monarchy, to which even the favoured name of "constitutional monarchy" cannot be refused. The true difference of these forms from genuine monarchy rests on the content of validated principles of right which the power of the State actualizes and guarantees. These principles are those developed earlier in the spheres of freedom and property and, over and above that, of personal freedom, the civil society, its industry and communities, and the regulated efficiency of official functions dependent on the laws.[11]

What Hegel is propounding is the theory of the rule of law under constitutional monarchy which, as he himself says, despotism equally with the anarchy of mob rule abolishes and destroys:

> Because the sovereignty is the ideality of all particular authority, the
> misunderstanding easily arises and is very common, of taking it for
> mere might and sheer arbitrary will, giving sovereignty the same
> meaning as despotism. But despotism means any state of lawlessness,
> where the particular will as such, be it of a monarch or of a people
> (ochlocracy) counts as law, or rather replaces law, while on the contrary
> it is precisely in legal, consitutional systems that sovereignty is the
> ideality of the particular spheres and functions.[12]

From these passages it is obvious that criticisms of popular government and of the "talk of 'sovereignty of the people' " that appear in the
Grundlinien (279, 301, 308) and in the *Geistesphilosophie* (loc. cit.) are
not directed against constituional democracy. In the context of these
very criticisms Hegel makes it clear that his objection is to unorganized
popular intrusion into the governmental process and not to the constituional structures of democratic rule. It is the aggregate of people as *vulgus*
and not the political unity of the people as *populus* that he excludes.
In the *Encyclopedia* (544) his criticism of the English system for giving
private persons a predominant share in public affairs, whether merited
or not, is immediately followed by the acknowledgment of the benefits
of participation by private citizens in public transactions. Essentially "it is
the right of the collective spirit to appear as an overt general will acting
in orderly and express efficacy for the public concern."

The use here of the phrase *allgemeine Wille* is (I suspect deliberately) reminiscent of Rousseau, and it is precisely Rousseau's distinction
between the General Will and the will of all on which Hegel is anxious
to insist. In his comment on Rousseau in the *Lectures on the History of
Philosophy* he is quite explicit:

> The universal will is not to be looked on as compounded of definitively
> individual wills, so that these remain absolute; otherwise the saying
> would be correct: "Where the minority obey the majority, there is no
> freedom." The universal will must be the rational will, even if we are
> not conscious of the fact; the State is therefore not an association that
> is decreed by the arbitrary will of individuals.[13]

One cannot reasonably doubt, in the light of these statements, that
Hegel's critique is not directed against the conception of sovereignty
of the people as it is advocated by Rousseau, but only against loose
and confused uses of the phrase that identify the people with a casual
association, an aggregate or a mob, or that fail to distinguish such an
aggregate from a genuine community.

Popper's typically wild and irresponsible allegation that Hegel voiced his criticism of popular sovereignty in order to please the Prussian King, to whom he was beholden for his academic position,[14] is stultified by the fact that the last installment of the posthumous essay on the English Reform Bill, despite its critical character, was suppressed by the Prussian censorship because it expressed approval of the genuinely democratic aspect of the advocated reforms and criticized the bill for failing to attack the root cause of the former abuses.[15]

The supremacy of the sovereign power of the state, as the highest mundane authority in the nation's internal affairs, in legislating, administering, and adjudicating the law, is a patent fact of modern history. There can be no right of defiance or revolt, for right is what the law recognizes and protects. Unrecognized rights may be claimed, but they become legal rights only when legally enforced; and no right of rebellion can be claimed because revolt is itself an abrogation of law and order, which, if it succeeds, becomes revolution, the dissolution of the state, and the substitution of a new political authority. That occurs and is justifiable when the General Will ceases to be realized by the existing government. For Hegel, if he ever considers its possibility, rebellion is just a rampant political disease and is justifiable in a conquered province because it is directed against a power that is strictly illegitimate.[16] In form, such rebellion belongs more properly to the sphere of external affairs and comes under the concept of war. To that sphere we shall next turn our attention.

International Relations and International Law

In external relations the state is sovereign, or it is not a state; and its sovereign status has to be recognized by other states. What is thus recognized is its independence and consequent freedom from subjection to any higher power or political authority. It acts *sui juris* and, as sovereign, cannot be made subject to any law superior to its own. It follows that its relations with other states are limited in form either to agreement, or treaty, entered into by its own will and determined solely by its own interest, or, where agreement fails, enmity and war. It is here that ordnance becomes *ultima ratio regum,* and Louis XIV is vindicated. To say this is not to glorify or to romanticize war; it is simply to recognize what is inevitably the case as long as states are sovereign. For, as Hegel, in company with Hobbes and Spinoza, quite clearly saw, where no superior authority regulates, the state of nature prevails.[17]

Treaties are observed, therefore, as they are entered into, only subject to the will and interest of the parties. Observance cannot be enforced, and the only sanction against breach is war. About all this Hegel was perfectly clear, and its truth is copiously illustrated in the facts of history.[18] For the sovereign state its own interests are paramount; hence there can be no community of sovereigns, because community implies a common interest which takes precedence over the particular interests of members. It is this common interest within the state that makes its sovereign authority supreme and is precisely what Hegel means by its ideality. If states were to become members of an international community, therefore, their sovereignty would be dissolved and some higher sovereignty would take its place. A community of sovereign states is thus a contradiction in terms.[19]

International law is not and cannot be the law of a community, because it lays down the proviso that its "subjects" can only be sovereign states (which, by definition, are subject to no superior authority). It is therefore not properly law in the political sense of that word. It is not positive law, for it cannot be imposed; it is not effective law because it cannot be enforced. It rests simply on treaty and agreement, subject to the particular wills of the participants, so it cannot regulate agreements or ensure the observance of treaties. Its primary principle, *pacta sunt servanda*, as Hegel puts it, "goes no further than the ought to be"—it is an empty aspiration. The principle cannot be an article of law because the law is itself a treaty that can hardly be the source of its own obligatoriness. In consequence, the actual situation, as Hegel tells us, alternates between the maintenance of treaty relations and their abrogation.[20]

In actual historical fact treaties are as often broken as observed, if not more often, and no less frequently are they denounced or ignored, as the interests of one party or another dictate. Each party can interpret their provisions as it thinks fit, and there is no disinterested arbiter. The worthiest and most respected statesmen have pronounced that no obligation to keep a treaty can be extended beyond the national interest. Among them were W. E. Gladstone, Theodore Roosevelt, and even Woodrow Wilson, chief architect of the League of Nations Covenant, itself a treaty, ostensibly to end all violations. But that no treaty could serve such a purpose Hegel had been well aware.

Above states, he reminds us, there is no judge or praetor, no power that can enforce a law or ensure the bond of contract. Enforcement upon a sovereign state is and can but be war; and when agreement fails the settlement of disputes can only be by force. It follows, therefore, as the night the day, that no league or confederation of states can secure peace, for every such association presupposes agreement, which itself depends on the particular sovereign wills and national interests. If that agreement fails, the alternative is war, to try forcibly to prevent which is to wage it.

The experience of the past century has borne this out, when the reasons for preventing war and the desirability of maintaining peace have been immeasurably greater than could have been conceived in Hegel's time. His analysis still holds good, and the mutual conduct of nations conforms to it to this day.

Kant's vision of perpetual peace involved the establishment of a world confederation, which could not be effective unless it involved the transference of sovereignty from the nation-state to an international body. But Kant is obviously confused on this point, for, while he clearly understood that states as sovereign cannot combine into a super-state without contradiction, he contemplated a "federation (*Föderalismus*) of free States", and he speaks of the federation as "a compact of the nations with each other," but one of a special kind, apparently more universal, seeking to put an end to all wars forever, not just to one. But if such a compact were more universal, Kant shows us no way in which it could be made more binding or enforceable. It is to be called a pacific federation (*Friedensbund*) but it will not aim, he says, at acquiring any of the political powers of a state. It will only be concerned with the maintenance and guarantee of the freedom of states without subjecting them to promulgated laws or coercion.[21] If that were so, it could at best be a kind of confederation or league of nations, the futility of which for its avowed purpose we, in our day, know only too well.

Because Hegel refers to the "pacific federation" as a *Staatenbund*, Popper accuses him of misrepresenting Kant.[22] But the misrepresentation is Popper's, for Hegel labored under no misapprehension. That was precisely the kind of body that Kant had described; and Hegel saw that no such arbitrating authority could have more effect than would be allowed by the particular wills of the sovereigns, the prior agreement of whom it must presuppose, and that it would, therefore, "remain infected with contingency."

Hegel's insight was corroborated a century later when between the two world wars of the twentieth century the League of Nations not only failed in its final outcome, but never genuinely conducted itself as a law enforcing authority and in no particular instance succeeded in converting international relations into anything other than power politics. The same has since been true of the United Nations which, as originally conceived, was to have been provided with "teeth" to remedy the impotence of the League. The teeth would not have been its own, but were to be provided voluntarily by its members and to remain under their control. Even that, however, was more than the sovereign nations could stomach, and the organization has remained toothless to this day. Even when all five permanent members of the Security Council unprecedentedly agreed to act against Iraq, the result was hardly describable as the maintenance of peace. These bald statements have been provided with supporting evidence and argument, not only by me,[23] but by more authoritative authors. Georg Schwartzenberger has shown that under the aegis of the League and the United Nations the relations between states have never been other than power politics in disguise. E. H. Carr develops essentially the same thesis, and a similar doctrine has been put forward by Bertrand de Jouvenel.[24]

War

That power politics is the inevitable character of the intercourse between states is not only shown by the historical record, it is inherent in the nature of sovereignty. The paramount concern of a sovereign state is to maintain its power, for without means of defense its independence is in perpetual jeopardy. Because its neighbors are obsessed with a like concern, because each of them acts in accordance only with its own will and interest, and further because no state can be trusted indefinitely to keep a treaty, each must regard potential rivals with constant suspicion and vigilance. As one augments its power so must the others keep pace. That national interests, in such circumstances, inevitably come into conflict is not surprising, and the very existence of a powerful neighbor may be regarded as a threat. Hegel understood all this unerringly:

> A State through its subjects has widespread and many-sided interests
> and these may be readily and considerably injured; but it remains
> inherently indeterminable which of these injuries is to be regarded as
> a specific breach of a treaty or an injury to the honour and autonomy
> of the State. The reason for this is that the State may regard its infinity
> and honour as at stake in each of its concerns . . . and it is all the more
> inclined to susceptibility the more its strong individuality is impelled as
> a result of long domestic peace to seek and create a sphere of activity
> abroad.[25]

Every state, in consequence, seeks to increase its power and to prevent its rivals from gaining an advantage. It becomes, with its rivals and potential enemies, involved in an uncontrollable arms race. All its policies, when carefully investigated, will be found to rest upon and to subserve this fundamental interest in power. All its external activities are power maneuvers, in one form or another; and the peace, while it lasts, is always a precarious power balance. Today, our political leaders acknowledge this fact in their constant pronouncements on the need to maintain the world balance of power, or that of a particular region (like the Middle East), and their expressions of fear for the breakdown of peace should that balance be unduly disturbed.

A state lacking power has no effectual voice in negotiations with others. "In the world today," said Neville Chamberlain in 1939, "an unarmed nation has little chance of making its voice heard." And the methods of negotiation involve the persistent use of threats, whether veiled or open, usually described euphemistically as "pressure," and necessarily backed by the potential use of force, without which no pressure can be exerted. The result is a constant series of intermittent crises threatening the maintenance of peace, and the eventual outcome can hardly fail to be open warfare. In short, Clausewitz's dictum in reverse is largely true of international relations, for here politics is war carried on by other means. Today this is no less true than it was when either Hobbes or Hegel wrote, and both of them understood perfectly the inevitable implications of relationships between sovereign states.

To see things as they are, however, is not necessarily to approve of their being so, and to realize the inevitability of war in interstate relations is not the same as to advocate it. There is nothing in Hegel's doctrine that actually glorifies war, and what he writes in its favor is consolation for an unavoidable evil. War, he says, is not to be regarded as an unmitigated evil, which is far from welcoming it as a positive good. It has an ethical aspect, which even today few would wish to deny, especially those who in Britain, during the perilous months of 1940 and 1941, experienced precisely what Hegel, in this connection, perspicaciously describes. Rather than providing a theoretical justification of Hitler and the Nazis, it would be more just to suggest that Hegel expounds the essentials of political character that were exemplified at that time by Churchill and the indomitability of the British.

When the existence and independence of a nation is endangered, the loyalties and devotion of its citizens are most readily called forth, the sacrifice of private interests to the preservation of the realm is most ungrudging, and the solidarity of the people is most fully realized and most intensely felt. All industrial and professional functions are subordinated to the public need, and life itself is held expendable in the national cause. The ethical aspect that Hegel stresses is that of sacrifice and service. He never glorifies (as did Mussolini and Hitler) the destructive and disruptive aspects of aggression. Nor does he hold, with Oswald Spengler, that man is by nature a beast of prey, or attempt to condone the element of hate and ferocity that war encourages. He seeks only to insist upon the altruistic virtues and patriotic loyalty that it requires and excites.

That war also involves harsh and undesirable aspects is not denied. It is the negative aspect of the state's external life, the incidence upon it of the Other which must be overcome and somehow reconciled. But as, for Hegel, the state was the ultimate unity of a nation's organized life, the only sublation of this negativity he could contemplate was that provided by world history. Here alone could the ultimate resolution of conflict be achieved in the hegemony of a nation embodying the dialectical phase of development of the *Weltgeist* appropriate to the age. It is for this reason that he saw *die Weltgeschichte als das Weltgericht.*

In the early nineteenth century war was a very different phenomenon from what it has become in the twentieth. In the eighteenth it had been little more than a dangerous but gentlemanly blood-sport. With Napoleon it became more generally destructive and horrible, but not until our own time has it developed into a universal disaster. Hegel could still point to mitigating advantages, the stiffening of the national moral fiber, the regeneration of the national spirit and the revitalization of cooperative solidarity. Today even these by-products are liable to be obliterated by the overwhelming holocaust that war is liable to bring.

Hegel knew nothing of nuclear weapons and intercontinental ballistic missiles; and short of these, could he have foreseen high explosives, aerial bombardment, fragmentation bombs, napalm, chemical and bacteriological warfare, he might well have concluded, as we should, that the patriotic virtues could be no countervailing advantages. So far as they encourage bellicosity, they might even themselves become part of the general menace. Could Hegel have foreseen the character of nuclear war as envisaged today by such prognosticators as Herman Kahn and Tom Stonier, he would have seen that the very enormity of the terror of modern warfare undermines and corrodes away these very virtues as, for instance, when citizens preparing to protect themselves against nuclear fallout contemplate shooting compatriots who seek to share their forlorn and dubious shelter.[26]

Hegel's general theory of international politics is sound and his insights are penetrating. Contemporary events still exemplify the principles he set out. His doctrine is not, therefore, in this respect obsolete. But the development of nuclear and other modern weapons has rendered obsolete the whole structure of politics, national and international, a structure which, nevertheless, we and our national leaders continue to preserve and implement. What is obsolete is not the theory, for sovereignty is still sought by national groups and still recognized in international affairs, and power politics are still the current practice. What has become a self-contradiction is the idea of nuclear war, even as a threat, a putative deterrent, or a means of self-defense, and its use, likewise for that reason, as an instrument of policy.

Until very recently it was evident that it was so used from the feverish competition among the great powers to develop vaster and vaster nuclear arsenals, with more powerful and more devastating warheads, along with more widespread and efficient systems of delivery. "When we deter the Soviets," wrote Herman Khan,

> by the threat that if they provoke us in a limited war, subsequent
> reprisals may blow up into an all-out thermo-nuclear war, we are
> deliberately or inadvertently using the threat, and therefore the
> possibility, of nuclear war. When we tell our allies that our Strategic
> Air Command protects them from Soviet aggression, we are in a sense
> using nuclear war.[27]

Yet it is generally admitted that the use of these weapons would destroy both attacker and defender, both potential victor and potential vanquished. *Ultima ratio regum* has become *ultima exitium nationum.*

Nevertheless national sovereign states remain in the state of nature, and the practice of power politics with its debilitation of international law continues. The recent changes in the Soviet Union and eastern Europe have, at any rate for the present, ended the Cold War and reduced the nuclear threat, although they have by no means removed it altogether. Nobody knows how long it may be before fresh changes and crises produce new dictatorships. There is still no guarantee against new threats and new wars (as we have just witnessed in the Gulf).

If contemporary mankind could pay closer attention to Hegel's teaching, a salutary lesson might still be learned, the lesson that national sovereignty is the greatest of all obstacles to world peace; and that might send us back to Kant for salvation and for the solution of international problems. A pacific federation is indeed what is required, but one that will not shrink from acquiring sovereign power and authority. The difficulties in the path of such a project may be formidable, and the obstacles to its establishment enormous—not the least is the widespread lack of belief in such an institution and of clear recognition of the nature of our present situation. But these difficulties cannot match the enormity of the alternative, whether it lies in the nuclear menace or the equally terminal threats from global warming, the loss of the ozone layer, and the general disruption of the earth's ecology. If that alternative could be somehow sufficiently impressed upon the minds of the peoples of the world, perhaps they would make a more determined effort to overcome the obstacles to world government. This is not the place to discuss its necessity and its advantages, or to set out the cogent reasons in its favor. I have attempted to do that elsewhere.[28] But if a sufficient number of people could be convinced of its necessity and if it could be brought about, *die Weltgeschichte* might indeed produce *ein Weltgericht* with some hope of genuine adjudication and of the maintenance of human rights. Morality would no longer be irrelevant to world-historical figures operating in an anarchical state of nature, where, Hegel tells us, no *Sittlichkeit* prevails, and the rationality of mankind—or, perhaps, nothing more than the cunning of reason, working through human fear and the instinct of self-preservation—might give new significance to the pronouncement that the real is the rational and the rational real.

12

Hegel on War:
Another Look

Steven Walt

Hegel's statements about war are as notorious as they are brief. They have also been subject to the most disparate interpretations. Hegel has, alternatively, been taken to glorify war and find a moral justification in it; to hold that wars may be morally justified in particular circumstances and hence that some but not all wars are morally justifiable; and to condemn war per se and hence to hold that wars are never morally justifiable. Indeed, these conflicting interpretations often result from equally conflicting interpretations of the same passages in Hegel's political and philosophical writings. Paragraph 324 in the *Philosophy of Right* is a case in point. From this crucial passage, where Hegel introduces the phenomenon of war and considers its philosophical significance, it is variously concluded that Hegel glorifies war and finds it "good in itself";[1] that Hegel considers defensive wars to be right and in fact periodically necessary;[2] and that, for Hegel, the philosophical significance of war is "completely devoid of the ethos of war itself."[3] These interpretations are important. They are important because it is in part from such textual evidence that Hegel, rightly or wrongly, is held to countenance a totalitarian or autocratic state, on the one hand, or an enlightened constitutional monarchy, operating in an essentially democratic state, on the other.[4]

Hegel's views on war are scattered throughout his writings. They appear in the early political tracts, in several explicit remarks in the *Phenomenology of Mind* and in under twenty paragraphs at the end of the

Philosophy of Right.[5] I want to examine in some detail in what follows mainly those remarks found in the *Philosophy of Right*. In doing so, I shall suggest that Hegel in fact has two independent arguments for the necessity of war: an argument from the (for Hegel) ethical relation of the individual to the state, and an argument from the nature of and relations between nation-states. Section I presents Hegel's argument for the necessity of war from the ethical relation of individuals to the state. Here I take a middle position, as it were, between those interpretations mentioned above. I argue that, although Hegel does find what for him is a philosophical justification of war in this relation, he does not glorify war or find it "good in itself." Section II briefly argues that Hegel's conception of how nations are recognized qua nations commits him to a view which endorses the necessity of war quite apart from the ethical relation of the individual to the state and the justification of war based on that relation. Commentators have not distinguished the two arguments.

I

It is crucial to understand Hegel's remarks on war within the context of what Hegel takes to be the concern of political philosophy and philosophy in general. For if the remarks are not interpreted within this context, the resulting interpretations will ascribe to Hegel views on war that he explicitly denies. Take, for example, his notoriously loose use of the term "necessity." Hegel claims that war, from a philosophical point of view, is a necessary phenomenon. The claim is made in the following paragraph:

> War is not to be regarded as an absolute evil and as a purely external
> accident, which itself therefore has some accidental cause, be it
> injustices, the passions of nations or the holders of power, etc., or
> in short something which ought not to be. It is to what is by nature
> accidental that accidents happen, and the fate whereby they happen
> is thus a necessity. Here as elsewhere, the point of view from which
> things seem pure accidents vanishes if we look at things in light of the
> concept and philosophy, because philosophy knows accident for a show
> and sees in it its essence, necessity. (324R)

If this claim is disassociated from what Hegel takes to be characteristic of philosophical statements, then it would seem to commit Hegel to the unlikely view that war is causally or in some sense logically necessary. But the necessity of war, for Hegel, is to be seen "in light of the concept and philosophy," as is in fact said above, and not on any other reading of "necessity." The concept, in the case of political philosophy, is the concept of right and the way it is realized in the world. The forms that the concept assumes in its development in the world are not only indispensable but necessary for its development and a philosophical knowledge of it (1, 2). One of the forms that the concept of right takes in its development is that of the state and its "accidental" activity—war. A philosophical understanding of right cannot therefore treat this form of the state's activity as accidental to the production of right in the world. Rather, it must consider war as somehow necessary for the realization of the embodiment of the concept of right: the idea of the state. Nor can philosophy pass normative judgment on war as an activity of the state. It cannot regard war as "something which ought not to be." Philosophical statements are, instead, descriptive just in the sense that they describe those forms that the concept of right *has* assumed, and not the particular facts in which those forms have manifested themselves (1; cf. 258A). (A philosophical treatment of war must "recognize reason as the rose in the cross of the present," as Hegel puts it elsewhere.)[6] Hegel therefore is not claiming that given particular conditions it is causally, much less logically, necessary that war occurs. He is not even describing the particular conditions under which nations go to war. Hence when Hegel talks about war being necessary when considered philosophically, the "necessity" here is different from that of causal or logical necessity. It is that of ethical necessity.

The notion of ethical necessity at work requires clarification. It is not immediately apparent in Hegel's treatment of war. It is even less apparent in commentators' treatment of the matter. The following four explications are candidates for Hegel's operative notion of ethical necessity:

1. War is good because it is required for . . .
2. War is good because it is required to produce the causal consequences that . . . , the consequence being good.
3. War is good because it is required to produce as a causal by-product . . . , the by-product being good.
4. War is good because it is required for the expression of some relationship . . . , the relationship being good.

The ellipses in each explication can be filled in by mention of the desirable features of war, if any. Now 1 is compatible with 2–4 above. For it is simply a more general formulation of any of 2–4. Any assertion concerning the ethical necessity of war entails 1. It is neutral between the sorts of justification offered in the other explications. Explications 2 and

3 incorporate instrumental notions of ethical necessity. Each takes war to be a necessary means of producing a desirable feature of a state of affairs, either as a causal consequence or by-product. War is good, on both 2 and 3, because it does so. Explication 4 incorporates a noninstrumental notion of ethical necessity. It stipulates a desirable feature constituted by an unspecified ethical relationship. The relationship is not itself a means of bringing about an independently desirable end. Hegel not only claims that war is in fact ethically necessary; he also does so by adopting explication 4, a noninstrumental notion of ethical necessity. To see this, take the claim and the noninstrumental notion in turn. Paragraph 324 contains the assertion that war is *ethically* necessary. To this extent, for Hegel there is a moral element in war. That Hegel allows for such an element in war is suggested in the passage from paragraph 324 cited above. There war is said not to be "absolutely evil." The implication is clearly that although war is in fact evil and so not wholly good, it is nonetheless good to some extent. That Hegel also holds that war is ethically *necessary* is evident several lines later when it is stated:

> It is necessary that the finite—property and life—should be definitely established as accidental because accident is the concept of the finite. From one point of view this necessity appears in the form of the power of nature, and everything is mortal and transient. But in the ethical substance, the state, nature is robbed of this power, and the necessity is exalted to be the work of freedom, to be something ethical. (324R)

Property and life are essentially accidental. By virtue of the nature of things, they perish through time or some mishap. Their demise is inevitable and is in this case an instance of "natural necessity." The state's disposal at will of life and property in war, however, is an instance of "unnatural" or ethical necessity. Hegel specifies the sense in which there is an ethical element in this necessity in the following important passage from paragraph 324. It is worth citing at some length:

> War is the state of affairs which deals in earnest with the vanity of temporal goods and concerns—a vanity at other times a common theme edifying sermonizing. This is what makes it the moment in which the ideality of the particular attains its right and is actualized. *War has the higher significance* that by its agency, as I have remarked elsewhere, "the ethical health of peoples is *preserved* in their indifference to the stabilization of finite institutions; just as the blowing of the winds preserves the sea from the foulness which would be the result of

prolonged calm, so the corruption in nations would be the product of
prolonged, let alone 'perpetual peace.' "[7] (324R, emphasis added)

This passage can be read as an elaboration on the assertion made earlier
in the same paragraph that "war is not to be regarded as an absolute evil."
Here Hegel is claiming that war is good to the extent that it is beneficial
to the "ethical health" of the citizens of nation states. Hegel therefore
cannot be interpreted as condemning war itself, as Avineri has it,[8] if the
waging of war is held to have some ethical value. Indeed, to condemn war
as such and not just particular features of it would be inconsistent with
Hegel's metaphilosophical dictum that philosophy should comprehend
what is and not what ought to be the case.[9] Where Hegel does seem
to condemn the waging of war, it is in fact the waging of continuous
or perpetual war and not war itself that is condemned. What he says is:
"Hence in war, war itself is characterized as something that ought to pass
away. It implies therefore the proviso . . . that the possibility of peace be
retained" (338). The emphasis here is on "in war" and not on "war itself."
Hence the passage is to be read as endorsing Kant's view that wars should
be fought in such a way as to allow for the possibility or their cessation.[10]
(In fact, when Hegel uses almost identical words in the *Encyclopedia*, it
is clear there that he is referring to "unchecked action," not "action,"
i.e. war, itself.)[11] Paragraph 338 does not endorse Kant's further view,
however, that war as such and not just particular wars should cease. Hegel
in fact rejects Kant's ideal of perpetual peace, since in paragraph 324
he explicitly claims that people would become corrupt as a result of an
extended of perpetual peace. The point is important. I shall return to it
in section II.

What is endorsed in paragraph 324 is the view that war maintains
the moral health of the citizens of a warring state. The simile cited above
suggests as much. War preserves the ethical health of a people just as
the wind preserves the sea from foulness. "Preserves" here suggests that
a people is ethically healthy *prior* to war just as the sea is in a "healthy"
condition *prior* to the coming of the wind. What war does in the one case
and the wind in the other is to maintain and not to strengthen these
respective conditions. Hence war has the valuable function of preserving
the ethical health of a people—a condition that would not, on Hegel's
view, be preserved in its absence. To be sure, in an early political tract
Hegel goes further. He suggests there that war does not even maintain
the ethical health of a people but simply tests its presence: "the health of
a state is generally revealed not so much in the calm of peace as in the
stir of war."[12] But in the *Philosophy of Right* something very different from
both these views is suggested: namely, that war does not just preserve or

merely test the ethical health of a people but also *improves* it. For in the addition to paragraph 324 Hegel claims that:

> In peace civil life continually expands; all its departments wall themselves in, and in the long run men stagnate. Their idiosyncracies become continually more fixed and ossified. But for health the unity of the body is required, and if its parts harden themselves into exclusiveness, that is death. . . . As a result of war nations are strengthened. (324A)

In times of peace, civil society, in Hegel's sense of the term, dominates the relationship of the citizen to the state. Individuals pursue their own interests, and their relation to the state is seen to be a contingent one which exists only insofar as such interests are satisfied (cf. 278). War, however, forces citizens to abandon their self-interest and adopt interests common to the state. In doing this they achieve a condition of ethical health lacking in peace, as the phrase "but for health the unity of the body is required" above suggests. The implication of the phrase clearly is that, although not dead, the ethical substance—the state—and, correspondingly, the ethical condition of its citizens is not fully healthy in peace. War, on this metaphor, can improve the health of the state and the ethical health of its citizens by bringing about the required healthy condition—by, that is, uniting the body of the state. To say this, however, commits Hegel to more than the claim made above: that war simply maintains or tests the ethical health of a people. It also commits him to the view that war, although not identifiable with the ethical health of a people, actually improves that health. Expanding this metaphor, for Hegel, then, war is not just a disease which, by attacking the body of the state and the ethical health of its citizens, maintains or tests that health. War is also a vaccination which, by generating antibodies, strengthens the body of the state and improves the ethical health of its citizens.

Hegel nowhere draws a further inference from this metaphor: that war is good *because* it is required to preserve the ethical health of citizens, and this either as a causal consequence or by-product. Doing so would commit Hegel to an instrumental notion of ethical necessity as it appears in either explications 2 or 3, respectively. Paragraph 324 only refers to war as having "the higher significance" of preserving the ethical health of citizens (cf. 351R). It adds that war serves the required function of uniting a people ("the unity of the body is required"). No normative endorsement follows or can be implied from either remark. So there is no commitment to instrumental notions of ethical necessity in paragraph 324.

This of course does not by itself show that Hegel is committed to a noninstrumental notion of ethical necessity. Other passages show as much. Sacrifice for the state in war is taken by Hegel to be a duty: "Sacrifice on behalf of the individuality of the state is the substantial tie between the state and all its members and so is a universal duty" (325). It forms part of the "doctrine of duties" Hegel expressly takes to apply to relationships characterized by ethical necessity (148R). Note the sort of duty identified here: a duty of sacrifice is taken to constitute the fundamental relationship between citizen and state ("is the substantial tie between"). It is not a means of furthering some goal, nor is sacrifice on behalf of the state a means of serving it. Hegel elsewhere rejects this instrumental reading:

> The state is not there for the sake of the citizens; one could say,
> it is the goal and they are its instruments. But this relation of
> means and ends is quite inappropriate here. For the state is not
> something abstract, standing over against the citizens; but rather they
> are moments as in organic life, where no member is end and none
> means.[13]

Paragraph 325, cited above, adds a further feature: that the noninstrumental, "organic" relationship between citizen and state *consists* in a duty of sacrifice in war. Hence it is the relationship in which citizens stand to state, not some independent goal, which is the basis of the resulting duty. Since the basis of the duty is noninstrumental, the operative notion of ethical necessity is not an instrumental one either. Instead, war for Hegel is justified because it is required for the expression of the substantial relationship between citizen and state. The content of the relationship consists in part in a duty of sacrifice in war. The justification, here as in explication 4 above, incorporates a noninstrumental notion of ethical necessity.

It is important to note that Hegel distinguishes between a philosophical justification of war and "mundane" justifications of particular wars. That war contributes to the ethical health of a people is, for Hegel, only a philosophical account of war. It is not a justification of specific wars. The distinction is evident in several lines that follow the part of paragraph 324 cited above. There Hegel says, referring to the philosophical account of war: "This, however, is said to be only a philosophical idea, or, to use another common expression, a 'justification of Providence,' and it is maintained that actual wars require some other justification. On this point see below" (324). Hence when Hegel claims that war is ethically necessary, he is not claiming that particular wars can be justified by using this "justification of Providence." In fact, he is denying it. What is being claimed, rather, is that there is some necessity attached to the occurrence of war, derived from a "philosophical idea" and so not applicable to specific outbreaks of war. (This is the way the statement "the fact remains that wars occur as the necessity of the case requires" [324A] must be interpreted. For it occurs in the addition to Hegel's philosophical justification of war and not in the later paragraphs where the ostensive justifications of actual wars are provided [334–37, 343].) The "justification" of actual wars—the "point seen below"—is given in paragraph 337 when Hegel says that:

> The substantial welfare of the state is its welfare as a particular state in its specific interest and situation and its no less specific foreign affairs, including its particular treaty relations. *Its government therefore is a matter of particular wisdom, not of universal Providence* [compare remark to paragraph 324]. Similarly, its aim in relation to other states and *its principle for justifying wars* and treaties is not a universal thought (the thought of philanthropy) but only its actually injured or threatened welfare as something specific and peculiar to itself. (337, emphasis added; cf. 340)

Two points about this passage are worth making. First, the putative justification of actual wars is not one which makes use of "universal Providence." "Universal Providence" is disparaged as a justificatory basis, as the ironic use of the term in paragraph 324 suggests. Use instead is made of the "particular wisdom" of the nations involved and therefore is not a philosophical justification of actual wars. Particular wars result from a conflict of specific interests and perceived threats between nations (334–35). This being the case, there is no necessity in the occurrence of actual conflicts. So Hegel is not committed to holding that this or that war is ethically beneficial to the peoples involved. To give a justification of war in terms of its ethical value, as Hegel clearly does, is not by itself to justify particular wars in terms of the ethical value they may or may not have.

Second, and more important, the justification of actual wars that Hegel provides in the above passage is not in fact a justification at all. Instead it is a *description* of two distinct elements: the reasons states use to justify particular wars and the features that induce a state to go to war. The former descriptive element is indicated when Hegel observes above that "its [i.e. a state's] principle for justifying wars and treaties is not universal thought . . . but only its actually injured or threatened welfare." To note the types of principles states use to justify wars or treaties is to describe, albeit in a general manner, the way in which particular wars are justified by participants. It is not to provide a justification of those wars. The latter descriptive element is indicated by Hegel's reference to a state's claim in relation to other states in paragraph 337, already cited. Similarly, Hegel's claim that nations are more prone to take offense over another nation's actions and start a war the longer they have maintained peace within their borders can be read in this way (334). That is, the claim can be read not as a justification of such a propensity but rather as a description of it as one of the factors inclining nations to go to war.

A close reading of paragraphs 349–51 provides further support. Paragraph 349 states as a necessary condition of statehood the presence of a well-defined system of laws and a rational constitution. Paragraph 350 requires that the instantiation of the requirement is taken to provide a justification for the treatment of "lesser" collectivities: "The same consideration justifies civilized nations in regarding and treating as barbarous those who lag behind them in institutions which are essential moments of the state" (351). The remark attached to the paragraph explains the importance of resulting wars: "When wars and disputes arise in such circumstances, the trait which gives them a significance for world history is the fact that they are struggles for recognition in connection with something of specific worth" (351R). No endorsement of such wars appears here. That resulting wars are struggles for "something of specific worth" is not said to justify them. Resulting wars are simply said to have "significance" for world history. Hence no inference can be drawn that resulting wars are morally permissible *because* they have world historical significance. The justification in paragraph 351 also is confined to the treatment of "lesser" collectivities prior to wars and disputes. It does not extend to the ensuing wars and disputes themselves, and, as confined, the justification is distinct from the reasons nations use as justifications. Civilized nations are taken to regard and treat "lesser" nations as barbarians. This describes the terms that nations use to justify particular treatment. The justification for the treatment is different. It concerns the requirement for the instantiation of the concept of right (350). No mention is or need be made of the cultural status of nations. Hence, unlike paragraph 337, justification and description are kept separate. But Hegel's practice here is the same as it is in paragraph 337: to characterize the reasons states use to justify particular actions.

The same descriptive element is evident in Hegel's rejection of normative laws characteristic of international law: "This universal proviso of international law [i.e., universal laws which ought to be binding between nations] therefore does not go beyond an ought-to-be, and what really happens is that international relations in accordance with treaty alternate with the severance of these relations" (333). "What really happens" in international relations is a description of those relations; it is not a justification of them. So when Hegel claims to be giving a justification of actual wars in paragraphs 324–37, the claim is misleading. What is given there is instead both a description of the sorts of reasons which figure in a nation's justifications of wars and of the sort of factors which incline nations to wage wars.

This is not to say, however, that Hegel refrains from making prescriptive remarks concerning the waging of war. He does not.[14] Hegel, characteristically, is not above insisting, for instance, that if a nation's autonomy is at stake, "all its citizens are duty bound to answer a summons to its defense" (326). But the point is that when Hegel discusses the *justification* of particular wars he describes how wars *are* justified and does not prescribe how their occurrence is to be justified. Hegel's discussion of actual wars need not therefore be taken to justify, much less glorify, the waging of particular wars. If anything, Hegel's discussion in the latter case (cf. 327–28, 327A) is to be interpreted as a discussion of how little glory there is in modern warfare.

If Hegel does not give a justification of particular wars, he does give a philosophical justification of war as such. The distinction between philosophical and nonphilosophical justification again is crucial for Hegel. This much is already evident from that part of paragraph 324 cited earlier, where Hegel insists that the notion that war is ethically necessary is a "philosophical idea" and that some *other* justification of actual wars is needed. The implication here is that although this "philosophical idea"—this "justification of Providence"—is in fact a justification of war, *another* sort of justification of the occurrence of particular wars is required. Indeed, Hegel provides the same sort of justification of war in the *Phenomenology*: "In order not to let them [i.e., the particular parts of civil society] get rooted and settled in this isolation and thus break up the whole into fragments and let the common spirit evaporate, government has from time to time to shake them to their very center by war."[15] Again, on Hegel's account, war is necessary, not by virtue of the nature of events. It instead is necessary by virtue of the fact that it is required to express a relation of duty between the citizen and the state. That is, war is necessary to express the unity of the state—for Hegel, the ethical health of its citizens. War, although for the most part an evil (cf. 339A), is good just to the extent that it fulfills this requirement. According to Hegel, this is the philosophical significance of war. But to say so is also, on Hegel's account, to give a philosophical justification of war; and this is true however unphilosophical or unacceptable that justification in fact may be. For Hegel's views on war can answer the question: why is war necessary and not just a recurring accident? Hegel's suggestion that war is necessary because it expresses the ethical bond between citizen and state and is to that extent good, is a moral justification. It is a moral justification even if it is also a philosophical account of war. This justification shares a feature that Hegel takes to be characteristic of all philosophical statements: both will be *ex post facto* accounts of that which has occurred and will not therefore be concerned with how the world or particular features of it ought to be. Hence the type of necessity and moral worth that Hegel finds in war is an *ex post facto* philosophical justification of war as it has occurred: it is not a justification, much less a glorification, of war as it will or ought to occur. Hegel has nothing to say about the latter issues.

II

Hegel justifies war, as has been shown, in terms of the ethical relation of the individual to the state which is strengthened or maintained by its occurrence. It is on this basis that Hegel rejects Kant's idea of perpetual peace in paragraph 324. Hegel also offers an independent argument against Kant's ideal. The argument depends on the nature of and relation between states, and not on the relation of citizens to the states of which they are members. This argument against perpetual peace, like the one on the basis of the individual's relation to the state, turns on Hegel's view that wars between states are ethically necessary, and hence that perpetual peace is unwelcome and impossible to achieve. But it also contains an extra component. For unlike the argument on the basis of the individual's relation to the state, it turns on Hegel's conception of how states are recognized qua states. Consider that conception first.

States, for Hegel as for Kant, share important features in common with individuals. One such feature is the way in which both are identified as states and persons, respectively. Just as individuals only exist, according to Hegel, insofar as they are recognized and distinguished from other individuals (cf. 71), so a state exists as a state only if it is recognized and distinguished from other states. States are, to this extent, simply individuals writ large. Here are two explicit statements of the view: (1) "Individuality is awareness of one's existence as a unit in sharp distinction from others" (322); (2) "A state is as little an actual individual without relations to other states . . . as an individual is actually a person without *rapport* with other persons" (331; cf. 322R). Now a person or state can be recognized as such by other persons or states, respectively, only if the latter are distinct from them. Hence independently existing states and persons are required in each case. An essential means by which individuals achieve a separate existence, on Hegel's account, is by opposition and struggle with other individuals. For it is only by opposition and struggle that individuals become conscious of themselves as persons, and Hegel claims that individuality just *is* a consciousness of one's existence as distinct from others. This much is evident in the first of the two passages just cited. It follows that it is only through struggle that individuals truly exist as persons. Hegel draws this conclusion when he notes: "The individual, who has not staked his life, may, no doubt, be recognized as a person; but he has not attained the truth of this recognition as an independent self-consciousness."[16] (Hegel does not say why this struggle and opposition need necessarily be a violent one.)

Since states are to be treated as individuals, the conditions of personhood also hold for them; and, as noted, recognition through struggle is a necessary condition of self-identification. A state must gain recognition through struggle if it is to achieve an independence required for self-identification—for personality, as Hegel calls it (35, 35R). Put anthropomorphically, a state only knows itself as a state in its opposition to and struggle with other states.[17] Hegel's argument above seeks to show that war is necessary between states. Its conclusion is that perpetual peace among states is in fact an impossible ideal to realize.

Notice the structure of Hegel's argument here. It in no way depends on the ethical relations that exist between a state and its citizens. For suppose that it is false that the individual stands in any ethical relation to the state. Consider now Hegel's argument just cited. That argument proceeds solely on the basis of the individuality. No mention is or need be made of the domestic character of the state at all, for if states are treated as individuals (cf. 321, 322); if "individuality essentially implies negation"; and if "negation" here has to involve war—then war is a necessary phenomenon quite apart from its ethical value to the citizens of any state. Hence war is a necessary condition of securing and maintaining that individuality. No mention is or need be made of the domestic character of the state at all, for if states are treated as individuals (cf. 321, 322); if "individuality essentially implies negation"; and if "negation" here has to involve war—then war is a necessary phenomenon quite apart from its ethical value to the citizens of any state. Hence war is a necessary means of securing and maintaining the self-identity of states qua states independently of its necessity for expressing an ethical relationship of duty between citizens and the state. It is also independent of the effect of maintaining or strengthening the ethical health of citizens. No assumption concerning the reactions of citizens to a state or their relation to it enters here. That is why Hegel's argument against Kant's ideal[18] does not stand or fall on the ethical argument, as it were, against the desirability of perpetual peace. That is also why Hegel holds and has to hold that war between states is necessary (in his sense of "necessity") and not just ethically necessary.

The above argument, as it turns out, has no force against Kant's ideal. For Kant's ideal of perpetual peace is one of perpetual peace within a world state and not among juridically independent nations.[19] (Characteristically, the notions of necessity and impossibility that Hegel employs are different from those Kant uses [cf. 330A].) At best, Hegel's argument succeeds only in showing that Kant's proposal for a league of nations—not necessarily a league of monarchs, as Hegel has it—is untenable as an attempt to realize perpetual peace. The argument does not show that the ideal of perpetual peace is untenable. But the important point is that Hegel would reject this ideal itself, both because he rejects the ideal of a world state (331) and because the ideal is metaphilosophically illegitimate, it being a claim about how things ought to be and not how they in fact are.

Hegel instead opts for a relation among nations midway between perpetual peace and perpetual war: the cross of the present. The requirement that states be recognized by other states in order to exist *qua* states is, for Hegel, fulfilled in war (338). This requirement, however, places limits on the extent of wars fought between states. A continuous war or war of extermination, like a world state, would remove the condition requisite to the existence of a state in the first place: the existence of other states. On the other hand, it is also necessary that a state go to war in order to exist as a state. The perpetual absence of war would bring about the same result as would be brought about by the absence of other states requisite to the existence of a state qua state. For the required recognition of statehood through violent struggle would be lacking. A war of extermination would (eventually) preclude the existence of a multiplicity of states. The perpetual absence of war would preclude the *recognition* of statehood by other states. In either case, a state would cease to exist as a state.[20] Hegel therefore arrives at the same conclusion on the basis of the relation between states as was arrived at on the basis of the relation of the individual to the state: war is necessary and so Kant's ideal of perpetual peace is to be rejected. The same conclusion is reached by a distinct argument.

Recognizing the distinctness of the arguments is not only important as a matter of logical structure. It is important for purposes of assessment. Hegel's metaphilosophical dicta as well as his empirical and normative claims can be set aside here. Each is eminently questionable. What is worth noticing is the difference between the two arguments with respect to the morally relevant features taken to establish the asserted necessity of war. Put anachronistically, the difference is one of the unit of moral concern identified. The argument in section I takes it to be one of *individual* citizens' duty to the state. There the asserted ethical necessity is one holding between a citizen and a duty of sacrifice in war. The argument from the individuality of states identifies a distinct moral concern: the concern with *institutions*. Here the asserted necessity deals with the preconditions for a set of institutions being a state. Hence the two arguments incorporate different types of morally relevant features, the former about individuals and the latter about institutions. Hegel makes claims about the ethical necessity of war by resorting to both features. Appraisals of his account of war should keep them apart.[21]

PART   4

THE MYTH OF THE END
OF HISTORY

13

The End of History and the Return of History

Philip T. Grier

I

Through the summer and fall of 1989, Hegel scholars in America were treated to the unusual spectacle of a debate in the mass media over the meaning and truth of Hegel's philosophy of history, a debate running through the pages of major daily newspapers, the weekly news magazines, and the journals of opinion. The occasion for this unaccustomed attention devoted to Hegel was the appearance of an article by Francis Fukuyama in the Summer 1989 issue of *The National Interest* entitled "The End of History?"[1]

Caught up in the spirit of the event, Irving Kristol, the publisher of *The National Interest*, generously announced in his comment on the Fukuyama article, "I am delighted to welcome G. W. F. Hegel to Washington. He will certainly help raise the intellectual level of the place. . . . Hegel is unquestionably a genius—along with Kant, the greatest philosopher of modernity" (26–27). The last sentence is, however, followed by this: "In a sense, all of us have to decide whether we are *pro* Hegel or *contra*, even if we have never read him, as not many of us have." Alas, most of the contributors to this episode would seem to be carrying out Kristol's injunction quite literally; as a consequence the recent extended public debate over "Hegel's theory of the end of history" has had almost nothing to do with Hegel.

In his essay Fukuyama aspires to identify "some larger process at work, a process that gives coherence and order" to our understanding of the events of history. He claims to have found such a "larger conceptual framework" (3) in Hegel's thesis of the end of history: "What we may be witnessing is not just the end of the Cold War, or the passing of a particular period of postwar history, but the end of history as such: that is, the end point of mankind's ideological evolution and the universalization of Western liberal democracy as the final form of human government" (4). This first statement by Fukuyama of what he means by "the end of history" appears to contain all the essential elements of his view. The story of human history is the story of our *ideological* evolution; that evolution culminates in *liberal democracy* ("the Western *idea*" [3]); history ceases because "the basic *principles* of the liberal democratic state [i.e., the ideals of the French and American Revolutions] cannot be improved upon" (5); there are no contradictions in human life that cannot be resolved in the context of the liberal democratic state (8); all important nations will either turn out to be liberal democracies, or, failing that, at least abandon their pretensions to represent any alternative or higher form of human society (13).

This theory supposedly reveals the larger significance of the observation that Western liberal democracy has now prevailed over every ideological alternative to it; "the remnants of absolutism, then bolshevism and fascism, and finally an updated Marxism that threatened to lead to the ultimate apocalypse of nuclear war" (3), have all been defeated. The twentieth century has turned out to lead neither to the "end of ideology" nor to "a convergence between capitalism and socialism . . . but to an unabashed victory of economic and political liberalism" (3).

This triumphant Western liberal democracy is distinctly *consumerist* in Fukuyama's conception of it, focused upon technical, economic problem-solving—"the satisfaction of sophisticated consumer demands" (18). At the end of the article, apparently forgetting his own dictum that this liberal democracy represents above all the achievement of the human values of freedom, equality and reason that "cannot be improved upon," Fukuyama falls into a bout of despair: "The end of history will be a very sad time" (18). Instead of the "struggle for recognition or the willingness to risk one's life for a purely abstract goal [*sic*]," life will consist of endless "economic calculation": "In the post-historical period there will be neither art nor philosophy, just the perpetual caretaking of the museum of human history" (18). Even sympathetic commentators immediately noticed that Fukuyama's *coda* had much in common with Nietzsche's idea of the "last man," and no discernible connection with Hegel.[2] In a sequel, "A Reply to My Critics,"[3] Fukuyama tried to restate his attitude toward the posthistorical condition of existence in a less provocative way without retracting his original remarks, leaving a certain ambiguity about his position (28). No significant changes were introduced in the sequel concerning his general conception of the end of history, nor was its attribution to Hegel qualified in any way.

II

Mainly under the spell of Fukuyama's article, one supposes, most commentators have seemingly accepted that his quick sketch of the end-of-history thesis is properly attributed to Hegel. Fukuyama himself betrays no doubt on this score; but his claim of attribution is at least indirect: It is Kojève's classic but highly eccentric *Introduction to the Reading of Hegel* which always figures as his explicitly cited authority for Hegel's views.[4] Fukuyama describes Kojève as, in essence, the last true Hegelian. He writes that most of us know of Hegel "primarily as Marx's precursor, and it is our misfortune that few of us are familiar with Hegel's work from direct study. . . . In France, however, there has been an effort to save Hegel from his Marxist interpreters and to resurrect him as the philosopher who most correctly speaks to our time" (4). He claims that it is *Kojève*, attempting "to resurrect the Hegel of the *Phenomenology of Mind*, the Hegel who proclaimed history to be at an end in 1806 [*sic*]" (4) who is most responsible for this effort.

Searching for a clue as to why Kojève, and not, say, the far more obvious candidate Hyppolite, should be accorded this honor, it emerges that Kojève is being contrasted primarily with Marcuse as a contemporary German interpreter of Hegel who "regarded Hegel ultimately as an historically bound and incomplete philosopher" (5, n. 2). In this company it becomes more understandable why Kojève might acquire this status as the last true Hegelian. But at the same time Fukuyama gives no particular sign of recognizing Kojève's *own* pronounced Marxist leanings, especially in his use of the master-slave dialectic as the prism through which the whole of Hegel's thought is to be viewed.[5] The more fundamental puzzle, though, would be to explain the source of Fukuyama's extraordinary confidence that Kojève's very eccentric reading of Hegel, especially on the theme of the end of history, could be accepted as an authoritative interpretation.

No serious reader of Hegel could fail to recognize that Kojève is as much creator as interpreter of the system he ascribes to Hegel. Kojève's entire reading of the *Phenomenology* revolves about the "master-slave" (*Herrschaft/Knechtschaft*) episode, treating it as a *passe-partout* for the whole. Kojève works it particularly hard in his exposition of the notion of history. He declares that "History began with the first Fight that ended in the appearance of a Master and a Slave" (Bloom, 43). Kojève insists that this fight is "a fight for pure prestige carried on for the sake of 'recognition' by the adversary" (Bloom, 11–12), that is, a fight not motivated by material or biological need, but a freely chosen one which puts everything at risk. The loss of the battle converts one of the combatants into a slave for the other, condemned to labor in confrontation with nature to satisfy the desire of the master. "History is the history of the working Slave" (Bloom, 20) articulated in a series of "slave ideologies" whereby the slaves seek to disguise their slavery from themselves. History comes to an end when the slaves eventually realize and assert their own intrinsically free being as citizens in a state in which all are equally free.

Kojève's end-of-history thesis has no obvious grounding in Hegel's texts, so the question must be asked: what led Kojève to this extraordinary view? The answer is not far to seek. Kojève himself declares (Bloom, 133–34; Queneau, 367) that "the source and basis of my interpretation of the *Phenomenology*" is to be found in an article which his fellow Russian émigré Alexandre Koyré wrote in the early 1930s on some of Hegel's Jena period texts which had recently appeared. Kojève gives no citation for the Koyré article, but there can be no doubt (on overwhelming internal as well as external evidence) that the article in question is "Hegel à Iéna," published originally in 1934.[6] It is evident that the source of Kojève's end-of-history thesis can be found in the final paragraph of Koyré's article.

Koyré was examining Hegel's treatment of time in the succession of manuscripts from the lectures at Jena in 1802, 1803–4, and 1805–6.[7] (Even though the 1802 date is no longer accepted as correct, the new dating does not materially affect Koyré's treatment of the texts.)[8] Koyré treated those manuscripts (lecture notes) as the first glimpse into Hegel's philosophical apprenticeship, our first opportunity to get behind the difficult and often obscure formulations of the mature system, to see the living process of its formation. At the same time he observed that there is a great risk in using these youthful works as an interpretive key to the mature system, namely the risk of "misunderstanding and misinterpreting" (150) the mature Hegel—and Koyré viewed the mature Hegel as above all the author of the *Science of Logic*, even more than of the *Phenomenology* (150, n. 4). On the other hand, Koyré was also inclined to treat the system of the *Encyclopedia* as problematic.[9]

The largest section of Koyré's article was devoted to the translation and exposition of passages on time from the *Naturphilosophie* of the *Jenenser Logik, Metaphysik, und Naturphilosophie* (i.e., sec. I.A.A.; Lasson, 203–6). He focusses especially on remarks Hegel made there concerning the relation of the finite to the infinite, time, and the relations of present, future, and past.[10] The present is described as an "empty limit" between the future and the past. "The past is this time returned in itself which has sublated in itself the two first dimensions [present and future]. The limit, or the Now, is empty; for it is absolutely simple or the concept of time; it realizes [*erfüllt*] itself in the future. The future is its reality" (169–70; Lasson, 204). Commenting on such passages Koyré remarks that it is not from the past that time comes to us, but from the future. "*La durée* does not extend itself from the past to the present" (176). "It is, on the contrary, from the future that it comes to itself in the present. The prevalent 'dimension' of time is the future which is, in some way, anterior to the past" (177).[11]

This treatment of past, present, and future was part of a larger argument by Hegel in the 1803 and 1804 versions of his *Naturphilosophie* dealing with the topic of motion in the solar system. Hegel treated the perfect periodicity of movement in the solar system as an image of the "true infinite."[12] As Harris puts it, "Periodic motion is what Hegel characterizes as the temporalizing of space and the spatializing of time" (244). Hegel wished to exhibit the conceptual connection between the two, and his discussion of time is part of that endeavor. All of this belonged to Hegel's attempt, presumably under the influence of Schelling, to treat nature as the realm of divine life. In this conception of nature, for example, Hegel depicted the aether as Absolute Spirit.[13] Though this theme of nature as the divine life underwent a certain development (diminution) during this time, the 1803 and 1804 philosophies of nature "represent a continuous development of thought that broke off some time in the spring of 1805" (Harris, 239). Harris also observes that the "system of 1805–6 proved to be the sunset of the Greek concept of nature as the divine life" (241).

Although Koyré, writing in 1934, did not have available the numerous scholarly investigations of the Jena period writings to which we now have access, and was not in possession of an entirely accurate chronology, nevertheless he correctly grasped the fact that the line of argument concerning time which so interested him disappears in the further development of Hegel's thought. First, the 1803–4 notes lack the corresponding section.[14] In the 1805–6 version of the *Realphilosophie* there is a discussion of time, but the nature of the text, as well as the argument, is quite changed. Space is no longer derived from time, but space is treated first, and time discussed afterward. The text is now divided into paragraphs, like those of the later *Encyclopedia*, and the style of writing is more public than private. Finally, in the corresponding *Encyclopedia* passages, these rich speculations concerning the priority of the future over the present and past have entirely disappeared (Koyré, 187).

Notwithstanding the evidence that he himself has assembled of Hegel having essentially discarded the argument on time from the "1802" notes, Koyré goes on to declare that, "It is this insistence on the future, the primacy accorded to the future over the past, which constitutes in our opinion, the greatest originality of Hegel" (177). In his concluding remarks Koyré curiously seems to speak as though Hegel had not discarded his doctrine of the primacy of the future, and treats that doctrine as ultimately leading to the failure of the system. "It is thus, in the Hegelian conception, that the dialectical nature of the instant secures the contact and the co-penetration of time and eternity. But it is also this which explains, in the final analysis, the failure of the Hegelian system. For if time is dialectical and is constructed *commencing with the future*, it is—whatever Hegel may say about it—eternally unfinished" (188–89). Since this is true, according to Koyré, the Hegelian system can be constructed only if history has been terminated, if there will no longer be a future, if time itself has stopped.

In his concluding paragraph Koyré observes almost casually:

> It is possible that Hegel believed in it [the end of history]. It is possible
> even that he believed not only that it was the essential condition
> for the system—it is only at night that the owls of Minerva (*chouettes
> d'Athéna*) begin their flight—but also that this essential condition had
> *already* been realized, that history had effectively ended, and that it was
> precisely because of that that he could—had been able to—complete
> it [his system]. (p. 189)

Since Koyré is obviously convinced on various grounds that the (*Encyclopedia*) system is a failure, and has just argued that the future cannot be foreseen, he has little interest in exploring the question of whether Hegel really believed that history had ended. (We must remember, of course, that the end of history is a precondition for the system only given Koyré's reading of the discarded "1802" passages on time as if they were a crucial element of Hegel's mature thought.) This possibility, which Koyré mentions just in an off-hand fashion, seems to have struck Kojève with the force of a revelation; it became the cornerstone for his interpretation of the *Phenomenology*.[15]

Kojève reveals only a fleeting awareness of anything odd about his procedure for interpreting the *Phenomenology*, namely, taking an obscure set of passages on time from a very early version of Hegel's *Naturphilosophie* which Hegel certainly rejected prior to writing the *Phenomenology*, and treating them as the basis for an interpretation not only of that work but of the whole of Hegel's philosophical position.[16] Kojève (and to some extent, it should be said, Koyré himself) seems to have entirely disregarded Koyré's warnings about the danger of applying these early and in some cases abortive writings of Hegel to the interpretation of the mature works.

Kojève goes on to develop Koyré's suggestions into an elaborate doctrine of the finite, empirical existence of time, history, and "man" (*l'homme*). He quotes Hegel as saying that "Time is the Concept itself which *exists empirically*" (Bloom, 136),[17] and argues that the empirical existence of time (history) entails that it must come to an end. Identifying the concept with work, Kojève argues that "the existence of Work in the World is the existence in this World of Time" (Bloom, 145). He further concludes on the same page that "if Man is the Concept, and if the Concept is Work, Man and the Concept are also *Time*." The empirical existence of time (history) thus also entails the empirical existence of work, and hence of man. Being empirical, each of these is also *finite*, hence coming to an end. "Therefore History itself must be essentially finite; collective Man (humanity) must die just as the human individual dies; universal History must have a definitive *end*" (Bloom, 148). This end of history, according to Kojève, constitutes the coming of the *wise man* (wisdom, Absolute Knowing). And this state of wisdom is eternal, posthistorical.

In the first edition of the *Introduction à la lecture de Hegel*, Kojève asserts that at the cessation of history, *l'homme* disappears. "Man remains alive as animal in harmony with Nature or given Being. What disappears is Man properly so-called—that is, Action negating the given, and Error, or in general, the Subject *opposed* to the Object" (Bloom, 158–59, n. 6). The disappearance of "man" in this sense means the disappearance of wars and revolutions, as well as philosophy. "But all the rest can be preserved indefinitely; art, love, play, etc., etc.; in short, everything that makes Man *happy*" (ibid.).

In a note to the second edition, Kojève modifies these conclusions rather drastically, acknowledging an obvious contradiction in them:

> If Man becomes an animal again, his arts, his loves, and his play
> must also become purely "natural" again. Hence it would have to be
> admitted that after the end of History, men would construct their
> edifices and works of art as birds build their nests and spiders spin
> their webs, would perform musical concerts after the fashion of frogs
> and cicadas, would play like young animals, and would indulge in love
> like adult beasts. (Bloom, 159 n.)

He declares the "American way of life" to be "the type of life specific to the post-historical period, the actual presence of the United States in the World prefiguring the 'eternal present' future of all of humanity. Thus, Man's return to animality appeared no longer as a possibility that was yet to come, but as a certainty that was already present" (Bloom, 160–61 n.). In the same remarkable note Kojève goes on to observe that following a trip to Japan in 1959, he became convinced that the Japanese had entered this posthistorical existence in the seventeenth century (!), with the cessation of all warlike or revolutionary fights, evolving a civilization grounded in the formalisms of pure *snobbery* (the Noh Theater, the tea ceremony, flower arranging, and ritual suicide).

At this point any reader possessing even a nodding acquaintance with the texts must recognize that Hegel has been more or less totally lost from view. Fukuyama himself has in fact used Kojève somewhat selectively in presenting his own end-of-history thesis; his own version seems to be a hodge-podge of Kojève and Marx, with a few vaguely Hegelian overtones. In view of all this, the question arises even more insistently: What on earth could have led Fukuyama with such careless confidence to attribute his own end-of-history thesis to *Hegel*?

A partial answer to that puzzle can be found in Bloom's introduction to the English edition of Kojève. (Bloom is evidently a mentor to Fukuyama as well as editor of this edition.) Bloom makes three claims there which help to explain why Fukuyama might have taken Kojève as an acceptable substitute for Hegel. First, he suggests that owing to the length and extraordinary difficulty of Hegel's texts, it is understandable that one might rely on an authoritative commentator: "Such a careful and comprehensive study which makes sense of Hegel's very difficult texts will be of great value in America where, though his influence has been great and is ever greater, very few people read, let alone understand, him" (Bloom, ix).

Second, Bloom presents Kojève as just such an authoritative interpreter. He describes Kojève's work as "the careful and scholarly study of Hegel" (Bloom, viii). Further: "Kojève's book is a model of textual interpretation; the book is suffused with the awareness that it is of pressing concern to find out precisely what such a thinker meant, for he may well know much more than we do about the things that we need to know" (Bloom, ix). Still more: "His own teaching is but the distillation of more than six years devoted to nothing but reading a single book, line by line. *Introduction to the Reading of Hegel* constitutes the most authoritative interpretation of Hegel" (ix). It is not quite clear what attitude one should take to these pronouncements by Bloom, given that in the same few pages he describes Kojève's interpretation of Hegel as *Marxist* ("Kojève is the most thoughtful, the most learned, the most profound of those Marxists who, dissatisfied with the thinness of Marx's account of the human and metaphysical grounds of his teaching, turned to Hegel as the truly philosophic source of that teaching" [viii]), *Heideggerian* ("One might ask whether Kojève is not really somewhere between Hegel and Heidegger, but it should be added that Kojève himself leads the reader to this question, which is a proper theme of philosophical reflection" [x]), and *Nietzschean* ("After reading it, one wonders whether the citizen of the universal homogeneous state is not identical to Nietzsche's 'last man,' and whether Hegel's historicism does not by an inevitable dialectic force us to a more somber and more radical historicism which rejects reason" [xii]). We are evidently meant to accept the implication that none of these recognizable tendencies affected the authenticity of Kojève's reading of Hegel.

Third, Bloom firmly endorses Kojève's treatment of the "end of history" motiv as authentically Hegelian: "Now the most striking feature of Kojève's thought is his insistence—fully justified—that for Hegel, and for all followers of Hegel, history is completed, that nothing really new can again happen in the world" (x). It is interesting to note, however, that in his recently published response to Fukuyama's article Bloom carefully describes the thesis in question as belonging to "Kojève and Kojève's Hegel" and declines to address the issue of whether it could be ascribed to Hegel himself.[18]

III

The genesis of Fukuyama's view is a puzzle of course, because neither Hegel nor Marx (nor possibly Kojève) could recognize Fukuyama's end-of-history thesis as his own. For Marx the relevant distinction is between *pre*history and history, rather than history and *post*history, but at the boundary there is indeed for Marx what Fukuyama attributes to Hegel: an irreversible, qualitative change in the nature of human action. Whereas prior to the communist revolution for Marx action is carried out with false consciousness, with a limited and defective comprehension of the human situation and of the consequences of action, after the event human social action is recognized for what it is, the free creation of humanity's nature itself in the choice of specific social institutions and practices. If there is an analogous change in the quality of human action for Hegel at the boundary between history and posthistory, then there should be an account of the changed nature of human action in posthistorical circumstances to be found in Hegel. But of course there is no such thing as an account of posthistorical existence in Hegel, precisely because there is no distinction between history and posthistory in his thought.

Recognizing this, we must then provide a very different explanation of the "end of history" in Hegel than the one Fukuyama ventured. One key to such an explanation lies in reading the "end" of history for Hegel as meaning its "*consummation*," and not its *cessation*. To read Hegel with insight on this issue, one must never forget his dictum in the preface to the *Philosophy of Right* that philosophy's comprehension of the world is always retrospective. Philosophy is always "its own time apprehended in thought," a summing-up which comprehends the present as having developed out of the past. But precisely because there are no "objective laws of historical development"—Hegel's "cunning of reason" (*die List der Vernunft*) is no such thing—there is never any basis for philosophy to predict the future; philosophy is and can be only a comprehension of what has been and not of what will be. An alleged "knowledge" of the "fact" that in the future there will be no more history could have no place in Hegel's scheme.

Instead there is a sense in which philosophy in each and every age, comprehending each present as the culmination of past development, could potentially be viewed as pronouncing the end of history, a pronouncement which would then be viewed as having been provisional, insufficiently concrete, by the succeeding age. This is a slightly fanciful way of reading Hegel, to be sure, if only because as he pointed out, the task of supplying an all-encompassing philosophy of world history was properly understood and undertaken for the first time in his own age. Of course Hegel did believe that there was a specific justification for the claim that the meaning of history had been "consummated" in his own age. It was his own age in which the standpoint of "Absolute Knowing" had been achieved (the culmination of the *Phenomenology*): the content of the objective world had at last been grasped as identical with Spirit's consciousness of self; Spirit had found itself "at home" in the world. It is this which constitutes the consummation of history for Hegel, Spirit's explicit realization of what it had implicitly been all along.[19]

From the standpoint of Absolute Knowing Hegel is able to develop the intricate detail of his account of reality as Absolute Spirit presented in his mature system, the *Encyclopedia*. Given that Hegel's system culminates in Absolute Spirit as an account of reality, many commentators have concluded that the historicist element of Hegel's philosophy is a kind of illusion, an illusion revealed by the culmination of the system in Absolute Spirit as a transcendent, eternal reality. Once the truth of Absolute Spirit is grasped, the argument runs, we now see that the historicist element of Hegel's argument is at most a kind of ladder which, once ascended, can be—must be—discarded. Whatever our attitude toward that history which culminates in the system of Absolute Spirit, if Hegel is correct then the rest of our human existence (the future) will be lived in the knowledge of the eternal truth of Absolute Spirit, and in this sense, history can contain no further revelations or surprises. On this reading there would, after all, be a form of posthistorical existence in Hegel.

But such a reading would require that we set aside Hegel's unmistakable claim that philosophy can offer only a retrospective comprehension of the world, a revision which I do not believe can be justified. Nor do I regard as justifiable the implication that Hegel's historicism is a kind of illusion. Both the retrospective nature of philosophical understanding and its historicist dimension can be taken seriously if we view the system of Absolute Spirit in a different light. The system of Absolute Spirit is Hegel's account of the nature of reality, grasped retrospectively as a process of development culminating in Hegel's present. But that in no way entails a cessation of history. In an often-cited passage from the *Lectures on the Philosophy of World History* Hegel remarks that, "it is up to America to abandon the ground on which world history has hitherto been enacted. What has taken place there up to now is but an echo of the Old World and the expression of an alien life; and as a country of the future, it is of no interest to us here, for prophecy is not the business of the philosopher."[20] From this and numerous other passages it is clear that Hegel would view any claim that history comes to a halt in the maturity of the Germanic Old World, or the Prussian state, as nonsense.

The sentence following the passage just quoted introduces a further important point: "In history, we are concerned with what has been and what is; in philosophy, however, we are concerned not with what belongs exclusively to the past or to the future, but with that which is, both now and eternally—in short, with reason." What proves to be so often overlooked by Hegel commentators, or proves difficult to digest, is just this conception of philosophy as concerned with what is, *both now and eternally*. In another passage in the same work he puts the point this way: "In our understanding of world history, we are concerned with history primarily as a record of the past. But we are just as fully concerned with the present. Whatever is true exists eternally in and for itself—not yesterday or tomorrow, but entirely in the present, 'now,' in the sense of an absolute present" (150). Hegel's endeavor is precisely to discover the absolute *in* history, *in* the world, not in some transcendental beyond.

Granting then that history never halts, that the future may indeed hold surprises, what attitude do we take toward the system of Absolute Spirit when that future has become for us the present? Do we treat the system as immune to revision, the revelation once and for all time of an eternal unchanging beyond? No. The system was after all for Hegel simply an attempt to set forth the logic, ontology, anthropology, and so on, which seemed inherent in an adequate philosophical comprehension of Hegel's own present—an articulation of the absolute inherent in that present. If—*a very important "if"*—Spirit has genuinely entered a new phase in our own present, then the simple conclusion must be that the system must be written anew—beginning with a new logic and ontology. If we are to retain Hegel's conception of the nature of philosophy, however, one condition must be set: that the new system of Absolute Spirit contain the previous one as *aufgehoben*.

Assuming the conclusion just reached is true, then Hegel's analysis points toward a significant question about our own historical present: has Spirit in fact entered a new phase, or are we still in essentially the same present with Hegel? That is, can an international order constituted of sovereign nation-states, where the nation-state is viewed as a (potential) realization of the values of freedom, self-determinination, and equality before the law, still be viewed as *rational*? Or has our historical experience driven us to the realization that only some transnational organization of humanity could be genuinely rational? Thus understood, the implications of Hegel's actual philosophy of history point to significant questions beyond any of those which Fukuyama entertains. And they also point to the inadequacy of Fukuyama's dismissal of the question of nationalism as no longer having any intrinsic importance in our day.

Perhaps enough has been said in my crude (but at least brief!) summary of Hegel to indicate why I believe that neither Hegel nor Marx could recognize Fukuyama's "end of history" as his own.

We should note a number of other difficulties with the attribution of Fukuyama's thesis to Hegel: (1) He seems unaware that Hegel is not a supporter but a *critic* of classical (Lockean or Hobbesean) liberalism. For example, commenting regretfully on the spiritual emptiness at the core of triumphant liberalism, he acknowledges that Rousseau was critical of this aspect of Lockean or Hobbesian liberalism—betraying no awareness that Hegel stands firmly with Rousseau on this point. (2) Hegel's "rational state" was not a reference to liberal democracy in the form we know it today, and not a reference exclusively to a form of political organization, but to the broader concept of *Sittlichkeit*, or concrete ethical life, of which the strictly political forms of organization were only one aspect. (3) Fukuyama operates for the most part with *Marx's* distinction between "consciousness" and the "real, material world," and despite one explicit attempt to acknowledge that Hegel would find the distinction specious in many contexts, does not really succeed in freeing himself from Marx's categories. (4) Hegel would not agree that liberal democracy is free from all essential contradictions, as Fukuyama argues. One of the motivations for Hegel's larger conception of *Sittlichkeit* was precisely that the liberal market economy, left to its own devices, would inevitably create an army of poor which it would be powerless to rescue. Fukuyama's own refusal to treat poverty as a systemic problem in liberal democracy ignores Hegel's argument (much amplified by Marx). (5) The history of humanity depicted by Hegel is not a history of the evolution of *ideology* (another bit of Marxizing terminology taken from Kojève), but rather, in the *Phenomenology*, initially, a succession of shapes of natural consciousness, and subsequently, a succession of shapes of a world, or of Spirit; and in the philosophy of history, a succession of nations and civilizations. Ultimately it is Spirit itself which develops through history, and not *ideologies.*

Since I have rejected Fukuyama's claim that there is any such thing as posthistorical existence in Hegel, I need not dwell on this theme further, but in his interpretation of posthistorical existence there is the peculiarity that in the future, only those nations would be allowed to have history whose history does not matter, as a witty colleague of mine expressed it. Fukuyama claims that his task is "not to answer exhaustively every crackpot messiah around the world, but only those that are embodied in important social or political forces and movements, and which are therefore part of world history. For our purposes, it matters very little what strange thoughts occur to people in Albania or Burkina Faso, for we are interested in what one could in some sense call the common ideological heritage of mankind" (9). The question then arises: what is the criterion of *importance*? The "common ideological inheritance of mankind" looks suspiciously like "the common ideological heritage of the Western liberal democracies" and thus begs the question. Hegel was similarly judgmental about the respective importances of the various nations in the history of Spirit, but his criterion for making such judgments was plain. Fukuyama takes up this point again in his "Reply," trying to explain why not every nationalist ideology possesses historical importance. There he argued that nationalist confrontations become important only when certain conditions are met: the nationalist ideology in question must belong to a large and powerful imperialist nation with universalist claims for its ideology; and the confrontation with other ideologies must involve threats of nuclear annihilation (27). "Important" here just means "universalist" and "powerful" in the military sense; but that is at most merely a gloss on the recently concluded Cold War between the superpowers and not a philosophy of history.

IV

The six or seven responses published along with the Fukuyama article turned out to be only the first trickle of what became a flood. In a relatively short time there were op-ed columns, editorials, more responses, and a continual stream of discussions in the opinion magazines. The *Washington Post* published an abridged version of the original essay; the *New York Times* printed excerpts in conjunction with an article on it by Richard Bernstein,[21] followed by an editorial entitled "Awaiting the Great Boredom,"[22] as well as a column by Flora Lewis, "The Return of History,"[23] and an article by James Atlas in the *Magazine*, "What is Fukuyama Saying?"[24] George Will weighed in with a column in *Newsweek*.[25] Essays have also appeared in *Encounter*, the *National Review*, *The Nation*, *In These Times*, *The Chronicle of Higher Education*, and *Time*, to mention only a random sample. "More Responses to Fukuyama" appeared in *The National Interest*, plus longer essays by Samuel P. Huntington and Leon Wieseltier.[26] Fukuyama's Winter 1989–90 "Reply" was excerpted in the *Washington Post* as "Beyond the End of History,"[27] and was followed by a further article in the *New York Times*, Bernstein's "The End of History, Explained for the Second Time."[28] The controversy will soon circle the globe, according to the *National Interest* editors,[29] with translations or reprints of Fukuyama's article being published in Paris, Tokyo, Rome, Sydney, and Amsterdam.

The discussion has predictably not risen to the philosophical level for the most part, but has remained at the level of mere ideology-cum-policy. A common theme of some neoconservatives has been to react suspiciously or negatively to the implication that the Cold War is over, presumably to forestall any threat of further diminution in defense expenditures, especially at the behest of a dead German philosopher. Other neoconservatives, perhaps already resigned to an inevitable decrease of defense expenditures on other grounds, have apparently welcomed Hegel's resurrection out of a conviction that his politics must be of the right, and that he is, by all reports, a profound thinker. On the other side of the spectrum, at least one unabashed liberal, Harvey J. Kaye, has decried the Fukuyama piece as part of a neoconservative, right-wing plot to "create a new, post-liberal consensus," displacing the liberalism which has reigned as the dominant consensus in America since the Second World War, both for our political life in general and for the profession of history in particular.

> The end-of-history thesis emanates from this neo-conservative attempt
> to fashion a new political consensus and governing narrative, and now
> after 10 years of rule by the Right, one specifically intended to sanctify

the present order of things. The goal is to portray it as the culmination of history, the best of all possible worlds, beyond which the choice is either more of the same or economic and political retrogression.[30]

On the other hand, if John Gray's "The End of History—or of Liberalism" is correct, liberals have nothing to fear from Fukuyama, for he is one of their own:

> Fukuyama's brilliant and thoughtful argument is a symptom of the hegemonic power of liberalism in American thought. So ubiquitously pervasive are liberal ideas and assumptions in American intellectual life, and such is their constraining power over public discourse, that it sometimes seems barely possible to formulate a thought that is not liberal, let alone to express it freely. The domination of the American mind by liberal ideology has fostered blind spots in American perception of the real world that have been immensely disabling for policy.[31]

In short, the recent debate over "Hegel's theory of the end of history" has had much about it that suggests confused armies clashing by night. Notwithstanding Irving Kristol's generous welcome of Hegel to Washington, D.C., we must conclude that G. W. F. Hegel has not yet arrived in this land of pundits. That is regrettable because Hegel offers us much wisdom concerning political order, morality, and history; and it is startling to discover in 1989 that Kojève's "commentary" is still being passed around as an acceptable substitute for Hegel. Nor was it an acceptable substitute in 1969.[32]

The greatest irony in Fukuyama's thesis of the end of history has to do with its seeming to turn a blind eye on the other theme that has been so much noticed and commented upon during the very same period: the return of history. As Flora Lewis argues in her *New York Times* article, we are living through an extraordinary period in which the prerogative of history to overturn established orders and systems, to frustrate the most relentless efforts of armies, police, or bureaucracies to prevent change has been strikingly reasserted. It happens that, on the same day as I write these lines, the Berlin Wall is being smashed open by the same authorities who erected it, desperate to forestall the spontaneous action of the East German people, and millions of East Germans are now allowed to do what none of us thought they would be able to do in our lifetimes. Flora Lewis quotes the French philosopher André Glucksmann as saying that "getting out of Communism is getting back into history." He in turn was echoing the Czech writer—now president—Václav Havel: "The totalitarian power brought a bureaucratic 'order' into the living disorder of history, as a result of which it was mummified as history. The Government has, so to speak, nationalized time, and so time has been struck by the sad fate of so much that was nationalized. It began to perish."[33]

One of the immediate Western victims of this particular return of history has been the intellectual luster of some of our "social scientific" theories of social and political organization. We now recognize that they have flourished in a period of relative historical stasis, and the return of history has reminded us of the limitations of this particular form of human "knowledge." We now remember that before there was "social science" there was narrative history, with its concern for events and periodizations of events, and that this particular perspective on history serves an essential function. But these changes in our consciousness are only a pale reflection of what has transpired in the experience of those in central and eastern Europe who are now once again directly confronting history.

14

Hegel and the End of History

Reinhart Klemens Maurer

Translated by Jon Stewart[1]

> The revolutionary desire to realize the kingdom of God is the
> elastic point of progressive education and the beginning of
> modern history.
>
> —F. Schlegel, Athenäumsfragm., 222

> One can only get at iron bones, containing the most noble
> marrow, by the combined biting of all teeth of all dogs. That is of
> course only a picture and an exaggerated one; if all teeth were
> ready, they would not even have to bite. The marrow would open
> itself up to the grip of the weakest puppy.
>
> —F. Kafka, *Forschungen eines Hundes*

I

With any talk about the end of history,[2] one must distinguish between
the three following meanings:[3]

    1. *The end of the world history of Europe*, which means the end of
that epoch in which the theoretical and practical "progress in the consciousness of freedom," i.e., the qualitatively and quantitively expanding
recognition of man as man, took place in Europe. Today world history in
this sense, defined with regard to its contents by Hegelian concepts, is no
longer limited to Europe and has in fact become world history. Almost
the entire earth is europeanized, so to speak (in large part due to the
powerful offshoots, America and Russia), and, moreover, it cannot be

discerned with sufficient clarity whether the consciousness of freedom is unfolding itself further either in Europe or anywhere else for that matter or if it is going to ruin in the inimical experiments of its worldwide organization, i.e., whether freedom fails in its very attempt at realization.

2. The "end of history" might also be taken to signify *the beginning of a new age* which is so very different from all those heretofore that it appears to be justified to call the past "history" in order to distinguish it from the present, which marks the beginning of posthistory. For example, the sociologist A. Gehlen, following Cournot, speaks of "*post-histoire*"[4] in this manner, a concept which on his description contains what he calls "cultural crystallization." A. Kojève, in his book *Introduction à la lecture de Hegel*,[5] speaks in a very similar fashion of the "disappearance of man at the end of history."[6] Behind these partly objective, partly prophetic, and partly sarcastic analyses stemming from an uncertain protest stands the claim of modern society that, through its coming on the scene, history no longer merely happens but rather is actively made by man. Clearly, the expression "man" is very imprecise in this context. "Man," understood as industrial society in general, can, according to these views, make history, which by this very fact stops being what it was heretofore (whatever that was) and is transformed into planned change.[7] This active history-making [*Geschichte-Machen*] compels mankind together into a collective whole, the freedom of which is above all the insight into the necessity of this process.

3. A third possible interpretation of "the end of history" would be *the new world-society as the final epoch of history*. The end of history can be represented in this manner either as the completion of humanity in an epoch of indeterminate or unlimited duration or as an historical period, with or without a completion, which leads to the destruction of mankind. According to the latter meaning, history would thus really come to an end without the "charming irresponsibility" or the "anonymous responsibility" (according to Jaspers a fundamental category of the new collective ethics) of a posthistory.

II

The question of my investigation is as follows: is it philosophically or philologically justified to associate Hegel with one or more of these meanings of the expression "the end of history" as has repeatedly been done? The aforementioned work by Kojève tries to interpret Hegel in this way based on Hegel's own doctrine as the bearer—a bearer having come about near the end of history—of an absolute knowledge about the unitary process of nature and history which encompasses God and the world. Similarly, Löwith[8] and Taubes[9] classify Hegel along with Marx and J. Burkhardt in the almost extinct sequence of eschatologically oriented occidental philosophies of history from the Greek Judeo-Christian tradition.[10] Likewise, M. Rubinstein, a link between the old and the new Hegelianism in Germany, wrote a treatise with the title "The Logical Foundations of the Hegelian System and the End of History."[11] According to R. Haym, in 1830 the Hegelians "with complete and bitter seriousness hashed out the question about what is likely to constitute the future contents of world history after World Spirit has passed through its goal, knowledge of itself, in the Hegelian philosophy."[12] And, likewise, a great many Hegel interpreters speak similarly of the Hegelian philosophy as the final synthesis of occidental Spirit or something like it.

Of all of these notions of the end of history that are attached to Hegel, the first meaning of this expression is clearly the most comprehensible. The other two (the beginning of posthistory and the last epoch of history, respectively) are problematic in connection with Hegel, since to use them demands an interpretation and application of what Hegel means when he speaks of the "coming-to-itself" ["*Zu-sich-selbst-Kommen*"] of Spirit or the realization of its realm. In fact, Hegel mentions the end of history directly only once. The passage at issue, which is rather dubious with respect to questions of authenticity, reads, "World history moves from east to west; for Europe is the end of world history plain and simple." This sentence, when applied to the three meanings mentioned at the outset, suggests various considerations. To begin with, it does not seem to mean that everything is at an end with Europe. It implies rather that Europe itself is the end. This means either if history itself continues after the end of Europe, it is merely posthistory, or the fall of the occident is also the actual end of history, i.e., the destruction of humanity. However, one ought not to insist on this sentence for the reasons mentioned above (cf. n. 2). The general sense of Hegel's theory of history precludes us all the more from overestimating this passage. Indeed, this sentence must be understood and put in the context of that theory. However, according to Hegel's theory of history (as well as his general theory of development which is based on that of Plato and Aristotle), the question about the end of history is of secondary importance.

Defined philosophically, and this means at the same time politically in accordance with the origin of philosophy from the polis, world history is, according to Hegel, "the progress in consciousness of freedom" (e.g., *Vern*, 63). Theologically, it is defined by its being the middle phase. "History goes to here and from there" (*WG*, vol. 11, 410), Hegel says about the incarnation that he understands philosophically as the revelation of the principle of "Spirit." Defined simultaneously theologically and philosophically, history is "this process of helping Spirit to itself, to its Concept" (*Vern*, 72; cf. 150ff.). In its essence Spirit is, as Hegel says, the "Concept of freedom" (*Vern*, 152). Here the impression might arise that the first and the third definition can be connected with the concept of a progressive process whose goal would be the realization of freedom in a sort of kingdom of God on earth. However, the understanding of history from its middle phase speaks firmly against this. In relation to this middle phase, everything earlier is prehistory and everything later posthistory, as the occidental calculation of time suggests. In Hegel, the concept of Spirit supplies, in fact, an entirely different form of secularization: it makes the middle of history the middle of every epoch and of every realizable present in every moment of the life and death of every individual. Moreover, it reconciles the different conceptions of history—above all the idea of progress which Löwith attributes to the Judeo-Christian tradition and the ancient idea of development and cyclical movement—into a higher concept of development, which brings together continuity and division. These other views of history merely cover up the break which lies for the one at the end of the cycles and for the other between them, and both are for this reason one-sided and false, since they are based on a geometrical model. However, talk about the end of history or of a history, insofar as it accepts an historical context at all, remains dependent upon either the idea of the rising, straight or (spiralling) winding line of the unitary process, which arrives at its goal, or according to the theory prepared by Nietzsche and made famous by Spengler, of a cyclical movement of culture, which takes as a model the geometrical schema in its biological embodiment.

III

On the face of it, Hegel derives his concept of development by applying the Greek, Aristotelian doctrine of becoming to history. The teleological concept of development brings history together logically as a totality, whereas history in its theological and political interpretation breaks it up, all in the medium of philosophy as a theory of self-negating reality or self-developing freedom.

First this is shown by the fact that Hegel often brings together Spirit and history in a simile taken from nature. For example, he writes, "And just as the seed carries the entire nature of the tree . . . in itself, so also the first traces of Spirit contain the whole of history" (*Vern*, 61; cf. *Vern*, 181ff.; and *WG*, vol. 10, 15ff. = *Syst. d. Philos.*, sec. 379, addition). Therefore, thanks to Spirit, totality does not need the completion of its development, although totality is meant in the temporal or rather historical sense.[13] As Spirit, the end is contained in the beginning or the beginning in the end (cf. *Vern*, 131) or in the middle or in the foundation of the whole process, which itself, even if it also seems to produce its presuppositions, in fact only unfolds its beginning.[14] In this vein Hegel writes, "The principle of development means that there is as a foundation an inner determination—a presupposition[15] existing in itself—which brings itself into existence" (*Vern*, 151). And Hegel can connect this foundation as "infinite possibility" with the "Aristotelian *dynamis* and *potentia*, that is force and potency" (*Vern*, 157). In the history of religion, Hegel explains the presence of the whole in the part, which moves or destroys both the whole and the part, with an example which departs from the realm of possible comparisons with nature as well as from an ontology of part and whole. In the introduction to the *Lectures on the Philosophy of Religion*, we read, "The different forms or determinations of religion are, on the one hand, moments of religion in general or of the completed religion. But they also have an independent form, such that religion has developed itself in them temporally and historically" (*WG*, vol. 15, 92). This is the theme of the *Phenomenology of Spirit*, perhaps the most fitting execution of Hegel's basic principle that essence must appear. In the *Phenomenology* itself, this thought of expressing the *immanence of the other* is declared in an even more *pluralistic* manner in the thesis which leads to *absolute* knowing: "The sequence of different religions which will come about represents only the different sides of a single and indeed of every single religion" (*Phä*, 481). It is the same dynamic structure which that movement has, which is often disparaged as the "dialectical method." The dialectic in Hegel is not a logical or material process of thesis, antithesis, and synthesis.[16] Rather, these inexact terms from formal logic may not be mentioned without their content, which is according to a formulation in the above mentioned introduction: (1) "the moment of presupposed unity"; (2) "the sphere of separation"; and (3) "the freedom reestablished in the separation" (the reestablished unity is more than the immediate unity; it is freedom) (*WG*, vol. 15, 86). These moments are a living process only as being contained in one another at each time. As Hegel directly says, "This rhythm, in which the whole of our science and the development of the concept moves, comes back again in each of the three given moments since each of them is in its determinacy the totality in itself until this totality is posited as such in the last moment" (*WG*, vol. 15, 76).

To this extent continuity can be traced. Now separation or division [*Entzweiung*] comes about. That is when there is a last moment in the account as in the historical sequence; then all mediation cannot remove this finite discontinuity. For this reason, it integrates the discontinuity, insofar as it is honest and thinks it through to the end. The omnipresence of the end is its immanent sublation. The end does not on this account lose its seriousness; since everything is for Spirit, self-consciousness belongs to Spirit and with it to fear. However, it may not matter with respect to the fear whether the self as a living thing dies or whether the world is destroyed. Death is its destruction of the world. Existentialism has as one of its favorite themes the immanence of the end as the presence of death. In Hegel, this presence means "separation." Negative, abstract reason [*Verstand*], freedom, and work are conceptually related to separation as a passage in the preface to the *Phenomenology* shows by virtue of the fact that its brings them all together. There we read,

> for only insofar as the concrete divides itself and makes itself unreal is it the self-moving. The activity of separation is the power and the work of abstract reason [*Verstand*]. . . . But that the accidental as such, separated from its context, which is bound together and wins its own existence and separate freedom only in connection with another real thing—this is the extraordinary power of the negative; it is the energy of thought, of the pure "I." Death, if we so call this unreality, is the most terrible. (*Phä*, 29)

The *Encyclopedia* of 1817 speaks of this negativity or freedom in the following fashion: "the highest form of nothingness for itself is freedom" (*WG*, vol. 6, 54). This freedom, according to Hegel, destroyed at first the polis and then, in the Reformation, the medieval fusion of religion and politics and then, in the industrial and democratic revolution, secular feudalism. According to everything Hegel says, it may even destroy an integration in the sense of a Marxist or American harmony of man, understood as society and (socially dominated) nature. No three-step law as in Comte forms the foundation of the Hegelian dialectic, and its third moment is based neither, as for the romantics, Feuerbach and Marx, on an immediately human or technically mediated return to nature[17] nor on a forward movement to a perfect natural system of humanity, whose ideologically (and thus not factually) ruling principle is the preservation of the life of all at any price.[18] Rather, the issue concerns the "impotence of nature" and the "impotence of life" (*Vern*, 58, 72, 169). This is due to the fact that nature does not see division in every development. Life as life knows nothing of destruction and transition. The development of nature is, therefore, in contrast to history, not a progress (except for the Spirit observing it and searching for its natural sources) (*Vern*, 153). Hegel calls the development of nature "immediate, without opposition and unimpeded," whereas the development of history is for him "mediated by consciousness and will," and this means division and alienation (*Vern*, 151ff.). Spirit wills alienation, and, as Hegel says, it is "proud and full of pleasure in this alienation of itself" (*Vern*, 152). The elimination of this would thus be fatal to Spirit itself.

First, this alienation is understood in the realm of nature, which is explained in natural religion as the holy and in magic as something at one's disposal—both are relations to nature, but identity and immediacy still predominate. "Only when Spirit has posited itself independently for itself, as free from nature, does this external other come on the scene" (*WG*, vol. 15, 97). Since separation is a characteristic of nature and since Spirit belongs to mankind right from the beginning, separation is just as much a category of universal history as of nature. The separation of nature which makes history is produced by nature. In its unfolding, however, it seems to become a purely historical category. The historical development of society destroys nature and with it ultimately its foundation since it separates itself from history, which was heretofore based on the symbiosis with nature as enslaved in a more and more perfect domination of nature. "We have in our consciousness two realms," Hegel writes, "that of nature and that of Spirit. . . . Although one may imagine all sorts of ideas about a kingdom of God, it is always a kingdom of Spirit, which should be realized in man and posited in existence by him" (*Vern*, 50). Insofar as this so produced kingdom becomes real in space, time, matter, and society, it is in nature and its restructuring; but it is also contrary to nature. If these two sides are not mediated (in which case the Hegelian externalization of the *Logic* and the *Philosophy of Nature* would be wholly incomprehensible), then the realm of Spirit, in accordance with its power, would destroy either itself, insofar as it has worldly existence, or would destroy not only its natural basis but all nature, which, created from nothing, could again go back to it. The realm of Spirit realizes itself in the collapse of the historical, naturally limited figures. As I have said, Hegel hardly speaks of the end of history; however, one can deduce from the analysis given so far that the actual end of history would be the earthly precondition for the only complete realization of this realm. All worldly complete (i.e., existing) realizations of the realm are provisional and should, conscious of their provisional nature, honor nature and life as the basis of finite Spirit and everything created by it, and should grant to them their proper development according to their own laws.

IV

Hegel's philosophy takes a positive view toward life and presupposes that something comes after it, but something that concerns a collapse [*Untergang*] in the sense of returning to the foundation or ground [*Zugrundegehen*]. The *Logic* frequently alludes to this, since this word "*Zugrundegehen*"[19] in the German language also means a "transition to the foundation" and thus to "a truer being." Philosophy is mediation and above all mediation between the two realms. However, precisely because of this, it can be pressed into the opposition by the total historicity that is overturned in the historical standstill of the end of history, since separation or division, as a purely historical category, makes such mediation dubious. Here separation implies that the long effective opposition only came to a head in modern times, and that, to use the language of Ritter's Hegel interpretation, an epoch approached, which would like to be based upon the end and upon the loss of its originary history. A history-making, unhistorical society comes on the scene with the claim to posit itself from itself; it is, as Hegel says, "the tremendous force, which seizes man, demands from him that he work for it and that he be everything through it and act through it." Philosophy distinguishes itself, on the one hand, just as much from the permanent revolution of society, which on account of the lack of recognition of its originary ground does not come to the realistic observation and use of its possibilities, as, on the other hand, from its attempts to identify itself with the process of its coming forth in a new integration of man (as species) and nature. At the end of his *Lectures on the Philosophy of History*, Hegel says, after he, like Kant,[20] starting with the antinomies of the total democracy first analyzed by Rousseau, distinguished between the world-historical development of the concept of freedom and the "objective," "real" freedom which is to be achieved—a distinction which lies particularly distant from modern political praxis: "From weariness of the movement of immediate passions in reality, philosophy comes around to observation; its interest is to recognize the course of development of the self-actualizing idea and, indeed, of the idea of freedom which is now the consciousness of freedom" (*WG*, vol. 11, 569). The conclusion of the *Lectures on the Philosophy of Religion* speaks even more clearly about a "dissonance" [*Mißton*] and a "decay" [*Verfall*], with respect to which philosophical reconciliation with reality can be "only partial and without universality" so that philosophy is "in this relation a separated sanctuary," and "its servants constitute an isolated caste of priests who isolate themselves from the external world" (*WG*, vol. 13, 354ff.). Thus, according to Hegel's late lectures, philosophy does not think much about the kingdom of God, since it turns itself instead to the historical and political reality and all the more since, as he writes in the introduction to the *History of Philosophy* from the Heidelberg period, it, "along with political and other interests bound to the common reality and also pure science, makes valid the free rational world of Spirit."[21]

Hegel's interpretation of the course of history as progress and as the realization of freedom for all, which came about principally with Christianity, remains tied to the *concept and the consciousness of freedom*. Freedom receives its reality less from the civil and societal institutions which are still good than from the individual consciousness according to the Spirit of a people and the person. The orientals "knew" that one was free, the Greeks that some were free, and "the Germanic nations in Christendom have come to the consciousness that man as man is free" (*Vern*, 62). To investigate who or how many knew how to develop these general possibilities does not, according to Hegel, fall within the realm of the philosophy of history, since it is not determined by the universal process. Likewise, the philosophy of history does not ask about the happiness of men but says only that the progress of freedom in consciousness does not mean an increase in happiness for some or all. Hegel writes, "History is not the ground for happiness. The times of happiness are empty pages in it" (*Vern*, 92; cf. 99ff.). Concerning all of these apparently comprehensible things of general interest, Hegel attributes neither to himself nor to the modern period any special position, which would make it possible to look back on history from its endpoint. Only in Spirit is the present, like every present, the kingdom of God.[22]

V

The much praised and much reviled sentence, "What is rational is actual; and what is actual is rational" (*Philosophy of Right*, preface), implies among other things that (1) the sort of rationality is irrational, which has no reality except in thought and therefore asserts that it is irrational to negate everything real and to have to start over again from the beginning; (2) the mere looking on is passionately concerned with the knowledge of that which exists and likewise changes like a collective social event; (3) the "best of all possible worlds" cannot be improved upon but at best can, by means of a realistic evaluation, be brought to its immanent good;[23] and (4) praxis without adequate theory, irrespective of any initial successes it may enjoy, leads to the unreal. As a rule, Hegel's writings are a "dialectic of the Enlightenment." This results from the demand that the Enlightenment be applied, which also means that the Enlightenment

must issue from antecedent, real, comprehensive, and foundational contexts and not merely from ones that are simultaneously posited by the application of the Enlightenment.[24] Should "applied Enlightenment"[25]—a
linguistically and logically somewhat unclear term—be understood as a
rational praxis at any price, even at the price of an extensive rationality?
There is also the question, according to Dahrendorf, whether, on the one
hand, such an unconditioned will to act is more dangerous or, on the
other hand, "Hegel's dialectical loops," will (according to Dahrendorf's
view) threaten to lead "thought only to the confirmation of the originally
unthought reality."[26] Experiments of the grand style belong only to the
Enlightenment understood in this way, and, in the social realm, experi-
ment anticipates action, which can only first begin when the attempt calls
forth positive results.

To what extent Hegel's "dialectical loops" also have, on the view of
Dahrendorf and others, a conservative or even revolutionary function
becomes clear when one imagines that they, just like the skepticism
against a realm of ultimately realized freedom, are based on the rejection
of an enthusiastically applied natural science. Hegel also held fast to this
from the period of his previously cited early writings onward, where he
describes one of the temptations of Christ "in a demythologized fashion":
"Once in the loneliness the thought came to him whether it was worth
the trouble to try . . . by the study of nature to change base materials
into noble ones, like for instance turning stone into bread, in order to
make them immediately useful for people and to make himself more
independent of nature in general. But he rejected this thought with the
observation of the barrier which nature has placed on man insofar as
man has power over it."[27] Indeed, Hegel later emphasizes, as has been
especially noted by interpreters inspired by Marx, that "liberation lies
in work,"[28] and in the *Philosophy of History* he traces the principle of the
industrial domination of nature from the ancient Phoenicians onward;[29]
however, the absolute positing of this principle is, for starters, precluded
by the reference to the New Testament passage, "provide not for your life,
become what you eat and drink . . ." (*WG*, vol. 11, 419), and in addition
by a general consideration of the Protagorean and Platonic distinction
between two civilizations (or cultures or even of civilizations of culture).[30]
W. Jaeger calls the first form "technical civilization" and, interpreting
Plato, explains that in spite of it "humans would have been condemned
to a lamentable destruction since they would mutually destroy each other
in terrible struggles if Zeus had not granted them the gift of law, which
made them capable of founding states and communities."[31]

For Hegel, the immediate Greek *nomos* breaks down into the
oldest moment of ethical life [*Sittlichkeit*] in the (Roman) moment of

abstract right and in the Christian, modern principle of moral subjectivity. In this breakdown, ethical [*sittlich*], self-ruling subjectivity stands over and against the outwardly directed object sphere that constitutes and dominates subjectivity. The historical development simultaneously runs its course in both of these spheres. When Hegel speaks of a realm of Spirit and of freedom brought about by the historical action of human agents, he does not mean the end of history or the producing of posthistory primarily by means of technology or social engineering, but rather he sets the realistic Christian position against such utopias,[32] which implies that history is only at an end with its own actual end and until then somehow goes on with or without technical domination of nature unless a change is made in the mutual recognition of individuals and in the insight of subjectivity into its posited interpretation of reality.

This point of view is just as fundamental for Hegel's theory of subjectivity as for Heidegger's and in a certain sense even for Plato's. In order for there to be objectivity, beings, or being for man at all, the "I" must (1) become conscious of its independence, isolation and one-sidedness; and (2) consciously externalize itself. In order that the externalization not be self-destructive alienation and enslavement to an object which is likewise to be destroyed, this process must be taken back to its origin. Hegel speaks of the "inner reversal" as the source of reconciliation. The *incurvatio in se ipsum* becomes a "process" in which individuals "complete this reconciliation in themselves such that they develop what they are, Spirit free in itself to its freedom—i.e. so that they reach the consciousness of heaven on earth, the elevation of man" (*WG*, vol. 19, 100).

In its sharpened Protestant form, this concept of reconciliation can easily pass over into a bad subjectivity such that "the subject in itself . . . is satisfied with itself just as it is with its own thoughts and desires, so that its knowing, its thought, and its conviction become the highest, and have the determination of the divine, i.e. of something valid in and for itself" (*WG*, vol. 19, 141ff.). Hegel, with this "new but one-sided" (*WG*, vol. 19, 142) form of reconciliation, touches on the danger point where what was originally religious individualism turns into the absolute positing of subjectivity as intersubjectivity,[33] thus into a religion whose highest entity is man as society.[34] Thus, the individual dissolves into a bundle of social mediations, and the freedom of the individual loses all substantial contents. It becomes something formal, determined by arbitrary, rational or irrational movements of the will, and turns into the social manipulation of everyone by everyone from which there are again smooth transitions to an open despotism.

But one can assume that for Hegel a progress (i.e., the increasing development and application of technological and social-technological means) without the "inner reversal" brings the kingdom of God nearer, for it is intended as something different from the "principle of hope." Working with the common ground of messianism, the Christians know, in contrast to the Jews, that even the God having become man, in order to get into his kingdom, must die according to the will of man. (He writes, "only as having died, is Christ represented as sitting to the right of God" [*WG*, vol. 11, 326]). The humanitarian demand "to minimize suffering," posited absolutely in social context, works, like a universally accepted hedonism, toward nothing else but collective euthanasia. It contains the deception—which, by the way, may be worth striving for— that course sufferings are merely replaced by more subtle ones, which are on the whole more dangerous to life, above all in ideologically concealed situations, since the former threaten life more from outside and produce resistance, whereas the latter can turn against life itself. Thus, the maintenance and support of life itself as the highest value of a societal ethic change into mass murder or mass suicide. Hegel writes, "What is limited to a natural life cannot by itself transcend its immediate existence; but it is driven beyond it by another and this being torn away is its death" (*Phä*, 69). A posthistorical existence of man who had become a satisfied animal would only be possible according to Hegel's considerations if this new animal really no longer had consciousness, for to continue with the passage cited above, "Consciousness suffers . . . this violence to spoil the limited satisfaction from him himself." The satisfied animal, "man," must, however, at least have a collective consciousness able to be controlled by mass-media, if it wants to perform the necessary domination of nature required for the self-preservation of the world society. Global destruction of this limited satisfaction would then correspond to the collective swallowing up of the individual in the process of self-preservation and in the principle of the minimizing of suffering. Whatever is still living, in order to be free, can only die. In Goethe's philosophical poem[35] we read, "For everything must collapse into nothingness, if it wants to persist in being." This is an axiom of classical thinking. And when it is simultaneously said that the stubborn persisting must pass because "the eternal moves on in everything," one is thus not assuming an absolute process still behind the rising and falling, but rather such a process would be the most fixed, especially since it is the universally interdependent self-preservation of all. Dialectical thinking is neither progressive nor reactionary nor conservative; it seizes the processualism as one side in itself but cannot be understood the other way around with categories that are oriented to the absolute process.

VI

Hegel, of course, knew (insofar as knowing is related to experiencing) the development of the modern society only as far as it had progressed up until his own time. He writes, "The philosopher is not concerned with prophesies. Rather, we are from the side of history concerned with what has been and with what is—in philosophy this means not with what merely was or will be but rather with what is eternal—with reason" (*Vern*, 210; cf. *WG*, vol. 11, 447). Without making prophecies about any further development, one cannot deduce the end of history or the privileged position of oneself or one's epoch either from the past and present or from eternal reason. In contrast to some of his successors, Hegel did not do this. After he called the last figure of the historical development the "most concrete," he says rather in the Berlin lectures notes from the introduction to the *History of Philosophy*: "It is . . . again no presumption of the philosophy of our time; for it is precisely the point of this whole account that the further developed philosophy of a later period in time is essentially the result of the previous work of the thinking Spirit" (*Einl*, 70).[36] In the conclusion of the *History of Philosophy* that bears the subtitle "Result" in the Glockner edition, Hegel makes a similar point: "This is now the standpoint of the present time, and the sequence of spiritual forms is now with this closed" (*WG*, vol. 19, 690). And elsewhere (*Vern*, 256ff.) there is talk of a final standpoint in the history "for us" and in the "progress of the idea." This conceptual progress of history has as its goal "that Spirit educates itself to a nature, to a world which is appropriate to it so that the subject finds its concept of Spirit in this *second nature*, in this reality produced by the concept of Spirit." Now the question would be whether "for us" means the same thing as "for now," that is, in the sense of "for us today," or whether it means "for us humans as spiritual individuals." In the latter case, "our" standpoint would not be historical. At best conditioned by nature, this standpoint would contain at the same time the thesis that Spirit has a mundane reality since human beings do exist. "For us today" contains an historical relativization, unless a unique privileged position in the progress of the idea were referred to by it, namely the point at which the goal is principally reached. The following formulation of Hegel speaks in favor of this view: "that work is still present, belongs to the empirical side." But what then does "principally" or "empirical" mean? The empirical is principally important when it concerns reality. Thus, with respect to this, the present time in the originally continuing development of the principle means merely an—obviously essential—developmental stage among others. The following passage in this context speaks for this interpretation, which I will discuss further below: "The length of time is something thoroughly relative, and Spirit belongs to eternity." Both interpretive possibilities should thus be taken together.

Beside the passage cited above at the end of the *History of Philosophy*, we read, "A new epoch has arisen in the world. It appears that world history has now been successful in doing away with all foreign objective essences and finally in comprehending itself as absolute Spirit and producing out of itself that which is objective to it, and in keeping it tranquilly in its power" (689). If one can interpret this in a purely economical, social and political fashion, one easily comes to the idea of this new epoch as a sort of posthistory, but Hegel, however, in what follows comes to speak about problems which have their place rather in the philosophy of religion. And in what follows this, where the discussion concerns the "goal" of history, the "it appears" is repeated. On the other hand, even without this addition stands the thesis that "at any given time, there has really been only one philosophy" (690), and the dialectical formulation of the same thought, which implies that the *sequence* of "spiritual figures of philosophy" is of such a sort that "it remains neither a plurality, nor a sequence as succession, but rather makes itself into a moment of the one Spirit, into one and the same present Spirit precisely in the process of recognizing oneself" (691).

Kojève sees Hegel as backing down from his otherwise allegedly basic idea of the "genetic self-creation" (of man as society) with this concept of immanence, which is mediated by consciousness, self-consciousness, and Spirit—the concept of immanence of the raising up of all individual reality to just this individual, historical reality, which Hegel following Plato calls the "Idea." Kojève writes, "Hegel does not always remain faithful to his guiding idea. Sometimes the historical evolution appears as the successive realization (in time) of an eternal idea . . . an ancient (pagan) notion in contradiction to that of the historicity of man from the Judeo-Christian tradition, according to which man is what he becomes."[37] This is, in fact, almost an inversion of what Hegel says often enough (e.g., *Vern,* 151; cf. *Phä,* 22): "Thus the organic individual produces itself: it makes itself into what it is in itself, thus Spirit." Indeed, whereas according to Kojève's interpretation of this tradition (apparently so formulated for the sake of the end of history of the Christian sublation of Jewish and ancient thought), "to become" [*werden*] is written, in contrast "to make oneself" [*sich machen*], which implies freedom, can be found in Hegel's "Heideggerian" conception. Man does not simply become what he is (i.e., ultimately nothing), but rather he makes himself what he is. And this conscious making implies an "absolute present."

The surmounting of the individual through the universal, which is posited in this idea, does not stop here, since the particular breaks up the universals just as much as the other way around. The totality, of which Hegel following Schiller speaks, is not the "bad infinity" of an unending temporal, causal, or mathematical sequence determined by its members running in their respective dimensions into endlessness, since it contains the infinite value of the individual. Referring to Hegel's phrase "the present is the highest" (*WG*, vol. 19, 686), Kroner, probably the most important representative of "modern Hegelianism," explains, "Indeed, it is true that every present is the product of the past," but in it "freedom comes into action in the course of history." The present is not history because it makes history.[38] It has in itself the certainty of the past, just as there is uncertainty of the future, and unifies reality and freedom against the will of man to certainty and change.

Hegel speaks directly of the "absolute present" only once (*Vern*, 181ff.). However, the present, presence, and objectivity belong indispensably to the basic concept of Spirit. And, likewise, Spirit and freedom belong together. If freedom is determined as being-with-itself (passim; e.g., *WG*, vol. 11, 44), then Spirit is the self-moving subject of freedom, since it is the "return into itself, to make . . . itself an object" (*Vern*, 181). And with the concept of "return," there is, as Hegel says, also "a certain cyclical idea" (181). For the sake of Spirit, which has itself as the center, the historical progress in the consciousness of freedom is not an indeterminate process into the infinite[39] (181), and it does not, on its account and measured by it, ever reach a situation that existed when Spirit was not already there first. In the historical self-fulfilled "now" the ideas both of a cycle and of infinite progress collapse. The "now" can, according to Hegel following Aristotle, be determined in a similar fashion as that in the return of the free self from externalization and alienation: "On the one hand, the now is equal to the point in space; but it is at the same time a part, it contains the future and the past, it is an other and a one at the same time" (*WG*, vol. 18, 383ff.). Freedom just as much as an open situation needs the present, which demands as a totality (eternity) something absolutely encompassing. Therefore, Hegel writes, so to speak, as if in an intentional distancing from Bloch's Marxist, mystical, and eschatological ontology of the being-not-yet[40] [*Noch-Nicht-Seins*]: "The idea is present, the Spirit immortal, i.e. it is not yet past and is not yet, but is essentially now" (*WG*, vol. 11, 120; cf. *Vern*, 22).[41]

VII

With this, the point is reached once again where separation must be thought. In Hegel we read, "In order to pick the rose in the cross of

the present, one must take the cross upon oneself" (*WG*, vol. 15, 293).
And the cross means the death of God, the division of the absolute,
the becoming unstable of everything to which one can hold fast, the
Phenomenology of Spirit as the "highway of despair" (*Phä*, 67); it means
at the same time the absolute present of suffering without hope of a
mundane improvement. Reason thus comes into history insofar as it is
concerned essentially with its destruction. The philosophy of history is
based directly on the observation and insight "that the richest creation,
the most beautiful life can find destruction in history, that we wander
among the ruins of the excellent . . . the passions have destroyed it. . . .
Everything seems to pass and nothing to remain" (*Vern*, 34ff.).

However, insofar as Spirit is at work behind the passions, the destruction [*Untergang*] is at the same time a "transition" [*Übergang*]. What
Hegel says about world-historical individuals—"that the special interest
of passion is thus inseparable from the activity of the universal" (*Vern*,
105)—is equally valid for groups, peoples, and cultures. The principal
meaning of the concept "the cunning of reason" lies in the fact that
it makes visible Spirit and the idea behind the passions as something
actually negating that undermines itself in the same way as it undermines
the passions.[42] With the concept of Spirit, for Hegel, we already have
the answer contained in the question, "Who or what actually acts, what
is the subject of history?" This moving principle, which everyone who
consciously acts shares, is for the sake of its positivity and freedom the
active negative. Hegel says, "This is Spirit itself . . . since it dissolves all
determinate content" (*Vern*, 178). For the "thinking subject and infinite reflection in itself," everything can in principle appear as merely
something "given, or immediate, an authority" with which it deals as a
limitation of its freedom or arbitrariness (*Vern*, 179). However, insofar
as the acting unity is a natural, finite being, the attempt to translate its
consciousness of freedom radically into practice means its destruction.
"The life of a people," writes Hegel, "brings the fruit to maturity. . . .
This fruit, however, does not fall into his lap, where it produced itself,
it does not receive it to enjoy it; on the contrary, it becomes for him
a bitter drink . . . the cost of the drink is its destruction" (*Vern*, 72). As
long as the spirits of peoples are limited, this destruction is, as we said
earlier, simultaneously the transition to a new historical form. With the
attempt to realize freedom for "all" through a world society, the problem
is created about what this encompassing totality could pass over into.
Spirit surmounts even this so that its negative power, as we can already
see, does not stop before it.

With Hegel used as the starting point, the question of the end of
history has been raised in its simplest and most acute form, although

Hegel himself had never posed the question in this way. The other meanings of the end of history mentioned at the beginning can also be explained based on Hegel, as has already been done by many commentators. Fundamentally, we can still hold fast to the fact that Hegel's philosophy of history is not eschatological in the same sense that Löwith and Taubes understand eschatology in the humanities or in the sense that Kojève understands it in the social sciences. In this connection, we should avoid saying Judeo-Christian, but rather we must differentiate between Jewish and Christian eschatology. According to the Christian understanding, which must be presupposed in Hegel, albeit in terms of a rather idiosyncratic interpretation, history does not come to completion in its final epoch but rather in passing through its actual end. The messiah was already there. The kingdom of God is not of this world. We do not need to worry about the point in time of its beginning. The remark of Herder which is thought wholly in the spirit of classical historicity is more human and more rational than the utopian concealment of the harshness of the destruction and than the blind aiming at the concealed end: "The father of the universe would have shown infinitely more care . . . if there were to lie in humanity an invisible seed for receiving happiness and virtue on the whole earth in all of its ages, which educates in different ways, and which appears in different forms, but which internally is only a measure and mixture of forces."[43] Accordingly, progress can at best prepare better conditions for old Adam.

Yet Herder and Hegel speak of progress, and Hegel attributes to his time, apart from its relative character as present, an absolute position, and so, as Brunstäd noted in his edition of Hegel's *Philosophy of History*, the question about the end of history, from which perspective one can ultimately understand the meaning of history, stands in intimate connection with the "theory of the historical possibility of the absoluteness of Christianity."[44] The end at which Hegel sees himself and his epoch standing is, for him, only the unfolded middle period of history. This middle, however, as the birth and death of God, is not the unfolding of a principle which was at work from the beginning of history. Insofar as the middle period is the progressive revelation of Spirit which was at work from the beginning, it causes the revelation and with it the sharpened claim *of separation*, which dominates through Spirit in nature. The incarnation leads this separation to its extreme (the death of God as "infinite loss"), to reconciliation. The reconciliation that Hegel sees completed religiously with the Reformation and politically with the bourgeois revolution (insofar as it is accompanied by a reformation) grows in the soil of the so reconciled, acute separation. To the extent that reconciliation consumes it, it reduces the possibility of its continued mundane existence.

Löwith cites Hegel's *Lectures on the Philosophy of History*: "The business of history is only that religion appears as human reason, that the religious principle which dwells in the heart of man be also brought forth as mundane freedom" (*Löw 2*, 60). Referring to J. Burckhardt, Löwith writes, "He was completely free of modern prejudices especially from that of Hegel, who saw in history a process of progressive development, through which the idea of Christianity is supposed to realize itself more and more in the world history" (*Löw 2*, 37). If the prejudice that is called "modern" here is supposed to be an exegesis or an interpretation of Hegel's doctrine, as the passage cited out of context by Löwith clearly says, then it should be pointed out that Hegel meant something different by it. In the *Philosophy of History* he does not speak primarily about the development of Christianity[45] but rather about the "progress in consciousness of freedom." This freedom is, however, *also* worldly, that is, more precisely political freedom, as the passage cited by Löwith shows. However, it does not say that "the religious principle" and "worldly freedom" are identical, nor does it say that the "religious principle" originates from the heart and because of this necessarily comes into reality radically changed. Hegel calls it rather the "folly of our time to want to create and develop civil constitutions independent of religion" (*Vern*, 123). (Elsewhere he writes, "States and laws are nothing other than the appearing of religion in the relations of reality" [*WG*, vol. 11, 524].) He criticizes the French Revolution for the "false principle that the chains of right and of freedom are cast off without the liberation of conscience, i.e. that a revolution can take place without a reformation" (*WG*, vol. 11, 564; cf. *WG*, vol. 10, 440). As long as it "holds out vis-à-vis religion in general, the concrete absolute content," the revolutionary principle of societal freedom remains merely "formal" (*WG*, vol. 11, 554). . . .[46]

IX

Hegel's philosophical history is a history of "reconciliation" from Christ on. That this concept is not easy to understand is shown first by the fact that the unfolding of reconciliation is simultaneously the history of the most radical and therefore necessary revolution, at least for as long as history lasts. With respect to radical passages in the gospels such as, for example, "You should not imagine that I am come to send peace to the earth . . ." (Matt. 10:34), Hegel says, "In this lies an abstraction from everything which belongs to reality, even from the ethical ties. One can say, never was there such revolutionary talk than in the gospels, for everything else of value is seen as something meaningless and not worthy of paying attention to" (*WG*, vol. 11, 420). For Hegel as for Rousseau[47] and in a certain sense also for Hobbes, who wanted to fence out this source of revolution once and for all, philosophy knows about this revolutionary radicalness which a priori has overtaken every political revolution. From it follows, for Hegel, the finite distancing of philosophy from the political reality of his time, in which Greek freedom in its Christian intensification and expansion to include all human beings seems to develop itself in grand style of democratic revolution. But political freedom and reconciliation are not the same, and, therefore, subjective freedom assumes the form of concrete, political mediation of the particular and the universal, to which belongs, according to Hegel, the "subordination of the arbitrary will" (*WG*, vol. 11, 568). In the *Philosophy of Right*, Hegel tries to work out the contemporary stage in the development of the concept of freedom in a concrete manner together with the "laws of real freedom."

Revolution and protest against the existing order issue from Spirit (although animals have needs and suffer like humans, they do not revolt). Political revolutions arise through a transference of innerness into action, through the temporarily equal connection of religion and politics, which is always in danger of being perverted into politics of religion[48] or religion of politics. Reconciliation, however, is first and foremost not of a political but rather of a religious nature. As such, it is the fulfillment of the "Jewish sentiment," which, according to Hegel, in contrast to the philosophy of the Greek and Roman world at the time, demanded a stoicism "hardened in reality and in it reconciliation" (*WG*, vol. 11, 412). However, in relation to this demand from which it grows, it is reconciliation of the sort that Hegel describes in the following passage: "The infinite loss only becomes compensated by its infinity and through it becomes an infinite gain" (*WG*, vol. 11, 413). The death of God even more than his birth grounds Christian knowing on the "unity of man and God" (*WG*, vol. 11, 414). His death is the worldly condition for the resurrection and for the beginning of the kingdom of God as kingdom of Spirit. Hegel says of the unity that is created by this, "Here one must remember the Greek anthropomorphism about which it is said that it did not go far enough" (*WG*, vol. 11, 414; cf. *WG*, vol. 11, 325). It went too far for the mass of Jews incited by their elders, since it did not fulfill their anthropomorphic hopes. Likewise, Hegel's "speculative Good Friday" (*WG*, vol. 11, 433) went too far for many of his contemporaries. In the later Hegel, the concept of "theodicy" as "justification of God in history" (*WG*, vol. 11, 569) is particularly troublesome in this context. However, it does not contain the presumption to want to justify God or the historical action of man before God or man taken together with God as mere host, but rather Hegel's account means "to see the worldly, the other in God, to know it as divine in itself, to make it divine" (*WG*, vol. 19, 100). Theodicy, as Hegel understands it, applies the separation to the absolute, which it cannot harm, and by applying the finite to the infinite, which by this is not made finite, it sinks the suffering of the world into the chasm of the infinite good, since it understands it as necessary for the mediation of the unity of man with God, the most important reconciliation. Just as man must assume the collapse of everything historical in order to recognize reason in history, so also reconciliation touches on the recognition of the necessity of suffering and collapse (as a presupposition for its sublation). Seen in this way, the secularized Jewish hope was illusory, and, on account of it, the chosen people prepared the death of the messiah who arose from it and was primarily thought by it, thereby initiating the reunification of man with God against its own concept of reconciliation. Its corrupted concept of reconciliation had received its right and had contributed to actual reconciliation. At the same time the Greek anthropomorphism and the late Greek, Roman ethic of stoicism were surpassed. The raised hopelessness in stoicism was just as sublated as confirmed, and Hegel in his *Logic* writes, "*si fractus illabatur orbis, impavidum ferient ruinae*, a Roman said, and the Christian is supposed to find himself even more in this indifference" (*Log*, vol. 1, 74).

With this sort of reconciliation, which seems to confirm Goethe's claim about the result of all historical observations "that it has been miserable in all times and in all countries" (quoted in *Löw 2*, 209), the end of history in itself is reached according to Hegel. The actual further development leads to the end, as present middle, into itself. Löwith also cites L. Bloy's claim, "Mankind began to suffer *in hope*, and therefore we speak of a Christian age" (*Löw 2*, 186). Hegel's concept of reconciliation means the same thing. The self-developing freedom makes possible this kind of suffering for all men. To juxtapose the stoic "*nec spe nec metu*" (*Löw 2*, 186) to this principle of hope which apparently but not actually alleviates suffering ("*contra spem in spem credere*," Paul says, Romans 4:18) means to pass by Hegel and a large chapter of European ethics, which Löwith, on the other hand, does not want to do. Not only is the end or the transition to the end-phase of history revolutionary, but the ever present middle is no less so. The change concerns primarily the subjectivity, the most inner space of freedom before itself. Starting from there, it can call forth material changes in society and the world, which nevertheless even turn over into unfreedom when they no longer come from that middle, when they, for example, reify present hopes in a detour over the future.

That Hegel did not tie the hopes of the bad infinite to the French Revolution, because it is for him the next most important stage in the development of that middle after the Reformation, is shown in, for example, the conclusion of that passage in the *Philosophy of History* which is often cited as testimony for his positive orientation toward the revolution which he maintained into the Berlin period. There we read, "a raised emotion was dominant at that time, an enthusiasm of the Spirit ran through the world as if it had only just come to the real reconciliation of the divine with the world" (*WG*, vol. 11, 557ff.). Concerning the "as if it had come," elsewhere (e.g., *Phä*, 413ff.) he expresses argued caution toward the bloody illusions and distortions of reconciliation and freedom. The revolution destroys its goal if it does not have as its basic principle the permanent reformation of the one Church, which Hegel described thus: "Everyone has in himself to complete the work of reconciliation . . . thus Christian freedom became real" (*WG*, vol. 11, 523; cf. 532). It is this sort of realizing repetition of the middle-historical reconciliation that is meant when Hegel speaks of the end of history.

To speak about this at all and even to orient the individual and political praxis in the present times[49] toward the goal of history must depend upon "whether one can recognize the time period . . . whether that, which is the final goal of the world, has really come into reality in a universally valid conscious manner" (*Vern*, 45). Hegel continues, "Now the characteristic thing of the Christian religion is that this time has come with it; this constitutes the absolute epoch in world history." Other formulations such as the following also aim at the historical, universal concept of the absolute epoch and the absolute present: "and with this, the new and last banner is formed around which the peoples gather themselves" (*WG*, vol. 11, 524), and "the Christian world is the world of completion; the principle is fulfilled and with it the end of days has become complete" (*WG*, vol. 11, 438). These passages speak of a middle-historically effective end and of a present redemption. Hegel held to this position from the beginning of his public philosophical activity in Jena, as is shown by a passage from this period which takes dialectical philosophy and religion together against philosophy of reflection. This passage is worth citing in full:

> Religion so little shares its view with this philosophy of absolute
> subjectivity that while the former understands evil as some merely
> accidental and arbitrary fact about nature already completed in itself,
> the latter on the other hand represents evil as a necessity of finite
> nature, as one with the concept of nature: but for this necessity it
> represents at the same time an eternal, i.e. not just one redemption

postponed in the infinite progress and never to be realized, but rather a truly real and present redemption; and it views nature, insofar as it is observed as finite and individual, as a possible reconciliation whose original possibility is the subjective posited in the original likeness of God; its objective side, however, is the reality in its eternal human value, the identity of that possibility and of this reality but through Spirit as the being-one of the subject with the man-become-God; so that the world reconstructed in itself redeems and is made holy in a completely different manner than always according to the ideal of the moral order of the world, that the volcanoes, etc. will not always remain as they are, that they will all gradually burn out, the hurricanes will become tamer, the illnesses less painful, the atmosphere of the forests and the swamps will become better, etc. (*WG*, vol. 1, 422ff.)

X. Conclusions

1. With this exposition, it cannot be doubted that "civil society" (the system of needs) can reach its goal, seen purely technologically or social-technologically, to be able to keep living all humans who are born until their natural death (insofar as they do not die from technological accidents, or new or still incurable diseases, suicide or war among competing ideological blocks) and to make possible for them a life of prosperity and growing leisure. Therefore, it really leads to a new historical epoch with respect to the basis of life. Concerning, merely the standpoint of technical possibilities, it cannot cease to amaze that this goal has not yet been reached. It appears that there are resistances of another sort which technical humanism can only understand as "irrational," thereby showing that it in fact does not understand them.

2. Civil society can be defined by its goals or by its common concept of freedom, which determines these goals so that it encompasses both the Western and Eastern forms of democracy. Its concept of freedom, heretofore more ideological than practical, guarantees to everyone a share in the decision about the social implications of his interests in survival, prosperity, leisure time, and education, by which education is understood in a mostly instrumental fashion vis-à-vis the first three. To the question, "For what purpose is this freedom?" the answer is in order of importance: life, prosperity, leisure time. This freedom makes the means of its fulfillment into its goal. Leisure time, indeed, seems to make being human possible outside of the world of means and work, and industrial civilization could even (again) plan for an unalienated

work, which, although it would be economically less efficient, would nevertheless provide people with the possibility of freely unfolding their energies in the realm of necessity; however, as long as the goals of the social process are effusive, the necessary ends and means become mixed up and mutually corrupt each other and force all spheres of life into their course. With the criticism of this secular chiliasm, Hegel can be consulted because he remains sober, since he is doing rational theology when he applies it to society.

3. Now it may have been necessary—as the maxim says, "ask the impossible so that the possible be done"—to bring about at first the process of the social domination of nature only through the confirmation of effusive hopes. But the result of this is that from a certain point on the problem arises or should arise in the "most advanced" countries about how one will exorcise the conjured spirit. And here the sciences, which take their presuppositions from the process itself, prove to be helpless. The only escape from all of these problems that they know is either in the direction which they—again using the orientation in the process heretofore—call "forward" or the indecisive "on the one hand and on the other hand," which is on every side conveniently protected from the dialectical conjunction of opposites. This indecisiveness changes nothing with its possibly additional, merely descriptive "at the same time."

4. However, it is not clear why there should be only these two directions, backwards and forwards, and not also sideways, upwards, or downwards. When the only alternative is either to let the large trend go on (liberalism, reform-conservatism,) or even to overtake it (revolutionary progressivism), one can assume that in this fashion an infinite progress arises but not one which approaches a determinate goal (e.g., the realm of freedom) but rather one that accelerates progress, not in the sense of a going forward [*Vor-schrittes*], but rather in the sense of a quicker and quicker progress, a flight from the already achieved. Every attempt to get the development under control, to subordinate it to determinate criteria and to direct it consciously in a direction which is thought to be good, must, on the other hand, appear increasingly reactionary, romantic or even naive.

5. When the process can only continue in the same direction as before—sometimes quicker, sometimes slower—and every kind of reversal of the trend is impossible, one can conclude from the disproportional increase of functional and instrumental reason which necessarily accompanies it that it becomes more and more a matter of chance whether the forces set free by the technical domination of nature are used for good or destructive purposes. Under such conditions, these forces become more and more dangerous in proportion to their size.

6. It would therefore be rational first to change the religious, ethical, and political presuppositions of the application of this means instead of expecting any improvement from its further growth. Since man is also nature, the growing social-technical possibilities do not solve the problem of *a domination of the domination of nature* but rather they make it more acute. Thus it becomes evident that the (Platonic) problem of a conscious synthesis of individual and political ethics lies at its foundation.

15

The End of History in Hegel

H. S. Harris

When we are studying Hegel's answer to any question, or his solution to any problem, we must always look first at the systematic context in which the problem is raised, or the question asked. Hegel's philosophy of world history comes as the climactic stage of the development of "objective spirit"; and it provides the transition to the spheres of "Absolute Spirit." The philosophical comprehension of political history provides the ultimate context for our political theory; and then it leads us on to the sphere in which we are directly aware of "the Absolute." Our political science comes to an end, when we recognize that "the world's history is the world's court of judgment." But that court of judgment has jurisdiction only over the objective forms of political and social organization. The judgment of history is not the "Last Judgment" for everything and everyone. There are modes of experience which emerge and develop in history, but which are recognized as transhistorical; and when philosophy, as the historical quest for wisdom, reaches its goal, we can see and say why Greek art has an enduring significance for us, even though the Greek religion (which their art expressed in its highest form) has passed over into history just as completely and irrevocably as the "city-state." Our political thought and action exists in the context of a religious ideal that will not allow us to divide the human community into "us" and "them," the freemen and the slaves, the civilized and the barbarians. But only the arrival of philosophical "wisdom" has enabled us to see and say what is "absolute" about our religion (just as it is we, and not the Greeks themselves, who have the "absolute" consciousness of Greek art).

We shall come back to the absolute judgment that is beyond the judgment of history. For the moment we should notice two things. First, that if there is a philosophical judgment that is transhistorical, then the idea of an "end of history" makes sense. For philosophy may be able to show us that there is a condition of things beyond which we cannot go, a condition from which any effective departure would be a regression. (I shall not need to persuade anyone that regressive departures are possible, since we are all conscious that history may come to its empirical end in our actual self-destruction.) Secondly, whatever is judged to be "absolute" cannot be historically dependent. For instance, a religion that necessarily requires the infallibility of its divinely authorized human head cannot be "absolute religion." (I refrain from saying "the absolute religion," precisely because the definite article tempts us to think of a determinately historical reference point—and that is a mistake.) Whatever the faith of the believer may say about its founder, the papacy is a human institution. So it is subject to the judgment of history. It may disappear. That, in itself, would not be a Last Judgment upon it. The logical difficulty about it is that we cannot know absolutely that its disappearance would be a regression.

What can we say rationally, to establish that something actual (and hence subject to the court of history) embodies an absolute value, so that its loss could only be a regression? This is the focal problem of the Hegelian philosophy of history. Hegel offered the philosophy of world history to his audience as a "theodicy." But he was speaking to an audience who were (at least nominally) believing Lutherans. When all of his talk of "theodicy" and "providence" came to the ears of a later generation for whom Marx and Nietzsche were already prophets, and Freud was soon to be one, they laughed him to scorn. The best minds who were sympathetic to Hegel in that generation, agreed with Croce that the speculative philosophy of history was a mistake. The Hegelian philosophy of history itself fell under the "judgment of history," and was seen not to be part of "Absolute Knowledge." In Croce's own language for the distinction, it was not "living" but "dead."

To Hegel's own Lutheran audience it was historically obvious that the providence of God had revealed the fallibility of the Pope—and even the Catholics in the audience were not at that time faithfully obligated to believe otherwise. To Croce, and to me, in our post-Hegelian world, it is logically (or philosophically) obvious—as it was to Kant and even to Lessing before Hegel—that the existence of the God who is to be "justified" in history cannot be established by appeal to history. But Hegel had read Lessing and Kant; and he put philosophy *beyond* religion. So his "Absolute Knowing" does not depend upon any form of "faith."[1]

Lessing was one of Hegel's earliest heroes;[2] and this present essay aims to make clear that he was still striving to be faithful (in his fashion) to Kant even in the years of his maturity and fame. The Providence whose existence is exhibited in history was the one defined by Kant. For Kant it was indeed an object of rational faith. But Hegel's way of being faithful to Kant was a lifelong struggle to eliminate the necessity for the "faith" for which Kant claimed to have made room. We can accept Hegel's doctrine of Providence without any act of faith in a controlling intelligence that is beyond or above our present world of experience (with its "boundaries" as set by Kant).

Once we accept the view that for Hegel himself the faith in Providence to which he appeals has already been transformed into the recognition of the objective presence of reason in our actual world of experience, it becomes clear that the proper way for us[3] to understand Hegel's philosophy of history is to grasp its relation to the problem that Kant set him. Kant's essay on world history was written in 1784 to defend the claim that "the ultimate purpose of the human race is to achieve the most perfect civic constitution."[4] This claim is reflected in his title: "Idea for a Universal History from a World-Citizen's Point of View." Kant begins with the "hope that if we attend to the play of freedom of the human will in the large, we may be able to discern a regular movement in it" (12).

The essay is organized as as sequence of nine theses; and the driving force of "the regular movement" is explained in the fourth thesis, which lays it down that "The means employed by Nature to bring about the development of all the capacities of men is their antagonism in society, in so far as this becomes in the end the cause of a lawful order among them" (15). By "antagonism" Kant means what he calls (in a phrase that has become proverbial) the "unsocial sociability of man" (15). This "unsocial sociability" is exactly what Hegel identifies as the dialectical phase of reason (as present objectively in the historical order of human life). Having pointed that out, we can pass straight on to Kant's fifth thesis, which states that "The greatest problem for the human race . . . is the achievement of a universal civil society that administers the right" (16).

Kant thought that the "complete solution" of this task was "impossible because from such crooked wood as man is made of, nothing perfectly straight can be built" (17–18). But his final thesis was that "a philosophical attempt to work out universal history according to a plan of nature that aims at perfect civil union in the human race must be regarded as possible, and as itself promoting this intent of nature" (23). In this connection he remarked that "a justification [*Rechtfertigung*] of nature—or better, of Providence—is no trivial motive for the choice of a standpoint towards World History" (25).

This was the challenge that Hegel accepted.[5] He set to work to interpret world history from this point of view in as much detail as he could. But he does not think of himself as possessing any standard of reason except the one that our "unsocial sociability" has already produced in our history. He is not already a "world-citizen" in an ideal, noumenal community of human moral reason. So he does not regard human nature as "crooked wood." What Kant sees as "crookedness" is only the dialectical structure of reason itself in history. Our rational comprehension of that structure is the perfection of reason (and the comprehension is not its straightening, but its circular closing). The contradictory nature that makes us want (through our substantial identification with our society) to be more than we naturally are, while at the same time we continue to want our own way in everything—the contradiction that Kant calls our "unsocial sociability"—is regarded by Hegel as nothing but the essentially dialectical structure of our practical rationality. Thus reason is the dialectical identity of the actual (*das Wirkliche*, or what works, what is effective) with the "rational" (*das Vernünftige*, our social goal of achieving the spiritual expression of our human nature and capacities). In this identity, the actual moment is whatever turns out to be effective. What is actual may be our own desires and will; or it may be whatever real complex of facts in the world prevails against our will. The rational moment is the spiritual aim of our social activity; and we are continually redefining that in terms of what we find to be possible, i.e., what projects we can actually realize.

"History" is properly the story of our gradual arrival at the clear consciousness of how the dialectical identity of the actual and the rational should be conceived and articulated. For this is the comprehension, the conceptual grasp, of our freedom. History can be said to "end," therefore, when we are universally aware of the conceptual structure of this identity. That will be the moment when Kant's "Nature, or better Providence" is no longer a necessary postulate, because we have understood our human situation, in the only "absolute" sense in which it is possible for us to understand it. Absolute Knowledge is the knowledge of what our human knowing is in principle (including the knowledge of its self-positing, or logically necessary limits). At the end of history we shall have understood why all of our historical action has the structure "Man proposes, Providence disposes." We shall be able to say, then, that Providence (like Sartre's hell) "is other people." Our achievements (like our failures) become the actual raw material for new rational purposes. That is the "cunning of reason." Once this structure of "infinite teleology" has been comprehended no yet higher purpose can declare itself in the later disposition of our own consciously world-historical activities. That is a logically necessary truth; and any merely imaginable knowledge that goes beyond this Absolute Knowing—the supposed divine knowledge of all future destinies, for example—is not "knowledge" for us at all because it violates our concept of knowing altogether. The Absolute Knowledge of our human goal (to be rational) leads us to our comprehensive logical concept of the knowing that is "absolute" for us. Its being "for us" does not make the "absoluteness" relative, because what we comprehend is precisely how this concept comprehends us, our world, and our knowing of both. It is precisely this necessary "overgrasping" of the "for us" relation, that logically requires us to reject any supposedly more comprehensive cognition as logically meaningless. This concept that comprehends all of our cognition is "the Idea," or the fully developed concept of reason.

Kant thought he knew what the human goal is, in principle. But he did not think that he was, or that we ever could be, at the end of history. He knew that we had not realized the goal, and he (probably) thought that we never would. Hegel, of course, cannot even suppose that he knows what the goal is, without holding that the goal is (in principle) realized. In terms of practical objectivity, Absolute Knowing is the coincidence of the actual with the rational, and of the rational with the actual. We need to speak of the identity in both ways (as Hegel did) because our "unsocial sociability" makes the two identities different. Soviet communism has finally come to grief because the party ideologues ignored the difference. That "the actual is rational" means that what drives us is rational, i.e., there is always an understandable necessity underneath the way things have turned out. That "the rational is actual" means that what pulls or draws us is comprehensively rational. For the two propositions to coincide harmoniously we must know both what social condition is universally desirable (since only what everyone desires can have an actually effective drawing power); and what bounding necessities we are subject to (since only when these driving necessities are assimilated can what is rationally desirable be effectively desired. The middle term, in which the efficient cause (or driving force) of history is properly reconciled with the final cause (or drawing force), is the rational state.

Hegel thought that he could define the middle term; he offered us his definition in the *Philosophy of Right*. But in his *Lectures on World History*, he did not say that "history has reached its end" (or, less paradoxically, that "the goal of Reason is fulfilled"). On the contrary, he concluded his lectures with a paragraph that ends in an appropriately Kantian way: "This is how far consciousness has come." We might well take this to imply that there is still a long way to go, perhaps a "bad infinite" distance (as Kant seems to have thought); but since Hegel thought that philosophy itself was "complete," a more modest hypothesis would seem to be indicated. Study of the *Philosophy of Right* suggests that a plausible case can be made for the view that Hegel was cautious about the end of history because in the Prussian state itself, the rational was not yet completely actual. Eduard Gans already took it that way.

Kojève applied the same hypothesis in his own reading. In his vision Hegel was the philosophical interpreter of the work of Napoleon.[6] That seems plausible to me, though my own interpretation does not require or depend upon any particular answer to the problem. Even if Kojève is right on that issue, he is mistaken about some deeper ones. This becomes clear when we examine the arguments of his latest disciple, Francis Fukuyama.

Fukuyama's theme is the universal triumph of Western culture. Current events have given a near-tragic pathos to the question he raises at the end of his article: "The real question for the future . . . is the degree to which Soviet elites have assimilated the consciousness of the universal homogeneous state that is post-Hitler Europe."[7] We have to notice, first, that Marxism (including Soviet Marxism) is a Western idea. It is a one-sided form of the Hegelian philosophy of history, in which far too much emphasis is put on the objective rationality of the actual. Fukuyama writes as if his own Hobbesian theory of possessive individualism is a more adequate comprehension of social reality than Marxism, but in the Hegelian perspective that does not appear to be the case. Kojève himself, we must remember, was a Marxist; and although his ontology will not permit him to appreciate the Hegelian thesis that it is the ethical substance that becomes equally "subjective" at the end of history, Kojève did retain the Kantian critical awareness of the human goal. Alan Bloom is right to protest that "There are elements of Kojève's thought about the end of history which Fukuyama does not give sufficient weight. The goodness of the end of history . . . consists in the possibility of unconstrained philosophizing and in the moral recognition of all human beings as ends in themselves."[8]

Fukuyama has taken over Kojève's interpretation of Hegel as a bourgeois political economist in the tradition of Adam Smith. All that Kojève discovered in Hegel was Kant's ideal of a universal civil society, shorn of its noumenal underpinning. "Western liberal democracy is the final form of human government" (4). Hegel recognized the work of Napoleon as "the universalization of the state incorporating the principles of liberty and equality" (5). The Marxist fraternity of Kojève and the Christian fraternity of Hegel are missing here. Fukuyama identifies Kojève's "universal homogeneous state" with the "universal civil society" of the world market. Now that history has ended "what remains is primarily economic activity" (5). It would be hard for Kojève as a scientific Marxist to reject this interpretation of his reading of Hegel. But something is missing. Calvin Coolidge said that "America's business is business." Now we are faced with an American who says that "Business is the only business of the world." Hegel called that view "barbarism," and Marx would have agreed.

We can see that there is something important missing, even without direct reference to the sphere of Absolute Spirit. Hegel himself was the son of a financial official; and he would certainly have approved of someone who left the academic life to become a civil servant (as Kojève did) when he saw that Absolute Knowledge had been reached. But Hegel would also have pointed out that being a civil servant represents a critical comment on the conclusion that "only business remains." For it implies that "being just" is different from, and more important than, "being rich."

Hegel himself was not a free market economist; and he did not think that political history had ended (or could end) because states were bound to make war on one another. This was necessary in order to make us aware of our substantial foundation in the objective way of life of our community (which war calls upon us to defend) and of our higher spiritual purposes beyond the economic sphere. It must be conceded that the First World War was a reductio ad absurdum of Hegel's concept of war. But in accepting the Marxist conclusion, Kojève was not just correcting an error—or a piece of Hegelian shortsightedness. He was abandoning Hegel's spiritualism—his belief that the rational is actual—altogether. Even Marx, for all his "historical materialism," did not abandon it so completely. Kojève, the world-citizen, uprooted from his substantial place by the war, understood the lesson of the war. But he learned it only negatively. He became a disillusioned Marxist—a Marxian skeptic. Marx was a somewhat better Hegelian than Kojève, because he was still an objective idealist. He believed in "fraternity" as the spiritual substance— the *Wirklichkeit* of reason. Kojève understood the drive of rational nature toward liberty and equality; but he did not comprehend the substantial pull of fraternity, because he knew by actual experience that Marx was mistaken in his belief that fraternity can be articulated and embodied by political action and institutions alone.[9] Marx had overlooked the unsocial side of our Kantian sociability. Like Kant's enlightened predecessors he thought that it was produced by history, rather than productive of history. Kojève grasped what Fukuyama aptly calls "the primacy of consciousness"; and he grasped Hegel's point in claiming that the life and death struggle is "the first experience of consciousness." The spiritual desire for freedom is more fundamental than the natural urge for self-preservation; but the drive for self-conscious freedom is primitively selfish.

Even in Fukuyama's proclamation of "the end of history" two non-economic sources of conflict remain: religion and nationalism. If we define "fascism" as a "natural religion" of the tribe or nation (in the Hegelian, not the enlightened, sense of "natural religion"), we can see that these two apparently disparate forces both belong to the range of the absolute concept of religion. The "homogeneous" state never will be actually "homogeneous" because the cultural differences that appear so irrational to an economic rationalist are manifestations of a spiritual freedom which logically belongs to the higher sphere. That higher sphere is more comprehensive; so it embraces everything that counts as irrational in the perspective of the universal civil society. "Religion" runs through a spectrum that goes all the way from the immediate substantiality of the "Light Essence" to the reciprocal self-surrender of the finite and the infinite consciousness in the gospel of universal forgiveness. But as soon as finite consciousness ceases to be simply a transient accident of substance—as soon as finite life counts for something positive—we are visibly in the world of "fraternity." We begin with the primitive fascism of the "animal religions"—in which every tribal group of "brothers" is engaged in a life and death struggle—and we move toward the recognized identity of God with his (or her) whole human family. The stages of religious development must go hand in hand with the stages of political evolution. Hegel thought that the French Revolution had failed in France itself, because the Reformation had failed in France. He would not be surprised by the political emancipation of the female sex without a violent revolution, because in the Lutheran vision, God is "the I that is We." (S)he rises in every finite consciousness.

On the other hand, the abolition of slavery—which Hegel took to be a definite mark of the maturity of the modern religious consciousness— could not take place in the United States without a violent upheaval of revolutionary proportions. Yet the United States was certainly closer to the Hegelian political ideal than Prussia. Moreover, since the political liberation of the slaves, the integration of their black descendants into the "universal civil society" has never been as "homogeneous" as the absorption of European immigrants of all kinds. Black poverty has some roots in the survival of the tribal consciousness of "animal religion." The natural difference of color is an alienating factor that tells against spiritual identity of moral feeling and rational substance. All differences of culture (and especially of language) operate in this same way. Differences of religion are—quite correctly—perceived as oppositions of will about conscious substantial identification. Living together and communicating effectively does weaken and wear down these substantial conflicts. But since it is humanly essential that there should be substantial identities (commitments for which individuals make serious sacrifices, and for which they morally feel that they ought to be prepared to die) it is quite unthinkable that all substantial conflicts should be worn away into the universal civil society in which the prevailing ideal is that of "telling the truth and paying one's debts." The cosmopolitanism of Marx and Kojève is as utopian as that of Kant (from whom they inherited it). Fukuyama is quite mistaken when he says that we do not need "the perspective of religion" in order to recognize the spiritual emptiness of economic liberalism" (14). It is not the recognition of the void but the filling of it that is the problem. We can all see that the breakup of the Soviet Union would make the problems of its many cultures and ethnic groups worse than they have always been.

Fukuyama writes as if that religious conflict can simply be ignored. He seems to think that economic liberalism will sublate religious and ethnic ties as soon as the "homogeneous" system exists. But the Arab world shows how a universal religion becomes communally particularized in obstinate resistance to liberal homogenization; so does Yugoslavia (or even Northern Ireland and Québec). Having grasped the "primacy of consciousness" Fukuyama can see that "the way in which any state defines its national interest is not universal but rests on some kind of prior ideological basis" (16); and he understands that the colonial imperialism of the nineteenth century was an ideology in which Hegel himself was still entangled. Yet he still affirms confidently that "International life for the part of the world that has reached the end of history is far more preoccupied with economics than with politics or strategy" (16). For him it is only a question of time before the market swallows politics.

China and the Middle East must obviously reach the end of history, if Fukuyama's thesis is to be validated. But he himself says that "it matters very little what strange thoughts occur to people in Albania or Burkina Faso" (9). This sounds "Hegelian" enough. But someone who knows the place of the philosophy of history in Hegel's system ought to reflect that Albania has already given us our most vividly obvious living saint; and no one would have expected a world savior to come out of Roman Galilee— so how can we be sure that a gospel of salvation (or damnation) will not emerge from Burkina Faso?

The Hegel of Kojève and Fukuyama is simply Hobbes reborn, but disguised in Hegel's mask and mantle. The masquerade gains much of its plausibility from the Hobbesian lesson that history has taught us since Hegel died. Hegel did not think that the end of philosophy spelled the end of history because he expected that history would continue to be the "world's court of judgment." Since his time a Hobbesian sovereign power has emerged from our political struggles in the shape of atomic war. We can no longer go to that court of judgment, because it offers only the monosyllabic verdict of the French Revolutionary Terror. In this way, one of Kant's enlightened deductions about the end of history has been validated: "In the end, war itself will be seen as not only so artificial, in outcome so uncertain for both sides, in aftereffects so painful in the form of an evergrowing war-debt that cannot be met—a new invention—that it will be regarded as a most dubious undertaking" (Beck, 23).

But this does not mean that the "end of history" is "the achievement of a universal civil society." Hegel saw clearly that world history (in the proper sense) began with that. The Romans established it in the imperial order where the history of God truly comprehended as Spirit began. In the world of the absolute religion—which has to become a philosophical ideal of universal fraternity in order to be absolute—a plurality of ideologies and cultures will continue to flourish, because the achievement of religious "absoluteness" involves the sublation of "superiority" and "authority." "Liberal democracy" cannot become the "guardian-ideal" of all cultures. Indeed it is already visibly inadequate for any of our multicultural communities.

The recognition of war as irrational changes the balance of state and church as Hegel envisaged it. We cannot say (at least I cannot) what the shape of the world will be now that we have been deprived of the category of a "just war." But the prognosis is hardly encouraging. The Gulf War gives us a nice case study. If we view it in Fukuyama's nonideological power perspective, the U.S. may seem to have come off well. The Bush administration managed to create a Hobbesian alliance of Arab states against the bully in the group; and they have certainly established that nothing can happen in the region that they do not like. But how long will this last? If we evaluate it in the Hegelian world-historical perspective of a fraternal community of ideologies it does not look good. In this perspective it is clearly the U.S. that is the bully; they have violated their own "Western idea" in going to war for the integrity of a community that is plainly not a state. Would it not have been better to win more slowly through economic pressure (as in South Africa)? Should we not recognize that all of the traditional societies must begin to constitutionalize themselves? (This follows just as readily from Fukuyama's Hobbesian argument as from my Hegelian-Christian one.) When and as they do, will not all of the constitutional regimes tend to be anti-Western? Are we not on the way to a Pan Arab bloc that is genuinely united ideologically? (One hopes that the Islamic republic of Iran is not a portent of what that means, but it may be—that may be the first decisive proof that Fukuyama is just another utopian idealist.) So who really won the war? It is hardly even over, and already we can see that the victory was Pyrrhic. "Reason" was far more cunning in 1945. That is the mark of how irrational war has become in the Clausewitz equation. War is no longer the successful continuation of any policy. The history of the Hegelian state has ended. But only because a new kind of Hegelian history has begun.

History will not cease to interest even the most systematic philosophers for a long time yet (if ever).

Postscript

Reading and discussing this essay at a conference of well-read Hegelian scholars has taught me that it deals with Hegel's political theory in a rather helter-skelter fashion. The "religious" language and context of the *Lectures on the Philosophy of World History* is explained here as clearly as I can manage it in a short compass. But then, the need to respond to an interpretation of Hegel that is conceptually stuck at the level of the "Truth of Enlightenment" (so that the crucial question becomes "does Hegel belong to the theistic or the atheistic party?") together with the arising of a new historical world in which the antithesis between the universal economic market and particular cultural traditions has become the problem of the time, forced me to treat Hegel's social theory in a manner that may appear to be as selective and arbitrary as that of the new apostles of Enlightenment.

As far as I can see, the best way to banish that impression is to give a schematic account of how politics and religion go hand in hand in the "science of experience" so as to produce the theory of the state in the "*Real Philosophie*." Then we shall be able to see how the basic thesis of my essay in "applied Hegelianism" expresses itself in our (essentially postpolitical) world. My basic thesis is that "the stages of religious development must go hand in hand with the stages of political evolution" (see above). Let us recapitulate, as briefly as possible, what this means in the "science of experience."

Political life begins in the polis (where else?). The polis is a community of "True Spirit." There is no sundering of political life from religion here. The people belong to their God. They are (in the noblest instance) Athena's people; to violate her temple is the ultimate political crime, and to violate the constitution is to violate the Virgin Goddess herself. But Athena's people is made up of families with their own private piety. The families produce citizens who will give their lives for Athena, because in their deaths they are assured of recognition as individuals in the family memory and the family cult; and the Athenian polis is one of many such communities which recognize the same gods and have the same family pieties.

This Hellenic community of communities is one that maintains its substantial plurality (Hegelian particularity) by warfare. So it essentially depends upon the absolute commitment of singular citizens. To the rulers of the cities it must appear therefore that any sacrifice can be demanded; and that upon one who violates the God of the city any penalty can be imposed. But every time that the universal pieties are violated by this fanaticism for the particular, it becomes apparent that the invisible individual's need for recognition is the absolute foundation of the system. The family, which secures that recognition, is already the focus of singular devotion on the part of the womenfolk. But it can become a community of hope (the future), not just a community of memory (the past). Antigone is devoted to a community of memory (her dead); but her story shows why the individual with a "future" consciousness is to be feared.

When the breakdown comes, the world does not revert to its pre-political communities of kinship. It is an imperial city that establishes the new order in which individuals receive recognition as soon as they are born (or even conceived). In that world of recognized statuses (from emperor to slave) all the pieties of true Spirit are sublated. The Gods have flown. But in this godless condition "the belief of the world" takes root that the one universal God has come to Earth—not as the emperor, but as a human individual who separated himself from all communities (even his family) and proclaimed that we are all equally children of God, who loves us as we must love Him.

We cannot trace here (even in outline) the complex story of the parallel evolution of the "civilized world" in objective actuality and of that Gospel in subjective consciousness. The story comes to its climax in a world of states which unify communities larger and more varied than the whole system of the warring poleis. The most advanced of these states is one in which (on one side) the religious blasphemy of a divine emperor has become political fact ("*L'état, c'est moi*"); while, on the other side, the faith of the Gospel has been replaced by a quarrel about the supposed choice between "*l'être suprême*" and the elementary being of matter.

The resolution of this antithesis is the Revolution; and instead of Napoleon then establishing the modern state as a self-conscious actuality it is Hegel who finds himself establishing it in thought. For that task it was appropriate to array the forms of religious life and thought as a series for which the defining criterion is: "To what extent does this ideology satisfy the need of reason for individual recognition?" So that was what Hegel did on the religious side.

His political theory is likewise the real philosophy of his actual world. It is not the theory of a homogeneous state. The female sex remains in a position analogous to that which it had in the world of true Spirit; the peasants and their noble landlords are completely differentiated from the civil society of the bourgeoisie; and that civil society itself is conceived as a functionally differentiated system of "corporations." This model is an idealization of the sociopolitical system of Prussia. Certainly it is not appropriate for our world. But the general principle of functional differentiation must be universally valid. Hegel's analysis of the Terror shows why he could never accept the democratic principle of "one person, one vote" as anything more than an "abstract right." This "equal recognition" must be mediated by some shared identity of interest if it is not to bring disaster upon the constitution. Kojève slides too easily from his "Napoleonic" Hegel to modern democratic "homogeneity."

Napoleon was the presiding genius of Europe until 1914. We can see this clearly in the Wilsonian program of the supposed settlement in 1919. So Hegel's political theory (with its implicit religious imperialism) was still appropriate, as it stood, for the world that actually perished between 1914 and 1945. But for our world, with its larger communities in which cultural "nations" (such as the ancient Hellenes) are thrown together with "barbarians" (who not only speak different languages, as in Hegel's European community, but worship other gods) the whole problem of social theory has been transformed. In particular, the arrival of the atom bomb means that our world has suffered (in its own way) the fate of the Greek cities. We cannot look to war to maintain social health.

Reliance upon international commerce to rationalize our world presupposes that the self-recognition mediated by Western civil society is the absolute (one and only true and logical) way in which the need for individual self-affirmation can be satisfied. If it does not actually pitch us into Armageddon, this comfortable "certainty" may indeed be verified. But the Hegelian philosopher should not put any stock in such future uncertainties as that. We must concern ourselves with the maintenance of a method that does not need to make assumptions (however comfortably certain they may appear). So we must study how individuality actually does form itself (in every tradition). All of the "forms of individuality" must be accepted as democratic equals. We ought therefore to do political theory with a proper consciousness of the fundamental status that substantial community (or religious "identity") enjoys in it. It is the conflicts of religious *Vorstellung* that have to be mediated first by philosophy—for when we are faced by the religious seriousness that is zealously determined to drive the infidels "across the river" or even "into the sea," we can see that the rhetoric of "democratic equality" and "forgiveness" is only the edifying babble that philosophy must at all costs avoid. We can no more accept religious persecution, than the British imperial power could accept *thuggee* and *sati*. But we must always begin by understanding it. It is idle to suppose that it would all go away if we could only guarantee an adequate supply of consumer goods. That hypothesis will never be tested, because in fact we shall never be able to do that. As Jesus said: "The poor ye have always with you." That fact alone may bring us to Armageddon, but we cannot alter it. Our business as philosophers is with the consciousness that we can alter (though only by raising it, or bringing it directly into being). Jesus is not (and does not deserve to be) noted as an economist. But he was a far better philosopher than Fukuyama; and he was better than all the students of Hegel's political theory who treat it as if it were just a document of the secular scientific enlightenment which can be abstracted from its systematic context. For it is the system (and only the system) that can make it relevant to our new day in which the nobility have no political power, while peasants and women have the vote; but in which the shadow of "holy war" can be seen everywhere we look, and the movements of the market make a mockery of political independence.

THE MYTH THAT HEGEL DENIED THE LAW OF CONTRADICTION

16

Hegel's Metaphysics and the Problem of Contradiction

Robert Pippin

egel's contributions to social and political philosophy and to the philosophy of history, his lectures on the history of philosophy, and his comprehensive analysis of the details of human history are fairly well known and often discussed. Many of his most original and provocative claims in these areas are found in his remarkable *Phenomenology of Spirit*, a work that has benefited from numerous, detailed commentaries. Much less noticed, especially in the twentieth century,[1] is that other of Hegel's only two real books, his *Science of Logic*.[2] This neglect is all the more remarkable since Hegel himself regularly claimed that the foundation for all other parts of his system were to be found only in the *Logic*, that its "metaphysical" arguments alone could establish finally much of what he wanted to say elsewhere.[3]

However, as even Hegelians sometimes complain, such neglect may be benign, given that work's often impenetrable terminology and the fact that much of Hegel's case in the *Logic* owes its peculiar form of expression to his comrades in German Idealism, Fichte and Schelling. Further, at times the *Logic*, like the *Phenomenology* (if one takes one's impressions from the commentaries), reads like an arcane *roman à clef*, requiring that subtle allusions to Greek metaphysics and nineteenth-century science and mathematics be revealed and discussed in detail if the work is ever to be understood. Indeed, even more problems await anyone interested in interpreting any one section, or idea, or topic. Such a topic would seem incapable of receiving a fair hearing on its own, given the constant

Hegelian insistence on seeing any "part" *only* in terms of the "whole." If we are to accept Hegel's claim that, in logic as in everything else, "*das Wahre ist das Ganze,*" no modest commentary on a single issue could hope to do justice to his intentions. Detailed connections with other, previous and subsequent "moments" in the movement of the whole must apparently be established, requiring a commentary at least as long as the *Logic* itself. Or, if one wants to do strict justice to Hegel's thought on some particular issue without such unextended analysis, one seems condemned, judging by many examples, to an opaque, brief, reshuffling of his own terms.

These problems, of course, reflect large, very difficult problems at stake in all Hegel interpretation, and they certainly cannot be resolved here. However, I think some progress can be made in interpreting Hegel's metaphysics on a particular point if some, albeit minimal, attention is paid to the structure and intention of the work as a whole, and if the problem Hegel is addressing is discussed, at least to an extent fair to his case, in less systematically specific language.

Indeed, there is one metaphysical issue in particular most in need of such isolated attention—Hegel's doctrine of contradiction. Hegel is well known, but often little understood, for claiming that any determinate thing's "identity" can be understood only as "contradictory," apparently meaning that some way must be found for intelligibly saying of anything that it both "is" and "is not" what it is. In his more Schellingean moments Hegel formulates this doctrine by insisting that "identity" can be understood only as an "identity of identity and nonidentity." His more familiar term of art for this "negation of negation," this logical doctrine that one can both posit and negate at the same time, is *Aufhebung* or "sublation." At bottom, though, this core of the Hegelian enterprise is defensible only if Hegel has made some case somewhere for the logical intelligibility of the "contradiction" involved in such a sublation. For Hegel, this contradiction emerges in "reflection" on "essence," and it is that case in particular that I want to explore briefly below.

I

I raise this issue not only since Hegel's remarks about the "dialectical" account required for "essence" are at the very center of his whole enterprise, but also because those claims can be, and have been, easily misinterpreted. Although it is true that *every* "transition" in the *Logic* ultimately depends on Hegel's infamously complicated doctrine of "contradiction," or, less flamboyantly, on his doctrine of "determinate negation," there is one section in the *Logic* where Hegel explicitly discusses and defends his interpretation of "contradiction"—in the context of Book 2's whole discussion of "essence." And there he makes some very surprising claims about that doctrine.

> But it is one of the fundamental prejudices of logic as hitherto
> understood and of ordinary thinking, that contradiction is not so
> characteristically essential and immanent a determination as identity;
> but in fact . . . contradiction [is] the profounder determination and
> more characteristic of essence; . . . contradiction is the root of
> all movement and vitality; it is only insofar as something has a
> contradiction within it that it moves, has an urge and activity.[4]

And, in even broader strokes, and with even stranger sounding consequences: "Only when the manifold terms have been driven to the point of contradiction do they become active and lively towards one another, receiving in contradiction the negativity which is the indwelling pulsation of self-movement and spontaneous activity."[5] Finally, Hegel concludes:

> In general, our consideration of the nature of contradiction has shown
> that it is not, so to speak, a blemish, an imperfection or a defect in
> something if a contradiction can be pointed out in it. On the contrary,
> every determination, every concrete thing, every notion, is essentially
> a unity of distinguished and distinguishable moments, which, by virtue
> of the determinate, essential difference, pass over into contradictory
> moments.[6]

To speak of a contradiction "in" a concrete thing is problematic enough, but to assert further that this contradiction is the "indwelling pulsation of self-movement and spontaneous activity" requires, to say the least, no little explanation. Again, though, such an explanation is indispensable if many of Hegel's well-known, and often more widely accepted, claims are to be defended. When Hegel asserts, for example, that the "absolute" both "is" and "is not" its appearances or shapes in history, he is making a claim that can be finally defended only by this "dialectical" account of the relation between "essence" and its appearances, or its "negations," which it, as essence, is *not*. However, again, Hegel's wholehearted embrace of "contradiction" seems very hard to take. Russell, in a famous swipe at the whole notion, writes impatiently that "this [Hegel's doctrine of contradiction] is an example of how, for want of care at the start, vast and imposing systems of philosophy are built upon stupid and trivial confusions, which, but for the almost incredible fact that they are unintentional, one would be tempted to characterize as puns."[7] The "stupid and trivial confusion" Russell alludes to is Hegel's supposed howler about the "is of predication" and the "is of identity," and it is a point to which we shall return shortly. First, some general remarks on Hegel's account of essence, the context for discussion of contradiction, are in order.

II

The explicit discussion of contradiction occurs in the second book of the *Logic*, entitled simply "Essence" (*Wesen*). This section is preceded by an account of "Being" (*Sein*) and is followed by the "subjective logic," or the "Notion" (*Begriff*). In the first section of this book on essence "contradiction" emerges as an "essentiality or determination of reflection," a "reflection" that Hegel has argued is necessary in order to distinguish "essential" from "unessential." His final claim about contradiction in this section is that any account of "what a thing essentially is," any attempt to determine not its mere "being" but at a "reflected" level its essence, must be committed to this "dialectical" contradiction. However, although such a claim sounds quite odd, not to say impossible, we should begin by noting that Hegel regards it as a consequence of his examination of some very traditional accounts of essence.

In fact, if we begin with certain basic aspects of the problem, we can detect two central traditional concerns throughout the first two books of the *Logic*. The first stems from considering the general problem of *change*, probably Hegel's central metaphysical interest. Some accounts of essence hold that there are some features of a thing which cannot change without that thing's ceasing to be what it is, and that there are other, manifold changes which do not affect such an identity (although, of course, such a substantial change could occur, and the thing literally could "become" something else). Hegel will initially accept this minimal, "substrate" requirement for essence, and indeed will present his own argument in favor of it in the transition from Book 1 to Book 2, as we shall see. To be sure, he develops his own version of "what it is" about a thing that makes it what it is throughout alteration, but the first point to be noticed here is that his doctrine arises directly from an interest in a traditional aspect of the problem—the "essence-accident" distinction. This is clear from his first definition of essence (*Wesen*) in Book 2 when he claims that "essence is past—but timelessly past—being."[8] Here he directly plays off the Aristotelian phrase for essence, *to ti ēn einai*, the "what it was to be" of a thing, and he even congratulates the German language for correctly preserving this temporal aspect by using a form of the past participle of the verb "to be" (*gewesen*) for essence. Essence must be explained as somehow outside the flux of accidentally acquired properties gained or lost *in time*. It is "timelessly past," or what a thing that changes *is*.

The second aspect of the traditional problem of essence arises out of the first. Besides a supposed need for essences to explain stability through change, a related aspect of this issue, the relation between "essence and appearance," must also be explained. At this point, though, the problem is hard to state precisely, since the philosophical vocabulary of the past two thousand years uses a variety of words, often in different senses, to make this point. Substance, attribute, essence, appearance, illusion, and other such terms are often no more uniformly used in Hegel than in the tradition to which he addresses himself. In general, though, there is a continuity of interest in the modern search for "substance," for that which exists independently, or by itself. (Even in Aristotle, a substance is not attributed of, nor does it exist in, a subject; it is what the subject is, just so that it may have properties.) This substance inquiry is for that which "really" is, or is "most of all." To use Aristotle's terminology, telling us the "what it was to be" of a substance is telling us its essence, what is true of the substance per se. And, in modernity as well as in Aristotle, this inquiry is after real, independent, determinate being, as opposed to merely accidental, derivative, or especially "apparent" being. It is this last designation that sets off the modern search for substance. From Descartes on, the question, "What is essential in phenomenal change?" came to mean, "What is true of the world of appearances independently of the way that world happens to appear to me?" In other words, the problem of contingency, or "nonessentiality," became a *subjective* problem. Locke's *je ne sais quoi*, Leibniz's inquiry into the well-foundedness of the merely phenomenal world, Hume's refusal to admit any substance, and Kant's *Ding an sich*—all indicate for Hegel the uniquely modern aspect of the problem of essence.

Thus, as in many such issues, Hegel takes himself to be solving in the *Logic* both the "ancient" and the "modern" versions of the problem of essence. He wants both to explain stability and identifiable determinacy through time and to show that the modern, epistemological question of "reality" can be solved without committing us to dogmatic appeals about the power of pure reason alone (as in rationalism), to an unknowable essence (Locke), or to ungrounded (Hume) or merely subjectively ungrounded phenomena (Kant). His main thesis in all of this, having distinguished essential from merely illusory being (*Schein*) as in skepticism, is to prove that "illusory being, however, is *essence's own positing*,"[9] and he calls this yet to be explained "showing of illusory being within essence itself" "*Reflection.*"[10] If Hegel's discussion of essence, then, is to be a valuable contribution, what he must show is that there is no essence for a thing as an unchanging, stable, eternal "form," *and* that there is no essence "behind" or beyond the phenomena, *but* that this claim does not mean that we are thus committed to Heracleitean flux or to the ungrounded *Schein* of skepticism and phenomenalism. This "contradiction"—that, even though there is a difference between essence and the nonessential, or mere appearances, there is also an "identity" between them—is what most needs explaining in Hegel's account of contradiction itself.

And, it is quite important to keep in mind that it is the problem of "essence" that makes such an account of "contradiction" necessary. Hegel does not claim that everything we say is contradictory and thus, in a straightforward sense of the term, meaningless. As we shall see, it is only in the metaphysical context surrounding any attempt to say just *what* something is that this problem arises. It is always worth remembering here that Hegel's whole metaphysical enterprise in the *Logic* begins with an unmistakably Aristotelian insistence on determinacy as a defining mark of any being. As with Aristotle, his attempt throughout is to specify those categories indispensably involved in the definition of "anything at all," and it is the attempt to give this *Kategorienlehre* that will lead to contradiction.

As I said, though, Hegel agrees with the modern (post-Cartesian) attempt to know this essence independently of "subjective" seemings and thus requires that this essence be "reflected" as that which "really" is. But it is this twin "metaphysical" interest in essence that sets the stage for the doctrine of contradiction and all the claims made for it.

We can take one final step in setting this stage by noting how Hegel thinks his own problem of essence arises. This occurs in an interesting passage called "The becoming of essence."[11] Without looking at this section in detail, its consequences are clear. Hegel agrees with the initial modern claim in science and philosophy that the appearances, the given, cannot be explained on their own terms. An explanation by "pure reason" for *why* the phenomena are related or relatable in certain basic ways is as important as telling precisely and predictably *what* those relations are. However, if we try to revert to an account based on what Russell called "internal relations" and claim that Y happens to X because it is in the "nature" of X for Y to happen to it, the problems becomes clear. Hegel calls it, in this section, the "indifference" of the substrate to its determinations. This charge of indifference is simply Hegel's way of claiming that such an internal explanation is really no explanation at all; it merely repeats that Y happened to X with no account of why. However, he is not willing to abandon all such attempts to show a relation between substrate and appearances because of such apparent indifference and opt for exclusively external relations, or opt for no metaphysics in the classical sense at all. Instead, he argues for pressing on to find the correct terms for the relationship between objective ground and subjective appearance. As he puts it,

> This unity [the unity of some phenomenal moment; e.g., all these determinations happen to this *one* thing, or this, specifically, is the cause of that] thus posited as the totality of the process of determining in which it is itself determined as indifference, is a contradiction in every respect; it therefore has to be *posited* as sublating this its contradictory character and acquiring the character of a self-determined, self-subsistent being which has for its result and truth, not the unity which is merely indifferent, but the immanently negative and absolute unity which is called essence.[12]

To sum up, what Hegel claims to have shown, prior to the explicit discussion of essence in book 2, is just why the modern essence-appearance distinction is required. Once the subjective, or reflective, turn is made and the appearances are, rightly, seen as always appearances to an observer, or as "subjectively mediated," the ground, or substrate or source, of that mediation must be explained. Or, the Aristotelian and post-Aristotelian inability to consider the role of the subject in fixing the difference between essential and accidental properties left that tradition wide open to the skeptical attack of the "new way of ideas." The distinction between essence and accident thus seemed arbitrary or "subjective," and the question of essence became explicitly epistemological or reflective; namely, a question of what could be established with certainly about the world, behind, or beyond, or posited as independent of subjective appearances. However, at this point such a reflective, second-level determination of essence can show no determinate connection between such essence and the world of experience around us. That relation is left indifferent (most dramatically, according to Hegel, in Spinoza, for whom the relation between substance and its determinations, or modes, *is* left indifferent, or inexplicable).[13] The same point is obvious in Descartes's attempts to make some transition between the *ordo cognoscendi* and the *ordo essendi*. It no more follows from the fact that I *know* myself clearly and distinctly as a *res cogitans* that I must *be* a mind distinct from body than it follows from the fact that I *know* the world clearly and distinctly as merely "extended" that it *is* only *res extensa*. But with such indifference skepticism about such a source reigns supreme and we are left with mere "*Schein*," or illusory being, ungrounded, without objective foundation.

We are thus left with unacceptable alternatives. We supposedly have come to realize the indispensability of inquiring after a substrate for changing appearances and to realize the need to specify the essence of that substrate, but we cannot explain how the mind could know such a substrate or such differentia apart from the way the world contingently and thus nonessentially happens to appear. We seem to be able to retain this line of inquiry only by becoming what Kant would call "dogmatists." On the other hand, when we confront this problem directly and turn our attention *first* to what the mind can know, we find that it can know only its own ideas, or that any access to an "exterior" ground seems prohibited. To continue this doubt is to become a skeptic.[14] To avoid both alternatives, Hegel must show that it does make sense to investigate the "essence" of appearances but that the relation between such a source and its results is neither unknowable, indifferent, nor merely external. In his own words, "The process of determining and being determined is not a transition nor an alteration, nor an emergence of determinations in the indifference, but is its own self-relating, which is the negativity of itself, of its merely implicit being."[15]

III

Any full account of this "self-relating," which is the "negating of itself" must take into account the philosophers who were, for Hegel, the most important philosophers of "reflection," especially Kant and Fichte. In lieu of such a larger analysis, however, this general sketch of Hegel's interest in the problem of essence should provide a sufficiently detailed context in which to discuss his "solution" to the problem of essence. Having, at this point in the *Logic*, determinately passed through ancient, early modern, and transcendental attempts, Hegel now considers that the solution lies ready at hand, staring us in the face if we will only see it. At first glance, it does seem as if this solution is simple, indeed almost simplistic. He argues that the "essence" of illusory being is, properly understood, the moments of *Schein* itself, that there is no essence behind the phenomena, but that essence is the "recollection" (*Erinnerung*) of the process of phenomenal change itself (when phenomenal is meant in its Kantian sense, or as subjectively conditioned appearances).[16] At bottom Hegel is here, in his own way, agreeing with Kant that the objectivity of phenomena can be established (that, basically, the distinction between real and illusory can be transcendentally established) *without* a dogmatic appeal to an unperceivable *jenseits*, or *Ding an sich*; but he now wants to deny Kant's skeptical remainder—the postulation of the existence of such an unnecessary entity. More straightforwardly, Hegel is asking empirical skepticism to take its own conclusions seriously.[17] It *is* true that the notion of an independent, *an-sich* substance is unthinkable, unknowable, even inconsistent, and finally unnecessary, since the basic structure and coherency of objective experience can be established without such a commitment. (This is precisely Kant's discovery in the Transcendental Deduction.) Given that, continued allegiance to such a notion occurs only because of Kant's unreasonable "reverence" for an unnecessary and outmoded conception of object.

Hegel realizes, of course, that such a claim for the "identity and difference" of essence and appearance commits him to an unusual "logic." In his own terms he claims that what determining reflection will establish, or what is arrived at as the basic "framework" or structure of experience (as in Kant's *Kategorienlehre*), "constitute determinate illusory being as it is in essence, essential illusory being. Because of this, determining reflection is reflection that has come forth from itself; the equality of essence with itself has perished in the negation, which is the dominant factor."[18] This last obscure phrase (from "the equality of essence" on) is the beginning of a larger claim that experience has been determinately grounded (by a detailed category analysis, as in the *Logic*), but not "indifferently." Or, as in the next section of the *Logic*, there is an "identity-in-difference" between appearance and essence, between what Hegel calls "positedness" or "negation" (the appearances, called negation because no one of the moments of such phenomenal change is what the whole is) and its "essence." He has an unusual, spatial way of putting the point: "It is positedness, negation, which however bends back into itself the relation to other, and negation which is equal to itself, the unity of itself and its other, and only through this is an essentiality."[19]

To understand this claim for the self-related, internal essentiality of *Schein*, we need to consider the large issue at stake for Hegel here and, as promised earlier, in the rest of his system. A reflective account of the "phenomena" cannot, as we have seen, merely describe what appears, or repeat the successive moments of what Hegel calls *Schein*. Although such a descriptive methodology (or "phenomenology" in the contemporary sense) is sometimes ascribed to Hegel in his *Phenomenology of Spirit*, it is clearly excluded as adequate precisely by the whole argument for "essence" (as well as by the presence of the interpreting *"wir"* in that book). On the other hand, though, Hegel's analysis and detailed *interpretation* cannot just *assume* a standpoint from which the "essence" of that progression is dogmatically made manifest. So, again, this claim for the logical relation between essence and appearance must be taken into account as the most thorough attempt at an answer to the much discussed interpretive question concerning the *Phenomenology*.

Also, in Hegel's philosophy of history the claim that there is "reason" in history means not that there is some external providence directing historical action, but that the process of historical events itself is rational, or is its own rationality. In the same way, Hegel's claim that in political philosophy "the real is the rational" would not be a reactionary or uncritical allegiance to "what happens," since there is a distinguishable, rational essence to the actual; but neither would reflection on that essence be an empty moralizing about some idle "ought," since that essence is determinate only *in* political actuality.

All of this, of course, raises numerous questions, many of which Hegel hardly had adequate answers for. It especially raises the problem of knowing in any detail how a correct description of some set of events can be defended as *correct*, if not empirically, rationally, or transcendentally. The more immediate problem for the moment, though, is whether the *very form* of the claim itself makes any sense. One might be tempted to say that such a claim that "essence" is and is not identical with its appearances is simply a contradiction. True to form, Hegel not only accepts such a characterization, he heartily embraces it.

IV

Ultimately, his full defense for such a claim is presented throughout the course of the rest of the *Logic*; indeed, the analysis of negation and contradiction is the primary theme of the whole work. But we can make some progress in analyzing the notion by looking at these initial claims.

For we have now arrived at a position where our general attempt to say "what anything is" appears to Hegel fully "contradictory," although in a very special sense. We already know: (1) that any attempt to specify the ground of appearances independently of an actual consideration of the phenomenal world itself is impossible (we end up with the "indifference" problem of rationalism); and (2) that the attempt by skepticism to eliminate any "ground" inconsistently leaves unexplained precisely what it needs to assume—the determinacy of the given. This means that any attempt to explain such a ground or essence must make determinate use of "what appears" in different contexts, even while admitting that any of these appearances *is not* that essence. In Hegel's infamous language, this means that anything "is what it is" and "is what it is not," or "everything is inherently contradictory."

This claim amounts to one of the most important, even if most obscure, things said in the *Logic*. To see it more clearly, we shall have to retreat somewhat for a moment from the details of this section of the *Logic* and examine the basic "logical" claim Hegel is making here concerning all discourse on "essence." Having done so, we can return to the general form of his argument. At bottom the simplest way to deal with this thesis about "contradiction" is to examine its relevance to some issues in standard, subject-predicate logic.[20]

Read straightforwardly, Hegel seems to be claiming that any attempt to say what a thing is—using, for the following example of his principle, some universal in the predicate position of a subject-predicate judgment—involves a dialectical, even contradictory, logic. Again prima facie, this must mean that saying

(i) *s* is *P*

must also mean

(ii) *s* is not *P*,

thus generating a "contradiction."

Item ii appears to be true because *P* is a universal and, in this example, *s* a particular. *S* as *s* "is not" completely *P*, just so that *P* can be attributed to particulars other than *s*. Thus

(i') Socrates is male

and

(ii') Socrates is not male,

since Plato, Alcibiades, and others are also male but are not Socrates. In language used earlier, any attempt to specify the essence of a thing makes use of determinations that "are not" what that particular *is* just so that we can, here, say something informative about Socrates. If such were not the case, "essential" statements would be tautologous and "empty," leaving us claiming only some version of

(iii) Socrates is Socrates.

At this point, however, Hegel's analysis seems not only confused but just wrong in an embarrassing way. Has he not obviously confused here, as Russell complained, the "is" of predication with the "is" of identity, a distinction he should be well aware of if he has read Plato, especially the *Sophist*, as carefully as is sometimes claimed? Why should the result of Hegel's analysis not be to show just that some individual (*s*) is not *identical* with some universal property (*P*), even while that property can be truthfully predicated of that individual (as in i)? No "contradiction" results as long as it is clear that we are expressing *only* this denial of identity in ii and are not, as we appear to do when i and ii are left unanalyzed, simultaneously predicating P of s and then denying that predication. There is thus no contradiction in admitting ii as long as we realize that the "is" negated is not meant to be taken in the same way as

    (iv) Socrates is not beautiful

or

    (v) Socrates is not tall.

The problem with such criticisms, however, is that far from having overlooked this issue, Hegel considers it as the heart of what he is interested in claiming. His whole point is that the "is" in question for an *essential* determination must always be the "is" of identity, and in that sense the contradiction does arise in just the way described. That is, in investigating some essence, Hegel insists that we can never be satisfied with simply predicating a universal of some particular (or of another universal for that matter, as in generic essences). As he has argued throughout, we are interested not in what properties s happens to have but in just what s *is* so that *it* can have properties. Thus the term in the predicate position will not say what s (*and nothing else*) essentially is, *unless* it expresses some identity between subject and predicate. But, again, if it expressed this identity merely tautologously, or nondialectically, or with no "difference" and just "identity," we end up with some version of the uninformative iii.

We need to be a little clearer here about why Hegel will not allow that essence judgments can be predicative. His central reason for that denial is that predicative or "Fa" paradigms for all, even essential, description commits us to a metaphysical position that is untenable and already overcome in the *Logic*. That position necessitates that if all "determination" occurs only by predication, the particular in question in this extended example must remain a "bare" particular, in itself essenceless, or ineffable, inarticulable, and known, if at all, only by some mysterious "acquaintance." Telling us what properties s has, but never what s is, is precisely the "indifference" relation Hegel has already criticized in the chapter on measure. At this point in the *Logic* Hegel takes it that he has shown why we must make determinate use of all those determinators, appearances, and properties which s is not (is not identical with) just in order to say *what s is* (to define s's identity). As he puts it at the conclusion of the chapter on contradiction, "Finite things, therefore, in their indifferent multiplicity, are simply this, to be contradictory and disrupted within themselves and to return to their ground."[21]

The clearest example of this internal "disruption" is, as it was for the Greeks, natural growth or change. Thus a plant "is not" its seed or blossom or fruit, but neither is it something "other" than the becoming of these moments.[22] But at this Kantian stage of the argument Hegel's point is also much more general. Expressed in that more general way, his claim is that the "framework" within which experience is apprehended and classified *itself comes to be* in the history of attempts at this apprehension and classification.[23] It is neither posited a priori, completely dispensable as in strict empiricism, nor just practically assumed or, in some inexplicable way, "more central" to our beliefs. As the ground of all experience, it develops from *its own* "contradiction," a contradiction that is not fully resolved until the whole, or Absolute, is expressed.

Now, of course, Hegel's full account of "negation" and "dialectic" involves much more than this. He is especially concerned elsewhere to explain how these contradictions come about, how any "position" short of "Absolute Knowledge" cannot successfully preserve this "identity and difference." But in this section of the *Logic* Hegel takes himself to have established the necessary form of this resolution—"contradiction"—and to have done so without any "stupid and trivial confusions."

V

What all this means in terms of Hegel's overall enterprise should now also be somewhat clearer. Having detailed what he regards as the proper, post-Kantian, or transcendental ground or essence, Hegel has now tried to show how that ground is *known*: that it is not merely posited, nor miraculously discovered by inspecting the table of judgments. Such a framework itself comes to self-consciousness in the phenomenon of knowledge's history and can be discovered, as he has already shown, by a "phenomenology" of such a progress by "Spirit."[24] What he takes himself to have done thus far in the *Logic* is to have defended the unique, dialectical way he examines such a progress, especially his own interpretive framework within which he looks for the "essence" of such becoming. If the interpretation begun above is correct, then, it is a serious misinterpretation of Hegel to accuse him of some extreme a priori constructivism in his interpretation of philosophy and history, as if the plot for such a story sprang full grown from his head. Neither would it be correct to claim that the arguments in the *Logic* themselves occur only because of some prearranged, arbitrary blueprint. Hegel's claim about essence should make clear that the evaluation of any of his arguments must occur *both in concreto* and in terms of the *whole* case for the development of theoretical and practical *Spirit.*

Now, I do not pretend that this is a fully adequate defense of Hegel, and it certainly is not close to the full Hegelian story. At this point in the *Logic* the "contradiction" doctrine arrived at—although a great improvement over previous positions, and a central, perhaps the decisive, turn to Hegel's own position—is still radically unstable and requires some four hundred more pages of analysis before the whole story is told. The most difficult problem remaining, even if this line of historical and metaphysical analysis can be continued, is how this "identity" and difference of "essence and appearance" can be determinately used in the analysis of some philosophical or historical context (or, as Henrich puts it, whether this claim for a "negation" of Kant's transcendental negation of skepticism has any "content," whether it amounts to any more than the claim *that* there must be such a further explanation).[25] I cannot pursue such issues here. However, I hope that enough has been said above to indicate the kind of relevance Hegel's *Logic* has for the rest of his work, to outline his interpretation of the problem of contradiction and to sketch and briefly defend his own initial position on that issue. The most important consequence of that position seems to me to be that, if followed through successfully, it allows Hegel to claim correctly that he has completely integrated the dominant themes of the history of philosophy into a unique position, and that he has thus earned his claim to be the first and last "philosopher of the history of philosophy," ending his case with, literally, no position of his own other than that recollected history. He would thus have shown some warrant for the claim, "It is of the greatest importance to perceive and to bear in mind this nature of the reflective determinations we have just considered; namely that their truth consists only in their relation to one another; without this knowledge, not a single step can really be taken in philosophy."[26]

17

From an Ontological Point of View: Hegel's Critique of the Common Logic

Robert Hanna

Hegel's logic, as developed both in the *Science of Logic*[1] and in the *Encyclopedia Logic*,[2] can be understood only as a criticism of what he calls the "common logic" (*EL*, 36/81) and also sometimes "formal logic" or "ordinary logic." Common logic is perhaps best exemplified by Kant's *Logic*:[3] it deals with the formal conditions of truth in judgments and includes the theory of the syllogism and identity.[4] Hegel's logic, as an ontological logic (*EL*, 36/81), manifestly goes far beyond the scope of the common logic; it is by no means either a bare denial or even a revision of common logic. Hegel's logic in fact preserves the entire edifice of common logic while still using the critique of the latter as a motivation for its own self-development toward a more comprehensive and radically new sense of logic. Many of the misunderstandings of Hegel's logic are based precisely on confusions concerning the equally critical and conservative character of Hegel's treatment of common logic. An explication of Hegel's unique ontological point of view should therefore go some distance toward removing the misunderstandings, and by implication, begin to give a proper sense of what Hegel's logic really is.

I

Logic—as common logic—is an ontologically undeveloped and naive science for Hegel. He points out that it has lagged behind "the higher standpoint reached by Spirit in its awareness of itself" (*SL*, 25/I, 13). In particular, the common logic has not been subjected to the same kind of critique as that leveled at traditional metaphysics by Kant. But in view of the importance of the common logic for the Kantian transcendental metaphysics, such a critique is demanded. Hegel fully agrees with Kant that an ontological logic is possible, but disagrees about the status of the common logic with respect to the higher logic. Hegel makes a crucial distinction between the activity of "understanding" insofar as it determines or merely fixes the characteristics of things, and the "reason" insofar as it is dialectical, dynamic, and speculative (*SL*, 28/I, 16–17; *EL*, 113–22/168–79). For Hegel, the understanding and the reason are not merely cognitive faculties, but determine ontological structures. The common logic clearly belongs to the activities of the understanding (*EL*, 255/344–45), while Hegel's logic belongs to the activities of reason. This means that the common logic and Hegel's logic *each* has an "ontological bias" toward understanding and reason, respectively, quite independently of its explicit recognition of this bias.

Hegel then articulates a basic contrast between Kant's transformation of the common logic of the understanding (which Kant calls "analytic general logic")[5] into a "transcendental logic," and Hegel's own critique and sublation of the common logic in the service of his logic of reason (*EL*, 65–94/113–47). The important difference between Kant and Hegel in this regard is that Kant did not see the common logic as ontologically naive and undeveloped, but rather as a well-grounded, necessary propaedeutic and foundation of his transcendental logic; by contrast, Hegel is quite clear that it is only by means of a *critique* of the common logic that the transition to the higher logic can occur. For the common logic has an unrecognized ontological bias toward the understanding which must be removed before a logic of the reason is possible. Therefore, insofar as Kant has not provided a critique of the common logic, his transcendental logic will be itself ontologically naive and undeveloped in direct proportion as it rests on the structures of the mere understanding. This means that any kind of Kantian "metaphysical deduction of the categories" whereby the forms of common logic are translated into forms of "all possible experience," is decisively rejected by Hegel.[6]

Thus Hegel sees his logic as a "completely fresh start" (*SL*, 27/I, 16) in philosophical logic, and therefore as a distinct movement beyond anything broached in the common logic. Philosophy does not so much borrow from common logic, as it consists in a free development of the content provided for it by common logic. We might then say that Hegel holds the common logic to provide a wealth of material in which certain ontological structures lie dormant. These structures must be worked up from a different perspective than that which produced the wealth of material in the first place. In short, Hegel's philosophical use of common logic is a higher-order activity than the common-logical activity, and does not therefore by any means *compete* with the common logic at its own level. Hegel's higher-order comments about the common logic are *ontological* remarks or recommendations, not *common-logical* remarks or recommendations.

This helps to make it understandable how Hegel can at once say that common logic is to be viewed as an "extremely important source [for Hegel's own logic], indeed as a necessary condition and as a presupposition to be gratefully acknowledged" (*SL*, 31/I, 19), and yet also say that "what it offers is only here and there a meagre shred or a disordered heap of bones" (*SL*, 31/I, 19). Indeed, Hegel even goes beyond the metaphor of common logic as a heap of bones to say: "the conceptions on which the [common] Notion of logic has rested hitherto have in part already been discarded, and for the rest, it is time that they disappeared entirely and that this science were grasped from a higher standpoint and received a completely changed shape" (*SL*, 44/I, 36). It is comments like these, I am sure, which have always misled interpreters of Hegel's logic. The apparent contradiction between common logic as a "necessary condition" and as a "disordered heap of bones," and again between common logic as a "presupposition to be gratefully acknowledged" and as something which should "disappear entirely" makes it seem that Hegel is either logically dense or seriously confused, or both. But this apparent contradiction can be dissolved simply by taking very seriously the "higher standpoint" of which Hegel speaks.

By establishing his own logic as a development beyond the common logic, and as a higher-order activity that consists in the "system of pure reason, as the realm of pure thought" (*SL*, 50/I, 44), Hegel is saying that the common logic can be viewed from two quite distinct perspectives. Viewed on its own terms and at its own level, common logic is simply a discipline among or "alongside" the other scientific disciplines (*SL*, 58/I, 54). As such its procedures and notions have a certain integrity and efficacy that cannot be denied. As Hegel puts it: "the purpose of the science [of common logic] is to become acquainted with the procedures of finite thought: and, if it is adapted to its presupposed object, the science is entitled to be styled correct" (*EL*, 22/75). But viewed from a higher viewpoint, namely that of ontology, the common logic can be seen to rest on certain enabling presuppositions which are also at the same time crippling limitations from an ontological point of view. These limitations prevent the common logic from passing directly over into philosophical significance: "they bar the entrance to philosophy [and must] be discarded at its portals" (*SL*, 45/I, 38). Only a transformation or "reconstruction" (*SL*, 52/I, 46) of the conceptions of the common logic by means of a thorough critique of it, can provide the basis of the transition from common logic to Hegelian logic. Thus in order to become adequately ontological or properly philosophical the common logic must "disappear." Again, this does not mean that Hegel is denying the efficacy and efficiency of common logic *at its own level*. He is denying only the implicit and therefore uncriticized claim of common logic to ontological adequacy.

It will soon be necessary to look more closely at some details of Hegel's critique and transformation of the common logic. As regards the tranformatory aspect, it is worth noticing from the start that Hegel's general procedure is to take a certain concept from the common logic, criticize it, and then to extend the meaning of the term over a much wider field which includes the initial meaning but is by no means reducible to it. It is precisely the misunderstanding of this procedure of Hegel's which has led to such claims as that Hegel "denies" the principle of noncontradiction, the law of identity, and so on. The misunderstanding stems mainly from the idea that the given term—say, "contradiction"— is being extended merely by taking the initial meaning as a model and then illegitimately widening the scope of its application. This is to get Hegel's approach quite backwards. To use rhetorical terminology, Hegel's treatment of the meaning of his logical terms is metonymic and not analogical. When Hegel uses a term like "contradiction" in *his* sense, it is because he has already shown that the original meaning of the term in the discourse of common logic was an abstract, partial, and specifically limited use of a much wider notion that can be named by the same word. In short, the narrow or "partial" use of the word gets its significance only *because* it is a narrowing of or participation in a much broader and more concrete notion which has been, as it were, "forgotten" in the ordinary business of common logic.

It can be seen here that Hegel's critique and transformation of the common logic has something in common with Heidegger's account of logic.[7] In a manner similar to Heidegger, Hegel is well aware that the common logic is a "derivative" or "founded" phenomenon, in the Hegelian sense that its ontological status and the meaning of its terms *consist* in the narrowing and limitation of the implicit absolute structures of the Notion (*Begriff*) and the Idea. As Hegel puts it: "the logic of mere understanding is involved in speculative logic, and can at will be elicited from it, by the simple process of omitting the dialectical and 'reasonable' element" (*EL*, 120/177). Hence Hegel's own usages of the common-logical terms should not be regarded as extensions in the sense of merely analogically "widening" the use of a term, but as extensions that refer metonymically "back into" the more complete original sense of the term—a sense that is recoverable from the standpoint of reason but not from the standpoint of understanding. Thus Hegel cannot be accused of twisting conceptions of common logic to his own purposes; he is rather resituating the notions in their proper sphere. From the ontological-philosophical (though not of course from the common-logical) perspective, it is precisely the common-logical uses of such terms as "contradiction" which are "twisted" owing to their abstract partiality.

In order to get a fuller sense of Hegel's critique of common logic, I shall focus on his criticism and transformation (or resituation) of the common-logical doctrines of (1) judgment, (2) syllogism, and (3) contradiction. (As regards Hegel's architectonic in the two *Logics*, the treatment of judgment and syllogism both fall under the logic of the Notion or Concept, in the Subjective Logic; and the treatment of contradiction falls under the logic of essence, in the Objective Logic. So far as I can determine, the relative positions of these topics in Hegel's overall logical system have no special significance for my account.)

II

It seems necessary to begin with Hegel's critique of the common-logical doctrine of the judgment for two reasons. First, the common logic is manifestly a logic of judgments in the sense that all of its logical operations begin and end with judgments. Hence, for Hegel to criticize the common-logical doctrine of judgment is to get at the basic "atomic parts" of the common logic. Secondly, the judgment is for the common logic the locus of truth, or as we would now say, the "truth-bearer." Both the common logician and Hegel himself would agree that "truth" is the central concern of all logic, be it common logic or Hegelian logic. For example, Kant in his *Logic* writes that logic is "rightly called the logic of truth" (*KL*, 18/438). Hegel too asserts that "truth is the object of logic" (*EL*, 26/68). But where Hegel and the common logician will disagree is over just "where" the locus of truth lies; that is, over just what deserves to be called the ontologically genuine "truth-bearer." In order to motivate his new conception, therefore, Hegel will have to criticize the traditional conception, which is to say that he will criticize the common-logical doctrine of judgment.

Thus Hegel in fact begins his own "critique of judgment" by questioning the truth-bearing capacity of the common-logical judgment. In the context of a discussion of metaphysical judgments such as "The soul is simple," Hegel raises a more profound problem by pointing out that "nobody asked whether such predicates had any intrinsic and independent truth, or if *the propositional form could be a form of truth*" (*EL*, 48/94, emphasis added). In short, Hegel proposes to circumvent the question of whether a given judgment is "true" or not by raising the more primordial question of whether any judgment can be "true" in any proper sense of the term. This is not meant as a form of logical skepticism by Hegel, but rather as a question about the possibility of an ontological limitation that is "built into" judgment merely owing to its "propositional form."

Now by "propositional form" in this context Hegel also means the "form of the judgment," as he himself points out (*EL*, 51/98). Hegel distinguishes between "propositions" and "judgments" by saying that whereas the former have a merely grammatical existence with correct syntactical form, the latter respond to some actual question about the world and reach out into the world in their reference (*SL*, 626/II, 305). It is worth making out this difference not only because it anticipates Austin's distinction between "sentences" and "statements,"[8] but so that it may be seen that Hegel is addressing his remarks primarily not to some imaginary construct or abstract entity but rather to a situated common-logical phenomenon.[9]

The common-logical judgment, as Hegel analyzes it, has both what can be called a "structural" and an "epistemic" component. These two components are nicely exemplified by Kant's doctrine of judgment. In his "Mistaken Subtility of the Four Syllogistic Figures," Kant writes: "Judgment is the comparison of a thing with some mark [or attribute]. The thing itself is the Subject, the mark [or attribute] is the predicate. The comparison is expressed by the word 'is' which when used alone indicates that the predicate is a mark [or attribute] of the subject."[10] This brings forward the "structural" element of the common-logical doctrine of judgment. The judgment is constituted by the linkage of a subject-thing to a predicate-thing by means of the "is" or copula. The predicate-thing or "attribute" is supposed to "determine" the subject-thing by its application to it.

Hegel points out in this regard that the etymology of *Urteil* ("judgment") implies an "original partition" (*EL*, 231/316). Hegel takes this to mean that the entity denoted by the subject-term of the judgment is partitioned or ruptured in its living concreteness by the application of the predicate to it. This thing is "ruptured" because a certain feature or aspect of the thing is thereby taken to characterize the *whole* thing. The thing is narrowed down in the judgment to a specific feature, as if it were being viewed out of the wrong end of a telescope. As Hegel notes: "Attribution is no more than an external reflection about the object: the predicates by which the object is to be determined are supplied from the resources of picture thought and are applied in a mechanical way" (*EL*, 50/96). What Hegel means by "external reflection" is the idea that a certain apparent feature of the object is elicited by the judgment, and is then hypostatized into a separate thing: the predicate. This hypostatized predicate is then *applied* to the thing as if it were simply another thing "over against" the original object. The "picture thought" which supplies the predicate is the activity of imagination governed by the understanding. This imagination "creates" predicates by taking concrete, embedded aspects of the thing and representing them as distinct things on their own. Hence the aspectuality (or relationality) of the thing is, as predicate, transformed into an "attribute" or "mark." The application of this predicative thing back to the original things is "mechanical" because the judgement is as it were *rebuilding* the object by means of the adhesive copula after having ruptured it in its primordial concreteness—or as Hegel would say, in its notion.

By contrast, for Hegel an adequate characterization of the object "must characterize its own self and not derive its predicates from without" (*EL*, 50/96). This does not mean that a totality of predicates should be listed for the object through "all possible" judgments about it. The thing is not a maximally large class of predicates. Hegel says that "even supposing we follow the method of predicating, the mind cannot help feeling that predicates of this sort fail to exhaust the object" (*EL*, 50/96). This means that *in principle* the judgment—even an infinite number of them—will not be able to characterize the object adequately. And this is not because—as in Husserl—we simply cannot grasp the "inexhaustible" object in all its "profiles." Rather it is because there is an ontological difference between an adequate characterization of the object and any predicative partition of it. The essential nature of the object simply *cannot* be grasped by positing any single predicative feature or even an infinite number of them.

Thus the difficulty with common-logical judgment lies not in the completeness or incompleteness of a list of possible judgments about a given object, but in the ontological bias of the judgmental form itself. Hegel writes: "The propositional form (and for proposition it would be more correct to substitute judgment) is not suited to express the concrete—and the true is always concrete—or the speculative" (*EL*, 51/98). The judgment is not suited to express the concrete because the (propositional) form of judgment itself contains an internal opposition or "contradiction" in the Hegelian sense (see sec. IV below). The judgment sets out to characterize a subject by means of a predicate. Hence implicitly the subject is taken to be a source or ground of this predicate. As Hegel puts it: "The predicate, as the phrase is, inheres in the subject. Further, as the subject is in general and immediately concrete, the specific connotation of the predicate is only one of the numerous characters of the subject. Thus the subject is ampler and wider than the predicate" (*EL*, 234/320). The subject is a source or ground of the predicate in the sense that the predicate by the structural intention of the judgment, is taken to "inhere" in the subject along with many other predicates. Thus the predicate must refer back to the subject and "belong" to it as a part belongs to a whole.

Yet as soon as the predication is carried out, the concreteness of the subject-whole passes over into the abstractness of the predicate. The concreteness of the subject is as it were "absorbed" by the predicate. So, in the movement from "The rose is . . ." to "The rose is *red*," we can see the concreteness of the subject being subordinated to the universal predicate " . . . is red." Thus "the predicate as universal is self-subsistent, and indifferent whether this subject is or not. The predicate outflanks the subject, subsuming it under itself: and hence on its side is wider than the subject" (*EL*, 234/321). In this way, the concrete whole of the subject becomes a particular as regards the abstract whole of the predicate. Hegel is clearly exploiting a crucial ambiguity here in the ontology of parts and wholes— an ambiguity which the common logic has not recognized—between concrete wholes or "individuals" and abstract wholes or "universals." The very subject-predicate form of the judgment embodies this ontological ambiguity insofar as it (1) denotes in the subject-term a concrete whole or individual in which it appears that the predicate must "inhere"; and (2) denotes in the predicate-term an abstract whole or universal, under which it appears that the individual subject must be subsumed. In short, to use spatial metaphors, the "in which" of attributive inherence conflicts with the "under which" of predicative subsumption. Or to put it another way: the individuality of the subject conflicts with its bare particularity with respect to the predicate. As a form, therefore, the judgment really cannot give an adequate characterization of the thing in its concreteness or indeed of the predicate in its abstract universality.

Having diagnosed the structural flaw in common-logical judgment, Hegel is able then to give a broader, ontological characterization of the difficulty by noting that the judgment in itself expresses what he calls the "determinate being or otherness of the Notion which has not yet restored itself to the unity whereby it is as Notion" (*SL*, 627/II, 306). This is an example of what I called Hegel's "resituation" of common-logical notions. The Notion, for Hegel, is the concrete synthetic unity of universal and particular, whole and part, genus and individual. As John Smith puts it:

"What Hegel called the Concept [or Notion] is *not* the abstraction of a feature common to many particulars, but a principle of order, structure and organization which specifies itself by determining the elements of the system it organizes."[11] With respect to judgment in particular, the Notion is the implicit, higher-order unity which makes it possible for the common-logical judgment to display itself as limited and internally oppositional in the first place. This aspect of Hegel's treatment of the judgment should not be taken to be a denial or discrediting of judgment, but only a diagnosis of its essential difficulties from an ontological point of view. To put it differently: the judgment of common logic is not *logically* flawed on its own terms; rather it is ontologically flawed insofar as it cannot adequately articulate the things of which it treats. The judgment is in fact the representative of the dirempted Notion, or the Notion as it shows itself in its onesidedness or otherness *prior* to the achievement of its own ultimate unity as Idea. Thus the judgment is seen by Hegel to be a kind of lower-order version of the Notion in its contradictory concreteness in much the same way that a two-dimensional photograph of a person is an inherently limited version of the three-dimensional living person who himself is incomplete in the sense that he has "many miles to go before he sleeps."

Owing to this ontologically limited, "contradictory" character of the judgment in its very form, it follows that for Hegel "every judgment is by its form one-sided and to that extent, false" (*EL*, 51/98). To the common logician this statement would seem to be a perfect example of Hegelian confusion and obfuscation. "Is he saying that even *true* judgments are false? How absurd!" But such a response would be based on a misunderstanding of Hegel's ontological analysis. To disentangle this misunderstanding, we must talk about the "epistemic" component of judgment mentioned above. In his *Logic*, Kant writes: "A judgment is a presentation [*Vorstellung*] of the unity of the consciousness of several presentations, or the presentation of their relation so far as they make up one concept" (*KL*, 106/531). Thus Kant is saying that a judgment is a representation of the unity of several representations. In the context of Kant's theory of knowledge, this means that a judgment is the holding-together of an intuitive representation of a thing-in-itself and an empirical concept. The thing-in-itself is beyond all possible experience and is given only representationally in intuition as an object of sense perception. The empirical concept is the synthetic act of the understanding in conjunction with the imagination. The upshot is that, as Hegel notes, "one's first impression about the judgment is the independence of the two extremes, the subject and the predicate. The former we take to be a thing or term per se, and the predicate a general term outside the said subject and somewhere in our heads" (*EL*, 231/316). In short, then, a certain epistemic view is implied by the common-logical judgment, a view in which the judgment seeks to apply a conceptual, "internal" predicate to a perceptual "external" subject.

This implicit epistemology of the judgment carries along with it a certain doctrine of truth. This is the doctrine of truth as "agreement" or "correspondence." Kant writes: "truth, one says, consists in the agreement of cognition with the object" (*KL*, 55/476). To put this formulation into the terminology of the present context, the truth of judgment consists in the successful application of the conceptual predicate to the perceptual subject. The "success" of the application is held to consist in some sort of mapping or matching of the conceptual predicate to the thing. It is absolutely crucial to note that Hegel's criticism of the truth of judgment does *not* amount to an attack upon the correspondence theory of truth. Instead, Hegel points out that such a view of judgmental truth relies upon a rather controversial doctrine of the relationship of thought and its object:

> The object is regarded as something complete and finished on its own account, something which can entirely dispense with thought for its actuality, while thought on the other hand is regarded as defective because it has to complete itself with a material and moreover, as a pliable indeterminate form, has to adapt itself to its material. Truth is [for the common logic] the agreement of thought with the object, and in order to bring about this agreement—for it does not exist on its own account—thinking is supposed to adapt and accommodate itself to the object. (*SL*, 44/I, 37)

The doctrine is "controversial" for Hegel not because it implies the falsity of the correspondence theory of truth, but because ontologically it sets two things apart—thought and its object—which for Hegel are never ontologically dichotomous. Hegel writes that the

> logic of understanding . . . believes thought to be a mere subjective and formal activity, and the objective fact, which confronts thought, to have a separate and permanent being. But this dualism is a half-truth: and there is a want of intelligence in the procedure which at once accepts, without inquiring into their origin, the categories of subjectivity and objectivity. (*EL*, 255/345)

For Hegel, thought is thought *of* objects, and objects become "objective" only *for* thought. Hence to claim that truth lies in the "agreement" or "correspondence" of thought and its object is to presuppose that they are apart in the first place, and thereby to say something which is ontologically naive or "wanting intelligence"—quite independently of any epistemic difficulties which a "correspondence theory of truth" might have.

Indeed, Hegel's treatment of the ontological naiveté of judgmental truth, far from denying the correspondence theory, in fact *preserves* it. Hegel does this by distinguishing between "truth" (*Wahrheit*) and "correctness" (*Richtigkeit*). Hegel writes:

> In common life the terms truth and correctness are often treated as synonymous: we speak of the truth of a content, when we are only thinking of its correctness. Correctness, generally speaking, concerns only the formal coincidence between our conception and its content, whatever the constitution of this content may be. Truth, on the contrary, lies in the coincidence of the object with itself, that is, with its notion. (*EL*, 237/323)

Several things must be said about this. First, it is clear that the distinction between truth and correctness enables Hegel to say that *all* judgments are "false" despite the fact that many of them may be "correct." They are "false" because they rely upon a view of thought and its object which is one-sided and ontologically inadequate. Secondly, however the correctness or incorrectness of judgments is preserved by Hegel as features of judgments considered wholly at their own level and not ontologically. Judgmental correctness, however its epistemic form be construed, is experimentally adequate—which is to say that it comports well with our various ordinary practices, especially those of the natural and pure sciences (*EL*, 32/75–76)—while it nevertheless remains ontologically inadequate. Finally, the concept of "truth" which is opposed here to mere "correctness" returns us to the idea that what judgment is always overlooking is the relationship between ordinary things and their Notions—that is, between things in their abstract immediacy and in their concrete articulated totality. The Notion of a thing is not something extra over against the thing but is the thing itself considered in its structural fullness and total relatedness to other things and to itself. This higher-order aspect of things is precisely what is overlooked by the common-logical doctrine of judgment and is therefore precisely where its ontological inadequacy lies.

Now that we have at length unpacked Hegel's criticism of common-logical judgment, it is worthwhile to look briefly at Hegel's own positive doctrine, which is correlative to the critique and is indeed negatively anticipated by it. For Hegel, the primary locus of truth is what he calls the "category" (*Gedankenbestimmung*). Hegel writes:

> To ask if a category is true or not, must sound strange to the ordinary
> mind: for a category apparently becomes true only when it is applied
> to a given object, and apart from its application it would seem
> meaningless to inquire into its truth. But this is the very question
> on which everything turns. (*EL*, 40–41/85)

It seems to be faithful to Hegel's doctrines to say that the category is the
judgment as taken up into the Notion, that is, the judgment as having
overcome its ontological limitations. Indeed as Hegel was no doubt aware,
the etymologies of "category" and "judgment" are intimately related,[12]
except that the former has always been taken to be an ontologically basic
version of the latter. For Aristotle, the categories are ultimate classes
of attributes of "substance." For Kant, the categories are the a priori
concepts of the understanding. Hegel would agree with Aristotle and
Kant on the idea that a doctrine of categories is somehow ontologically
basic, but would notice that for both Aristotle and Kant, their categories
are modelled too closely on the common-logical doctrine of judgment.
Using the terminology developed in this paper, we might say that Aristotle's categories are too "objective" and manifest the structural flaws of
judgment; while Kant's categories are too "subjective" and manifest the
epistemic flaws of judgment. Be that as it may, what *is* absolutely clear from
a Hegelian point of view is that both Aristotle's and Kant's doctrines of
categories participate in the ontological naiveté of the common-logical
doctrine of judgment.

By contrast Hegel's idea is that "the principles of logic are to be
sought in a system of thought-types or fundamental categories in which
the opposition between subjective and objective, in its usual sense, vanishes" (*EL*, 37/81). Hegel's "thought-types" (*Denkbestimmungen*) or categories are like Aristotle's categories in that they describe "generic traits
of existence"—to use Dewey's phrase—and also like Kant's categories in
that they are "forms of thought" (*SL*, 33/I, 22). But the "generic traits"
are dynamic rather than static for Hegel, and the "forms of thought"
are by no means limited to individual human subjects. The categories
are simply the "moments of the Notion" (*SL*, 28/I, 38), which is to say
that they express the actualized natures or essences of things insofar as
thought has manifested itself in these things (*EL*, 237/323–24). Categories are "true" precisely because they have captured these natures or
essences. Thus categories play the same role relatively to Hegel's logic
that judgments play in the common logic. Hegelian categories are, as it
were, "ontologized judgments"—where it is of course understood that
the inherent ontological limitations of judgment have been overcome in
the "ontologization."

III

It was noted above that all of the operations of the common logic begin and end with judgments. This of course implies a process or procedure of operation which takes one in a systematic way from judgment to judgment. This process of the systematic "movement" of the judgment is the syllogism. In his *Logic* Kant writes: "A syllogism is the cognition of the necessity of a proposition by subsumption of its condition under a given general rule" (*KL*, 125/551). That is, by means of a syllogism, a logically necessary relation is established between a single judgment and other judgments. The single judgment results from the logical interaction of other judgments, and in the canonical Aristotelian case, two other judgments. This interaction is conceived by the common logic as the specification of a judgment (minor premise) under a general rule (major premise). By actually running through this specification, the common logician is able to obtain a single judgment as a conclusion. Kant says: "By concluding is to be understood that function of thought in which one judgment is deduced from another. A conclusion in general is thus the deduction of one judgment from another" (*KL*, 120/545). Now Kant is speaking here of an "immediate" syllogism in which the conclusion is drawn directly from a single premise. But this single premise is typically the conjunction of the two premises of the standard syllogism, so the normal structure of the syllogism is implied. A judgment is thus "deduced" as a conclusion from two other judgments which are its premises. As is well known, the deduction is successfully carried out or "valid" so long as it cannot be the case that when the premises are true, the conclusion is false. Now while not all deductions are syllogisms, every syllogism properly carried out is a deduction; the syllogism with its threefold form traditionally stands forth as a paradigm of deduction.

As in the case of judgment, Hegel is by no means interested in criticizing the syllogism in its ordinary functioning; he grants the syllogism its common-logical integrity as a particular relationship between judgments. Rather Hegel is interested in criticizing the syllogism insofar as it betrays a certain ontological bias or naiveté. As we saw, the judgment contains an ontological limitation in its very structure and also in the epistemic views with which it is closely associated. A similar state of affairs holds for the syllogism. But whereas for judgment the limitation had both a structural and an epistemic aspect, the limitation in the syllogism is purely structural.

The structural limitation of the syllogism from an ontological point of view displays itself in two ways. The first way has to do with the relationship between the three judgments of the syllogism, while the second way has to do with the dimension of truth in the syllogism.

As for the relationship between the three judgments in the common-logical syllogism, Hegel wants to say that the very externality of these parts of the syllogistic whole is misleading for any adequate characterization of the relationships between phenomena:

> If we stop short at this form of the syllogism, then the rationality in it, although undoubtedly present and posited, is not apparent. The essential feature of the syllogism is the *unity* of extremes, the *middle term* which unites them, and the ground which supports them. Abstraction in holding rigidly to the *self-subsistence* of extremes, opposes this *unity* to them as a determinateness which likewise is fixed and *self-subsistent*, and in this way apprehends it rather as a *non-unity* than as a unity. (*SL*, 665/II, 353)

What is crucial for Hegel here is that the common-logical syllogism is used by the common logic and indeed by philosophical logicians as a model for the movement of thought and thereby as a model for the relationships between things (since even for Kant there is a strong connection between thought and things). But the very triplex form of the syllogism implies that such relationships can be determined as merely external relationships between two "self-subsistent" extreme terms (i.e., the major premise and the conclusion) and a self-subsistent middle term (the minor premise). Insofar as each of these is presented as self-subsistent, the actual internally related movement of thought and things is ruptured. If the major premise is a universal judgment and the minor premise and conclusion are particular judgments, this seems to indicate that the universal and particular are somehow related only externally.

Moreover, the form of the common-logical syllogism requires that the middle term become a virtual barrier between the major premise and the conclusion. Hegel writes:

> The expression *middle term* (*media terminus*) is taken from spatial representation and contributes its share to the stopping short at the *mutual externality* of the terms. Now if the syllogism consists in the *unity of extremes* being *posited* in it, and if, all the same, this unity is simply taken on the one hand as a particular on its own, and on the other hand as a merely external relation, and non-unity is made the essential relationship of the syllogism, then the reason which constitutes the syllogism contributes nothing to rationality. (*SL*, 665/II, 353)

The syllogism "contributes nothing to rationality" in this regard essentially because the extremes are not united in some encompassing third thing, but rather are externally related over against one another *through* the middle term. In a word, it conceives relationships as the understanding does, not as the reason does. It presents an obviously naive picture of mediation as requiring a third *distinct* thing (*tertium quid*) in order to relate the two extreme terms. But if the middle term is a distinct thing, then clearly it can be put over against each of the extreme terms, thus requiring a new "third thing" or middle term to relate the original middle term to each of the extreme terms. A viciously infinite "third man" regress of relations is thereby engendered.

In general, the common logic suffers ontologically from having misunderstood the interest which reason takes in the syllogism. What reason is interested in is the movement of things in their general notional relationships; but the common logic portrays this movement and relationship as a rigid formalism. Hegel writes:

> To regard the syllogism merely as consisting of *three judgments*, is a formal view that ignores the relationship of the terms on which hinges the sole interest of the syllogism. It is altogether a merely subjective relation of the terms into separate premises and a conclusion distinct from them. . . . This syllogistic process that advances by means of separate propositions is nothing but a subjective form; the nature of the fact is that [in] the differentiated Notion determinations of the fact are united in the essential unity. (*SL*, 669/II, 358)

Thus Hegel here exposes in the very idea of the common-logical syllogism a crucial ambiguity in the way rational relationships are conceived. It is not at all clear how the common logic can reconcile its idea of reason as syllogistic deduction with the traditional concept of reason as the progress toward completed totalities (as Kant would express it). For Hegel, the unnecessary limitation in the syllogism consists in the overly great emphasis upon the bare externality of the syllogistic form as a model for reason. Indeed Hegel sees the syllogism of the common logic as being really a disguised syllogism of the understanding: "What the Formal Logic usually examines in its theory of syllogism, is really nothing but the mere syllogism of understanding, which has no claim to the honour of being made a form of rationality, still less to be held as the embodiment of all reason" (*EL*, 245/334). This transposition of the understanding for the reason, and the consequent ontological restriction of reason, is typical of the common logic. In the Kantian case of the development of the common logic into propaedeutic of all philosophy, the consequence is that even though Kant has recognized the ability of reason to comprehend a totality, this ability is essentially truncated and is viewed merely as a constant approach to the infinite totality which never actually obtains the totality.[13] Thus for Kant it is as if reason were a common-logical syllogism with a maximally broad major premise and an infinite number of middle terms. The very possibility of what Hegel would call the "spurious infinity" (*SL*, 137/I, 149) seems to lie in the structure of the common logical syllogism owing to the externality of its terms.

By contrast, Hegel would like to see the syllogism properly interpreted as anticipating the notional fusion of universality and particularity which issues into individuality. This would involve seeing the "middle term" as an encompassing dynamic unity which links the two extreme terms in a totality. Hegel even writes: "Everything is a syllogism, a universal that through particularity is united with individuality" (*SL*, 669/II, 359). Clearly, Hegel is carrying out here what I have called a "re-situation" of the common-logical terms, an insertion of the common-logical notion back into the basic ontological structure from which it arose as an abstract form. Another way of saying this is to say that the abstract understanding presupposes concrete structures of reason of which it is not aware. In the case of the syllogism, Hegel is thus able to "repatriate" the syllogism from the understanding to the reason by showing that the threefold structure of the common-logical syllogism implies the threefold structure of the Notion in general. The triad "major premise/minor premise/conclusion" can be "mapped" back onto the notional triad "universal/individual/particular." Again, it should be remembered that Hegel's re-situation of the term "syllogism" is not meant to imply that henceforth the common-logical syllogism should be regarded as somehow more profound and powerful in a common-logical sense; he is only providing an ontological commentary on the concept of a syllogism.

As regards the ontological limitation implicit in the dimension of truth in the common-logical syllogism, Hegel notices that what is a banality for the common-logician—namely, the syllogism's "truth preserving" character—is of great ontological significance. A syllogism is "valid" just in case it cannot happen that when the premises are all true, the conclusion is false. This of course means that when the premises are true, the conclusion *must* be true if the syllogism is to remain valid. But this by no means guarantees the truth of the conclusion just in case one of the premises is false, nor does it guarantee the truth of the premises and conclusion. As Hegel notices, this "truth-preserving" but not "truth-guaranteeing" character of the syllogism means that false conclusions can be validly drawn from a true major premise merely by using a false minor premise:

It is justly held that there is nothing so inadequate as a formal syllogism
of this kind, since it is a matter of chance or caprice which middle
term is employed. No matter how elegantly a deduction of this kind
has run its course through syllogisms, however fully its correctness may
be conceded it still leads to nothing of the slightest consequence, for
the fact always remains that there are still other middle terms from
which the exact opposite can be deduced with equal correctness. (*SL*,
671/II, 361)

Now, as usual, the common logician would yawn at such an observation on
Hegel's part. But it must be reemphasized that Hegel is not attempting to
disclose anything "new" to the common logician in point of logical fact
or technique. What he is indicating is the ontological weakness of the
syllogism as regards truth—and truth is the stated objective of all logic.

The truth of the conclusion of a syllogism is guaranteed, as we
have seen, only if the premises are also true. This casts the "burden of
truth," as it were, back upon the separate judgments of the premises.
But this means that, so far as syllogistic form is concerned, each of the
premises will have to be itself derived from a further syllogism in which
both premises are true. It can easily be seen from this that an infinite
regress of justificatory prosyllogisms will be required to guarantee the
truth of any given conclusion (*SL*, 672–73/II, 362–63). This regress in
justification illustrates how the primary question of truth in the common
logic is forever delayed by the very form of the syllogism. Now of course,
this is a "delay" only in an ontological sense, since as we have seen, the
common logic appeals to its own "correspondence" theory of truth for
judgments. But Hegel wants to say that it is essential to the very conceptual
structure of the common-logical syllogism that it never deals directly with
the notion of truth.

The "ontological delay" of truth in the syllogism is closely bound up
with the syllogism's character as a tool for the manipulation of judgments.
By means of the syllogistic apparatus and its various modes and "figures,"
arguments may be formally "tested" for their validity by monitoring the
"distribution" of the middle term. Such testing relies heavily on the
syntactical character of the propositions that represent judgments in
the syllogisms. This partial reliance upon syntax and the regularity of the
syllogistic figures gives the syllogism a mechanical, calculative dimension.
Hegel writes:

In judgments and syllogisms the operations are in the main reduced
to and founded upon the quantitative aspect of the determinations;
consequently everything rests on an external difference, on mere

> comparison and becomes a completely analytical procedure and
> mechanical [*begriffloses*] calculation. (*SL*, 52/I, 47)

Here it is clear that while Hegel of course has no conception of a
purely truth-functional logic, nevertheless he has anticipated the modern
development of logic as the construction of formalized languages and
propositional calculi. Hegel's criticism of this idea has nothing to do
with a Luddite objection to the mere fact of logical mechanization,
as if there were something inherently wrong with formalization and
mathematization. Rather Hegel is concerned *only* with the illegitimate
extension of such structures into ontological realms where they do not
belong, namely the realms of organic relationships, dynamic process, and
concrete truth.

In this regard, Hegel refers to Leibniz's idea of a "*characteristica
universalis*" or what would now be more commonly called an "ideal
language":

> The extreme example of this irrational treatment of the Notion
> determinations of the syllogism is surely Leibniz's subjection of the
> syllogism to the calculus of combinations and permutations. . . .
> Connected with this was a pet idea of Leibniz, embraced by him in his
> youth, and in spite of its immaturity and shallowness not relinquished
> by him even in later life, the idea of a *characteristica universalis* of
> Notions—a language of symbols in which each Notion would be
> represented as a relation proceeding from others or in relation to
> others—as though in rational combinations, which is essentially
> dialectical, a content still retained the same determinations *that it
> possesses when fixed in isolation.* (*SL*, 684/II, 378–79)

It is the last sentence of this quotation that is crucial for Hegel's critique
of the ontological bias of the syllogism conceived as a *characteristica
universalis.* The error of an "ideal language" which is conceived as a
calculus is the ontological error of imposing a model which functions
in a mechanical sense onto a content which functions not in a mechanical sense but in an organic and teleological sense. The Notion for
Hegel is among other things the self-development of a phenomenon
from potentiality to actuality. Notional truth lies in the completeness
or perfection of this self-development (*EL*, 237/323–24). The Notion is
also the principle of organic totality whereby a whole and its parts are
internally related. The mechanical and quantitative structural aspects of
the syllogism conceived as a *characteristica universalis* cannot capture the
organic and irreducibly qualitative aspects of the Notion. The proposed

"ideal language" therefore fails as "ideal" because it cannot adequately describe large ontological domains.

In light of the critique of the syllogism, Hegel can again anticipate an aspect of his speculative logic. We saw above that in the critique of the common-logical judgment ontological limitations were exposed which called out for an ontologically adequate correlative of judgment—this was the "category" in the Hegelian sense. Similarly in the case of the syllogism, the critique has revealed an ontological lack in the syllogism, namely its externalism, formalism, "delay" of truth, and "calculative" character. This lack of course tends to call out what is *lacking*, which as we saw was an idea of reason developing its Notion in an internalistic, material, truthful, and organic way. For Hegel, the ontological correlative of the common-logical syllogism is the idea of a "system" in which the phenomena display their rationality by means of internal, articulated, organic connection. The system, for Hegel, is the ultimately adequate locus of truth (as opposed to correctness):

> Truth, then, is only possible as a universe of totality of thought; and
> the freedom of the whole, as well as the necessity of the several
> subdivisions, which it implies, are only possible when these are
> discriminated and defined. Unless it is a system, a philosophy is
> not a scientific production. (*EL*, 20/59–60)

Such a speculative-logical system is constructed of categories in a way partially analogous to that in which the syllogism is built out of judgments. But a system in Hegel's sense does not merely "preserve" the truth of categories; rather it *guarantees* their truth. This is because, unlike the syllogism, the categorial "parts" anticipate the systematic whole (the Notion or Idea) and the systematic whole is manifested in every one of the categorial parts. In short, for Hegel the speculative-logical system reproduces in essence the structure of organic totalities and therefore overcomes the ontological inadequacy of any "ideal language."

IV

By having first developed Hegel's critique of the common logic with respect to judgment and the syllogism, I hope to have prepared a climate of receptivity for that *bête-noire* of Hegel's doctrine, his critique of common-logical contradiction. Russell's cheeky remarks in "On Denoting" implying the absurdity of Hegel's "denial" of the principle of noncontradiction[14] have long stood in the way of a fruitful understanding of Hegel's logic. But as we have seen, Hegel's account provides a critique of the common logic from an ontological point of view alone, and is by no means a "denial" of *any* principle of the common logic. This goes as much for contradiction as it does for judgment and the syllogism. Thus Hegel escapes the charge of absurdity by having a wholly different critical project in mind than the one Russell implicitly attributes to him.

In order to understand Hegel's critique of the common-logical concept of contradiction, however, a few preliminary historical remarks are absolutely necessary. For there is a troublesome distortion regarding Hegel's critique of contradiction which stems merely from the development of the science of common logic between Kant's day and the modern period. For the modern common logic, (1) negation is an operation applied only to propositions (or more accurately, to sentences of the formal language—formulas not containing free variables—where "sentence" means in addition to simple sentences, also conjunctions, disjunctions, negates, and conditionalizations of sentences) and results in the reversal of the truth-value of that proposition; (2) contradiction is a conjunction of a proposition and its negate; and (3) the theory of identity is regarded as being separate from the central subject matter of common logic.[15]

But for the common logic of Kant's day, the concepts of identity and of contradiction are closely connected. In his *Logic*, Kant includes as the first of the "three principles of universal, merely formal or logical criteria of truth": "The principle of contradiction and identity (*principium contradictionis* and *identitatis*), by which the inner possibility of a cognition is determined for *problematic* judgments" (*KL*, 58/479). Hegel also accepts this basic unity of the concepts of contradiction and identity: "The other expression of the law of identity: A cannot at the same time be A and not-A, has a negative form; it is called the *law of contradiction*" (*SL*, 416/II, 45). Now what is important about this assimilation of identity and contradiction for my purposes is the idea that contradiction may apply equally to *things* and to *propositions*. For identity is explicitly a relationship between things (or between a thing and itself), and on this view if a thing is non–self-identical, it is contradictory. Thus it follows that for Kant's and Hegel's common logic, negation can be construed as an operation either upon propositions (or judgments) or as an operation upon things insofar as they are nonidentical with other things.

Quite independently, then, of the logical correctness of this assimilation of contradiction and identity, it must be understood that Hegel (just as does Kant) *assumes* this to be the case, and his entire critique of the common-logical concept of contradiction presupposes it. It is therefore wrongheaded or at least in interpretive bad faith to criticize Hegel for "muddling" the principle of noncontradiction by applying it indifferently to things and propositions (or judgments), when it is explicitly part of Hegel's critical method to assume that the common logic must be analyzed *as it stands* and not be intrinsically disturbed by his analysis.

Having said this, we can now turn back to Hegel's account of common-logical contradiction. It should be clear by now that Hegel's critique of common-logical contradiction cannot be wholly split off from his treatments of identity and negation, since the common logic posits an intimate relationship between these three notions. In particular, it can be said that in the common logic, contradiction is construed as the negation of self-identity, where "identity" can be taken to encompass both things and propositions (or we might simply say that propositions are a special subclass of things). Thus, in order to criticize the common-logical notion of contradiction, we must first turn to Hegel's critique of the common-logical notions of identity and negation.

Hegel formulates the common-logical law of identity in the following way: "Thus the essential category of identity is enunciated in the proposition: everything is identical with itself, A = A" (*SL*, 409/II, 36). Now Hegel's criticism of common-logical identity really has two parts, one of which is concerned with the "material" aspect of the general law "A = A" and the other of which is concerned with its purely "formal" aspect. The material aspect of the law of identity is that it asserts an absolute identity between a thing and itself (which I shall call "simple identity"), or between two things (which I shall call "complex identity") in such a way that no difference whatsoever between the things is possible. This abstraction from all possible difference is what Hegel calls the "abstract identity of understanding" (*EL*, 166/237). It is "abstract" precisely because of the abstraction from all difference. As J. N. Findlay puts it: "On the degenerate interpretation [i.e., the interpretation held by the common logic] the Law of Identity merely bids us identify objects referred to by means of one term or concept with objects referred to by the *same* terms or concept."[16] Thus identification occurs merely through the criterion of sameness alone. And yet the very fact of the repeatability of the second term in simple identity ("A = A") and the bringing forward of the distinct second term in complex identity ("A = B") seems to presuppose the dimension of difference. For in simple identity, repetition is still *different* from the mere presence of an object, and the relation a thing bears to itself is still *different* from its mere existence; and in complex identity the mere presence of a second thing (or on the Fregean interpretation, a second name with a distinct sense but the same denotation) is sufficient to indicate at least a prima facie difference (even if only a difference in the Fregean sense) from the first thing, despite their identity. Hegel objects therefore not to the bare idea that a thing is identical to itself, or that two things can be identical to one another (or put in a Fregean way, there is but one thing, referred to by two different names), but rather to the covert ontological assumption that identity can be "pure" in the sense of excluding all difference.

Hegel then goes on to give an account of how it is that the common logic thinks itself able to propose a "pure" law of identity. He writes:

> This Identity becomes an Identity, in form only, or of the understanding, if it be held hard and fast, quite aloof from difference. Or, rather, abstraction is the imposition of this Identity of form, the transformation of something inherently concrete into this form of elementary simplicity. And this may be done in two ways. Either we may neglect a part of the multiple features which are found in the concrete thing (by what is called analysis) and select only one of them; or, neglecting their variety, we may concentrate the multiple characters into one. (*EL*, 166/237)

In short, the crucial thing about common-logical identity is that it utilizes a principle of abstraction without explicitly admitting to it. In this abstraction it either neglects the variety of features of things in favor of one particular feature which it then fixates upon and calls "identical" across implicitly suppressed differences; or it overlooks the prima facie differences between the features of a thing and collapses them into a single homogeneous feature which is then held to be "identical" with another similarly reduced class of features.

The "formal" aspect of the common-logical notion of the law of identity is that it presents itself as formally or logically necessary, or as Hegel puts it: "This proposition in its positive expression A = A is in the first instance, nothing more than the expression of an empty tautology" (*SL*, 413/II, 41). That is, the common logic wants to put the principle of identity forward as necessary purely in virtue of its logical form alone, or as the contemporary terminology would have it, as necessary owing to its "analyticity." But Hegel is suspicious about the analyticity or tautologousness of the law of identity, because he holds that the very form of the proposition in which an identity is expressed is sufficient to imply the nonanalyticity or "syntheticity" of the proposition. He writes:

> In the *form of the proposition*, therefore, in which identity is expressed, there lies *more* than simple, abstract identity; in it, there lies this pure

> movement of reflection in which the other appears only as illusory
> being, as an immediate vanishing; A *is*, is a beginning that hints at
> something different to which an advance is to be made; but this
> different something does not materialize; A *is*—A; the difference is only
> a vanishing; the movement returns into itself. The propositional form
> can be regarded as the hidden necessity of adding to abstract identity
> the more of that movement. (*SL*, 415–16/II, 44)

Thus the common logic has not realized that there is something "built
into" the very form of the proposition which prevents the law of identity
from being a mere tautology or analytic proposition. This "built-in"
component is the bipartite subject-predicate structure of the proposition
which requires that something *distinct* from the subject-term be applied
to the subject in the predicate-term. Hence the ontological structure
of difference is implicit in the very syntax of the proposition. Hegel
of course recognizes that there are differences between the existential,
veridical, predicative, and the identifying uses of "is"; but he is well aware
that these uses are not ontologically so split off from one another as
the common logician supposes. In this way Hegel is able to say that the
syntactical structure of predication is implicit in every identifying use
of "is" (or its symbolic correlative "="). This makes every superficially
"analytic" statement of identity into a "synthetic" statement at a deeper
level. Hegel writes:

> From this it is evident that the law of identity itself, and still more the
> law of contradiction, is not merely of *analytic* but of *synthetic* nature.
> For the latter contains in its expression not merely empty, simple
> equality-with-self, and not merely the other of this *in general*, but what is
> more, absolute *inequality, contradiction per se*. But as has been shown, the
> law of identity itself contains the movement of reflection, identity, as a
> vanishing otherness. (*SL*, 416/II, 45)

For "contradiction" in the above quotation, read "internal self-opposi-
tion"; I will deal with Hegel's own notion of contradiction below. At
present, it is necessary only to see that Hegel has detected within the
very form of the principle of identity a structural characteristic which
opposes the apparent "pure" analyticity of identity.[17]

Hegel's critique of the common-logical negation has to some extent
been anticipated by the account I have just given of identity. For Hegel,
the contrary of sameness is difference, and an obvious parallelism arises
from his critique of identity: just as there can be no "pure" identity
such that one can have sameness quite apart from difference, so there

is no "pure" negation such that one can have difference quite apart from sameness. Another way of saying this is that for Hegel negation is never mere difference without some implicit determinate content or sameness.[18]

The common logic, however, puts its doctrine of negation forward in such a way as to suggest that negation is something quite apart from any "ontic commitment" or sameness. The common logic views negation as an "indifferent difference" which can be applied to things or propositions. In order to capture the important distinction between the negation which implies determinate things and the negation of the common logic which is an "indifferent difference," Hegel proposes a distinction between "difference" (*Unterschied*) and "diversity" (*Verschiedenheit*). Here we can see that Hegel's critique of common-logical negation consists in the re-situation of the abstract common-logical doctrine into a more concrete ontological doctrine of negation as "difference." Of difference Hegel writes:

> That which is different from difference is identity.[19] Difference is
> therefore itself and identity. Both together constitute difference; it
> is the whole, and its moment. It can equally be said that difference,
> as simple, is no difference; it is there only when it is in relation with
> identity; but the truth is rather that, as difference, it contains equally
> identity and this relation itself. (*SL*, 417/II, 47)

And of diversity, Hegel writes that "in diversity, as the indifference of difference, reflection has become, in general, external to itself" (*SL*, 419/II, 48). Whereas difference determinately refers to things in their concreteness, diversity at best indeterminately refers to them. Whereas difference has an internal relatedness to things it operates upon, diversity has only an external relatedness.

"Diversity" is for Hegel an ontological term which refers to the negation which is utilized by the common logic. Where common-logical negation is to be criticized is not in the fact that it is used in assertions of nonidentity or in negates of propositions, but rather in the fact that it does not recognize itself to be only "diversity" and not "difference." Put differently, negation in the common-logical sense puts itself forward as ontologically basic, but is in fact an abstract, static concept which, in its indifference to the things it negates, ontologically distorts the actual concrete relations of difference which things have to one another. Thus for Hegel diversity is not "wrong" but is rather ontologically limited. To take diversity as exhaustive of the whole idea of the negative is simply to cover over an entire region of reality named by "difference." Of this ontological region Hegel writes:

> All that is necessary to achieve scientific progress—and it is essential
> to strive to gain this quite *simple* insight—is the recognition of the
> [speculative] logical principle that the negative is just as much positive,
> or that what is self-contradictory does not resolve itself into a nullity,
> into abstract nothingness, but essentially only into the negation of its
> *particular* content, in other words, that such a negation is not all and
> every negation but the negation of a specific subject matter which
> resolves itself, and consequently is a specific negation, and therefore
> the result essentially contains that from which it results. (*SL*, 54/I, 49)

The essential aspect of difference for Hegel is that it consists in an active
rejection of a determinate content; thus the "negative is just as much
positive." What this means is that things are to be construed for Hegel
in their sameness with themselves only because they positively exclude
other things, and define themselves as against those other things.

This concrete dimension of the negative is also inherently active
because when a thing changes or moves it does so obviously by not-being
what it was, or by striving to be what it currently is not. Thus Hegel can
speak of difference as the "inner negativity of the determinations [of the
understanding] as their self-moving soul, the principle of all natural and
spiritual life" (*SL*, 56/I, 52). We are verging here upon an essential aspect
of Hegel's own speculative logic, the aspect of dialectical negativity. In an
adequate account of this, much would need to be said about negativity or
difference as the motor of the dialectic, and about the inherent tendency
of the understanding to give rise to this dialectical dynamism. For the
present purposes, however, all we need notice is that common-logical
negation implicitly avoids the concreteness and dynamism of difference
by its ontological bias toward "indifferent difference." The awareness
of this avoidance is sufficient for Hegel's critique of common-logical
negation as ontologically limited.

We now have the materials for an adequate discussion of Hegel's
critique of the common-logical notion of contradiction. Insofar as the
common logic defines contradiction in terms of common-logical identity
and negation, it will presuppose whatever the latter presuppose. We have
seen that common-logical identity is ontologically biased in its claim to
be "pure" and to be analytic. We have also seen that common-logical
negation is abstract and avoids the concrete dimension of difference.
Consequently, common-logical contradiction will be ontologically biased
in its "purity" and analyticity, and will also avoid the concrete ontological
region of difference. Here we can see that the law of noncontradiction
will continue to work undisturbed in the logical practices of the common
logic. Hegel's critique does not make logical contradictions such as
"Socrates is mortal and it is not the case that Socrates is mortal" into

noncontradictions. All Hegel is doing is to point out that common-logical contradiction is as it were only the very most abstract tip of the ontological iceberg, and therefore must not be taken to stand in for the whole iceberg.

Hegel's critique of common-logical contradiction centers on the fact that in the common logic contradiction is presented in an overly abstract way. For the common logic, a contradiction is a necessary falsehood, whether by non–self-identity or by the conjunction of a proposition and its negate. But this leaves the terms of the contradiction in a merely external relationship to one another. As Hegel puts it, in the common logic, contradiction

> remains an external reflection which passes from likeness to unlikeness, or from the negative relation to the reflection-into-itself, of the distinct sides. It holds these two determinations over against one another and has in mind *only them*, but not their *transition*, which is the essential point and which contains the contradiction. (*SL*, 441/II, 77–78)

In short, the two terms of the common-logical contradiction face one another as merely exclusive. There is no sense of the "transition" between the two terms which would show *why* the two terms are in fact mutually incompatible. This of course has no impact upon the common-logical contradiction in its propositional form, but it does seem to imply that the things *referred* to by the common-logical judgment will be as externally related as the terms in the proposition. Here again we see the implicit translation of syntactical form into ontological structure. To make the law of noncontradiction ontologically basic (as in Aristotle) is to impose an ontologically biased structure on the world. As Hegel will show, when two aspects of a phenomenon mutually exclude one another within the same phenomenon, they do so because of some internal characteristic of one aspect which cannot "tolerate" some internal characteristic of the other aspect. Common-logical contradiction is a formal, externalized *expression* of the ontological reflexive intolerance or internal self-resistance, not the *reason* for it. Thus common-logical contradiction replicates at best the mere form of a more concrete relationship arising within a single phenomenon, and cannot be said to be basic to that phenomenon.

By contrast, then, in his usual move of ontological re-situation, Hegel can state his own ontologically more adequate account of contradiction:

> The self-subsistent determination of reflection that contains the opposite determination, and is self-subsistent in virtue of this inclusion, at the same time also excludes it; in its self-subsistence, therefore,

it excludes from itself its own self-subsistence. For this consists
in containing within itself its opposite determination—through
which alone it is not a relation to something external—but no less
immediately in the fact that it is itself, and also excludes from itself
the determination that is negative to it. It is thus *contradiction*. (*SL*,
431/II, 65)

Since the re-situated idea of contradiction is central to Hegel's speculative
logic, it is worth paraphrasing what he is saying here. In a nutshell, Hegel
is saying that when a phenomenon excludes itself by virtue of what it
includes, and includes itself by virtue of what it excludes, it is "contradictory" in his sense. That is: a phenomenon is contradictory when the very
conditions of its own existence necessitate its own nonexistence, but the
conditions of its nonexistence are sufficient to provide its existence.

Thus it can be seen that for Hegel a contradiction—or as G. R. G.
Mure calls it, a "dialectical contradiction" in contradistinction from
common-logical contradiction[20]—is not merely a necessary falsity, but
rather involves the internally destructive character of a thing whereby it
continually posits and negates itself. As Hegel put it in the *Phenomenology
of Spirit*:

We have to think . . . antithesis within the antithesis itself, or
contradiction. For in the difference which is an inner difference, the
opposite is not merely *one of two*—if it were, it would simply *be* without
being an opposite—but it is the opposite of an opposite, or the other is
itself immediately present in it.[21]

This is what I referred to above as "ontological intolerance" or "self-
resistance." Hegel's dialectical contradiction, as J. N. Findlay has noticed,[22] is very close in certain ways to what modern logicians call a
"paradox" or an "antinomy." What is important about such paradoxes
and antinomies is not that they generate a particularly vicious form of
truth-functional inconsistency (indeed, only some of the antinomies are
truth-functional), but that they undo themselves by means of the very
same functions and conditions by which they establish themselves. As
Quine has pointed out, such paradoxes and antinomies are at the limits
of logical comprehension, and yet are somehow basic to logic.[23] In a
very similar way, the Hegelian contradiction is a notion that confounds
the logic of the understanding, and yet from the standpoint of reason
is ontologically basic. For as Hegel points out, "everything is inherently
contradictory" (*SL*, 439/II, 74). This is far from being the ridiculous claim
that it seems to be, for it is only saying that everything is a complementary

blend of sameness and difference, and both posits and negates itself in its every activity.

A final difference between dialectical contradiction and common-logical contradiction brings forward the "dialectical" dimension of Hegel's speculative logic. Whereas common-logical contradiction is static and "linear" (in Bosanquet's sense),[24] dialectical contradiction is dynamic and developmental. It is dynamic and developmental because for Hegel all motion and process, interpreted ontologically, contain within themselves an essential aspect of internal negativity or difference. In this light, dialectical contradiction is seen as the most acute form of difference—a kind of boiling-point of difference, as it were. This "boiling-point" erupts into activity when the negativity is sufficiently involuted. Hegel writes: "Contradiction is the root of all movement and vitality; it is only insofar as something has a contradiction within it that it moves, has an urge and activity" (SL, 439/II, 75). What Hegel means is that contradiction is not only the reflexive intolerance of things, but is also intolerable *for* things, and that a new level or state of development will be forced into existence through the pressure of dialectical contradiction. Such development is for Hegel a "dialectical" development.

This aspect of contradiction may seem intolerably metaphorical; and indeed from a restricted common-logical point of view it *is* vague and unsatisfactory. But ontologically speaking, Hegel's doctrine of contradiction points to that aspect of things which we all recognize in our struggles with conceptual knots and which we also recognize in the irreducible phenomena of conflict and crisis in the process of development of organic nature. Therefore, insofar as Hegelian contradiction at least gives us a way of talking about these things, the ontological adequacy of Hegel's account is not impaired by criticism based on the ontological "clarity" of any ontology based on the common logic. Such ontologies cannot even begin to *speak* of such things: "what we cannot speak about, we must pass over in silence."[25]

V

From the perspective of Hegel's critique of the common logic, we can now see Hegel's own logic as the attempt to establish an ontological logic over and above the common logic. This involves the resuscitation of ontological structures that have been narrowed or even positively distorted by the common logic. This supposes that the common logic is not "ontologically neutral" but is rather in fact ontologically biased insofar as it implicitly treats of things from the standpoint of understanding as opposed to that of reason. In the process of his critique, Hegel has re-situated the concepts of judgment, syllogism, and contradiction back into his own speculative logic, and has thereby prepared places for his ontological doctrines of categories, system, and dialectic, respectively.

What is perhaps more important, however, than Hegel's re-situation of common-logical concepts or his anticipation of his own ontological doctrines, is his critical conservatism with respect to the common logic. This allows him to expose the ontological bias of the common logic and hence remove its suitability for translation into ontology, without thereby disturbing the common logic itself. Thus the Hegelian logic is not a competitor of the common logic—not some grandiose "alternative logic"—but is rather the result of a more adequate *ontological* reflection on the common logic.[26]

PART   6

MISCELLANEOUS MYTHS

18

Hegel and the Seven Planets

Bertrand Beaumont

My reason for raking up this story is that no one in this country seems to have got it right. It also, I think, contains material of some interest to historians and philosophers of science, and to all interested in nature and human nature. The reader will also understand that biographical details are merely introduced as a way of opening out the subject.

One of the first phrases I heard McTaggart utter was "I am a Hegelian." In a later book on Hegel's logic he expressed the opinion that Hegel had come nearer to the true nature of reality than any other philosopher before or since. Now all young wits in their first year enjoy nothing better than a story which reflects in any way on their elders, especially those of some repute. Here was one! "Hegelian, is he: why, that's the man who gave an a priori proof that there were, and could be, only seven planets." And some versions added the surprising news. "And in that very year the eighth (or maybe *an* eighth) planet was discovered." As I knew nothing then of the dates, I accepted the story, and as one of the would-be wits, passed it on.

In later life, having discovered that this same Hegel had a volume of 700 pages on the philosophy of nature, and knowing of no other philosopher who goes anything like so far to meet the naturalist, I decided to look into the matter. I found much that was weird and wonderful, and here and there some quite good empirical material, even about the planets, but nothing approaching such an a priori proof as I was looking for. There did not even seem to be anything that could be misunderstood or twisted into such. But there was a reference to a much earlier "Dissertation on the Orbits of the Planets," with a remark that

Hegel no longer held some of the opinions there expressed. And as the dissertation was in Latin I had to let the matter drop.

But other people still kept flogging the dead horse. Neurath of Vienna, in *Erkenntnis* about 1930, repeats the story about both the a priori proof and the contemporary discovery of an eighth planet. And Sarton in a quite recent book pours sarcasm on Hegel apparently believing in this alleged proof. Meanwhile, I had come across and read Lasson's German translation of the dissertation. The translation is very free, and the work itself does not give one a very good impression of German university standards round 1800.

I shall attempt to give the reader the historical background for appreciating the point at issue. The Pythagoreans had discovered the connection of mathematics with musical scales. Kepler and other moderns were greatly interested in such harmonies. Newton gave us his seven colors, later correlated with wavelengths of light. Then there were intervals between the planetary orbits; surely there must be some plan in them, some simple law or laws, in finding which we should be "thinking God's thoughts after Him." For long all efforts were baffled; then in 1772 came a ray of light, Bode's Law. Studying the not very accurate data then existing, Bode found a rule which fitted fairly well. If we call the average distance of Mercury from the Sun "a," and that of Venus "a + b," and take a = 4, and b = 3; then for the planets known in 1772 we get:

	Bode's Law		Actual Distances E = 10
Mercury	a	4	3.87
Venus	a + b	7	7.23
Earth	a + 2b	10	10.00
Mars	a + 4b	16	15.24
	[a + 8b]		
Jupiter	a + 16b	52	52.03
Saturn	a + 32b	100	95.39

Note that the "b"s are as $2^0: 2^1: 2^2: [2^3]: 2^4: 2^5$. Notice also the gap for "a + 8b," for that is the cause of all the trouble. God surely wouldn't leave a gap in such a delightful scheme. Now if we go in thought another step we shall get:

	Bode's Law		Actual Distance
Uranus (1781)	a + 64b	196	191.90

Thus Uranus, discovered after the rule, also conforms approximately. So when Hegel took up the matter there were eight terms, but only seven planets. But there were a priorists in those days who were not content with this. They (not Hegel) said: "There *must* be *an* eighth planet; not eighth in the series, but between Mars and Jupiter (i.e., fifth). Admittedly, it is quite invisible with existing instruments, and exercises no gravitational perturbation. But it must be there!"

To complete the historical sketch: two other planets have been discovered since Hegel's death; and precisely by means of the perturbations exercised (at least this is true of Neptune, 1846, if not also of Pluto, 1930). This completes our table.

	Bode's Law		Actual Distances
Neptune	a + 128b	388	300.70
Pluto	a + 256b	772	394.60

Note that *the* eighth planet came fifteen years after Hegel's death, so cannot be the one referred to in the story. And even the approximate rule no longer holds.

But we must now return to Hegel and 1801, and forget Neptune and Pluto. Some readers may be surprised that Hegel was not on the side of the a priorists. He accepted Uranus on the empirical evidence, and there is every reason to believe that he would have accepted, or even welcomed, Neptune, as I shall show later. But he decided to beat the a priorists at their own game. There is a much simpler a priori series of powers in Plato's *Timaeus*, stemming from the Pythagoreans.

$1, 2, 3, 2^2, 3^2, 2^3, 3^3$, etc.

$1, 2, 3, 4, 9, 8, 27$, etc.

(This series need not be limited to 7 terms.)

Now Hegel substitutes 16 for 8, and so fakes a series of 7 terms which approximately (or so he tries to show) fits the existing 7 planets. And his quite good conclusion is: "There is no need to worry about the missing eighth (or fifth) planet."

Now what was it that happened in the same year 1801, for it was not the discovery of *the* eighth planet? But something was discovered that year, on New Year's Day; a small piece of rock called Ceres, in the gap between Mars and Jupiter, "a + 8b." This, and many similar fragments discovered since are variously termed "asteroids," "planetoids," or even "minor planets." But they are *not* counted in the series of planets. But Hegel accepted them as closing the gap, and (for him) the argument. Note "a + 8b" = 28. Humboldt in his *Cosmos* gives the actual distance as 27.68.

It only remains to refer briefly to what Hegel did say about the planets in his lectures on philosophy of nature. He gives (1) an inner series of 4: Mercury, Venus, Earth, Mars; (2) the asteroids Ceres, Pallas, Juno, Vesta, also 4, which happened to be all Hegel knew; (3) an outer series, Jupiter, Saturn, Uranus (and . . . ?). I think Hegel would have welcomed Neptune as completing his third set of 4. Sets of 12 are not unknown even in the *Logic.* Three, not seven, is Hegel's number; and often in the field of nature four. It was Newton, Hegel's bugbear, who went in for seven! Whereas 12 can be made up of 3 fours or 4 threes, 7 would have to be 3 and 4 and this only gives 2 terms. Hegel would not have liked 7 in one row like the spectral colors. Even the five senses have to be triadized: (1) Touch, (2) Smell and Taste, (3) Sight and Hearing.

To sum up: Had Hegel any special weakness for the number 7, he could rightly have dismissed Ceres, etc. as not being genuine planets. Instead he accepted without demur the *empirical* evidence that there was something in the gap and later gave a list of 11, including 4 planetoids. If then I have got the story right, he was not trying to prove anything a priori or otherwise. He was merely demurring to the a priori assertion that there were 8, made before there was any empirical evidence. If, as is possible, I have not got the story right, I hope someone will correct me.

19

A Semi-Legend: The "Divinity" of the State in Hegel

Franz Grégoire

Translated by Jon Stewart

egel's statements about the divinity of the state are in everyone's
memory. They have been cited more than enough by both the
adversaries of the totalitarian state as well as certain of its partisans.
I recall two passages from the *Philosophy of Right*: "One must honor the
state as a divine element on earth" ("*Man muss den Staat wie ein Irdisch—
Göttliches verehren*").[1] Elsewhere in the same work, Hegel opposes those
doctrines "which destroy the state, the divine which is in and for itself, its
absolute authority and majesty" ("*das an und für sich seiende Göttliche und
dessen absolute Autorität und Majestät*").[2] The expression "the divine in and
for itself" means, as we know from Hegel, the divine as something wholly
actual in opposition to something that is only potential. I would like to
make a few observations about the precise interpretation that I believe it
is necessary, in all disinterestedness, to give to these celebrated passages
and others with a similar tone.

Let us begin first by recalling that Hegel's works are usually divided
chronologically into three groups: first, the early writings, then a transi-
tional work, the celebrated *Phenomenology of Spirit*, and finally the mature
works. I will only be concerned with the latter, among which figures the
most important work for our purposes, namely, the *Philosophy of Right*.
This book appeared in 1821. At that time and since 1818, Hegel taught
philosophy at the University of Berlin, and there he seemed to be the
official philosopher of the king of Prussia, Frederick Wilhelm III.[3] Hegel

remained in Berlin until his death in 1831. The other mature works, which are important in differing degrees for the problem of the state, also come from this Berlin period. They are the *Philosophy of History*, the *History of Philosophy*, and the *Philosophy of Religion*. All these works develop a text in a series of lectures on the whole system (and thus they also lay out the logic and the philosophy of nature). This text is often called the *Encyclopedia*, and the second and third editions of it appeared likewise during the Berlin period. The *Encyclopedia* renders us a great service as well in our attempt to solve the problem at issue. We observe straightaway that during the Berlin period there is no trace of a notable evolution in Hegel's thought on the issue that concerns us.

Before saying a word about the method that we are going to employ, this is the place to give an account briefly of the initial facts of our problem. In addition to statements about the "divinity" of the state and statements with a more or less similar tone, we read very often in Hegel that the state is the "substance [*Substanz*] of the individuals" and likewise, just as often that the state is their "final end" [*Endzweck*]. The term "substance" easily evokes the meaning of "first cause" that the word had for Spinoza. It is from this that the impression arises that the state is, for Hegel, the fundamental initial and permanent cause of the properly human development of mankind and his education. Since in the European philosophical tradition, it is the character of the first cause to be a classical attribute of the divinity, and that goes as well for the other characteristic that we have just mentioned, i.e., that of the final end, then we see that these two qualities, *Substanz* and *Endzweck*, both attributed to the state, seem to furnish the basic commentary on its "divinity" [*Göttlichkeit*].

What is really the case? In order to respond to this question and a number of other equally difficult ones that pose themselves with respect to Hegel's thought in general, it is necessary to refer to two complementary methods. The first consists in establishing with as much care as possible the sense of all of the relevant terms with a technical meaning employed by the philosopher. This procedure, indispensable with regard to any philosopher, is particularly appropriate for those of us concerned with what is imagined to be Hegel's strongly personal terminology, which has produced so many obscurities and equivocations. With respect to this procedure, one can speak of "the philological method" that we might employ when writing articles for a Hegel lexicon. Moreover, in order to understand with exactness the ideas of our author, it is also necessary to be constantly aware of the general structure of his thought. This rule, also one of universal application, is required especially when, as here, it is a question of a thought that is at once very complex and very systematic and at the same time strongly interwoven. The philological method and this, so to speak, "ideological method" form, moreover, a circle in the sense that these methods not merely complement each other by the convergence of their conclusions, but also it happens that the former is necessary for the very exercise of the latter, and, depending on the case, the latter for exercise of the former.

Let us begin with the philological explication.[4] It is necessary first to observe that parallel to properly philosophical language, Hegel often expresses himself, as he himself informs us, in the language of religious "representation," which is in reality that of then current Lutheran preaching. (Of course, we must recall that Hegel in his youth had completed the course of studies of a priest at the University of Tübingen.) Now what can we glean from the passages written in this style? The state is called "divine," but it is far from being the only reality that is so named. For example, the same thing goes for human nature, in consequence of the rank that it occupies in the cosmos,[5] for human reason,[6] and for other elements as well. The expression is supposed to be understood in accordance with the religious teaching for which, as Hegel himself notes, "things are what they are because of the divine . . . creative thoughts."[7] For his part, Hegel during the Berlin period had long since renounced the Christian beliefs, taken in their traditional sense, of his youth. The Absolute became for him a first reason, not endowed it seems with its own consciousness, and which expresses itself through the cosmos and most particularly through human Spirit, where it becomes conscious of itself. The cosmos, an expression of Absolute Reason, is thus completely rational and completely satisfying for human reason. All the aspects and all the sections of the cosmos are, insofar as they are rational, unmistakable elements properly constitutive of the rational totality or of the Absolute, of "God." In this sense they are "divine." To use the philosophical language which Hegel deliberately transposes to traditional religious language (in the same way that his philosophy is a deliberate transposition of traditional religion), this is why numerous realities, and not only the state, are called "divine." Nature in its totality is "divine";[8] the spiritual life of the human person is "divine";[9] this even holds true for the family as well.[10] What does this all mean? The answer can be found in what Hegel very clearly says about education, which accustoms the individual to attach himself to the collective interests: education is "an immanent moment of the Absolute."[11] This expression is taken up again precisely with regard to the state, "a moment, a determination, of the divine essence."[12] All these things can, in Hegel's eyes be called "divine" because as he notes, a thing can be divine without its being exhaustive of the divine.[13]

Under these conditions we have hardly advanced because the whole question is going to be to know, with respect to the value of the state, if it, qua "divine," understood doubtless in the general sense which we have just indicated, should be considered as *sovereignly* divine or in any case as *eminently* divine. In order to find a response, it will be necessary to pursue our investigation in other directions.

As we have said, the very frequent expression, "the state is the substance of the individuals," immediately presents itself. But concerning this, problems abound. Generally speaking, the term "substance" means in Hegel a unique and permanent element affected by multiple and transitory modalities. Depending on the case, it can be a unique *cause* of multiple effects, or a unique and important *value* with respect to other subordinate values, or a unique and constant *end* with respect to various means, and so on. The state is at once called the "substance" of the individuals in order to express the fact that it is, through history, the sole and constant *cause* of all their education. But in this case, we are rather concerned with the state as a community that is the incarnation of a whole civilization and not merely the political state. Now, whatever may be the precise relation that he sees between civilization and political state, Hegel in any case distinguishes them clearly. (Indeed, the reality of the situation obliges him to do so. Was not Germanic civilization, i.e., the community of Germanic peoples, during that epoch divided into a series of politically independent states which were sometimes at war with one another: Germany, Sweden, England?) The political state as such with its own constitution, its independence, its prestige, and its own power is, for Hegel, an original value. Moreover, it is this which is almost always called the "state." It is this to which the solemn statements about the divinity of the state refer.

Now, when the political state is named the substance of the individuals, it is not considered so much as a cause of the education of men as the *end* of their will. It is the "substance of their will," an expression synonymous with the "substantial object of their will," that is, an object valuable in itself, a unique and permanent object of their desire (a value and end in itself, *stans*, subordinated to other goals, *sub-stans*). This leads us to prove the equivalence of the expression the state as "substance" with the third term which we have discussed, namely, the state as "final end." At the same time, the conundrum about the use of the word "substance" is to a certain degree clarified. It remains to be seen in the final analysis in what sense the state is the "final end."

In order to show with a final remark on the word "substance" that this question will not be simple either, let us note right from the beginning that if the political state is called the "substance" of the individuals, exactly the same thing holds true for the family, and it thus seems that it too is an object valuable in itself, a unique and permanent object of individual wills. Are these two realities, the state and the family—which are each valuable in their own right and each "divine," "holy," and "substantial"— "final ends," the one for the other? And if so, what would this mean? Are we on the path toward a plurality of final ends, toward a pluralism of absolute values? In this case, how do these diverse absolute values arrange themselves with respect to each other?

After this account of the philological method, the time has come to go back to the ideological method and start once again from the beginning. Now, we are going to examine the general structure of Hegel's system in order to see which hypotheses it gives rise to concerning the question of the value of the state. In reality, we are going to be concerned with much more than working hypotheses but rather with very pressing suggestions. We will need to verify them as we go on to the extent possible by Hegel's explicit statements concerning the place and the role of the political state and other connected questions. Fortunately, such declarations will not be wanting.

Thus, furnished with a knowledge, which can still be only very scant, of the "dialectical" procedure of thought via thesis, antithesis, and synthesis,[14] let us take a glance at the table of contexts of the *Encyclopedia*. We see there an outline of the structure of the becoming of the totality of the real. From triad to triad, this outline raises some of the most general aspects of things (being, nothing, becoming, quality, quantity, etc.) in passing through the aspects and elements of a nature lower than man (space, time, gravitation, electricity, vegetable life, animal life, etc.) until we reach man himself considered in his individual life, his social life, the history of civilizations, and the higher forms of his spiritual life.

In order to interpret this immense succession of stages and levels, of structures and rhythms with some precision, it is necessary to remember that beginning with the level where a concept has made its appearance, it contrives to apply itself to all the following levels. Thus, from the moment when the idea of finality has risen up in the construction, all the higher layers are marked with finality: the theses and antitheses are by an immanent tendency oriented toward the synthesis as toward an end. The same thing goes for the general notion of the organism which specifies, at a higher level, the notion of finality and which will prove to be key for the problem that we are concerned with. At first, let us define this idea of an organism. Taking up again and expounding the Kantian definition of organism, Hegel sees in an organism a collection such that each element is for its part and in its own way at once the cause and the end of each of the others, whence it results that the said collection is both the effect and the end of each of its elements. It follows that from the moment when this very general idea of organic totality has made its appearance in the system, all the triads are so structured that not only, as we said above, the synthesis constitutes the end of the thesis and the antithesis, but also each of the three terms constitutes the end of the other two, however, with a certain prevalence placed on the synthesis over the first two terms. For example, let us say that for Hegel, in biological life each organ is at once the cause and the immanent end of each of the others, with there being a prevalence of the higher organs.[15] I forego treating this in detail.

This being so, let us consider the supreme triad of the system. We see represented there the religious, artistic, and philosophical life, respectively. The final element forms the synthesis, the fulfillment, the accomplishment, the keystone of the triad (and at the same time of the totality of things). With what concerns religion (here above all traditional Christian religion), it takes the place of philosophy for the nonphilosophers, and the philosophers themselves should nourish the nonphilosophical sectors with their spirit, their imagination, and their sensibility. Hegel calls this triad the "Absolute Spirit." For the sake of convenience, we will call this the "spiritual life" of the person. We must leave our subject for a moment to describe with precision the organic relations that unify the three terms: philosophy, religion, and art. It is preferable, moreover, to turn our attention toward the triad immediately below this one where precisely the political state appears. It forms there the figure of the synthesis vis-à-vis the family (thesis) and civil society (antithesis). Hegel understands by civil society [bürgerliche Gesellschaft] the collection of institutions such as the corporations, the police, the judiciary, and the municipalities. Likewise, for the sake of convenience, rather than speaking as Hegel does of "objective Spirit" here, we will call this "the sphere of social relations" or "social morality" (Sittlichkeit, in Hegel's own language).

Since these two spheres, that of the spiritual life of the person and that of social morality, constitute a part of a larger triadic structure of which spiritual life is the synthesis, one sees immediately how, in virtue of our general hypothesis, the relations between the political state and the spiritual life of persons come to establish themselves. Spiritual life will have its value in itself, irreducible to all others, and will therefore be a final end for itself. The state will have for an end, in part at the very least, the spiritual life of its members. Besides, the state with its internal political life and its independence, its prestige and power, will have a value in itself, irreducible to any other and will thus be a final end for itself, to be sure partially, since it already has for its final and principal end the spiritual life of its members. Finally, philosophy, religion, and art will have for their final end, partially and in a more or less secondary manner, the political state.

Such is the first suggestion, derived from the general structure of the system, concerning the place of the state. Is this suggestion collaborated by specific and explicit textual examples? Without a doubt. Hegel repeatedly praises Christianity for having placed at the summit the things of value of the human person in his moral and religious life. And he notes in his *Philosophy of History*, if the divine unfolding of the history of civilizations and of empires seems to hold the human individual at very little value, it is only an appearance which concerns the spiritual life of man, which can be taken above all contingencies. And one sees Hegel, the celebrated philosopher, great bourgeois and servant of the Prussian grandeur, write this remarkable sentence: "The religiosity, morality of a limited life—that of a burgher, of a peasant—concentrated in his interiority and in the limits of a few situations and entirely simple, possess an infinite value, and the same value as the religiosity and morality of a perfectly cultivated spirit and an existence opulent in the extensiveness of its relations and of its works."[16] If this is the value of the spiritual life, one wants to see what the figure of the end in itself would look like for the political state. And this is, indeed, what Hegel declares with solemnity in the inaugural lesson in his *Lectures on the Philosophy of Religion*. Religion, "the final unconditioned end," is "the center" of all other "manifestations of Spirit: the sciences, the arts, etc. . . . . and the interests of political life."[17] To be sure, as he will explain in the final lessons of the same course, religion in the highest sense is philosophical thought and, more widely, the philosophical life dedicated to the cult of the total rationality by contemplation and by action.

The duties of the state with respect to religious confessions and institutions of education, in particular universities, proceed from these principles. The state should respect the autonomy of these institutions (except in the case of doctrines contrary to life in society) and should accord them its protection.[18] We will not go into detail on this since it is the general principles alone which are important for us here.

Therefore, in virtue of our hypothesis about the pluralism of absolute values, as we have said, we must now expect that spiritual life for its part will be assigned in a reciprocal manner as a partial end to the political state in view of itself. And this is indeed what we have proved. In conformity with their nature, philosophy and religion should render the state the practical and secondary service, notes Hegel, of supporting its authority in the opinion of the citizens.[19] But especially, they perform for the state the service, which is eminent, of doctrinally grounding its value. This is what philosophy does when it establishes the character of the reality of the highest rationality which marks the state, and this is what religion, in particular the religion of Luther, also does in its own way in presenting the state as an institution willed by God.[20]

With the relations between the state and the highest forms of life of Spirit so elucidated, the question arises about the relations of the state to other aspects of human beings. If the state is supposed to accept the *sharing* of its quality as the final end with *the spiritual life of persons*, would it not seem to be the final end *without sharing* at the very least with those among its members *who do not coincide purely and simply with its life of Spirit*? Or, in order to express the same question in words which will be very influential and which we already find in Hegel himself,[21] if the "person" escapes the state, is it not necessary to say that the "individual" should be entirely consecrated to it? In order to respond to this question, it is now necessary to examine the internal structure of the sphere of social relations, a structure composed, we recall, of the state, the family, and the civil institutions.

Like the state, the family, we have already noted, is called a "substantial object" of value. As a result, it has a value in itself, irreducible to another part, and it is not therefore purely and simply in the service of the state. On the contrary, the state is for one part in the service of the family in view of the family itself. We will not insist on this question in order to pass over to the examination of the relations between the state and the civil institutions, because it is with respect to this that the relations become elucidated between the state and the individual considered in that which is not his spiritual life and thus in that which we can call his individual exterior goods (his life, his goods, his capacity to come and go, his reputation, etc.). In fact, according to Hegel, whereas the state and the family have an original and ultimate value in themselves, the civil institutions (police, courts, corporations, etc.) are pure means in the service of individuals. Their value is that of simple utility. This being the case, in the triad of social relations that we have been examining, the antithesis, which on the face of it is constituted by the civil institutions, in fact resides in the individuals themselves, envisioned according to their nonspiritual advantages. And the question comes up here: what is the status of the individuals in view of and with respect to the state? Do they have some value in themselves, and, as a result, are they in a certain measure a final end for the state? One will immediately perceive our line of interpretation, since the notion of the three members of a triad of partial final ends, the one for the other, leads to the idea that if the political state is an eminent end in itself for the individuals, then it is at the same time, in part, organized with a view toward the individuals in view of themselves. This confirms once again that in the state the individuals have rights that do not derive solely or in the final analysis from their quality as members of the state, i.e., as useful to the state, to its prestige and power, but rather from their quality as man, a value in itself. Once again, the individuals do not have only duties with respect to the state, with the only right being to the necessary conditions for fulfilling their duties. And from its side, the state does not have only rights with respect to the individuals, with the only duty toward them being to act in their best interests. The individuals possess unconditional rights with regard to the state, and correlatively the state has unconditional duties with respect to them. (And it is by the mediation of the civil institutions that the state exercises these duties toward the individuals.) Such is the conception that the structure of the Hegelian system naturally leads to. And one finds it very clearly expressed in the texts.[22]

The ancient idea of the state, which sees in the city the final end without reciprocity is, Hegel supposes, once and for all a thing of the past. In the modern state, the individual is seen to recognize the "subjective freedoms" (that is to say the civil and political rights) which belong to him. Neither Plato nor Aristotle nor Roman law ventured to see the basis of law itself as the "infinite" value of the human person envisaged in his own "particularity." One owes to Christianity this chief discovery, which philosophy then furnished with a fully rational status.[23]

Starting from this principle, we see that Hegel is concerned with a whole series of "subjective freedoms," and he attaches to them explicitly and on many occasions the dignity of man as such: the right to the free disposition of oneself with the condemnation of slavery, the right to property, the right to choose one's profession, the right to express personal opinions and to pursue individual fantasies, and so on.[24] Before the law, he writes, "what should exist are not Jews, Catholics, Protestants, Germans or Italians, but men, and this consciousness of equality of man as such is one of infinite importance."[25] And it is, among other reasons, in virtue of the Jews' quality as men that Hegel declares himself a partisan of granting them civil rights.[26]

In fact, concerning political rights, one can only say that Hegel showed himself to be quite liberal. He was, in any case, appreciably more liberal than the king of Prussia in whose service he was. Indeed, the constitutional monarchy, such as he conceived it, featured a permanent national assembly, public debates, freedom of the press (considered by Hegel as a political right), and trial by jury, all institutions that were absent in the Prussian state of the day. These political rights, like civil rights, are in their principle the special attribute of the human person as such. With respect to sovereignty, the *first* root of political power, it is necessary to see it as unequally shared, in the monarch, the constitutive bodies, and the sum of the citizens. With this doctrine, Hegel tries deliberately to find a middle way between the ancient conception of the state as an end without reciprocity and the conception, at the close of the eighteenth century, of individuals as ends without reciprocity, who represent the end to which the state is totally ordered.[27]

Has he, to the point of making it explicit (or almost), rescued the idea of the state and the individual as final reciprocal ends? Unquestionably he has in our view. Two chief passages which have been little noted state in effect the precise relation which is at work between the individual and the state.[28] There we are concerned with talk of "organism" and of the "organic relation." But Hegel by no means wants to imply by this that individuals are simple members of a whole. The state will only have value precisely in its members without any of its own emergence, so to speak, outside of the whole. Such was, Hegel notes, the error of Aristotle. There is here an organic relation, i.e., a relation of member to member, not between individuals inside of the state as a whole, but rather between the state and the individual. The totality is not in the occurrence of the state, but in the state-individual pair. This is, Hegel observes, a "higher organic relation," which is to say again that in this pair each of the two terms is an end for the other. The idea expressed here by Hegel can appear subtle. It is, however, clear and very significant, since it rejects the notion of the state organism precisely in favor of another more flexible application of the same category of organic relation. Thus, for one part—a preponderant part—the state is the final end of the individuals, considered in their exterior advantages, and for the other part—a lesser part—the individuals are the final end of the state.

We need to make this sharing of ends more precise. With respect to the chief of state and the individuals, one sees immediately that the question is about the rights to different objects or the rights to different portions of the one and the same divisible object. And it is, indeed, thus that Hegel envisages things. In his eyes the preponderance of the state is manifested above all in the right which it has to demand that the individual, in case of war, risk his life (a right which is obviously without univocal reciprocity in the person of the chief of state) in the same way that it can demand a considerable sacrifice of his goods in the form of war contributions.

Let us observe that with respect to the case of war a sort of *ad hominem* argument is furnished to Hegel in favor of the idea of the state as end in itself and as the preponderant end. According to him, the true foundation of this idea is, it is true, in the eminent rational character of the state, an issue which we cannot hope to understand or resolve here. But to address those persons who will be insensitive to this reason,

Hegel remarks that if they admit, as is more often the case than not, that the state can under certain conditions legitimately demand that the individual risk his life in war, one can see no other possible foundation for such a demand than to consider that the state in its independence, as an end in itself, prevails over individuals.

We cannot at present indicate the motives, for which, despite the chief restrictions which we have indicated, Hegel sees in the state an eminent element of the rational totality, a highly divine element of the divine whole, and why also he sometimes speaks with a certain emphasis concerning this "divinity."

The political state is the highest incarnation of reason before spiritual life proper. It is the highest human society. This is why it cannot consent to any alienation of authority to the advantage of a league of nations.[29] The eminence of this sovereign society is so uniform that it is metaphysically inevitable and morally profitable that it manifest itself in war. (One sees things made more precise here in a very important manner which concerns war above.) Hegel does not want in any way to legitimate just any war. But the principle is set out: war alone, by the sacrifice that it requires of the individual, proves to the eyes of all the eminence of the state and leads the individual to recognize it, practically while leading him to his death.[30] One sees it is not merely a question here of accepting war as an inevitable evil, which would have this indirect consequence more or less as a compensation, but it would not be desirable under this form to bring to light the value of the state to arouse the courage of the individuals. Moreover, the value of the state is such that war, which renders it manifest, is an element of the rational perfection of the universe and an indispensable factor of civic education. By this right, war is desirable in principle and regardless of whatever the concrete conditions are when it can legitimately release itself. This understanding helps to explain, we think, the emphatic statements about the divinity of the state. It is necessary still to add that Hegel, by his rebuke, knew how to react against the anarchic tendencies which he perceived in the German youth of his epoch.

Let us sum up. The state, for Hegel, is not divine in the sense that it is the highest reality there can be as the unique final end of man. Spiritual life is higher than the state, and many other values still are values in themselves alongside the state. It follows that the state is not divine in the sense that its authority is totalitarian. The state is divine in that it is an element and an eminent element of the divine whole and an important part of the final, total end of man. It is divine to the extent that war might be in principle desirable.

Finally, let us add one last restriction. What is divine in its occurrence is the idea, i.e., the ideal of the state, and the real state is divine only to the extent to which it incarnates this ideal. This extent can be notably imperfect, as Hegel teaching at the university of the King of Prussia well knew.[31] That Hegel has seen nothing of sacrilege in this understanding testifies in its own way to the fact that the state in order to be divine, as it was in his eyes, was only a semi-divinity. Because of this, one is indeed still free to suppose that semi-idolatry is still idolatry.

20

The Hegel Legend of "Thesis-Antithesis-Synthesis"

Gustav E. Mueller

Hegel's greatness is as indisputable as his obscurity. The matter is due to his peculiar terminology and style; they are undoubtedly involved and complicated, and seem excessively abstract. These linguistic troubles, in turn, have given rise to legends[1] which are like perverse and magic spectacles—once you wear them, the text simply vanishes. Theodor Haering's monumental and standard work has for the first time cleared up the linguistic problem. By carefully analyzing every sentence from his early writings, which were published only in this century, he has shown how Hegel's terminology evolved—though it was complete when he began to publish. Hegel's contemporaries were immediately baffled, because what was clear to him was not clear to his readers, who were not initiated into the genesis of his terms.

An example of how a legend can grow on inept reading is this: translate "*Begriff*" by "concept," "*Vernunft*" by "reason," and "*Wissenschaft*" by "science"—and they are all good dictionary translations—and you have transformed the great critic of rationalism *and* irrationalism into a ridiculous champion of an absurd panlogistic rationalism and scientism.

The most vexing and devastating Hegel legend is that everything is thought in "thesis, antithesis, and synthesis." A prominent illustration of this interpretation is W. T. Stace's *The Philosophy of Hegel*.[2] He first supposes that he has to construe Hegel's philosophy in "triads of thesis, antithesis, and synthesis" (97), then he finds that Hegelian texts do not follow this "ideal, method," and what is his conclusion?

> These irregularities do not indicate, however, that our description of
> the dialectic method is wrong. What they do show is that Hegel has not
> himself been able to carry out his own dialectic method with absolute
> consistency in all cases. This is of course an imperfection in his system.
> (Ibid.)

And although he claims that his chapters "embody all the essential principles," nevertheless, he does admit that they "can give little idea of
the vast fields which Hegel covered, the profuse wealth of his concrete
illustrations, the enormous learning which he brought to bear upon these
studies, the profundity and breadth of his vision" (viii). This abstract
separation of "principles" and "vision" is utterly un-Hegelian. The actual
texts of Hegel not only occasionally deviate from "thesis, antithesis, and
synthesis," but show nothing of the sort. "Dialectic" does not for Hegel
mean "thesis, antithesis, and synthesis." Dialectic means that any "ism"—
which has a polar opposite, or a special viewpoint leaving "the rest" to
itself—must be criticized by the logic of philosophical thought, whose
problem is reality as such, the "world-itself."

Hermann Glockner's reliable *Hegel Lexikon*[3] does not list the Fich-
tean terms "thesis, antithesis, synthesis" together. In all the twenty volumes
of Hegel's "complete works"[4] he does not use this "triad" once; nor does
it occur in the eight volumes of Hegel texts, published for the first time in
the twentieth century. He refers to "thesis, antithesis, and synthesis" in the
preface of the *Phenomenology of Mind*, where he considers the possibility of
this "triplicity" as a method or logic of philosophy. According to the Hegel
legend one would expect Hegel to recommend this "triplicity." But, after
saying that it was derived from Kant, he calls it a "lifeless schema," "mere
shadow" and concludes:

> The trick of wisdom of that sort is as quickly acquired as it is easy to
> practice. Its repetition, when once it is familiar, becomes as boring
> as the repetition of any bit of sleight-of-hand once we see through
> it. The instrument for producing this monotonous formalism is no
> more difficult to handle than the palette of a painter, on which lie
> only two colors.[5]

In the student notes, edited and published as *History of Philosophy,*
Hegel mentions in the Kant chapter, the "spiritless scheme of the triplicity of thesis, antithesis, and synthesis" (*geistloses Schema*) by which the
rhythm and movement of philosophic knowledge is artificially pre-scribed
(*vorgezeichnet*).[6]

In the first important book about Hegel by his student, intimate friend and first biographer, Karl Rosenkranz (*Hegels Leben*, 1844), "thesis, antithesis, synthesis" are conspicuous by their absence. It seems Hegel was quite successful in hiding his alleged "method" from one of his best students.

The very important new Hegel literature of this century has altogether abandoned the legend. Theodor Haering's *Hegels Wollen und Werk*[7] makes a careful study of Hegel's terminology and language and finds not a trace of "thesis, antithesis, synthesis." In the second volume there are a few lines (118, 126) in which he repeats what Hegel in the above quotation had said himself, i.e., that this "conventional slogan" is particularly unfortunate because it impedes the understanding of Hegelian texts. As long as readers think that they have to find "thesis, antithesis, synthesis" in Hegel they must find him obscure—but what is obscure is not Hegel but their colored glasses. Iwan Iljin's *Hegels Philosophie als kontemplative Gotteslehre*[8] dismisses the "thesis, antithesis, synthesis" legend in the preface as a childish game (*Spielerei*), which does not even reach the front-porch of Hegel's philosophy.

Other significant works, like Hermann Glockner, *Hegel*; Theodor Steinbüchel, *Das Grundproblem der Hegelschen Philosophie*; Theodor Litt, *Hegel: Eine Kritische Erneuerung*; Emerich Coreth, *Das Dialektische Sein in Hegels Logik*; and many others have simply disregarded the legend.[9] In my own monographs on Hegel,[10] I never found any "thesis, antithesis, synthesis."

Richard Kroner, in his introduction to the English edition of selections from Hegel's *Early Theological Writings*, puts it mildly when he says:

> This new Logic is of necessity as dialectical as the movement of thinking itself. . . . But it is by no means the mere application of a monotonous trick that could be learned and repeated. It is not the mere imposition of an ever recurring pattern. It may appear so in the mind of some historians who catalogue the living trend of thought, but in reality it is ever changing, ever growing development; Hegel is nowhere pedantic in pressing concepts into a ready-made mold. The theme of thesis, antithesis, and synthesis, like the motif of a musical composition, has many modulations and modifications. It is never "applied"; it is itself only a poor and not even helpful abstraction of what is really going on in Hegel's Logic.[11]

Well, shall we keep this "poor and not helpful abstraction" in our attic because "some historians" have used it as their rocking-horse? We rather agree with the conclusion of Johannes Flugge: "Dialectic *is not* the scheme of thesis, antithesis, and synthesis imputed to Hegel."[12]

In an essay by Nicolai Hartmann, *Aristoteles und Hegel*, I find the following additional confirmation of all the other witnesses to the misinterpretation of Hegel's dialectic: "It is a basically perverse opinion [*grundverkehrte Ansicht*] which sees the essence of dialectic in the triad of thesis, antithesis, and synthesis."[13] The legend was spread by Karl Marx, whose interpretation of Hegel is distorted. It is Marxism superimposed on Hegel. Thesis, antithesis, synthesis, Marx says in *Das Elend der Philosophie*, is Hegel's purely logical formula for the movement of pure reason, and the whole system is engendered by this dialectical movement of thesis, antithesis, synthesis of all categories. This pure reason, he continues, is Hegel's own reason, and history becomes the history of his own philosophy, whereas in reality, thesis, antithesis, synthesis are the categories of economic movements.[14] The few passages in Marx's writings that resemble philosophy are not his own. He practices the communistic habit of expropriation without compensation. Knowing this in general, I was also convinced that there must be a source for this "thesis, antithesis, and synthesis," and I finally discovered it.

In the winter of 1835–36, a group of Kantians in Dresden called on Heinrich Moritz Chalybäus, Professor of Philosophy at the University of Kiel, to lecture to them on the new philosophical movement after Kant. They were older, professional men who in their youth had been Kantians, and now wanted an orientation in a development which they distrusted; but they also wanted a confirmation of their own Kantianism. Professor Chalybäus did just those two things. His lectures appeared in 1837 under the title *Historische Entwicklung der speculativen Philosophie von Kant bis Hegel, Zu näherer Verständigung des wissenschaftlichen Publikums mit der neuesten Schule*. The book was very popular and appeared in three editions. In my copy of the third edition of 1843, Professor Chalybäus says: "This is the first trilogy: the unity of Being, Nothing and Becoming . . . we have in this first methodical thesis, antithesis, and synthesis . . . an example of or schema for all that follows" (354). This was for Chalybäus a brilliant hunch which he had not used previously and did not pursue afterwards in any way at all. But Karl Marx was at that time a student at the University of Berlin and a member of the Hegel Club where the famous book was discussed. He took the hunch and spread it into a deadly, abstract machinery. Other left-Hegelians, such as Arnold Ruge, Ludwig Feuerbach, and Max Stirner use "thesis, antithesis, synthesis" just as little as Hegel.

But "thesis, antithesis, synthesis" is not the only Hegel legend fabricated by Marx. Brutal simplifications are Marxistic specialties. "Thesis, antithesis, synthesis" is said to be an "absolute method" of Hegel's alleged "rationalism." Marx says: "There is in Hegel no longer a history in the order of time, but only a sequence of ideas in reason." Hegel, on the contrary, says: "The time-order history is distinguished from the sequence in the order of concepts."[15]

A third minor legend is innocently taken for granted in the recent work by R. Tsanoff. "Actually the closing pages of the *Philosophy of Right* review in rapid survey the historical evolution of mankind—and discover 'the unity of the divine and human' in the German Empire! All these stiff Prussian notions are recorded in Hegel's works: they cannot be ignored."[16] In the first place, Hegel is not a Prussian, but a Swabian, and he is not stiff, but flexible. "Actually" the text referred to contains not a word justifying the accusation. "*Germanische Welt,*" as Hegel calls it does not mean German ("*Germanisch*" is not "*Deutsch*"), but simply refers to the incontestable historical fact that various German tribes after the disintegration of the Roman Empire reconstituted Europe or what we now call "the West," in distinction from the Arabic and Slavic worlds. Germany is not even mentioned, let alone Prussia. Hegel's theme, further, is not "the historical evolution of mankind" culminating in some particular state, but the omnipresent self-manifestation of the Absolute—always submerged in the distortions of irrationality. This interpretation is, in its origin, a vicious Marxistic smear: it occurs almost verbatim in Friedrich Engels's crude diatribe "Ludwig Feuerbach and the Exit of Classical German Philosophy" (1847). To him, Hegel's organic conception of the state is, of course, a hated bulwark against the totalitarianism of his "economic class-interests."

Once the Hegel legend was established, writers of textbooks in the history of philosophy copied it from their predecessors. It was a convenient method of embalming Hegel and keeping the mummy on display for curious visitors of antiquities. Hegel's dialectic was inconvenient for a century in which philosophers liked to belong to partisan schools and abstract "isms," such as idealism, realism, objectivism, subjectivism, rationalism, skepticism, and so forth. In Hegel's dialectic, philosophy had matured beyond such one-sided possibilities. Hegel's dialectic means that philosophy has found its own logic, as Croce proclaimed in his book *What is Dead and What is Alive in Hegel,*[17] with which the Hegel Renaissance of the twentieth century was initiated.

21

Hegel and the Myth of Reason

Jon Stewart

The oeuvre of Hegel, like that of many thinkers of the post-Kantian tradition in European philosophy, has been subject to a number of misreadings and misrepresentations by both specialists and nonspecialists alike that have until fairly recently rendered Hegel's reception in the Anglo-American philosophical world extremely problematic.[1] These often willful misrepresentations, variously referred to by scholars as the Hegel myths or legends,[2] have given rise to a number of prejudices against Hegel's philosophy, primarily, although by no means exclusively, in the English-speaking world.[3] Among the caricatures that have enjoyed the widest currency are the following: that Hegel denied the law of contradiction;[4] that his dialectical method of argumentation took the form of the thesis-antithesis-synthesis triad;[5] that he saw the end of history in his own philosophical system;[6] that he tried to prove a priori the number of planets;[7] that he was a reactionary apologist for the Prussian state,[8] or worse, a protofascist;[9] finally, that he was a kind of pre-Kantian metaphysician[10] or "cosmic rationalist"[11] who believed like Schelling and some of the romantics in a metaphysical world soul.

One of the most pervasive of the famous Hegelian myths is that Hegel was an archrationalist and the last great spokesman for reason before the full-scale attack on rationality by Schopenhauer, Kierkegaard, Nietzsche, Heidegger, Freud, Sartre, Foucault, Derrida, and others. According to this myth, Hegel, as the last *Aufklärer*, believed in the all conquering force of reason and gave in his philosophy a description of the march of reason in history. As one commentator writes, "The whole thrust of his thinking was an affirmation of absolute reason. With him, moreover, belief in reason was at the highest summit."[12] We are told from another expositor, "For Hegel, if reason is rightly understood, it is sovereign."[13] On this view of Hegel, everything is reducible to reason or to what Hegel calls the concept (*Begriff*). One writer characterizes this purportedly Hegelian view by saying, "The 'concept' meets with no opposition in Hegel's system that it cannot overcome; it holds a position of power that no other thinker before ever dared ascribe to it, that no one had ever claimed that it possessed. The concept is omnipotent."[14] Allegedly, Hegel was wholeheartedly and naively under the spell of all-powerful reason. According to this myth, not only does Hegel's philosophy purport to demonstrate reason in history, but it also affirms it normatively.[15] By gaining an insight into the rationality in history we are then reconciled with the world as it exists.[16] The normative side of Hegel's account with its unqualified acceptance and approval of reason appears on this view particularly naive and vulnerable to criticism. Nietzsche's analysis of how unrelenting Socratic rationality destroyed Greek tragedy by demanding that it live up to reason's own ideals of intelligibility and self-reflectivity, and Foucault's analysis of the subtle and ubiquitous forms of contemporary power relations that have resulted largely from the pernicious employment of instrumental reason are seen as two corrective accounts of Hegel's unreflective and overenthusiastic view of reason. I would like to show that this oversimplistic view of Hegelian philosophy vastly underestimates and, indeed, ignores Hegel's own criticism of reason and its purportedly positive effects. What I ultimately wish to suggest is that Hegel is very aware of the pernicious aspects of reason, and thus is best seen not as the last *Aufklärer* but rather as a forerunner of the so-called "irrationalist tradition."[17] Thus, the tradition that is inaugurated after Hegel is most accurately understood not as a new beginning or a radical break with the past but rather as something continuous with what preceded it.[18]

I

I wish simply to put to the side whatever historical accidents might have played a role in the distancing of Hegel from the existentialist tradition;[19] instead, the question I wish to concentrate on for the moment is what in Hegel's philosophy itself has been the cause of his having been tagged with the label of archrationalist. The tendency to see in Hegel a naive proponent of the Enlightenment has doubtless been largely due to a widespread misinterpretation of his famous claim, "What is rational is actual and what is actual is rational."[20] The common understanding of this famous Hegelian maxim, made famous by Rudolf Haym's interpretation,[21] is that everything that exists or that is "actual" has its own reason and internal justification. Thus, existing practices and institutions would seem to be above reproach.[22] This would seem to imply an extreme conservatism and a callous, Panglossian theodicy, since in this maxim we could find a justification for oppressive institutions and needless human suffering. On this view, totalitarian states with all their abuses would be rational simply because they exist.[23] To make such a claim seriously would be to support some kind of naive whigish stance and to be guilty of a naive optimism purportedly characteristic of the Enlightenment.[24] Blinded by his overpowering belief in reason, Hegel allegedly was entirely uncritical or unfeeling not to see the obvious evils of the world around him, in particular, the evils of the contemporary Prussian state. One commentator writes, "In their post-Enlightenment optimism all but a few modern philosophers have ignored or denied the demonic. Hegel's philosophy— which unites Christian religious with modern secular optimism—is the most radical and hence most serious of this modern tendency."[25] Hegel, due to his belief in the omnipotence of reason, was thus purportedly blind to the evil or "demonic" aspects of culture, history, or society.

This view of Hegel as a naive optimist or as a nineteenth-century Candide is still quite common, although, as recent interpreters have made clear, this certainly cannot be what Hegel meant in the famous or, perhaps better, infamous, passage cited above.[26] In his discussion of this disputed dictum in the *Encyclopedia*, Hegel makes it clear that he is not so naive as to believe that everything that exists is rational and thus beyond reproach simply by virtue of its existence: "for who is not acute enough to see a great deal in his own surroundings which is really far from being as it ought to be?"[27] Clearly, Hegel recognizes that there are injustices, atrocities and crimes that exist and for which there can be no justification, rational or otherwise. Moreover, in a passage from the *Philosophy of Right*, Hegel refutes precisely this position that he is accused of holding. In distinguishing between the philosophical and the historical approach to law, he argues that laws and institutions cannot be justified by an appeal to their mere existence and by uncovering their historical origins in the world:

> When those who try to justify things on historical grounds confound
> an origin in external circumstances with one in the concept, they
> unconsciously achieve the very opposite of what they intend. Once
> the origination of an institution has been shown to be wholly to
> the purpose and necessary in the circumstances of the time, the
> demands of history have been fulfilled. But if this is supposed to pass

for a general justification of the thing itself, it turns out to be the opposite, because, since those circumstances are no longer present, the institution so far from being justified has by their very disappearance lost its meaning and its right.[28]

Thus, for Hegel, historical justifications fail on their own terms; simply laying bare the historical origins of an institution is not enough to justify it since in this way we could justify all existing institutions: "A particular law may be shown to be wholly grounded in and consistent with the circumstances and with existing legally established institutions, and yet it may be wrong and irrational in its essential character."[29] The historian is only able to see a given law in its particular social-historical context and thus can never critically judge it; on the other hand, the philosopher, for Hegel, is able to examine the specific laws against an independent criterion, i.e., that of the concept of right itself. Thus, he clearly could not have held that whatever law or state exists is by mere virtue of its existence just and right. His general claim that there is reason in history ought not to be construed as meaning that every single historical event is rational; likewise, his claim that the state as a concept is rational does not mean that every single existing state is rational. Precisely this misunderstanding has promoted the picture of Hegel as a naive and anachronistic *Aufklärer*.

Admittedly, Hegel's use of the term "reason" (*Vernunft*) is not always as clear as it might be; however, he does tell us that it is synonymous with his term of art the "Idea" (*Idee*).[30] In his philosophy, the "Idea" is a two-sided concept: on the one hand, it is the form or abstract concept of thought, but, on the other hand, it is also the concrete content in which reason, implicit in thought, is embodied in reality.[31] The Idea is then the marriage of the abstract concept with the concrete actuality which is mediated by reason. Insofar as reason is both in the abstract concept and in the concrete actuality, it is synonymous with the Idea. This rather abstract notion of reason in Hegel then comes in the following way to be associated with the conception of reason that we are more familiar with, (i.e., reason understood as reflection or critical self-consciousness): the task of philosophy, for Hegel, is not to posit utopias or some world beyond our own[32] but rather to examine reality or what is the case and to find the reason that is in it. In order to discover reason in the manifold of concrete contents, the philosopher must understand this manifold conceptually. Hegel writes concerning the study of nature, "people grant . . . that nature is inherently rational, and that what knowledge has to investigate and grasp in concepts is this actual reason present in it."[33] The task of the speculative philosopher is then for Hegel by means of reflection and criticism to examine reality and deduce its implicit rationality. Through this critical reflection the philosopher is also then participating in that rationality. Thus, rationality also takes on the sense of critical observation or reflection for Hegel. In this sense, Hegel's conception of rationality resembles Socratic rationality, which applies the dialectical criticism to all institutions and beliefs to see if they rest on a rational basis. It is Hegel's purportedly unqualified positive assessment of reason in this sense that I wish to analyze.

In this paper, I wish merely to suggest that Hegel is in fact aware of the pernicious aspects of history and culture as well as the negative aspects of reason itself, understood in the aforementioned sense of philosophical reflection. This should suffice to convince us that the myth of Hegel as an archrationalist at least minimally is in need some serious qualification if it is not to be dismissed altogether, although it may leave the question open concerning to what degree Hegel ascribes to reason and what precisely the conception of reason is that he ascribes to.[34] The modest objective of this paper is simply to provide sufficient grounds for rejecting this myth and thus to call for a reevaluation of Hegel's advocation of reason along the lines indicated above. It would be impossible here to give an overview of Hegel's philosophy to the end of discussing the role of reason and rationality in it. My argumentative strategy will be instead to analyze a few passages from Hegel's account of the conflict between the Enlightenment and religion in the *Phenomenology of Spirit*.[35] Short of giving us an overview of Hegel's use and understanding of these very broad concepts, this analysis will provide us with sufficient counterevidence to expose this Hegelian myth and will allow us to see the connections between his thought and that of the so-called "antirationalistic" thinkers listed above.

I do not wish to imply that Hegel has not been seen in some regards as an important forerunner of the irrationalist or existentialist movement, since this connection is a well-known fact to most intellectual historians. Clearly, Hegel's account of, for instance, the master-slave dialectic[36] or the unhappy consciousness[37] has had a profound influence on existentialist philosophy and psychology. His dialectical methodology and his view of the situatedness of human knowledge have also found positive resonance among the existentialists. However, with respect to the question of reason, Hegel has been, for whatever reason, presented as the typical *Feindbild* by commentators of this tradition. Thus, despite the many continuities that can be found in Hegel's thought and that of the existentialists, the important difference is usually thought to lie in Hegel's allegedly unreflective view of reason which is contrasted to the existentialists' disabused, hard-headed, critical assessment of it. This, in my view, is a part of the Hegelian myth of reason, which can be debunked by an analysis of his portrayal of reason in a few carefully selected *loci* in his philosophical *corpus.*

II

In the section entitled "Self-Alienated Spirit" of the "Spirit" chapter in the *Phenomenology*, we find an extended account of the Enlightenment and the French Revolution. The preponderance of this material is dedicated to an account of the Enlightenment's conflict with what it perceives as the simple superstition of religion. I do not wish to go into detail about Hegel's account of how the Enlightenment misses the point of religion and continually erects a straw man that it uses as a ready foil for its criticisms.[38] These passages show us merely that Enlightenment rationality is limited in its approach to Christianity and fails to see religion's truth in falsity, so to speak. Moreover, I do not wish to go into Hegel's criticism of the unrestrained madness of Enlightenment reason during the reign of terror since that has been fairly well documented.[39] I wish instead to focus on a specific passage in the *Phenomenology* which, in my view, best illustrates Hegel's awareness of the pernicious nature of reason. Before we examine this passage, however, it will be useful to see how Hegel expresses the same thought elsewhere in his *corpus.*

Hegel clearly recognizes the destructive power of rational thought and reflectivity on cultural institutions in a provocative *Zusatz* in the *Encyclopedia Logic.* He writes,

> In earlier days men meant no harm by thinking: they thought away
> freely and fearlessly. They thought about God, about Nature, and the
> State: and they felt sure that a knowledge of the truth was obtainable
> through thought only, and not through the senses or any random ideas
> or opinions. But while they so thought, the principal ordinances of life
> began to be seriously affected by their conclusions. Thought deprived
> existing institutions of their force. Constitutions fell a victim to thought:
> religion was assailed by thought: firm religious beliefs which had been
> always looked upon as revelations were undermined, and in many
> minds the old faith was upset. The Greek philosophers, for example,
> became antagonists of the old religion and destroyed its beliefs.[40]

Here Hegel portrays philosophical reflection as a destructive influence on various aspects of society and culture at large. When reason examines specific institutions in the social order and demands that they give an account of themselves, it invariably finds many of them to be wanting in rational justification. From the perspective of reason, the institutions in question seem arbitrary and are no longer viewed as legitimate. At this point the institutions lose their cultural meaning and gradually fall into desuetude. Reason and reflective thought are thus destructive forces in traditional societies. Hegel sees this dynamic of awakened rationality as destroying traditional beliefs and customs in the Greek world. This same thought about the destructive nature of reason is expressed in the *Phenomenology*, but there reason and reflection are characterized in a different way.

In the section on "Self-Alienated Spirit" from the "Spirit" chapter of the *Phenomenology*, Hegel uses a provocative and, for some perhaps, surprising set of metaphors to describe the subtle encroachment of skeptical, scientific reason into traditional areas of religion and ethical life. He writes,

> It is on this account that the communication of pure insight is comparable to a silent expansion or to the *diffusion*, say of a perfume in the unresisting atmosphere. It is a penetrating infection which does not make itself noticeable beforehand as something opposed to the indifferent element into which it insinuates itself, and therefore cannot be warded off. Only when the infection has become widespread is that consciousness, which unheedingly yielded to its influence, *aware* of it.[41]

Here he uses two metaphors for reason: a perfume and an infection. Like a perfume, "pure insight," Hegel's synonym for Enlightenment reason, works its way initially unimpaired into the ways of thinking and acting that form the matrix of our ethical life. Religion is simply a part of the passive and "unresisting atmosphere" which reason interpenetrates, since the former does not perceive the imminent danger that rationality presents to its most dearly held beliefs and institutions. But gradually reason, like a perfume, diffuses itself silently and insidiously into all aspects of culture.

Hegel then changes the metaphor from that of a benign diffusion of perfume in space to the clearly negative image of an infection. According to this metaphor, Spirit is conceived of as an organic system that is attacked from the inside by a deleterious force, i.e., a cancerous disease. But this disease is latent and goes long undetected by spiritual doctors with even the greatest prognostic acumen. When the illness is finally detected, the disaster and the lasting damage therefrom have already occurred:

> Consequently, when consciousness does become aware of pure insight, the latter is already widespread; the struggle against it betrays the fact that infection has occurred. The struggle is too late, and every remedy only aggravates the disease, for it has laid hold of the marrow of spiritual life, viz. the Notion of consciousness, or the pure essence itself of consciousness. Therefore, there is no power in consciousness which could overcome the disease.[42]

Just as self-awareness comes about only after the original sin, so also aware-ness of the destructive nature of reason comes only after the damage has already been done. Here the remedies to save religion from the onslaught of reason are ineffectual, since religion attempts to defend itself using the tools of reason, thus giving away the game from the start. Religion attempts to justify itself with rational argumentation and scientistic reason in order to show that it can hold up under the test of this scientistic rationality, yet this betrays that the attempt at defense or treatment has come about entirely too late, since even the defenders of religion have already unknowingly come to accept the basics of Enlightenment ration-ality and its methodology and criteria for truth as their standard.[43] Thus, the disease is only aggravated: far from erecting an effective defense, the defenders of religion unknowingly ally themselves with the enemy. By using reason as its standard, religion destroys itself, since at its heart are mystery and revelation, which are by their very nature irreducible to logical categories and rational explanation. Reason has by this time so permeated our way of thinking that we cannot imagine anything else as a viable option. As Hegel puts it, reason "has laid hold of the marrow of spiritual life." Thus, the spiritual life of religion cannot be rescued since it has become unable to defend itself, having been so infected by the foreign principle of thought. Reason here is clearly portrayed as something subtle, insidious, and destructive, and this account stands squarely in opposition to the myth of Hegel's unqualified advocation of reason outlined above.

Hegel also uses the Biblical image of the serpent to describe the status of reason after the capitulation of religion. For the disabused, religion remains but a hollow husk lacking any substantial meaning and alive only in memory and in history books: "Memory alone then still preserves the dead form of Spirit's previous shape as a vanished history, vanished one knows not how. And the new serpent of wisdom raised on high for adoration has in this way painlessly cast merely a withered skin."[44] Here reason frees itself of religion and superstition just as the serpent sheds its skin. Religion is merely a dead form of Spirit that falls away when it is no longer of use. This image suggests that in fact religion and reason are in a sense the same thing, i.e., the same serpent with a new form. This new form of religion then simply replaces the old form.[45] Dostoevsky describes the zealous belief in technology and in scientific rationality that he sees embodied in the hustle and bustle of the city of London likewise as a new sort of religious affirmation: "You feel that a great amount of spiritual fortitude and denial would be necessary in order not to submit, not to capitulate to the impression, not to bow down to the fact and not to worship Baal."[46] For Dostoevsky, science and reason are the new Baal in which London has corrupted itself, just as for Hegel they are the new serpent of wisdom. Both images imply a deception or a seduction, and both clearly indicate the pernicious side of reason.

III

The metaphor for reason or reflectivity as an illness and a disease links Hegel with the more recent thinkers in the European philosophical tradition who unambiguously place emphasis on the pervasive and deleterious force of rationality. This illness metaphor has been a dominant one the philosophical and literary schools of existentialism and phenomenology. I wish simply to trace this image in a handful of thinkers in order to show that they make use of this metaphor in the same way as Hegel does, i.e., to represent the destructive or pernicious force of reason. By pointing out the similar use of the illness metaphor in Hegel and in the "irrationalists," I do not mean to imply that the latter self-consciously made use of Hegel's metaphor or even that they read the passages cited above. My claim is merely that the similarity in language and in meaning with respect to this issue of reason and its effects that can be located precisely in this metaphor reveals that Hegel has more in common with the "irrationalist" tradition than is commonly acknowledged, and that Hegel was not the naive advocate of reason that he is often caricatured as being. This analysis of the illness metaphor will then help us to establish a hitherto unseen connection between Hegel and this tradition with respect to this issue of reason.[47]

Dostoevsky's criticism of modern science and rationality and the schools of Marxism, utilitarianism, socialist utopianism, and so on that labor under their banner is well known. His portrayal of this criticism through the underground man in *Notes from Underground* takes on an interesting form which invites comparison with the passages from Hegel cited above. Dostoevsky's underground man characterizes himself as suffering from the disease of reflectivity or what he calls "hypercon-sciousness" by virtue of which he differs from the normal man. The underground man writes, "I swear to you, gentlemen, that to be hyper-conscious is a disease, a real positive disease. . . . I am firmly convinced not only that a great deal of consciousness, but that any consciousness, is a disease. I insist on it."[48] Here we see critical rationality in the form of self-consciousness, which the underground man says leads to a negative, pernicious, hyperconsciousness that precludes action and inhibits social intercourse. Like a disease, consciousness begins innocently and unsus-pectingly as simple reflection, but then it spreads to a global reevaluation of one's life and social interactions. After the onset of this illness, one cannot return to the naive prereflective life of custom and habit. Reflec-tion then comes to have a paralyzing effect on the individual, who can no longer immediately engage in and enjoy communal life. It incapacitates the underground man in his feeble attempts at human interaction. It renders him a pathetic and jaded intellectual, alienated from all ordinary human contact. Thus, even the unreflective lives of the underground man's former schoolmates begin to look attractive insofar as they, unin-fected by the disease of hyperconsciousness, are able to engage in the social world spontaneously and are able to attain a kind of immediate fraternity regardless of its superficiality or want of a rational basis.

The concepts of scienticity, objective thought, and rationality are also well-known targets for Kierkegaard. In *The Sickness unto Death*, he develops at great length the metaphor of rational reflection as an illness in a way that is strikingly similar to Dostoevsky's account.[49] In his pref-ace, Kierkegaard writes, "once and for all may I point out that in the whole book, as the title declares, despair is interpreted as a sickness."[50] Just as Dostoevsky's underground man suffers from despair which is a symptom of the disease of hyperconsciousness, so also despair is for Kierkegaard strongly associated with rational reflection:[51] "Conscious-ness is decisive."[52] The spread of the "dialectical disease" of despair is traced in what might be seen as Kierkegaard's phenomenology of despair. In analyzing the vertical path of despair, the degrees of despair and thus of the sickness are correlated with the degrees of consciousness: "The ever increasing intensity of despair depends upon the degree of consciousness or is proportionate to its increase: the greater the degree of consciousness, the more intense the despair."[53] Increased reflection and rationality are here again portrayed as the spreading of a disease.

In *The Birth of Tragedy*, Nietzsche argues that self-reflection and reason led Socrates to demand of every custom and tradition in Greek life that it give a self-justifying rational account of its existence, and in his portrayal of this cultural movement he uses the same illness metaphor.[54]

With this demand, Socratic rationality thus destroyed the immediate primordial nature of Greek tragedy in the satyric chorus, which for Nietzsche was one of the original "irrational" Greek institutions, which originated from the inebriated and orgiastic Dionysian rites in which the follower found "a mystic feeling of oneness"[55] or a "primal unity"[56] in the community of fellow revelers. He writes, "might not this very Socratism be a sign of decline, of weariness of *infection*, of the anarchical dissolution of instincts?"[57] The new scientistic rationality, called by Nietzsche the "logic and logicizing of the world,"[58] which was embodied by Socrates, functioned like an irreversible infection on Greek tragedy and on the immediate irrational impulse for which tragedy provided a forum. As soon as there was reflectivity, the immediate unity with the whole was broken and the Apollinian principle of individuation set in again. The infection had become fatal. Rationality and science thus destroyed Greek tragedy and became a threat to all immediate forms of art which aimed to overcome this individuality and to wallow in a primeval universality and harmony. Scientistic, Socratic rationality, which was a disease in the Greek world, then spread into a plague for the Western world as a whole:

> We see clearly how after Socrates, the mystagogue of science, one philosophical school succeeds another, wave upon wave; how the hunger for knowledge reached a never-suspected universality in the widest domain of the educated world, became the real task for every educated person of higher gifts, and led science onto the high seas from which it has never again been driven altogether. . . . For if we imagine that the whole incalculable sum of energy used up for this world tendency had been used *not* in the service of knowledge but for the practical, i.e., egoistic aims of individuals and peoples, then we realize that in that case universal wars of annihilation and continual migrations of peoples would probably have weakened the instinctive lust for life to such an extent that suicide would have become a general custom . . . as a remedy and a preventive for this breath of *pestilence*.[59]

For Nietzsche, scientistic rationality in the West has not been used to improve mankind's lot but rather, like a growing plague, has been an increasingly destructive force.[60]

Camus in his criticism of reason makes use of the same metaphor. He writes in the introduction to *The Myth of Sisyphus* about the object of his inquiry: "There will be found here merely the description, in the pure state, of an *intellectual malady*."[61] This intellectual malady has its origin in consciousness or reflectivity: "For everything begins with consciousness and nothing is worth anything except through it."[62] It is through reason or reflectivity, which Camus here describes as "consciousness," that we are jarred out of our daily routine and habit and come to recognize the contingency of our goals and projects. The dominant metaphor used to describe consciousness and the use of reason as a universally critical tool that undermines transcendent values and causes us to see the absurd in human existence is that of an illness. In *The Plague*, Camus's character Tarrou equates self-reflection with a disease as well. He explains how he long lived in innocence until reason and reflectivity caught up with him: "Then one day I started thinking."[63] Thus he explains to the valiant Doctor Rieux: "I had plague already, long before I came to this town and encountered it here."[64] The plague he refers to is not that which affects Oran but rather that of reflectivity. Camus here uses the plague as a fitting symbol for the cause or occasion of the self-reflection which reshapes the life of the existential hero Tarrou, and which jars the townspeople of Oran out of their complacency and lack of reflection. Camus, like Dostoevsky, views this new lucidity about the disjointedness between man's nostalgia for unity and comprehension of the universe and the utter indifference of the universe to our demands as a positive insight that leads to liberation. The goal then is not to backslide into some form of what Nietzsche called "metaphysical comfort," but rather to keep the paradoxical or absurd nature of the human condition continually in focus. Camus writes, "The important thing . . . is not to be cured, but to live with one's ailments."[65] For Camus, many existentialist philosophers are guilty of what he calls "philosophical suicide," since they offer a *cure* to this disease by positing some form of hope in spite of the original recognition of the absurd. Here, the disease is the awareness, brought about by critical reason, of the indifference of the world to our hopes and values, and the existential task is to live unflinchingly with this awareness.

Sartre uses the metaphor of a particular kind of illness—the nausea—to describe the awareness of consciousness via the employment of reason.[66] Sartre's first person narrator Roquentin in the novel *Nausea* explains the origin of his condition: "Something has happened to me, I can't doubt it any more. It came as an *illness* does, not like an ordinary certainty, not like anything evident."[67] Nausea, like the plague, is a disease of consciousness which comes on secretly and unexpectedly. Nausea arises covertly and perniciously for Roquentin. One feels the nausea when contemplating the banality of the facticity of our existence. When one *via* reason and reflection realizes the lack of transcendent meaning or the nothingness in the world around oneself, the disease sets in. The disease of reflectivity leads to the realization of the contingency of human existence and to the existential requirement of positing human values in place of any divine meaning. Roquentin's rational reflection on the nothingness of existence hinders his ability to act in the world. He describes his failed attempt to write as follows: "An immense sickness flooded over me suddenly and the pen fell from my hand, spluttering ink. What happened? Did I have the Nausea?"[68] The vertigo of the nausea is brought on by the over-reflectivity of consciousness. Roquentin, like Dostoevsky's underground man, is hyperconscious, as is evidenced in his narrative:

> How serpentine is this feeling of existing—I unwind it, slowly. . . . If I could keep myself from thinking! I try, and succeed: my head seems to fill with smoke . . . and then it starts again: "smoke . . . not to think . . . don't want to think . . . I think I don't want to think. I mustn't think that I don't want to think. Because that's still a thought." Will there never be an end to it?[69]

Despite his mental exertions, Roquentin cannot stop reflectivity or the existential disease of nausea with a simple act of will. Like many a physical disease, the nausea runs its own course and is not within our control.

The use of this dominant metaphor throughout the existentialist tradition provides us with a point of contact or overlap between this tradition and Hegel's thought with respect to the conception of reason. Hegel's portrayal of reason as a malady and as a destructive force clearly reveals his awareness of its darker aspects, and this awareness associates him with the existentialists and the self-avowed irrationalists and distances him from the caricature of the naive *Aufklärer*. The continuity of Hegel and these later thinkers in the European tradition is most obviously seen in the common use of the illness image to portray the spread of reason. We can thus see Hegel, instead of as the great enemy of the irrationalist tradition and as the bitterest opponent of Kierkegaard and Schopenhauer, as in fact an important forerunner of the existentialist tradition on this issue as on many others. This insight will then help us to lay to rest one of the better known Hegel myths and will afford us a fresh opportunity for evaluating Hegel's significance with respect to the question of reason. The difficult and controversial road that Hegel studies has come in the Anglo-American philosophical world has only added to the intrinsic difficulty of Hegel's own texts in our effort to achieve a sober assessment of his thought. We can only do this to the degree to which we are able and willing to put aside the Hegel caricatures, legends, and myths, and to the degree to which we are willing to stop viewing him as an angel or as a devil, as a Candide or a Hitler.[70]

Notes

Jon Stewart, Introduction

1. Walter Eckstein, "Hegel, Georg Wilhelm Friedrich," *Collier's Encyclopedia*, vol. 12 (Crowell-Collier Publishing Company, 1964), 14.

2. Ibid., 15.

3. Ibid.

4. Robert C. Solomon, "Teaching Hegel," *Teaching Philosophy* 2 (1977–78), 213–24. See also his "Approaching Hegel's *Phenomenology*," *Philosophy Today* 13 (1969), 115–25.

5. E.g., John N. Findlay, "Hegel and Modern Preconceptions," in his *The Philosophy of Hegel: An Introduction and Re-Examination* (New York: Collier Books, 1966), 13–24; originally, *Hegel: A Re-Examination* (New York: Macmillan, 1958); Wilhelm Seeberger, "Vorurteile gegen Hegel," in his *Hegel oder die Entwicklung des Geistes zur Freiheit* (Stuttgart: Ernst-Klett Verlag, 1961), 42–70.

6. Benedetto Croce, *What Is Living and What Is Dead in the Philosophy of Hegel*, trans. Douglas Ainslie (New York: Russell and Russell, 1969), 217.

7. James Hutchison Stirling, *The Secret of Hegel: Being the Hegelian System in Origin, Principle, Form and Matter* (London: Longman, Green and Longman, Roberts and Green, 1865).

8. William H. Goetzmann, ed., *The American Hegelians: An Intellectual Episode in the History of Western America* (New York: Knopf, 1973). David Watson, "Hegelianism in the United States," *Bulletin of the Hegel Society of Great Britain* 6 (1982), 18–28. David Watson, "The Neo-Hegelian Tradition in America," *Journal of American Studies* 14 (1980), 219–34.

9. See John E. Smith, "Hegel in St. Louis," in *Hegel's Social and Political Thought*, ed. Donald Phillip Verene (New Jersey: Humanities Press, 1980), 215–25.

10. See Loyd D. Easton, "Hegelianism in Nineteenth-Century Ohio," *Journal of the History of Ideas* 23 (1962), 335–78.

11. Oxford: Clarendon Press, 1883.

12. Glasgow: MacLehose, 1877.

13. Edinburgh: W. Blackwoods and Sons; Philadelphia: J. B. Lippincott, 1883.

14. New York: Macmillan and Co.; Glasgow: MacLehose, 1893.

15. Glasgow: MacLehose, 1904.

16. London: H. S. King and Co., 1876.

17. All of these texts appeared at Cambridge University Press.

18. See for instance Peter Hylton, *Russell, Idealism and the Emergence of Analytic Philosophy* (Oxford: Clarendon Press, 1992).

19. London: George Allen and Unwin, Ltd., 1918.

20. *The Open Society and Its Enemies*, vol. 2: *The High Tide of Prophecy: Hegel, Marx and the Aftermath* (London: Routledge and Kegan Paul, 1944–45).

21. London: Methuen, 1966.

22. Rudolf Haym, *Hegel und seine Zeit: Vorlesungen über Entstehung und Entwicklung Wesen und Werth der hegelischen Philosophie* (Berlin: Rudolf Gaertner, 1857; modern edition, Hildesheim: Georg Olms Verlagsbuchhandlung, 1962), 357ff.

23. Ibid., 365.

24. Cf. Hubert Kiesewetter, *Von Hegel zu Hitler: eine Analyse der Hegelschen Machtstaatsideologie und der politischen Wirkungsgeschichte des Rechts-Hegelianismus* (Hamburg: Hoffmann and Campe, 1974).

25. Walter Kaufmann, *Hegel: A Reinterpretation* (Garden City: Anchor Books, 1965), 290.

26. See Marcel Régnier, "Hegel in France," *Bulletin of the Hegel Society of Great Britain* 8 (1983), 10–20.

27. Cf. Mark Poster, *Existential Marxism in Postwar France: From Sartre to Althusser* (Princeton: Princeton University Press, 1975), 8.

28. Alexandre Kojève, *Introduction à la lecture de Hegel: Leçons sur la Phénoménologie de l'esprit professées de 1933 à 1939 à l'École des Hautes Études*, ed. Raymond Queneau (Paris: Gallimard, 1947, 1971). In English as *An Introduction to the Reading of Hegel*, ed. Alan Bloom, trans. James H. Nichols, Jr. (New York: Basic Books, 1969).

29. Alexandre Koyré, "Hegel à Iéna (à propos de publications récentes)," *Revue philosophique de France* 59 (1934), 274–83; reprinted in *Revue d'histoire et de philosophie religieuse* 15 (1935), 420–58.

30. Jean Hyppolite, *Genése et structure de la "Phénoménologie de l'esprit" de Hegel* (Paris: Aubier, 1946). In English as *Genesis and Structure of Hegel's "Phenomenology of Spirit,"* trans. Samuel Cherniak and John Heckman (Evanston: Northwestern University Press, 1974). N.b. Hyppolite still owes much to Kojève's account of Hegel and the end of history.

31. Pierre-Jean Labarriére, *Structures et mouvement dialectique dans la Phénoménologie de l'esprit de Hegel* (Paris: Aubier, 1968).

32. E.g., *Kant and the Philosophy of History* (Princeton: Princeton University Press, 1980).

33. Bloomington: Indiana University Press, 1967.

34. *Das Scheitern einer Einleitung in Hegels Philosophie: Eine Analyse der Phänomenologie des Geistes* (Munich and Salzburg: Verlag Anton Pustet, 1973); *Individuum und Gemeinschaft bei Hegel*, vol. 1: *Hegel im Spiegel der Interpretationen* (Berlin: Walter de Gruyter, 1977).

35. *Hegel's Philosophy of Right* (Oxford: Clarendon Press, 1952).

36. Oxford: Clarendon Press, 1935.

37. Walter Kaufmann, *Hegel: A Reinterpretation* (Garden City: Anchor Books, 1965).

38. *Études hégéliennes: Les points capitaux du système* (Louvain: Publications Universitaires de Louvain, 1958).

39. Shlomo Avineri, *Hegel's Theory of the Modern State* (Cambridge: Cambridge University Press, 1972).

40. *Hegel's Recollection: A Study of Images in the "Phenomenology of Spirit"* (Albany: State University of New York Press, 1985).

41. *Hegel's Social and Political Thought* (Atlantic Highlands: Humanities Press, 1980).

42. Nietzsche, *Untimely Mediations,* vol. 2: "The Use and Abuse of History," §8.

43. Francis Fukuyama, *The End of History and the Last Man* (New York: Free Press, 1992). See also Fukuyama, "The End of History," *The National Interest* 16 (Summer 1989), 3–18.

44. Second edition (Freiburg: Karl Alber Verlag, 1980).

45. H. S. Harris, *Hegel's Development: Toward the Sunlight, 1770–1801* (Oxford: Clarendon Press, 1972); Harris, *Hegel's Development: Night Thoughts, 1801–1806* (Oxford: Clarendon Press, 1983).

46. Cambridge: Cambridge University Press, 1989.

47. English translation: "G. W. F. Hegel: *Philosophical Dissertation on the Orbits of the Planets* (1801), Preceded by the 12 Theses Defended on August 27, 1801," trans. Pierre Adler, *Graduate Faculty Philosophy Journal* 12 (1987), 269–309.

48. J. M. E. McTaggart, *A Commentary on Hegel's Logic* (Cambridge: Cambridge University Press, 1910), §4: "The whole course of the dialectic forms one example of the dialectic rhythm, with Being as Thesis, essence as Antithesis, and Notion as Synthesis. Each of these has again the same moments of Thesis, Antithesis, and Synthesis within it, and so on."

49. Walter T. Stace, *The Philosophy of Hegel: A Systematic Exposition* (London: Macmillan and Co., 1924; reprint, New York: Dover, 1955), cf. §§126, 166.

50. *Hegel Denkgeschichte eines Lebendigen* (Munich: Francke Verlag, 1959). In English as *Hegel: The Man, His Vision and Work* (New York: Pageant Press, 1968); *Hegel über Offenbarung, Kirche und Philosophie* (Munich: E. Reinhardt, 1939); *Hegel über Sittlichkeit und Geschichte* (Munich: E. Reinhardt, 1940).

51. Kaufmann, *Hegel: A Reinterpretation,* 290.

52. See Henry Harris, "The Hegel Renaissance in the Anglo-Saxon World Since 1945," *The Owl of Minerva* 15 (1983), 77–107; Frederick G. Weiss, "A Critical Survey of Hegel Scholarship in English: 1962–1969," in *The Legacy of Hegel: Proceedings of the Marquette Hegel Symposium 1970,* ed. J. J. O'Malley, et al. (The Hague: Martinus Nijhoff, 1973), 24–48.

M. W. Jackson, Hegel: The Real and the Rational

1. Avineri (1970, 124) is one of the very few scholars who have noted this misquotation.

2. References to *The Philosophy of Right* are to sections, not pages. Hegel's remarks are indicated with an R and the additions based on students' notes with an A. His footnotes are marked with an N.

3. Sandars (1855, 215) thought Hegel's government institutions were copied from the British example.

Works Cited

Aris, R. (1936). *History of Political Thought in Germany from 1789 to 1815*. London: Cass.

Artz, F. (1934). *Reaction and Revolution, 1815–1832*. New York: Harper.

Avineri, S. (1970). *The Social and Political Thought of Karl Marx*. Cambridge: Cambridge University Press.

Barker, E. (1914). *Nietzche and Treitschke*. Oxford: Oxford University Press.

———. (1915). *Principles of Social and Political Theory*. Oxford: Oxford University Press.

Berki, R. (1968). "Political Freedom and Hegelian Metaphysics." *Political Studies* 16, 365–83.

Brudner, A. (1978). "The Significance of Hegel's Prefatory Lectures on the Philosophy of Law." *Clio* 8, 41–48.

Burno, B. (1961). "Morale e stato." *Rivisita Rosminians* 63, 57–67.

Bullock, A. (1962). *Hitler*. New York: Harper and Row.

Catlin, G. (1962). *Systematic Politics*. London: Allen and Unwin.

Catt, E. H. (1962). "Democracy Re-considered." *Power and Civilization*. Ed. A. Cooperman and F. V. Walter. New York: Crowells.

Champion, R. (1985). "The Purpose of Popper." *Age Monthly Review* 5, 11–13.

Coker, R. (1932). "Pluralistic Theories and the Attack upon State Sovereignty." *Principles of Social and Political Theory*. Ed. C. Merriam. Oxford: Oxford University Press. 80–119.

Cole, G. (1934). *Some Relations Between Political and Economic Theory*. London: Macmillan.

Copleston, R. (1963). *A History of Philosophy*. Vol. 7. Garden City: Image Books.

Cousin, V. (1866). "Souvenirs d'Allemagne." *Revue de Deux Mondes* 75, 594–619.

Ebenstein, W. (1956). *Great Political Thinkers*. 3d ed. New York: Rinehart.

Elliott, William Y., and N. MacDonald. (1950). *Western Political Heritage*. Englewood Cliffs: Prentice Hall.

Engels, F. (1888). *Ludwig Feuerbach und der Ausgang der Klassischen Deutschen Philosophie*. Berlin: Verlag furliteratur und politik.

d'Entrèves, A. (1967). *The Notion of the State*. Oxford: Oxford University Press.

Findlay, J. N. (1962). *Hegel*. New York: Collier.

Fisk, M. (1980). *Ethics and Society*. Sussex: Harvester.

Fleischmann, E. (1964). *La philosophie politique de Hegel*. Paris: Plon.

Gooch, G. F. (1920). *Germany and the French Revolution*. London: Cass.

Goodwin, B., and K. Taylor. (1982). *The Politics of Utopia*. London: Hutchinson.

Gordon, S. (1980). *Welfare Justice, and Freedom*. New York: Columbia University Press.

Gottfried, P. (1978). "Marx, Hegel and the Philosophy of Right." *Modern Age* 22, 177–86.

Grégoire, F. (1962). "L'état hégélien est-t-il totalitaire?" *Revue Philosophique de Louvain* 60, 244–53.

———. (1955). "The Use and Misuse of Philosophy and Philosophers." *The Third Reich*. Ed. E. Venneil. London: Weidenfeld and Nicholson.

Haym, R. (1857). *Hegel und seine Zeit*. Berlin: Guertner.

Hegel, G. (1895). *The Ethics of Hegel*. Boston: Ginn.

———. (1896a). *Hegel's Lectures on the History of Philosophy*. London: Routledge and Kegan Paul.

———. (1896b). *Philosophy of Right*. London: Bell.

———. (1952). *Hegel's Philosophy of Right*. London: Oxford University Press.

———. (1955). *Die Vernunft in der Geschichte*. Hamburg: Neimer.

———. (1970). *Grundlinien der Philosophie des Rechts*. Frankfurt: Suhrkamp.

———. (1974). *Hegels Vorlesungen über Rechtsphilosophie*. 4 vols. Stuttgart: Frommann.

———. (1975a). *Hegel's Aesthetics*. Vol. 2. London: Oxford University Press.

———. (1975b). *Hegel's Logic*. London: Oxford University Press.

———. (1977). *Hegel's Phenomenology of Spirit*. London: Oxford University Press.

Heiden, K. (1944). *Der Fuehrer*. New York: Fertig.

Hobhouse, I. (1918). *The Metaphysical Theory of the State*. London: Allen and Unwin.

Hocking, W. (1926). *Man and the State*. New Haven: Yale University Press.

Hoffmeister, J. (1963). *Hegel: Correspondence*. Vol. 2. Paris: Gallimard.

Holborn, H. (1969). *A History of Modern Germany, 1648–1840*. New York: Knopf.

d'Hondt, J. (1968). *Hegel et son Temps*. Paris: Editions sociales.

Hook, S. (1970). "Hegel and his Apologist." *Hegel's Political Philosophy*. Ed. W. Kaufmann. New York: Atherton. 87–104.

Inwood, M. (1983). *Hegel*. London: Routledge and Kegan Paul.

Joad, C. (1938). *Guide to the Philosophy of Morals and Politics*. London: Gollancz.

Joll, J. (1960). "Prussia and the German Problem, 1830–1866." *New Cambridge Modern History*. Vol. 10. Ed. J. Bury. Cambridge: Cambridge University Press. 493–522.

Kaminsky, J. (1962). *Hegel on Art*. New York: State University Press of New York.

Kaufmann, W. (1959). "The Hegel Myth and Its Method." *From Shakespeare to Existentialism*. Boston: Beacon. 137–71.

Keily, G. (1978). *Hegel's Retreat from Eleusis*. Princeton: Princeton University Press.

Knox, T. (1957/1958). "Hegel's Attitude to Kant's Ethics." *Kant-Studien* 40, 70–81.

Kohn, H. (1967). *Prelude to Nation-State*. Princeton: Van Nostrand.

Kolakowski, L. (1981). *Main Currents of Marxism*. Vol. 1. London: Oxford University Press.

Kierkegaard, S. (1941). *Concluding Unscientific Postscript*. Princeton: Princeton University Press.

Laski, H. (1935). *The State in Theory and Practice*. London: Allen and Unwin.

Lichtheim, G. (1967). *The Concept of Ideology*. New York: Vintage.

MacKintosh, R. (1903). *Hegel and Hegelianism*. Edinburgh: Clark.

MacIver, R. (1926). *The Modern State*. London: Oxford University Press.

Magee, B. (1979). *Popper*. London: Woburn.

Maritain, J. (1960). *La philosophie morale.* Paris: Gallimard.

Mead, G. (1936). *Movements of Thought in the 19th Century.* Chicago: University of Chicago Press.

Miewald, R. (1984). "The Origins of Wilson's Thought." *Politics and Administration.* Ed. J. Rabin and J. Bowman. New York: Dekker. 19–30.

Miliband, R. (1977). *Marxism and Politics.* London: Oxford University Press.

Morris, G. (1887). *Hegel's Philosophy of the State and of History.* Chicago: Griggs.

Muirhead, J. (1915). *German Philosophy in Relation to the War.* London: Murray.

Nelson, B. (1982). *Western Political Thought.* Englewood Cliffs: Prentice Hall.

Neumann, F. (1942). *Bebemouth.* New York: Oxford University Press.

Pateman, C. (1979). *The Problem of Political Obligation.* New York: Wiley.

Pavon, D. (1971). "La Filosofia Politica de Hegel en Relacion con 'La Constitucion de Alemania.' " *Revista de Estudios Politicas* 178, 5–87.

Peters, R. (1966). "Hegel and the Nation-State." *Political Ideas.* Ed. D. Thomas. New York: Basic. 134–47.

Pfannenstill, B. (1936). *Bernard Bosanquet's Philosophy of the State.* Lund: Ohlsson.

Popper, K. (1966). *The Open Society and its Enemies.* Vol. 2. 5th ed., London: Routledge and Kegan Paul.

———. (1976). *Unended Quest.* London: Collins.

Quinton, A. (1976). "Karl Popper." *Contemporary Political Philosophers.* Ed. A. Crespigney and K. Minogue. London: Methuen.

Reyburn, H. (1921). *The Ethical Theory of Hegel.* London: Oxford University Press.

Riedel, M. (1984). *Between Tradition and Revolution.* Cambridge: Cambridge University Press.

Rose, G. (1981). *Hegel Contra Sociology.* London: Athlone.

de Ruggiero, G. (1959). *The History of European Liberalism.* Boston: Beacon.

Russell, B. (1945). *A History of Western Philosophy.* New York: Simon and Schuster.

Ibid. (1947). *Philosophy and Politics.* London: Cambridge University Press.

Ryle, G. (1947). "Critical Notice." *Mind* 55, 167–72.

Sabine, G. (1937). *A History of Political Theory.* London: Harrop.

Sandars, T. (1855). *Oxford Essays.* London: Parker.

Sartori, G. (1962). *Democratic Theory.* New York: Praeger.

Seeley, J. (1878). *The Life and Times of Stein.* Cambridge: Cambridge University Press.

Shirer, W. (1961). *The Rise and Fall of the Third Reich.* London: Secker and Warburg.

Simon, W. (1953/1954). "Variations in Nationalism during the Great Reform Period in Prussia." *American Historical Review* 49, 305–21.

Sturt, H. (1906). *Idola Theatri.* London: Macmillan.

Treitschke, H. von (1916). *History of Germany in the 19th Century.* 2 vols. London: Harrold.

Tucker, D. (1980). *Marxism and Individualism.* Oxford: Blackwell.

Vaughan, C. (1925). *Studies in the History of Political Philosophy.* Vol. 2. Manchester: Manchester University Press.

Viereck, P. (1965). *Meta-Politics.* Rev. ed. New York: Capricorn.

Voegelin, E. (1968). *Science, Politics and Gnosticism.* Chicago: Regnery.

Watkins, F. (1967). *The Political Tradition of the West.* Cambridge: Harvard University Press.

Weldon, T. (1946). *State and Morals.* London: Murray.

Wells, G. (1959). *Herder and After.* The Hague: Mouton.

Yirmiahu Yovel, Hegel's Dictum that the Rational is Actual and the Actual is Rational

1. This paper sums up in part a large essay, a first draft of which appeared in *Hebrew Philosophical Quarterly, Iyyun* (Jerusalem 1976). The full-length English version is in progress.

2. By this term I mean a set of objectives and strategies of discourse, to which a given message is related and which must be part of its interpretation. It is not the same as "context" in the sense of the textual environment of a phrase (passage, chapter, etc.). It is closer to the "pragmatic context" of an utterance. Only it does not relate to utterances as one-time events but to repeatable items of discourse such as sentences, slogan-phrases, and so on.

3. This does not abolish, of course, the interest of the textual discovery, but puts it in the right perspective; it brings out and confirms that which was there all along. However, neither the original nor the revised formula in itself is a valid source for understanding the system.

4. Section 3 will be given here in full, sections 1 and 2 only in summary.

5. I use the double-headed arrow to indicate equivalence, and the one-headed arrow to indicate an implication whose converse is false.

6. Work on this paper was helped by the Centre Nationale de la Recherche Scientifique (C.N.R.S.), to which thanks are due.

Emil L. Fackenheim, On the Actuality of the Rational and the Rationality of the Actual

1. Hildesheim (Olms, 1962). Photomechanical reproduction of the original 1857 edition.

2. Sidney Hook, "Hegel and the Perspective of Liberalism," in *A Hegel Symposium*, ed. C. D. Travis (Austin: University of Texas, n.d.), 51.

3. Munich and Berlin: Oldenbourg, 1920.

4. Cf., e.g., Hook, "Hegel and the Perspective of Liberalism," 45. Hook's case is instructive because, obviously relying on memory, he is well enough served by it to quote the German text accurately—but not its order.

5. See below, sec. 7.

6. G. W. F. Hegel, *Encyclopedia of Philosophical Sciences* par. 6. *Hegel's Logic, Being Part One of the Encyclopedia of the Philosophical Sciences,* trans. William Wallace (Oxford: Clarendon, 1975) §6.

7. G. W. F. Hegel, *Werke*, vol. 11 (Berlin: Duncker and Humblot, 1840–47), 222ff.

8. Ibid., vol. 12, 336.

Henning Ottmann, Hegel and Political Trends

1. This essay was a contribution to the conference "Politics and German Idealism" (11–14 October 1978), which was supported by the Thyssen Foundation and organized by W. Jaeschke and K. R. Meist.

2. B. Willms suggests these images of Fichte in *Die totale Freiheit: Fichtes politische Philosophie* (Cologne, 1967), 1ff. See also the overview by H. Verweyen, *Recht und Sittlichkeit in J. G. Fichtes Gesellschaftslehre* (Freiburg, 1975), 9ff.

3. E. Topitsch, *Die Sozialphilosophie Hegels als Heilslehre und Herrschaftsideologie* (Neuwied, 1967), 5ff.; see also his "Über Leerformeln," in *Probleme der Wissenschaftstheorie*, Festschrift für Viktor Kraft, ed. E. Topitsch (Vienna, 1960), 251ff. Popper bases the empty formula criticism on the criticism of dialectic, since the dialectic, according to Popper, rests on contradictions, which allow "any conclusion." K. R. Popper, "Was ist Dialektik?" in *Logik der Sozialwissenschaften*, ed. E. Topitsch (Cologne, 1968), 262ff.

4. Above all H. Heller, *Hegel und der nationale Machtstaatsgedanke in Deutschland* (Leipzig, 1921).

5. This is asserted in all seriousness with appeal to Buchheim by A. v. Martin, *Macht als Problem: Hegel und seine politische Wirkung* (Mainz, 1976), 5. Martin continues the argumentation here which allowed him in 1948 to see in Hegel one who paved the way for the German disaster. A. v. Martin, *Geistige Wegbereiter des deutschen Zusammenbruchs: Hegel, Nietzsche, Spengler* (Recklinghausen, 1948).

6. While Popper grounds this thesis in its strong form in complete ignorance of the non-Hegelian ideologues of national socialism and with reference to the false chief witnesses such as the antisemites Fries, Schopenhauer, and Wagner (*Die offene Gesellschaft und ihre Feinde*, vol. 2: *Falsche Propheten: Hegel, Marx und die Folgen* [Bern, 1957; 2d ed. 1970]), the last version of this "from Hegel to Hitler" literary genre is more carefully formulated. Right Hegelianism is for Kiesewetter only one of the tributaries from which the river of national socialism was formed (H. Kiesewetter, *Von Hegel zu Hitler* [Hamburg, 1974], 19); however, Hegel's ideology for the authoritarian state is supposed to have also been "constitutive" for the Third Reich (ibid., 21).

7. Paulus in his attack on the motto from the preface about the identity of reason and reality already foreshadows the criticism of accommodation; the anonymous reviewer "Z.C." uses the word "*accomodieren*" as early as 1822: "Such a philosophy can clearly accommodate itself to everything, which is precisely the order of the day. This philosophy will teach that liberal principles rule in the world." Cited from K.-H. Ilting, ed., G. W. F. Hegel, *Vorlesungen über Rechtsphilosophie*, vol. 1 (Stuttgart, 1973), 403. For Paulus's critique see ibid., 565ff. Thaden reports the following to Hegel as early as 1821: "You are decried both as a royalist philosopher and as a philosophical royalist" (ibid., 394–95). We can, in agreement with Riedel, probably designate the first book reviews of the *Philosophy of Right* as an "unsuccessful reception." M. Riedel, ed., *Materialien zu Hegels Rechtsphilosophie*, vol. 1 (Frankfurt, 1975), 17ff.

8. J. E. Erdmann, *Die deutsche Philosophie seit Hegels Tode* (Berlin, 1896). Reprint with an introduction by H. Lübbe (Stuttgart, 1964), 710.

9. This controversy can be followed in the selections in the Riedel collection, 209ff.

10. See ibid., 267ff. Hegel himself responded only ironically to the confused attacks (ibid., 219).

11. Typical are the encomiums which Ruge still struck up for Prussia in 1838, which as a protestant progressive state justified the double meaning of the words "reformation" and "reform" at the same time; A. Ruge, *Preußen und die Reaktion* (Leipzig, 1838), 92ff. In 1867 he himself admitted that the later left Hegelians had been still "Prussian orthodox" and "Hegelian Christians" at that time (ibid). Cf. *Aus früher Zeit*, vol. 4 (Berlin, 1867), 484.

12. We can see the great expectations that were cultivated with the succession to the throne in F. K. Koeppen, *Friedrich der Große und seine Widersacher* (Leipzig, 1840), which is dedicated to his friend "Karl Heinrich Marx."

13. One should recall the excellent accounts of G. Mayer, "Die Anfänge des politischen Radikalismus im vormärzlichen Preußen," in *Radikalismus, Sozialismus und bürgerliche Demokratie* (Frankfurt, 1969), 20ff.; see also his "Die Junghegelianer und der preußische Staat," *Historische Zeitschrift* 121 (1920), 413ff. See also H. Rosenberg, "Arnold Ruge und die *Hallischen Jahrbücher*," *Archiv für Kulturgeschichte* 20 (1930), 281ff. For an understanding of the left Hegelians see also S. Hook, *From Hegel to Marx* (New York, 1958, 3d ed.); D. McLellan, *Die Junghegelianer und Karl Marx* (Munich, 1974); and of course K. Löwith, *Von Hegel zu Nietzsche* (Stuttgart, 1969, 3d ed.). The relatively mild application of the decrees of the censorship in the year 1842 probably delayed the migration to the left; the denial of a professorship to Ruge, the dismissal of Bruno Bauer, and the difficulties with the censorship experienced by all progressive journals such as the *Hallische Jahrbücher*, the *Rheinische Zeitung*, and the *Königsberger Zeitung* made complete the degree of disappointment with the policy of the Ministry of Culture and the King. For an instructive source, see also B. Bauer, *Vollständige Geschichte der Parteikämpfe in Deutschland während der Jahre 1842–1846* (Berlin, 1847; reprint Aalen, 1964).

14. The wide currency of the philosophy of action, which at first was systematized by Cieszkowski and then was supposed to be a characteristic of all left Hegelians, has already often been excellently treated. For example, H. Stuke, *Philosophie der Tat* (Stuttgart, 1963); J. Gebhardt, *Politik und Eschatologie* (Munich, 1963), 130ff.; N. Lobkowicz, *Theory and Practice* (Notre Dame, 1967), 167ff.; McLellan, *Die Junghegelianer*, 18ff.

15. According to Ruge in his decisive article, "Die Hegelsche Rechtsphilosophie und die Politik unserer Zeit," *Deutsche Jahrbücher* (1842), 763.

16. *Aus früher Zeit*, 497. Engels, when he still wanted to oblige young Hegelianism to the synthesis of Hegel with Börne, judges as early as 1841: "Strauss in the theological field, Gans and Ruge in the political, will remain epoch-making. Only now are the dim patches of the fog of speculation dispersing into the shining stars of ideas, which are supposed to light the way of the movement of the century" (F. Engels, "Ernst Moritz Arndt," in *MEW-Ergänzungsband*, part 2 [Berlin, 1967], 124).

17. F. Engels to Marx, 8 May 1870, in *MEW*, vol. 32 (Berlin, 1973), 501.

18. K. Marx, "Zur Kritik des Hegelschen Staatsrechts," in *MEW*, vol. 1 (Berlin, 1969), 283ff., 355, 363, 369ff.

19. F. Engels, "Ludwig Feuerbach und der Ausgang der klassischen deutschen Philosophie," in *MEW*, vol. 21 (Berlin, 1973), 265ff.

20. The criticism of accommodation and the rejection of the theological philosophy of origin (and its political consequences) characterizes also the present, ambitious Hegel interpretations of the left Hegelians. In Lukács Hegel is almost a Marxist political economist and an ideologue for the capitalist society; for Marcuse he is almost the father of critical theory and an authoritarian philosopher of the system; for Adorno he took away the negative dialectic and preached a reactionary system of identity. In Bloch, who perhaps most resolutely tries to break through the division of method from system (philosophy of origin), there ultimately remains the division of the emancipatory, utopian Hegel from the antiquarian system. Also in Habermas, despite his adoption of the Hegel of the Jena period and of the realistically applied program which recalls the *Phenomenology of Spirit*, one can sense the hostility toward the philosophy of origin, which sees emancipatory freedom dissolve in World Spirit and in history not completely abandoned to man. The division of system from method is also often handed down in its simple form. E.g., G. Lukács, *Zur Ontologie des gesellschaftlichen Seins* (Neuwied, 1967), or R. Garaudy, *Gott ist Tot* (Frankfurt, 1965).

21. Stuke works this out clearly. See *Philosophie der Tat*, 82ff.

22. Cf. Mayer, "Die Anfänge des politischen Radikalismus," 27ff.

23. In view of the criticism of accommodation and of the later radicalism of the Hegelian left, even historians have underestimated the quite possible and in part existing alliances of Hegelianism with liberalism. Mayer eliminated the alliances of Hegelianism with liberalism when he connected liberalism with Kant, radicalism with Rousseau and the young Hegelians (ibid., 27). Neher tried to separate the early liberalism of Ruge from that of Schön and Jacoby. Yet in 1840, Ruge still seems to speak for many of his comrades in arms when he calls for freedom of the press, public opinion, and a national assembly: "Zur Kritik des gegenwärtigen Staats- und Völkerrechts," *Hallische Jahrbücher* (1840), 1210ff. Even in 1841 he still calls Hegel's concept of the state "the most unshakable foundation of liberalism" (ibid., 137). In the same year he spread Jacoby's "Vier Fragen" in Halle, and in 1846 he dedicated to Jacoby the fourth volume of his work (Neher, "Zur Kritik," 71).

24. *Briefwechsel zwischen Bruno Bauer und Edgar Bauer während der Jahre 1839–1842 aus Bonn und Berlin* (Charlottenburg, 1844), 163.

25. "I have ploughed through the *Staatslexikon* and have seen more and more the shallowness of this book, its unphilosophical smoke screen (one reads only invective against Hegel) and the bombastic haughtiness of the proponents of constitutionalism. A terrible and powerful bombardment must be opened up against this. . . . The whole would be a victory over these scheming, provincial southerners" (ibid., 173–74).

26. E. Bauer, *Die liberalen Bestrebungen in Deutschland*, vol. 1: *Die ostpreußische Opposition*; vol. 2: *Die badische Opposition* (Zurich, 1843).

27. A. Ruge, "Eine Selbstkritik des Liberalismus," *Deutsche Jahrbücher* (1843), 1ff.

28. Stirner under the title "the free" settles the score with all forms of a political, social, or human liberalism in the name of the individual. M. Stirner, *Der Einzige und sein Eigentum und andere Schriften*, ed. H. G. Helms (Munich, 1968), 72ff.

29. K. H. Scheidler, "Hegelsche Philosophie und Schule," in *Das Staatslexikon*, vol. 6, ed. C.v. Rotteck and C. Welcker (Altona, 1847, 2d ed.), 608.

30. R. Haym, *Hegel und seine Zeit* (Berlin, 1857), 365.

31. Ibid., 466, 5ff. Ironically Haym seems to believe in the judgment of history about Hegelian idealism since the "idealism" of 1848 is supposed to be a failure (6).

32. *Briefe von und an Hegel*, vol. 2, ed. J. Hoffmeister (Hamburg, 1969, 3d ed.), 432ff., 455ff. In addition to Hoffmeister, J. D'Hondt has also treated the persecution of Hegel's students as well as Hegel's attempts to intercede for them: J. D'Hondt, *Hegel in seiner Zeit: Berlin 1818 bis 1831* (Berlin, 1873), 96ff.

33. D'Hondt, *Hegel in seiner Zeit*, 36ff.

34. Ibid., 56ff. Also Gebhardt, *Politik und Eschatologie*, 153ff. Avineri has taken up the motifs of D'Hondt once again: S. Avineri, *Hegel's Theory of the Modern State* (Cambridge, 1972), 130ff. Stahl must—in contrast to the widely held view—be counted among Hegel's opponents and not among his students. With respect to Haller and his supporters, there can be no doubt about the enmity: "Haller's followers and the men who flock around Jarcke's *Berliner Politisches Wochenblatt* blame Hegel for the secret political liberalism which concerns state, church and ethical life" (H. Rosenberg, "Zur Geschichte der Hegelauslegung," in his *Hegel und seine Zeit* [Leipzig, 1927], 526–27).

35. J. E. Erdmann, *Philosophische Vorlesungen über den Staat* (Halle, 1851), 37, 40, 57.

36. J. E. Erdmann, *Preußen und die Philosophie: Akademische Rede gehalten zum Geburtstage Sr. Majestät des Königs* (Halle, 1854), 11, 20.

37. Neher, "Zur Kritik," 222ff. V. Henning, once persecuted as a demagogue, had already made the move from left to right in the 1840s. He became a follower of the corporate monarchy. See H. Lübbe, *Politische Philosophie in Deutschland* (Munich, 1974, 2d ed.), 66. Edgar Bauer after his liberal phase became a communist, a democrat, an anarchist, a conservative, and a Guelf. His brother in old age worked for the *Kreuzzeitung* and with the follower of Bismarck, Wagener, edited the *Staats- und Gesellschaftslexikon* and offered an orientation for the new age: *Zur Orientierung über die Bismarcksche Ära* (Chemnitz, 1880; reprint Aalen, 1969); also see his *Disraelis romantischer und Bismarcks sozialistischer Imperialismus* (Chemnitz, 1882; reprint Aalen, 1969). For the changes in Bauer's views, see E. Barnikol, *Bruno Bauer: Studien und Materialien, aus dem Nachlaß ausgew. und zusammengest. von P. Reimer und H.-M. Saß* (Assen, 1972).

38. R. Haym, "An Hegels hundertstem Geburtstag," in *Hegel und seine Zeit*, 478.

39. G. Rümelin, "Über Hegel," in *Reden und Aufsätze* (Freiburg, 1875), 60–61: "A Schwäbish thinker first recognized in the Prussian state the structure for a

higher world historical calling and declared over it, as it were, the consecration and blessing of German thought."

40. R. Haym, "An Hegels hundertstem Geburtstag."

41. Ibid., 478–79.

42. Rößler's career and his intimacy with Bismarck is treated by H. Delbrück, "Constantin Rößler," in *Erinnerungen, Aufsätze und Reden* (Berlin, 1902), 439–63. As early as 1858 Rößler had written a pamphlet, *Preußen und die italienische Frage*, which was generally taken to be one of Bismarck's works. When he saw the long awaited new era of Prussia dawning in 1860, he left the university and dedicated himself wholly to journalism. In 1862, with a view toward Bismarck, he demanded anonymously "a dictatorship for one man." In 1865 he was appointed to the Prussian embassy in Hamburg for affairs of the press. In 1877 he was the head of the literary office, which supplied the King and the ministries with newspaper excerpts. At the age of seventy-two he transferred again into the foreign office for two more years as legation councilor. In the 1890s in his work *Die Sozialdemokratie*, he was still demanding a dictatorship!

43. C. Rößler, *System der Staatslehre* (Halle, 1857), 320ff. An exerpt from this important work, which is supposed to be reproduced as a whole, is found in *Die Hegelsche Rechte*, ed. H. Lübbe (Stuttgart, 1962), 270–320.

44. A. Lasson, *System der Rechtsphilosophie* (Berlin, 1882), 104ff.

45. Rößler, *System der Staatslehre*, 547ff.; A. Lasson, *Das Kulturideal und der Krieg* (Berlin, 1868); A. Lasson, *Prinzip und Zukunft des Völkerrechts* (Berlin, 1871).

46. Haym, *Hegel und seine Zeit*, 273ff.

47. K. Rosenkranz, *Hegel als deutscher Nationalphilosoph* (Leipzig, 1870; reprint Darmstadt, 1965); cf. also K. Köstlin, *Hegel in philosophischer, politischer und nationaler Beziehung* (Tübingen, 1870), a book which promises much but delivers little.

48. C. L. Michelet, "Festrede an Hegels hundertjährigem Geburtstag," *Der Gedanke* 8, no. 3 (1871), 127, 156.

49. For accounts of these "ideas" see Kjelléns, Plenges, and others: Lübbe, *Politische Philosophie in Deutschland*, 171ff. G. Lasson says in a review of a book by Plenge, "Hegel is the intellectual father of the thought about the state in 1914. Without a doubt Plenge has furnished proof of this" (G. Lasson, "Hegel und die Ideen von 1914," *Hegel-Archiv* 3, no. 2 [1916], 57). Also see T. Ziegler, "Hegels Anschauung vom Kriege," *Archiv für Rechts- und Wirtschaftsphilosophie* 6 (1912–13), 88ff. Georg Lasson, the son of Adolph Lasson, together with Kaufmann in the first years of the Weimar Republic passed on Hegel's doctrine of the totalitarian state. See G. Lasson, *Einleitung des Herausgebers zu Hegels "Grundlinien der Philosophie des Rechts"* (Leipzig, 1911); G. Lasson, *Hegel als Geschichtsphilosoph* (Leipzig, 1920); E. Kaufmann, *Das Wesen des Völkerrechts und die clausula rebus sic stantibus* (Tübingen, 1911). The renewed interest in Hegel was then carried on by neo-Kantianism and "*Lebensphilosophie*": see H. Levy, *Die Hegelrenaissance* (Berlin, 1927).

50. How the juristic neo-Hegelians used Hegel's *Philosophy of Right* to make formal right substantial and as a means of political pressure toward integration is

treated by Rottleuthner, who also provides an extensive bibliography of relevant works: H. R. Rottleuthner, "Die Substantialisierung des Formalrechts: Zur Rolle des Neuhegelianismus in der Jurisprudenz," in *Aktualität und Folgen der Philosophie Hegels*, ed. O. Negt (Frankfurt, 1970), 211ff. Kiesewetter describes the struggle of these Hegelians against the state of the parties and the parliamentary democracy (Kiesewetter, *Von Hegel zu Hitler*, 203ff.). The leading heads were probably Binder and Larenz. Haering's great work *Hegel: Sein Wollen und sein Werk*, 2 vols. (Leipzig, 1929, 1938) was still free of national socialism; however, during the war there followed unambiguous opuscula.

51. The National Socialists "regretted" that Hegel did not recognize "the Jewish question" as a problem of race and did not accentuate the "natural side" of the "people" better. See W. Schönfeld, *Die Geschichte der Rechtswissenschaft im Spiegel der Metaphysik* (Stuttgart, 1943), 510; K. Larenz, "Die Bedeutung der völkischen Sitte in Hegels Staatsphilosophie," *Zeitschrift für gesamte Staatswissenschaft* 98, no. 1 (1938), 135.

52. K. Larenz, *Hegelianismus und preußische Staatsidee* (Hamburg, 1940). As Larenz emphasizes with an appeal to the continuity in Hegel's thought and the difference between Hegel's state and Prussia, Hegel did not sell out to the existing powers; his doctrine corresponds to the "spirit of Prussia which is not bound up with any particular age" (ibid., 8).

53. Above all K. Larenz, *Rechts- und Staatsphilosophie der Gegenwart* (Berlin, 1931); see also his *Deutsche Rechtserneuerung und Rechtsphilosophie* (Tübingen, 1934) and "Volksgeist und Recht: Zur Revision der Rechtsanschauung der historischen Schule," *Zeitschrift für deutsche Kulturphilosophie* 1, no. 1 (1935), 40ff. See also J. Binder, *Grundlegung zur Rechtsphilosophie* (Tübingen, 1935) and his *System der Rechtsphilosophie* (Berlin, 1937, 2d ed.).

54. G. Dulckeit, "Hegel und der preußische Staat: Zur Herkunft und Kritik des liberalen Hegelbildes," in *Zeitschrift für deutsche Kulturphilosophie* 2, no. 1 (1935), 63ff. The terminological distinction between concept of right [*Rechtsbegriff*] and figure of right [*Rechtsgestalt*] was indirectly aimed against the left Hegelian criticism of the system of accommodation which metaphysically transfigured empirical reality. See G. Dulckeit, *Rechtsbegriff und Rechtsgestalt* (Berlin, 1936).

55. Cf. B. Knoop, *Hegel und die Franzosen* (Stuttgart, 1941). Knoop obviously analyzes this reaction under the aegis of national socialism.

56. J. Dewey, *German Philosophy and Politics* (New York, 1915); L. T. Hobhouse, *Die metaphysische Staatstheorie* (Leipzig, 1924); C. E. Vaughan, *Studies in the History of Political Philosophy before and after Rousseau*, vol. 2 (New York, 1920, 2d ed.), 143ff; G. H. Sabine, *A History of Political Philosophy* (New York, 1962, 3d ed.); S. Hook perhaps most resolutely contests any chance to see in Hegel anything other than the state philosopher of Prussia and the proponent of Bismarck's totalitarian state: "Hegel and the Perspective of Liberalism," in *A Hegel Symposium*, ed. D. C. Travis (Austin, 1962), 39ff., and in his contributions to *Hegel's Political Theory*, ed. W. Kaufmann (New York, 1970), 55ff., 87ff. Carritt's criticism appears in the same volume (30ff., 48ff.); G. P. Plamenatz, *Man and Society*, vol. 2 (Oxford, 1968).

57. F. Meinecke, *Die Idee der Staatsraison in der neueren Geschichte* (Munich, 1924), 459. Meinecke, who took up Ranke's criticism of the mediating of the epochs and individuals in Hegel's philosophy of history (as early as *Weltbürgertum und Nationalstaat* [Munich, 1915, 3d ed.], 173), and who even after the Second World War made Hegel responsible for the German catastrophe (*Die deutsche Katastrophe* [Wiesbaden, 1946]), had in any case claimed only that Hegel celebrated the "national culture" and not yet the national power as such.

58. In Heller, Hegel's "national culture" (discussed by Meinecke) has already become the "national power." We are probably most fair to Heller when we, like Rosenzweig, assert that in Heller one can observe "how Hegel might have thought, if he had not been Hegel but rather a national liberal Hegel of the Bismarck era" (F. Rosenzweig, *Kleinere Schriften* [Berlin, 1937], 509).

59. While Hook and Plamenatz are satisfied to attack Hegel simultaneously as the state philosopher of Prussia and the ideologue of Bismarck's authoritarian state, for most critics of Hegel as national socialist it is customary to attack him for the total array of legends, as for example Popper, Topitsch, Kiesewetter and V. Martin. See also W. M. McGovern, *From Luther to Hitler* (Boston, 1941; New York, 1973, 2d ed.), 259ff. Somewhat more balanced, since other sources of the power ideology and totalitarianism are at least mentioned, are the following: W. Apelt, *Hegelscher Machtstaat und kantisches Weltbürgertum* (Munich, 1948); and E. Cassirer, *The Myth of the State* (New York, 1955, 2d ed.).

60. Marcuse has shown this with respect to the influential ideologues of the Third Reich such as Rosenberg, Schmitt, Krieck, Boehm, and Hitler himself: H. Marcuse, *Reason and Revolution* (Boston, 1969, 7th ed.), 409ff.

61. In Heller, Popper, Kiesewetter, and v. Martin the procedure employed is that of *post hoc, ergo propter hoc*, which Kaufmann has already emphasized in his devastating criticism of Popper's attacks on Hegel: W. Kaufmann, "Hegel: Legende und Wirklichkeit," *Zeitschrift für philosophische Forschung* 10, no. 1 (1956), 191ff.

62. For Erdmann "humanity" was still the highest ideal of the nation: J. E. Erdmann, "Das Nationalitätsprinzip," *Ernste Spiele* (Berlin, 1890, 4th ed.), 206ff. A. v. Martin has great difficulties dissolving the Prussian conservatism of Erdmann into the Bismarck Hegelianism: v. Martin, *Macht als Problem*, 100ff. In Rößler and Lasson the connection of power with spirit and ethical life remained at least in part intact, just as also man as moral agent should not subordinate artists, scientists, and believers to the power claims of the state: Rößler, *System der Staatslehre*, 235ff., 354; Lasson, *Das Kulturideal und der Krieg*, 14.

63. E.g., G. Lukács, *Schicksalswende* (Berlin, 1948), 37ff.

64. P. Herre, ed., *Karl Rosenkranz: Politische Briefe und Aufsätze 1848–1856* (Leipzig, 1919), xi.

65. K. Rosenkranz, *Apologie Hegels gegen Dr. Rudolf Haym* (Berlin, 1858), 33ff., 51ff.

66. Rosenkranz, *Hegel als deutscher Nationalphilosoph*, 301ff.

67. Ibid., 161.

68. Ibid., 152.

69. Ibid., 162.

70. K. Rosenkranz, *Meine Reform der Hegelschen Philosophie* (Königsberg, 1852), 69.

71. Lübbe, *Politische Philosophie in Deutschland*, 62ff.

72. C. L. Michelet, *Die Geschichte der Menschheit in ihrem Entwicklungsgange seit dem Jahre 1775 bis auf die neuesten Zeiten*, part 2 (Berlin, 1860), 586ff.

73. Instructive for the reports of the discussions of the "Philosophy Club" is "Über den Begriff der Nationalität in der Rechtsphilosophie," *Der Gedanke* 2, no. 3 (1861), 242ff.; concerning the change in meaning of Hegel, see *Der Gedanke* 2, no. 1 (1861), 76ff.; F. Förster, *Hegel als Hofphilosoph* 4, no. 1 (1863), 76ff.

74. Since I cannot hope to demonstrate the well-known development of the latest Hegel research here in detail, let me simply refer the reader to my book *Individuum und Gemeinschaft*, vol. 1: *Hegel im Spiegel der Interpretationen* (Berlin, 1977), 261ff.

75. To summarize the results of middle Hegelianism from Rosenkranz via Rosenzweig up through the modern Anglo-Saxon and French research with respect to these arguments, one can say that the continuity of Hegel's thought between Jena and Berlin can be established with respect to the doctrine about religion and church and in part in the conception of the classes, the estimation of the civil servants, the enmity with Fries, and the doctrine of the hereditary monarchy. With all perspectives of systematic philosophy aside, strong criticisms result from this against the last form of the critique of accommodation in Ilting, who sees an in principle liberal Hegel in 1819 guilty of accommodation. (My article attempts an extended criticism of this view: "Hegels Rechtsphilosophie und das Problem der Akkomodation," *Zeitschrift für philosophische Forschung* 35, no. 2 [1979], 227–43). In addition there is evidence for the distinction between the politics of Hegel and of Prussia which can be documented not only by Hegel's lack of popularity among the parties of the time and not only by his intercession for the sake of his progressive students, but also by his lack of interest in many questions which were relevant to the Prussian state of the day (regulation of the budget, universal military service, the issue of unified states or Prussian states). Since Michelet's and Rosenzweig's remarks, it has become urgent to work out for once the influence on Hegel (an influence which he shares with many of the Prussian reformers) of the English situation (the view of self-administration, of voting, of the social question, of the two house system, and of representatives).

76. Concerning Ritter, see Ottmann, *Individuum und Gemeinschaft*, vol. 1: *Hegel im Spiegel der Interpretationen* (Berlin, 1977), 229ff. Lübbe, Saß, Kriele, and Marquard, following Ritter, have shown (ibid., 369ff.) how Hegel's political views can be interpreted in a liberal-pragmatic sense as an obstacle to right- and left-wing totalitarianism, as a defense against historical reaction and as an indirect mediation of society and state.

77. M. Riedel, *Studien zu Hegels Rechtsphilosophie* (Frankfurt, 1969).

78. These are the consequences of the theological and political Hegel interpretation in Rohrmoser, Maurer, and Theunissen which expand on Ritter's account (see Ottmann, *Individuum und Gemeinschaft*, vol. 1, 239ff.).

79. Z. A. Pelczynski, ed., *Hegel's Political Writings*, introduction (Oxford, 1964), 134.

80. Apart from the fact that (like Ritter himself) one usually disregards the nonliberal institutions in Hegel's doctrine of the state, external signs of this tendency can be discerned in the apologetics, which acknowledges the fraternities and Fries only as right-wing liberals, antisemites, and pro-Germans (e.g., Avineri, Taylor), and declares Prussia of around 1820 as the most progressive state in Europe (Weil) or tries to disarm Hegel's account of "international law" with renewed sallies.

81. G. W. F. Hegel, *Enzyklopädie,* Jubiläumsausgabe, vol. 10, ed. H. Glockner (Stuttgart, 1958), §433.

82. M. Theunissen, *Hegels Lehre vom absoluten Geist als theologisch-politischer Traktat* (Berlin, 1970), 444.

83. Ilting, *Vorlesungen über Rechtsphilosophie*, vol. 1, 330.

84. For the latter, see G. Heimann, "The Sources and Significance of Hegel's Corporate Doctrine," in Pelczynski, *Hegel's Political Writings*, 11ff.

85. *MEW-Ergänzungsband*, part 1 (Berlin, 1973), 608. I am thankful to M. Rubel for his making me aware of this verse.

86. Charles Taylor, *Hegel* (Cambridge, 1975), 375.

T. M. Knox, Hegel and Prussianism

1. *Philosophical Theory of the State* (London, 1930), 230ff.

2. *German Philosophy and the War* (London, 1915).

3. *Les doctrines politiques des philosophes classiques de l'Allemagne* (Paris, 1927), 110ff.

4. E.g., S. Hook, *From Hegel to Marx* (London, 1936), 19.

5. E.g., Aldous Huxley, *Ends and Means* (London, 1938), 58, 171; E. A. Mowrer, *Germany Puts the Clock Back* (London: Penguin Books, 1938), 38–39.

6. This is the work referred to in this article as the *Philosophie des Rechts*. The only English translation—*Hegel's Philosophy of Right*, trans. S. W. Dyde (London, 1896)—has long been out of print. A new translation, with commentary, by the writer of this article is in preparation. [*Hegel's Philosophy of Right*, trans. T. M. Knox (Oxford University Press, 1967).—Ed.]

7. The letter is printed, with an introduction and notes be E. Crous (on which I have drawn for the facts about the Carlsbad Decrees and the subsequent censorship), in Lasson's *Hegel-Archiv* 1, no. 2 (Leipzig, 1912), 18ff. This letter was first brought to my notice by Professor Sidney Hook of New York, whose kindness I acknowledge all the more readily in that I have come to different conclusions from his about Hegel's political objectivity.

8. Ibid., 57. (Here again the writer is indebted for the reference to Professor Hook.)

9. Copies were in Hegel's hands, however, before the end of 1820. See a letter to him (*Briefe von und an Hegel*, vol. 2 [Leipzig, 1887], 32–33), dated 18 December 1820, acknowledging a complimentary copy of the book.

10. By 1824 the censorship was considerably relaxed (Lenz: *Geschichte der Universität zu Berlin*, vol. 2 [Halle, 1910], 183), but I cannot find that it was relaxed earlier, and I therefore assume that it was still rigid in 1821, and that Hegel's book was submitted and passed.

11. *Hegels Nürnberger Schriften*, ed. J. Hoffmeister (Leipzig, 1938), 470.

12. English translation, vol. 1 (London, 1929), 63.

13. *Morals and Politics* (Oxford, 1935), 107.

14. *Proceedings of the Aristotelian Society* (1935–36), 230.

15. Haym, who, in his *Hegel und seine Zeit* (1857), employs every available weapon to attack what he holds is Hegel's "servility" and conservatism, and makes much use of the preface, never mentions the sentence that I have been endeavoring to explain. Had he interpreted it in Carritt's sense, would he not undoubtedly have added it to his armory?

16. The evidence for this is quoted in a note by H. Falkenheim, in Kuno Fischer, *Hegels Leben und Werke* (Heidelberg, 1911), 1232.

17. This fact and those in the next paragraph for which I have quoted no reference are taken from an article by D. J. Hoffmeister in the *Geist der Gegenwart* supplement of the *Kölnische Zeitung*, 12 December 1937.

18. Rosenkranz, *Hegels Leben* (Berlin, 1844), 318.

19. *Hegel-Archiv*, vol. 1, no. 2, 21.

20. Ibid., 31–32.

21. These three are singled out for mention by Treitschke in his *Deutsche Geschichte im neunzehnten Jahrhundert*, vol. 3 (Leipzig, 1919), 721. In what follows references in parentheses to numbered paragraphs are to the paragraphs of the *Philosophie des Rechts*.

22. In his Berlin lectures on the history of philosophy, Hegel says that Prussia is *auf Intelligenz gebaut*. This remark is doubtless to be explained in the light of the passage, in his *Philosophy of History*, treating Prussia as the embodiment of *Protestantism*.

23. *Morals and Politics*, 114. Citations could have been made from authors other than Carritt, but I take them from him because of recent English scholarly writings on Hegel his are probably the best known of those which adopt the point of view attacked in this article.

24. *Proceedings of the Aristotelian Society* (1935–36), 236.

25. I am glad to find my argument here supported by a recent keen critic of Hegel—J. P. Plamenatz—in his *Consent, Freedom and Political Obligation* (Oxford, 1938), 33.

26. *Morals and Politics*, 108.

Walter A. Kaufmann, The Hegel Myth and Its Method

1. Princeton University Press, 1950, in one volume (the English volume has two). There are twenty-five chapters: ten each attacking Plato and Marx, two on Aristotle and Hegel, and three presenting some of the author's conclusions. The notes are gathered together at the end of the volume (467–726) and printed very

readably (much better than the English edition); and the publisher has made it exceedingly easy to match them up with the text.

2. *Open Society*, 253.

3. Hegel, *Sein Wollen und sein Werk: Eine chronologische Entwicklungsgeschichte der Gedanken und der Sprache Hegels*, 2 vols. (1929–38), 785, 525. This interpretation has been countered from a Marxist point of view by G. Lukács, *Der junge Hegel* (1948), 718. In English, a brief account of Hegel's social philosophy against the background of his intellectual development may be found in Sabine, *A History of Political Theory* (1937), chap. 30. There is also an English version of Hegel's *Early Theological Writings* (1948), which contains well over half of Nohl's German edition. The titles of both editions are, however, misleading: "Early Antitheological Writings" would have been more accurate, although these writings are admittedly not antireligious.

4. *Hegel Selections*, 227. What Hegel is reported by Gans to have said is merely that it is the way of God with the world that there should be the State. Cf. my *Nietzsche* (1950), 84. Popper's one major deviation from the *Selections* consists in his profuse capitalization of nouns, which makes the passages he quotes from Hegel look absurd. When quoting Popper, I have of course reproduced his translation, but all other translations from the German in this article are my own.

5. *Phänomenologie*, ed. Lasson (1907), 294f. Cf. H. G. ten Bruggencate, "Hegel's Views on War," *Philosophical Quarterly* (October 1950), 58–60.

6. Popper, *Open Society*, 227.

7. *Ideas and Men*, 473.

8. Popper employs composite quotations on 227, 252, 257, 259, and 266 (cf. notes 8, 64, 69, 71, and 84). To cite even one of these fully, and to analyze each of its components in terms of its original context, would take far too much space here. As it is a principle that concerns us here, rather than a particular author, it may be permissible to offer instead a brief observation on Brinton's second composite quotation from Nietzsche, on 473 of *Ideas and Men*. It is introduced, "In fact, Nietzsche wrote a whole platform for totalitarianism of the Right a generation before it came to power"; it begins with a line referring to Prussian officers; and it proceeds from there to four passages dealing with "war" and "peace." The quotation as a whole leaves no doubt but that Nietzsche meant literally "war." I have tried to show in my *Nietzsche* (337ff.) that, when some of these remarks about war are considered in their context, it becomes clear that Nietzsche did not mean war in the literal sense of the word; and, in a very kind review of my book (*Saturday Review of Literature*, 13 January 1951), Brinton apparently accepts my demonstration and concludes: "So when Nazis like Haertle or Baeumler quote him on war they quote the words but distort the meaning." And what, for all their good intentions, of anti-Nazis like Brinton or Popper?

9. Popper, *Open Society*, 256 and n. 66; n. 25 reveals that Hegel held theories which are "unmistakably Bergsonian."

10. Ibid., 225 and n. 6. I am matching up n. 6 with a reference to the "evolutionists," although there is a 7 in the text, and assume that n. 7 refers to another 7, on 227. The note for the 6 on 225 was apparently omitted inadvertently.

11. Kolnai also claims that the two men who contributed most "to the rise of National Socialism as a creed" were "Nietzsche, perhaps the greatest Satanist of all times, and Stefan George, less great but, perhaps because of his homosexuality, more directly instrumental in creating the Third Reich" (14); that Nietzsche was a "half-Pole" (453); that H. S. "Chamberlain was a mellow Englishman tainted by noxious Germanic influences" (455); and that Jaspers is a "follower" of Heidegger (207). Under the circumstances, it would seem advisable to check the context of his quotations before using them. Whether Popper did this is far from clear, and it is not easy to understand his note: "I am greatly indebted to Kolnai's book, which has made it possible for me to quote in the remaining part of this chapter a considerable number of authors who would otherwise have been inaccessible to me. (I have not, however, always followed the wording of Kolnai's translations.)"

12. Popper, *Open Society*, 269f.

13. Ibid., 266.

14. Ibid., 271.

15. Ibid., 270.

16. Ibid., 223.

17. *Über die Gefährdung des Wohlstandes und Charakters der Deutschen durch die Juden*, published simultaneously as a pamphlet and in *Heidelbergische Jahrbücher der Litteratur* (1816), 241–64, where it is printed as a review of a book by Friedrich Rühs and does not have this title. Fries's ideas are of interest here also because they supply a much needed background for an adequate appreciation of Hegel's whole position and *niveau*, for Fries had been his predecessor at Heidelberg. (The page references for the following quotations are to the *Jahrbücher*.) The Jews "were and are the bloodsuckers of the people" (243). "Not against *the Jews*, our brothers, but against *Jewry* [*der Judenschaft*] we declare war. . . . Jewry is a remnant from an uneducated primeval past and should not be confined but totally exterminated. . . . Jewry is a disease of peoples [*Völkerkrankheit*]" (248). "The Jewish religion . . . *ought not to be tolerated*" (251). "The Jews do not at all live and teach according to Mosaic doctrine, but according to the Talmud" (251). The following comments on the Talmud, and not only these, are quite on the level of Streicher. "Thus the Jewish caste . . . *should be exterminated completely [mit Stumpf und Stiel ausgerottet] because it is obviously of all secret and public political societies and states within the state the most dangerous*" (256). "Any immigration of Jews should be forbidden, their emigration should be promoted. Their freedom to marry should . . . be limited. . . . It should be forbidden that any Christian be hired by a Jew" (260). And one should again force on them "a special mark on their clothing" (261). In his preface to the *Philosophy of Right*, Hegel repudiated Fries's substitution of "the pap of 'heart, friendship, and enthusiasm' " for moral laws; and it would surely have been unwise of "the Jews, our brothers" to rely on Fries's brotherly enthusiasm. Hegel's often obscure style may have evened the way for later obscurantism; but Fries's and Schopenhauer's irrationalism is, stylistically, too, much closer to most Nazi literature.

18. Popper, *Open Society*, 226.

19. Hoheneichen-Verlag (1940), 525, 527. The book was published originally in 1930; 878,000 copies had been printed by 1940.

20. Ibid., 288. Rosenberg also emphasizes and excoriates the "Socratic" elements in Plato.

21. H. Holtorf, *Platon, Auslese und Bildung der Führer und Wehrmänner: Eine Auswahl aus dem "Staat"* ("Eclogae Graecolatinae," Fasc. 73, 2d. ed.; Teubner, 1936); and *Platon, Über die Grundsätze artgemässer Staatsführung: Eine Auswahl aus den "Gesetzen"* ("E.G.", Fasc. 74). In his preface to the first work, the editor also recommends some of his articles which are relevant: "Platon im Kampf gegen die Entartung der nordischen Rasse," *D. Phil.-Blatt* 42 (1934), 269ff.; and "Der Schicksalsweg des griechischen Volkes und der letzte Sinn des platonischen Denkens," *Völk. Beob.* (Hitler's own paper), no. 67 (8 March 1935), 5. Holtorf also refers to an essay, "Das Beamtenideal bei Plato und seine Bedeutung für die Gegenwart," in *Theodor von der Pforten an die deutsche Nation*, five essays with an introduction by Staatsminister Dr. Hans Frank (J. Schweitzer Verlag, 1933).

22. *Platon als Hüter des Lebens: Platons Zucht-und Erziehungsgedanken und deren Bedeutung für die Gegenwart* (1928; 2d ed., 1935). For Günther, cf. also my *Nietzsche*, 256.

23. Popper, *Open Society*, 3.

24. Ibid., 249.

25. Ibid., 244.

26. Ibid., 253; cf. 269.

27. A detailed account of Hegel's almost incredibly unemotional style as a lecturer has been given by one of his students, H. G. Hotho, and is quoted in Glockner's *Hegel*, vol. 1 (1929), 440ff., and also in Kuno Fischer's two-volume *Hegel*.

28. Popper, *Open Society*, 227.

29. Ibid., 272.

30. Ibid., 244.

31. Ibid., 227–28.

32. Ibid., 241.

33. Besides the works already cited, cf. T. M. Knox, "Hegel and Prussianism," *Philosophy* (January 1940), and the Discussion with Carritt (April and July 1940).

34. Popper, *Open Society*, 235.

35. Ibid., 237.

36. Ibid., nn. 11, 43.

37. Ibid., 271.

38. Ibid., n. 65.

39. Ibid., 262.

40. *Scholasticism and Politics* (1940), 147.

41. Popper, *Open Society*, 237.

42. Ibid., 231.

43. Ibid., 236.

44. Sec. 6.

45. Popper, *Open Society*, 252.

46. Hegel, *Philosophy of Right*, §3.

47. Ibid., §66.

48. Ibid. Cf. also §77.

49. Ibid., §137.

50. Ibid., §209; cf. §270 n.

51. Ibid., §258 n.

52. Marcuse, *Reason and Revolution: Hegel and the Rise of Social Theory* (1941), 180f.

53. Popper, *Open Society*, 260.

54. Hegel's distinction, of course, raises grave difficulties; but no interpreter can afford simply to ignore it.

55. Hegel, *Philosophy of Right*, §270.

56. Popper, *Open Society*, 258.

57. Ibid., 4.

58. Ibid., 5.

59. Ibid., 254.

60. Ibid., 260.

61. Ibid., 233 and n. 11.

62. Ibid., 263.

63. Ibid., n. 77.

64. Ibid., 233.

65. Ibid., 252.

66. Hegel, *Encyclopedia*, §550.

67. Hegel says: "The self-consciousness of a particular people is the carrier of the current stage of development of the universal spirit as it is present, and the objective actuality into which this spirit lays its will." In Scribner's *Selections* this becomes " . . . in which that spirit for a time invests its will." And in Popper it becomes "the Spirit of the Time."

68. Popper, *Open Society*, 258.

69. This notion was adapted by Stefan George and, with the individual prophet in the place of a whole people, became part of the creed of his *Kreis*: "In jeder ewe / Ist nur ein gott und einer nur sein künder" (In every epoch / There is but one god, and but one his prophet). This seems even more obviously false than Hegel's view—and doubly ironical because, even in the relatively narrow field of German poetry, George was no solitary giant and was probably inferior to Rilke.

70. Hegel, *Philosophy of Right*, §347.

71. At the outset of his *Study of History*, Toynbee seeks to show that England is no intelligible field of study, while Western civilization is. Had he taken Spain as his example, he could scarcely have arrived at the latter conclusion.

72. Popper, *Open Society*, 266f.

73. Ibid., 239.

74. Popper's version of this passage (ibid., 267) makes nonsense of it: "In public opinion all is false and true."

75. Ibid., 237.

76. Ibid., 268.

77. Ibid., 250.

78. Ibid., 268.

79. Hegel, *Philosophy of Right*, preface.

80. Quoted by Popper, *Open Society*, 269.

81. Ibid., 262.

82. Hegel, *Philosophy of Right*, §324.

83. Hegel, *Sämtliche Werke*, vol. 14, ed. Glockner, 354f. The epics of the past referred to are the *Iliad* and the *Cid*, and Tasso's, Ariosto's, and Camoëns' poems.

84. Ibid., vol. 11, 128f.

85. Popper, *Open Society*, 245.

86. Ibid., 246.

87. Ibid.

88. Ibid., 226.

89. Ibid., 251.

90. Rosenberg, *Der Mythus*, 527.

91. Marcuse, *Reason and Revolution*, 179f.

92. Hegel, *Philosophy of Right*, §270 n.

93. Popper, *Open Society*, 252.

94. Ibid., 228.

95. Ibid., 256.

96. Ibid.

97. Ibid.

98. Mure, *A Study of Hegel's Logic* (1950), 360.

99. On the jacket of the English edition of 1949. The book received many other encomia, and I am not implying that the attack on Hegel is representative of the caliber of the whole work.

100. Popper, *Open Society*, 247.

101. Ibid., 435f.

Franz Grégoire, Is the Hegelian State Totalitarian?

1. J. Maritain, *La philosophie morale: Examen historique et critique des grands systèmes.* (Paris: Gallimard, 1960).

2. Ibid., 159–262.

3. Ibid., 219, n. 1.

4. I have criticized this interpretation in a succinct manner in a communication to the Belgian Royal Academy: "Une semi-légende. La 'divinité' de l'État chez Hegel," in the *Bulletin de L'Académie royale de Belgique, Classe des Lettres et des Sciences morales et politiques*, 5e série, t. 41, 1955, 6, 315–35, and I have taken up this issue again in more detail in my *Études hégéliennes: Les points capitaux du système* (Louvain-Paris, 1958), 285–300. Maritain rejects the first of these accounts and does not seem to be aware of the second.

5. Maritain, *La philosophie morale*, 207–21.

6. Ibid., 196, n. 2.

7. Cf. *Études hégéliennes*, 285–92. For Maritain, the conception that Hegel constructs of the person is not satisfactory, since Hegel characterizes the person by his belonging to the human species and not by his ineffable incommunicability (*La philosophie morale*, 196, n. 2, to the end, *et alibi*). Here the question is obviously different from that of knowing whether or not Hegel accords to the person his own value in the face of the state or of landed rights.

8. Specifically slavery: *La philosophie morale*, 196, n. 2. This exception remains without influence on the interpretation of the relationships between the individual and the state which Maritain consequently gives.

9. Cf. *Études hégéliennes*, 293–94.

10. Cf., e.g., *Recht* §260, Gl, 7, 337. [Grégoire cites from Hermann Glockner's edition of the *Philosophy of Right*: *Grundlinien der Philosophie des Rechts oder Naturrecht und Staatswissenschaft im Grundrisse*, vol. 7 of *Sämtliche Werke: Jubiläumsausgabe in 20 Bänden* (Stuttgart: Friedrich Frommann Verlag, 1927–40), which he abbreviates as "Gl."—*Trans.*]

11. Grégoire, *Études hegeliennes*, 294–96.

12. Maritain, *La philosophie morale*, 219, n. 1.

13. *Weltg*, vol. 1, 91. [Grégoire cites from Georg Lasson's edition of the lectures on the *Philosophy of History*: *Vorlesungen über die Philosophie der Weltgeschichte*, 4 vols. (Hamburg: Meiner Verlag, 1934), which he abbreviates as *Weltg*.—*Trans.*]

14. Here is the text: "The state does not exist with a view to the citizens." (Hegel means in his emphatic style that the state does not exist purely and simply not even principally with a view to the citizens.) "One could say that the state is the goal and the citizens the instruments. However this relation of end and means is not applicable here at all. Because the state is not an abstract term" (Hegel means "separate") "which is found over and against the individuals, but they" (the individual and the state, and not, as Maritain reads it in *La philosophie morale*, 219, n. 1, the individuals, one in relation to the other) "are the moments" (an expression drawn from the theory of lever mechanics and which in Hegel simply refers to correlative terms) "as in an organic life where no member is the ends and none the means."

15. The living thing is a whole of which the elements are reciprocally ends and means by immanent relation. Hegel cites this definition several times (e.g., *Encyclopedia*, vol. 1, §57; Gl, vol. 8, 156) and makes great use of it in his *Philosophy of Spirit.* (Cf. my *Études hégéliennes*, 250–51 where I indicated why this notion is important for Hegel.) [The reference to the *Encyclopedia* is also from the Glockner edition of Hegel's works.—*Trans.*]

16. *Gesch. Philos.*, vol. 2; Gl, vol. 18, 399–400.

17. In a "highest organic life" the autonomy of members is reconciled with the raised unity of the whole (cf. *Weltg*, vol. 1, 123). This notion of a highest organism conforms to two general principles of Hegel's system: no category is applied as such to the levels which are higher than it, not even the category of organism; Spirit is characterized simultaneously by the autonomy of its elements and by the profundity of their union in the self-consciousness and the will of the individual. In the state, the members are perfectly autonomous, but, in addition,

they are united by the fact that they all have consciousness of the value of the state and all will it (and, in this sense, the state has in them consciousness of itself and wills itself).

18. This *vollkomme Selbstständigkeit* of the individuals refers to *bürgerliche Freiheit* with which we are concerned in the text immediately above and not as Maritain understands it (*La philosophie morale*, 219, n. 1), the spontaneous compliance with the state, i.e. the *höhere Freiheit* which then appears and which is conditioned precisely by the *bürgerliche Freiheit*, recognized by the state. Here is the text: "Bürgerliche Freiheit . . . ist ein nothwendiges Moment, das die alten Staaten nicht kannten: oder nicht diese vollkommene Selbständigkeit der Punkte, und eben größere Selbständigkeit des Ganzen—das höhere organische Leben. Nachdem der Staat diess Princip in sich empfangen, konnte höhere Freiheit hervorgehen."

19. Extolled principally by J.-J. Rousseau (*Gesch. Philo.*, vol. 1; Gl, vol. 17, 295).

20. The only freedom of the individual with regard to the state in Hegel which might be underlined by Maritain consists in spontaneously willing the state for itself and in thus participating in its autonomy (*La philosophie morale*, 211–12; 219, n. 1). In fact, I think there we find the highest freedom of the individual in his relation to the state, which Hegel calls "objective freedom." To be free for the individual is above all to direct oneself freely to a free state with a view to this state itself (cf. *Études hégéliennes*, 274–76). And it is in this context that we must interpret what Hegel means in the emphatic passages cited by Maritain (ibid., 210). "All that a man is, he owes to the state. He has only his being in himself. All the value that a man possesses, all his spiritual reality, he has only for the state" (*Weltg*, vol. 1, 90). "With the state being objective Spirit, it is only as one of its members that the individual himself possesses objectivity, truth and ethical life" (*Recht*, §258; Gl, vol. 7, 329). (Here we are only concerned with—and Maritain admits as much, cf. below—the sphere of conduct of ethical life, i.e., *Sittlichkeit*, prior to and lower than the theoretical life consisting in art, religion, and philosophy.)

But there are—and it is this which escapes Maritain—"subjective freedoms" which form a synthesis with "objective freedom," with which we are concerned. These "subjective freedoms," which are, to be sure, not as high and which are the rights of man as man, are recognized by the state (and form the *bürgerliche Freiheit* which he treats in the n. 18). These "subjective freedoms" are said to be united with "objective freedom" in (among others) precisely the second passage cited by Maritain. (In another sense, "subjective freedom" is the free and rationally motivated decision of dedicating oneself to the state, a decision that is united in "objective freedom" and forms there a synthesis with the value of the state in itself [cf. *Études hégéliennes*]. The "subjective freedoms" in the first sense indicated and "subjective freedom" in the sense which we have just discussed have in common the attributes of the will of the individual conscious of himself, of its emanating from "subjectivity." The two fields in question about "subjective freedom" are expressly brought together by Hegel (e.g., *Recht*, §§124, 258; Gl, vol. 7, 182–83, 329).

21. *Gesch. Philos.*, vol. 2; Gl, vol. 18, 293–94.

22. Cf. *Études hégéliennes*, 286–90.

23. Let us recall some of the most significant passages that Maritain fails to take up.

"Before the law and the courts," writes Hegel, "that which ought to exist, are not Jews, Catholics, Protestants, Germans, Italians, etc., *but men as such*, and this awareness of the value of the thought *is of infinite importance*." (my italics) ("Der Mensch gilt so, weil er Mensch ist, nicht weil er Jude, Kathokliek, Protestant, Deutscher, Italianer, u.s.f. ist—dies Bewußtsein, dem der Gedanke gilt, ist von unendlicher Wichtigkeit") (*Recht* §209; Gl, vol. 7, 286). Here it is obvious that we are a long way away from the individual having value and rights only as a member of the state. It is not, however, necessary for all that, notes Hegel next, to fall into an "abstract cosmopolitanism, contrary to the concrete life of the state." This doubtless means that the citizens of a state should enjoy—as citizens—certain advantages that Hegel does not expand upon and which in all likelihood have reference to political rights.

Moreover, concerning the Jews, Hegel writes, when one wants to refuse them civil rights "with the argument that they are considered not a simple religious faction but rather as members of a foreign people," one "forgets that they are above all *men*" ("dass sie zu allererst Menschen sind") (*Recht*, §270, rem.; Gl, vol. 7, 354). Moreover, this is only one of the reasons invoked by Hegel in this passage in favor of granting civil rights to Jews, and even this reason he treats with a certain disdain with respect to the other reason, which is the interest of the state.

Concerning the right to property in particular, Hegel writes, "it is *man* (and not as in Greece, Rome, etc., only *some* men) who is recognized as a person and which counts before the law" ("dass es der Mensch ist (und nicht, wie in Griechenland, Rom, u.s.f., nur einige Menschen) welcher als Person anerkannt ist und gesetzlich gilt") (*Encycl.*, vol. 3, §539; Gl, vol. 10, 412). And he adds that this recognition "is the result of the awareness of the most profound principle of Spirit" (i.e., freedom).

Generally, "in the state man is recognized and treated as an intelligent being, as free and as a person" (*Encycl.*, vol. 3, §432, Zus.; Gl, vol. 10, 284).

24. It is in this way that I believe it is necessary to interpret the *Philosophy of Right*, §260 (Gl, vol. 7, 338): "The principle of modern states possesses the power and extraordinary depth of allowing the principle of subjectivity to progress to the extreme of autonomy of personal particularity, and yet at the same time it brings it back to the substantial unity and so maintains this unity in the same principle." The principle of subjectivity is pushed "to the extreme of autonomy of personal particularity" by virtue of the fact that the state not only accords to the individual all the "subjective freedoms" (it is these that we are concerned with in the text) which are compatible with the state's interest in the individual, and, moreover, which are demanded by that interest itself—by virtue of his being a member of the state—but also by virtue of the fact that he is a man. (The same remark is in *Encycl.*, vol. 3, §537; Gl, vol. 10, 410.) The "substantial unity," which

we are concerned with in the text cited, is the unity of the one unique and stable end in itself. For an account of the meanings of the difficult term "substance" as applied to the state, see *Études hégéliennes*, 232–34. In fact, the sentence that we just discussed is a continuation of another where one sees the recognition of the state by the individual united with the recognition of the individual by the state. Now, we know that the recognition of the individual by the state is his recognition as man. (See the last text cited in the preceding note.)

The recognition of the individual by the state—and therefore the "subjective freedoms"—and the recognition of the state by the individual—and therefore "objective freedom"—together constitute (according to this same §260) "concrete freedom." In it the two freedoms in question form a synthesis, a "penetrating unity" (*Recht*, §258; Gl, vol. 7, 329), not by a simple coexistence (that which would hardly be Hegelian) but rather I think by reciprocal conditioning. One sees, in fact, the subjective freedoms condition objective freedom (*Gesch. Philos.*, vol. 2; Gl, vol. 18, 400) as much as they themselves are conditioned by it (*Encycl.*, vol. 3, §539; Gl, vol. 10, 414; *Recht*, §261; Gl, vol. 7, 341).

Generally, Maritain, like many other interpreters of Hegel, and as a result of Hegel's own language, speaks as if when one passes from a lower sphere to a higher one, the first, because it has been sublated (*aufgehoben*, which as one knows means at once to abolish and preserve), is abolished or at the very least loses its own character. This is, however, only true in certain cases. Thus, according to Hegel, by the advent of dialectical idealism, Christian dogmatism loses its character of absolute truth in order to become a mere symbol of philosophical truths or simple "picture thinking." But in other cases, it happens differently, and the lower term loses only its exclusive character. For example, the father of the family still remains the father of the family while also being a citizen; the citizen still remains a citizen while also being, possibly, a philosopher (even if at the moment when he is sunk in his philosophical contemplation, he has no thought of his quality of being a citizen). Similarly, the value of man as such is by no means abolished by the value of the state, although the dignity of the member of the state might be higher than the simple dignity of man, which Hegel sometimes calls "superficial and abstract" (*Recht*, §270, rem.; Gl, vol. 7, 354). (One would hope that an author would undertake a systematic examination of the different forms of *Aufhebung* in Hegel.)

For an account of the reasons for the general idea of the state being more intensively an end for the individual than the inverse, see my *Études hégéliennes*, 298–300. This becomes a question above all with the state, in case of war, requiring the individual to sacrifice his goods and his life.

25. With respect to the relations between man and God, Maritain correctly notes, "it is essential . . . to Hegelian thought to refuse the simple 'yes' and the simple 'no.' (This is because, we are concerned with a truly philosophical position. Hegel is reassured about the truth of what he says only in testing the destructive and the negative power of his own mental word, and in using rather distended language for strengthening the emphasis on maintaining the 'no' under the 'yes' and the 'yes' under the 'no')" (*La philosophie morale*, 162, n. 2). This observation holds perfectly true, in my view, with respect to Hegel's view of the state and the individual as man, each a value in itself and an end in itself.

26. Cf. *Études hégéliennes*, 239–64.

27. Maritain, *La philosophie morale*, 219, n. 1.

28. Ibid., 224–25. Maritain then makes more precise his claim (ibid.) that, for Hegel, the individual personality of the sage becomes volatilized (the expression is mine) [*"se volatise"—Trans.*] in philosophical contemplation. I also believe, at the very least in this sense (and it is doubtless this sense that Maritain means), that the sage loses reflected consciousness of himself in a sort of ecstasy.

29. On this last point see *Études hégéliennes*, 246–48.

30. I have explained the uncertainty that Hegel leaves concerning the authority of the state in *Études hégéliennes*, 317–20.

31. For example, concerning the relation between the demands of conscience and obedience to the state in Hegel (*La philosophie morale* 205–6), and also the relation between the obedience to the state and the submission to the rational development of history (ibid., 248).

Shlomo Avineri, Hegel and Nationalism

1. This is an extended version of a paper read before the Israel Historical Association in Jerusalem. I am deeply indebted for the help I was privileged to receive from Professor J. L. Talmon, under whom this study was conducted. I am further indebted to Professor Karl Popper of the London School of Economics, Dr. J. Rodman of Harvard University, Dr. Z. A. Pelczynski of Pembroke College, Oxford, and Mr. R. Friedman of Johns Hopkins for the stimulating discussions I had with them. That we sometimes had to agree to differ did not diminish the value of those discussions in clarifying my own ideas.

2. *Briefe von und an Hegel*, vol. 1, ed. J. Hoffmeister (Hamburg, 1952), 120.

3. Ibid., vol. 1, 137.

4. Ibid., vol. 2, 6.

5. Ibid., vol. 2, 27.

6. Ibid., vol. 2, 14–15.

7. Ibid., vol. 2, 23.

8. *Hegels Schriften zur Politik und Rechtsphilosophie*, ed. G. Lasson (Leipzig, 1913), 159.

9. G. W. F. Hegel, *Vorlesungen über die Philosophie der Weltgeschichte*, ed. G. Lasson (Leipzig, 1920), 937 (subsequently referred to as *Weltgeschichte*).

10. *Hegel's Philosophy of Right*, trans. T. M. Knox (Oxford, 1945), §322.

11. Ibid., §209; cf. also §270. See Avineri, "The Hegelian Position on the Emancipation of the Jews," *Iyyun* 25, no. 2. (1960), 134–36 (in Hebrew).

12. G. W. F. Hegel, *Die Vernunft in der Geschichte—Einleitung zur Geschichtsphilosophie*, ed. J. Hoffmeister (Hamburg, 1955), 159 (subsequently referred to as *Einleitung*).

13. K. R. Popper, *The Open Society and Its Enemies* (Princeton, 1950), 255–73.

14. H. Heller, *Hegel und der nationale Machtstaatsgedanke in Deutschland* (Leipzig and Berlin, 1921).

15. E. F. Carritt, "Hegel and Prussianism," *Philosophy* 15 (January 1940), 51–56; J. Bowle, *Politics and Opinion in the 19th Century* (London, 1954), 34–50; W. M.

McGovern, *From Luther to Hitler* (New York, 1940), 317–55; cf. also the recent work by A. Hacker, *Political Theory: Philosophy, Ideology, Science* (New York, 1961), 438–45. This view, however, is by no means unchallenged. Cf. Georg Lukács, "Der deutsche Faschismus und Hegel," in his *Schicksalswende: Beiträge zu einer neuen deutschen Ideologie* (Berlin, 1948), 37–67; H. Marcuse, *Reason and Revolution*, 2d ed. (London, 1955); W. Kaufmann, *From Shakespeare to Existentialism* (New York, 1960); also F. Meinecke, *Weltbürgertum und Nationalstaat*, 3 Aufl. (Munich and Berlin, 1915), 275ff.

16. R. Haym, *Hegel und seine Zeit* (Berlin, 1857).

17. H. V. Treitschke, *Politics*, vol. 1, trans. B. Dugdale and T. de Bille (London, 1916), 22–23, 53.

18. K. Köstlin, *Hegel in philosophischer, politischer und nationaler Beziehung* (Tübingen, 1870), 158–65, 174.

19. *Hegels Schriften zur Politik und Rechtsphilosophie*, 24–25.

20. G. W. F. Hegel, *On Christianity: Early Theological Writings*, trans. T. M. Knox and R. Kroner (New York, 1961), 69.

21. Ibid., 77.

22. Ibid., 152.

23. Ibid., 158–59.

24. Ibid., 146.

25. Ibid., 149.

26. Quoted by Köstlin, *Hegel*, 170 (my italics).

27. For the connection between the Historical School and political romanticism and nationalism, cf. C. Schmitt, *Politische Romantik*, 2. Aufl. (Munich, 1925), 46ff. For the indebtedness of the Nazi lawyers to this tradition, see O. Dietrich, *Die philosophischen Grundlagen des Nationalsozialismus* (Breslau, 1935); H. Nicolai, *Die rassengesetzliche Rechtslehre* (Munich, 1933).

28. G. Rexius, "Studien zur Staatslehre der historischen Schule," *Historische Zeitschrift* 107 (1911), 520; H. V. Kantorowicz, "Volksgeist und historische Schule," ibid., 108 (1912), 303ff.; S. Brie, *Der Volksgeist bei Hegel und in der historischen Rechtsschule* (Berlin and Leipzig, 1909), 25ff.

29. §§33, 331, addition to 259.

30. Cf. J. Löwenstein, *Hegels Staatsidee—Ihr Doppelgesicht und Einfluss im 19. Jahrhundert* (Berlin, 1927), 41–42.

31. *Reason and Revolution*, 237.

32. *Philosophy of Right*, §§349–50.

33. Ibid., §211.

34. Ibid., introduction, 10; §§258–59.

35. Ibid., §211. The unreformed English Common Law is frequently used by Hegel as an example of the anxiety, irrationality, and eventual cruelty of uncodified customary law. He kept a whole collection of press-cuttings illustrating some of the more blatant absurdities of early nineteenth-century Common Law. These cuttings have been published in *Hegels Berliner Schriften*, ed. J. Hoffmeister (Hamburg, 1956), 718–24.

36. *Philosophy of Right*, §213. Hegel's disciple, Edward Gans, held the same

position in his introduction to his master's *Philosophy of Right*, xiii–xiv, as well as in his own work, *Erbrecht in weltgeschichtlicher Entwicklung* (Berlin, 1824), vol. 1, vi.

37. This has been characteristically criticized as being contradictory to Hegel's system by Ferdinand Lassalle, *System der erworbenen Rechte*, 2. Aufl., I, xv–xvii, 58–61. Lassalle, in spite of his Hegelianism, was very much influenced by the Historical School (his book was dedicated to one of its leading members), and his concept of *Volksgeist* is identical with their and with the general romantic outlook. Those interested in the involved problem of Lassalle's nationalism may find this of some interest.

38. *Hegels Schriften zu Politik und Rechtsphilosphie*, 199. That this attitude is very far from a Burkean one should be borne in mind, especially by those who tend to see in Hegel strong traces of Burke's influence. The fact that Hegel accepted rational criteria for a critique of social conditions should make his attitude quite distinct from Burke's, in spite of the fact that Hegel did not go very far in applying those criteria to immediate reality.

39. *Philosophy of Right*, addition to §211.

40. Meinecke, *Weltbürgertum und Nationalstaat*, 275. Cf. also F. Rosenzweig, *Hegel und der Staat* (Berlin, 1920), vol. 2, 5.

41. *Einleitung*, 250; *Weltgeschichte*, 705, 711.

42. *Philosophy of Right*, §347.

43. *Einleitung*, 174.

44. *Weltgeschichte*, 533–42.

45. *Hegel's Philosophy of History*, trans. J. Sibree (New York, 1956), xv, 341. I have refrained from using this translation, and rendered my own translation of the passages quoted from the various parts of *Philosophy of History*, because of the rather unreliable and fragmentary German edition which served as a basis for Sibree's translation. See Hoffmeister's appendix to his edition of the *Einleitung* for a detailed account of these problems.

46. *Weltgeschichte*, 758.

47. Ibid., 775.

48. Ibid., 774ff.

49. Ibid., 761.

50. *Philosophy of Right*, addition to §339. A similar note is voiced by Hegel in his *Aesthetics*: "In contemporary Europe, every nation is limited by another one, and cannot, therefore, embark on a course of war against another European nation" (*Werke*, ed. Glockner, vol. 14, 335). Cf. *Weltgeschichte* 761, and Avineri, "The Problem of War in Hegel's Thought," *Journal of the History of Ideas* 22 (1961), 463–74.

51. *The Modern Democratic State* (London, 1943), vol. 1, 146–49.

Shlomo Avineri, The Problem of War in Hegel's Thought

1. See, e.g., H. Heller, *Hegel und der nationale Machtstaatsgedanke in Deutschland* (Leipzig, 1921), 118; W. M. McGovern, *From Luther to Hitler* (New York, 1941); K. R. Popper, *The Open Society and Its Enemies* (Princeton, 1950), 259. This

opinion, uncritically accepted, found its way into general text books of political philosophy, e.g., J. Bowle, *Politics and Opinion in the 19th Century* (London, 1951), 43. The opposite opinion is no less widespread; see F. Rosenzweig, *Hegel und der Staat*, 2 vols. (Munich, 1920); H. Marcuse, *Reason and Revolution*, 2d ed. (London, 1955); E. Weil, *Hegel et l'État* (Paris, 1950). Cf. also Georg Lukács's "Der deutsche Faschismus und Hegel," in his *Schicksalswende* (Berlin, 1948), 37–67.

I wish to express my gratitude to Prof. J. L. Talmon for the help and advice I was privileged to receive from him while doing research on this subject under his supervision.

2. D. A. Routh, "The Philosophy of International Relations," *Politica* (September 1938), 223–35.

3. *Hegels Schriften zur Politik und Rechtsphilosophie*, ed. G. Lasson (Leipzig, 1913), 470.

4. Ibid., 432.

5. G. W. F. Hegel, *The Phenomenology of Mind*, 2d ed., trans. J. B. Baillie (London, 1949), 474.

6. H. Treitschke, *Politik*, 5th ed., ed. M. Cornicelius (Leipzig, 1922), vol. 1, 24, 39, 60; vol. 2, 362, 371, 519.

7. Cf. Mussolini's article "Fascismo," in *Enciclopedia Italiana*, vol. 14 (Rome, 1932), 847–50, for the strong emphasis on "positive" values of war. See also W. Ebenstein, *Modern Political Thought* (New York, 1958), 330–37.

8. A. Müller, *Elemente der Staatskunst*, vol. 1, ed. J. Baxa (Jena, 1922), 5, 7, 85ff. Meinecke, in *Weltbürgertum und Nationalstaat*, 146, sees in Müller the forerunner of Ranke's thoughts on war, while Hegel's thought, which is free from the romantic obsession with the vitalistic and organic growth of the state, is of a completely different mold. This seem to be true in spite of Hegel's remark that literature, and mainly epic literature, is nourished by wars of conquest (*Werke*, vol. 14, ed. Glockner [Stuttgart, 1928], 354, recently quoted and discussed by W. Kaufmann, *From Shakespeare to Existentialism*, 122–24). It seems that here, once more, a mere statement of what seemed to Hegel to be an historical fact was construed as if it meant moral approval.

9. *Hegel's Philosophy of Right*, trans. T. M. Knox (Oxford, 1945), 12. On the specific Lutheran connotations of this expression, which occurs also in Goethe, cf. K. Löwith, *Von Hegel bis Nietzsche* (Zurich, 1941), 24.

10. Montesquieu is perhaps the first among the moderns who sees in war a result of the social condition of man, and not a relapse into some traumatic presocial state. *L'Esprit des Lois*, vol. 1, chaps. 2–3.

11. *Philosophy of Right*, §338; see also addition to §339.

12. Ibid., §324. Without directly drawing on this paragraph, this utilitarian-liberal argument was criticized on the more general level of political obligation by Hegel's English disciple, B. Bosanquet, *The Philosophical Theory of the State* (London, 1958), 76, n. 1.

13. *Philosophy of Right*, §36; Hegel's *Enzyklopädie*, §49. Compare this with the Nazi maxim: "The individual as such has neither a right nor a duty to exist, as all the rights and duties derive exclusively from the community," stated by the

Nazi jurist Otto Dietrich in his article in the *Völkischer Beobachter* (11 November 1937).

14. *Philosophy of Right*, §324.

15. Ibid.

16. Ibid., addition to §324.

17. Ibid., §324. It is interesting to note that Popper (*Open Society*, 262, 269) did not make the distinction, falling therefore into the pitfall of identifying Hegel with Treitschke and Moeller van den Bruck.

18. *Philosophy of Right*, §323.

19. Ibid., §331. Hegel writes: "Das Volk als Staat . . ."; since Knox translated that as "the nation-state," which only begs the question, I have had to render my own translation of the phrase.

20. Ibid., addition to §324.

21. Ibid., The Korean and Congolese experiences might perhaps be cited as illustrations to Hegel's contention how the existence of an international organization might enmesh this very organization in what is to all practical purposes an act of war. Assertions that those experiences tend to strengthen the authority of the UN only corroborate Hegel's insight, as the same might be said of an individual state confronted by the challenge of war.

22. Ibid., §71.

23. Ibid., §323.

24. Cf. the interesting study on this subject by Dr. Adam von Trott zu Solz, *Hegels Staatsphilosophie und das Internationale Recht, Abhandlungen des Seminars für Völkerrecht und Diplomatie*, Heft 6 (Göttingen, 1932), 87–91.

25. For the difference, according to Hegel, between law and contract, see his *Enzyklopädie*, §§493–95.

26. *Philosophy of Right*, §333.

27. Ibid., §338 (my italics). Cf. also the addition to this paragraph, as well as §339. This is strikingly similar to clause 6 of Kant's "Preliminary Articles of Perpetual Peace" in his *Perpetual Peace*, trans. M. Smith (London, 1903), 114.

28. *Elemente der Staatskunst*, vol. 1, 9.

29. *Philosophy of Right*, addition to §338.

30. Ibid., §268.

31. *Hegels Schriften zur Politik und Rechtsphilosophie*, 99–101 (my italics).

32. *Philosophy of Right*, §334.

33. Ibid., §335.

34. Ibid., §334.

35. Ibid., §337.

36. Ibid., §§325, 328.

37. Ibid., §327.

38. Ibid., addition to §271.

39. Ibid., addition to §339. Hegel uses a similar expression in his lectures on aesthetics when he remarks: "In contemporary Europe every nation is limited by another one, and cannot, therefore, embark on a course of war against another European nation" (*Werke*, vol. 14, ed. Glockner, 355).

40. G. W. F. Hegel, *Vorlesungen über die Philosophie der Weltgeschichte*, ed. G. Lasson (Leipzig, 1920), 761 (my italics). I have had to render my own translation, as this passage, like so many others, does not appear in Sibree's English translation, which was based on the very fragmentary early German edition of Hegel's lectures on the Philosophy of History. Only at the beginning of this century did Lasson compare this edition with Hegel's own notes and publish the fuller edition. It is a pity that the English-reading public has to rely on such an incomplete version. Cf. also Hegel's opposition to the claim for "natural" frontiers, most vociferously claimed in Germany by Arndt. Hegel contends in this *Philosophy of Right*, §247, that such a claim only causes endless dangers and provokes further wars, as there exists no objective criterion for the "naturalness" of the frontiers. It is fascinating how deeply an early nineteenth-century philosopher could foresee the hollowness of this nationalistic catchword, so much still *en vogue* in our own century.

41. Cited in T. Klein, *1848—Der Vorkampf deutscher Einheit und Freiheit* (Munich, 1914), 294–95. On this problem in the history of modern, and especially German, nationalism, cf. J. L. Talmon, *Political Messianism: The Romantic Phase* (London, 1960), 479–86.

42. H. Haupt, *Quellen und Darstellungen zur Geschichte der Burschenschaft und der deutschen Einheitsbewegung*, vol. 2 (Heidelberg, 1911), 37. For Hegel's attitude to the extreme nationalism of the Fraternities, see my "The Hegelian Position on the Emancipation of the Jews," *Zion, Quarterly for Research in Jewish History* 30 (1960), 134–36 (in Hebrew).

D. P. Verene, Hegel's Account of War

1. For example, Karl R. Popper, *The Open Society and Its Enemies*, vol. 2: *The High Tide of Prophecy: Hegel, Marx and the Aftermath* (London, 1945), chap. 12. See also Hans Kohn, "Political Theory and the History of Ideas," *Journal of the History of Ideas* 25 (1964), 305. Kohn's criticism is directed against the defense of Hegel's views on war in John Plamenatz, *Man and Society*, vol. 2 (New York, 1963).

2. I take this to be the standard or most frequently held view. See, e.g., F. S. Northedge, "Peace, War, and Philosophy," *The Encyclopedia of Philosophy*, vol. 6 (New York, 1967), 63–64; George H. Sabine, *A History of Political Theory* (New York, 1937), 664–67, 753; J. N. Findlay, *Hegel: A Re-examination* (New York, 1962), 331.

3. See Shlomo Avineri, "The Problem of War in Hegel's Thought," *Journal of the History of Ideas* 22 (1961), 463–74. That Hegel's political thought is part of the mainstream of Western European political theory not incompatible with that of Hobbes, Locke, Montesquieu, and Rousseau is argued by Z. A. Pelczynski in his introductory essay to *Hegel's Political Writings*, trans. T. M. Knox (Oxford, 1964). See the exchange over Pelczynski's interpretation between Hook and Avineri in Sidney Hook, "Hegel Rehabilitated?" *Encounter* 24 (January 1965), 53–58; Shlomo Avineri, "Hook's Hegel," *Encounter* 25 (November 1965), 63–66. Reprinted in *Hegel's Political Philosophy*, ed. W. Kaufmann (New York, 1970).

4. *Political Writings*, 143–44, 208–10. See also the quotations from "The System of Ethics" (*System der Sittlichkeit*) and "On the Methods of Scientific Treatment of Natural Law" (*Über die wissenschaftlichen Behandlungsarten des Naturrechts*) in Avineri, "The Problem of War in Hegel's Thought," 463–64.

5. For a compilation of quotations on war from Hegel's lectures, see H. G. ten Bruggencate, "Hegel's Views on War," *Philosophical Quarterly* 1 (1959); and Constance I. Smith, "Hegel on War," *Journal of the History of Ideas* 26 (1965), 284–85.

6. Hegel's views on war in the *Philosophy of Right* are also stated in the third part of the *Encyclopedia*. See William Wallace, *Hegel's Philosophy of Mind* (Oxford, 1894), §§545–47.

7. *Hegel's Philosophy of Right*, trans. T. M. Knox (Oxford, 1942), §324. See also Herbert Marcuse, *Reason and Revolution: Hegel and the Rise of Social Theory* (Boston, 1960), 55.

8. *Philosophy of Right*, §324.

9. See the concluding comments to the preface to the *Philosophy of Right*, especially the owl of Minerva metaphor, 12–13, and also Hegel's description of the purpose of philosophy in *The Phenomenology of Mind*, trans. J. B. Baillie, 2d ed. (London, 1949), 80–91.

10. *Philosophy of Right*, §§1–2.

11. *Phenomenology of Mind*, 497.

12. Ibid., 474. See also *The German Constitution* in *Political Writings*, 143–44.

13. *Philosophy of Right*, §324 and addition. Hegel's discussion of war in the *Phenomenology of Mind* (466–99) and in the section of *Philosophy of Right* titled "Sovereignty *vis-à-vis* foreign States" (§§321–29) seems primarily directed to the relation of the individual and the state. His discussion of war as a feature of the relations between states occurs primarily in the section on "International Law" in the *Philosophy of Right* (§§330–40).

14. *Philosophy of Right*, §340.

15. Ibid., §334.

16. Ibid., §338.

17. Smith, "Hegel on War," applies this distinction to Hegel's statements on war to show that at least in his later works Hegel's intent was to describe, not prescribe. I agree with Smith that this distinction is useful for structuring approaches to Hegel's views on war, but the reasons that follow below do not find it, as does Smith, a sufficient mechanism for solving the problem of the logical status of Hegel's statements.

18. *Phenomenology of Mind*, 139–45.

19. Ibid., 84, 120–21.

20. Ibid., 88–91.

21. The first part of the system is presented in the *Phenomenology of Mind* (see 95, 806–8). The second part of the system is presented in the *Science of Logic* (vol. 1, trans. W. H. Johnston and L. G. Struthers [London, 1929], 37) and the *Encyclopedia of Philosophical Sciences* (the first book being a restatement of the larger logic and the second and third books being the *Philosophy of Nature* and the

Philosophy of Spirit or *Culture*). The *Philosophy of Right* is an expanded statement of section 2 of the *Philosophy of Spirit* and, Hegel states, is intended systematically to present those remarks he would normally present verbally in lecturing on that section of the *Encyclopedia* (*Philosophy of Right*, 1). Hegel regards the *Philosophy of Right* as based on an extension of the principles established in the *Science of Logic*, the foundation work of the second part of the system.

22. *Science of Logic*, 37.

23. In speaking of Hegel's political philosophy here, I am not including his shorter political writings which are not directly part of his system and are generally empirical in character. As Z. A. Pelczynski argues in his introduction to *Hegel's Political Writings*, these show a different side to Hegel's political thought (see 134–37). However, as mentioned earlier, the content of Hegel's statements on war in these shorter writings does not differ from those made in the works of his system.

24. The importance of not approaching Hegel's political theory as a set of empirical generalizations is well realized by Irving Louis Horowitz, "The Hegelian Concept of Political Freedom," *The Journal of Politics* 28 (1966), 3–28. Horowitz states:

> The Hegelian approach assumes completeness in that all relevant concepts and relations which would be required in empirical undertakings are worked out. This special sense of methodology as ideal typification should be kept in mind when examining Hegel. What we are provided with is a systems approach rather than empirical analysis. Few commentators have viewed the directly political and social writings of Hegel as an extension of his more abstract works. (3)

25. (BB.), VI, A. "Objective Spirit: The Ethical Order."

26. (A.), II, "Perception, Thing, and Deceptiveness."

27. *Philosophy of Right*, §§333–34. See also §324, remark.

28. Ibid., §333.

29. *Perpetual Peace*, ed. Lewis White Beck (New York, 1957), 24.

30. Ibid., 17, 46.

31. See preface, 10 and §29.

32. *Philosophy of Right*, §346.

33. Ibid., §349.

34. Ibid., 11.

35. It is interesting to note that Kant in the *Critique of Judgment* makes comments similar to Hegel's regarding the stagnation of nations during prolonged periods of peace that are quite in contrast to his approach in *Perpetual Peace*. See the *Critique of Judgment*, §22 (83). For remarks on these passages, see Albert William Levi, *Humanism and Politics: Studies in the Relationship of Power and Value in the Western Tradition* (Bloomington, 1969), 268–69.

36. Karl Jaspers, *The Future of Mankind* (Chicago, 1951), 45 (my italics).

37. (B.), IV, A. "Independence and Dependence of Self-Consciousness: Lordship and Bondage."

38. See *The Future of Mankind*, chap. 4.

39. *Philosophy of Right*, §328. See also the addition to §327.

40. As Hegel points out, the honor or interest of the state may be seen by it as at stake in any of its dealings with other states. See ibid., §334.

41. See *Phenomenology of Mind*, 233. For a discussion of some of the perspectives from which Hegel's master-slave relationship can be viewed and some of the difficulties of developing social hypotheses from it, see George Armstrong Kelly, "Notes on Hegel's 'Lordship and Bondage,' " *Review of Metaphysics* 19 (1966), 780–802.

42. See *Phenomenology of Mind*, 238.

43. For an analysis of the mode of being of the warrior, see J. Glenn Gray, *The Warriors: Reflections on Men in Battle* (New York, 1959), esp. conclusion.

44. See Ernst Cassirer, *The Myth of the State* (New Haven, 1946), 274.

Errol E. Harris, Hegel's Theory of Sovereignty, International Relations, and War

1. *Grundlinien der Philosophie des Rechts*, 279.

2. Ibid., 333.

3. London, 1949.

4. Ibid., 278.

5. Cf. Ibid.: "In former times of feudal monarchy, the State was certainly sovereign in external affairs, but internally neither the monarch nor the State was sovereign." Cf. also *Encyclopedia*, 544.

6. *Studies in History and Jurisprudence*, vol. 2 (Oxford: Clarendon Press, 1901), 86.

7. *Grundlinien*, 279; words omitted from the opening quotation above.

8. Ibid., 278.

9. Cf. *Critique of Hegel's Philosophy of Right*, trans. Annette John and Joseph O'Malley (Cambridge: Cambridge Universisty Press, 1970), 23.

10. Cf. *The Open Society and Its Enemies*, vol. 2 (London, 1942), 54.

11. *Encyclopedia*, 544.

12. *Grundlinien*, 278. "Ideality" here clearly means ideal unity.

13. E. S. Haldane and F. H. Simpson's translation (London 1896; reprinted 1968), vol. 3, 402.

14. *The Open Society and Its Enemies*.

15. Cf. Shlomo Avineri, *Hegel's Theory of the Modern State* (Cambridge: Cambridge University Press), chap. 2.

16. Cf. *Grundlinien*, n. to 281.

17. Cf. T. Hobbes, *Leviathan*, chap. 13; Spinoza, *Tractatus Politicus*, chaps. 3, 13; Hegel, *Rechtsphilosophie*, 333.

18. Cf. my *Survival of Political Man* (Johannesburg: Witwatersrand University Press, 1950), chaps. 3, 4; *Annihilation and Utopia* (London: Allen and Unwin, 1966), chaps. 5, 6.

19. Cf. ibid.

20. *Grundlinien*.

21. Cf. Kant, *Zum Ewigen Frieden*, sec. 2, art. 2.

22. Popper quotes Hegel in Knox's translation which advisedly uses the phrase "League of Nations," and Popper was writing at a time when the League of Nations set up after the First World War had signally failed to prevent World War II.

23. *The Survival of Political Man*, chap. 5; *Annihilation and Utopia*, chap. 10.

24. Cf. G. Schwartzenberger, *Power Politics*, 2d ed. (London: Stevens and Sons, 1951); E. H. Carr, *The Twenty Years' Crisis* (London: Macmillan, 1946); B. de Jouvenel, *On Power* (Geneva, 1945; Boston, 1962).

25. *Rechtsphilosophie*, 334, Knox translation.

26.

> In Las Vegas, J. Carlton Adair, the head of the local civil defence agency, announced that a militia of 5000 volunteers would be necessary to protect residents in the event of thermonuclear war against an invasion, not by a foreign enemy, but by refugees from Southern California, who, he said, would come into Nevada like a swarm of locusts. In Hartford, Connecticut, at a private meeting of citizens to consider civil defence, one man maintained that firearms were standard equipment for shelters as a means of repulsing the inroads of people maddened by the effects of wounds or radiation. One's own family, so it was argued, must be protected because there would be only sufficient food and water for them. Neighbours caught in the open by warning of attack, who might rush to friends for shelter must, therefore, be shot down. (*Annihilation and Utopia*, 121f.)

27. *Thinking about the Unthinkable* (London and Princeton, 1962), 101.

28. In the works cited above. Cf. esp. *Annihilation and Utopia*, pts. 2 and 3.

Steven Walt, Hegel on War

1. Karl Popper, *The Open Society and Its Enemies*, vol. 2 (New York, 1967), 68; and Hans Kohn, "Political Theory and the History of Ideas," *Journal of the History of Ideas* 25 (1964), 305.

2. Constance Smith, "Hegel on War," *Journal of the History of Ideas* 21 (1965), 283; and H. G. ten Bruggencate, "Hegel's Views on War," *Philosophical Quarterly* 1 (1950), 58; cf. Edward Black, "Hegel on War," *Monist* 57 (1973), 580–81.

3. Shlomo Avineri, "The Problem of War in Hegel's Thought," *Journal of the History of Ideas* 22 (1961), 467. Avineri also holds that Hegel condemns war itself (ibid., 465).

4. Both views are defended in the various debates included in *Hegel's Political Philosophy*, ed. Walter Kaufmann (New York, 1970).

5. All unidentified references cited in the paper will be to the paragraph numbers in G. W. F. Hegel, *Philosophy of Right*, trans. T. Knox (Oxford, 1978). Paragraph numbers followed by an "A" will be to the additions to those paragraphs. Paragraph numbers followed by an "R" will be to the explanatory remarks to

the corresponding paragraphs. Bruggencate cites relevant passages on war from several of Hegel's other writings (Bruggencate, "Hegel's Views on War," 59–60).

6. Hegel, *Philosophy of Right*, preface, 12.

7. Cf. G. W. F. Hegel, *Phenomenology of Mind*, trans. J. B. Ballie (New York, 1967), 497, where Hegel says:

> War is the spirit and form in which the essential moment of ethical substance, the absolute freedom of ethical self-consciousness from all and every kind of existence, is manifestly confirmed and realized. While, on the other hand, war makes the particular sphere of property and personal independence, as well as the personality of the individual himself, feel the force of negation and destruction, on the other hand, this engine of negation and destruction stands out as that which preserves the whole in security.

8. See n. 3, above.

9. Hegel, *Philosophy of Right*, 12.

10. Hegel probably had in mind the sixth article of Kant's *Perpetual Peace*: "A state shall not, during war, permit hostilities of a nature that would render reciprocal confidence in a succeeding peace impossible: such as employing assassins, poisoners, violation of capitulations, secret instigation of rebellion" (Immanuel Kant, *Perpetual Peace*, original translation [Morningside Heights, 1939], 7.)

11. G. W. F. Hegel, *Philosophy of Mind*, trans. W. Wallace (Oxford, 1971), art. 547.

12. G. W. F. Hegel, "The German Constitution," in *Hegel's Political Writings*, trans. T. Knox (Oxford, 1964), 143–44. Avineri argues on the basis of this passage and par. 324 that Hegel's view is that war *only* has the function of testing the ethical health of a people (Shlomo Avineri, *Hegel's Theory of the Modern State* [Cambridge, 1972], 196, 199.)

13. G. W. F. Hegel, *Die Vernunft in der Geschichte*, par. 112, cited in Charles Taylor, *Hegel* (Cambridge, 1975), 380.

14. Many of Hegel's statements concerning the prescriptions governing the waging of war (e.g., that envoys be respected, that war be waged by standing armies and not against domestic institutions [326, 338, 339]), however, may be read not as prescriptive statements *simpliciter* but as descriptive statements concerning the prescriptions nations in fact usually abide by in war. Smith notes the descriptive character of some of Hegel's statements without identifying the content of the descriptions (Smith, "Hegel on War," 284). Verene argues that Hegel's statements here are neither descriptive nor prescriptive but instead are characteristic of what Hegel takes to be philosophical statements. The passages which he cites to support this view, however, are taken from the *Phenomenology*; and it is not clear how they apply to those ostensibly descriptive or prescriptive statements in the *Philosophy of Right* (Donald P. Verene, "Hegel's Account of War," in *Hegel's Political Philosophy*, ed. Z. Pelcynski [Cambridge, 1971], 172–75).

15. Hegel, *Phenomenology*, 474. Defenders of Hegel who dismiss this passage as being representative of Hegel's early writings on war and not of those found in the *Philosophy of Right* fail to note the similarity in language between this passage

and the beginning of the addition to par. 324. In particular, they fail to note the similarity of the "spirit evaporating" as a result of the isolation of the parts of civil society from the state to the demise of the body as a result of the parts of civil society " 'walling themselves in' from the unity of the state" (cf. Bruggencate, "Hegel's Views on War," 58; Avineri, "The Problem of War in Hegel's Thought," 464, 467).

16. Hegel, *Phenomenology*, 233; cf. the whole section "Lord and Bondsman," 228–40.

17. "This negative relation [i.e., "this entanglement with chance events coming from without"] is that moment in the state which is most supremely its own, the state's actual infinity as the ideality of everything finite within it" (323).

18. Immanuel Kant, *The Metaphysical Elements of Justice*, trans. J. Ladd (Indianapolis, 1965), 128.

19. Referring to perpetual peace, Kant says, for example: "Only through the establishment of a universal union of states (in analogy to the union that makes a people into a state) can these rights [i.e., the property rights of nations] become peremptory and a true state of peace be achieved" (ibid., 123–24).

20. This of course is not to say that states would cease to exist as nations. Nor does Hegel say so. He clearly distinguishes states from nations (cf. 324).

21. I thank the anonymous referees for their helpful comments on a previous draft of this chapter.

Philip T. Grier, The End of History and the Return of History

1. Francis Fukuyama, "The End of History?" *The National Interest* 16 (Summer 1989), 3–18; "[Six] Responses to Fukuyama," 19–35. The author is described as "deputy director of the State Department's policy planning staff and former analyst at the RAND Corporation." *The National Interest* is published four times per year in Washington, D.C.

2. The comparison of Kojève's "posthistorical man" to Nietzsche's "last man" was originally suggested by Allan Bloom in his editor's introduction to the English edition of Kojève's *Introduction to the Reading of Hegel*, trans. James H. Nichols, Jr. (New York: Basic Books, 1969), xii.

3. Francis Fukuyama, "A Reply to My Critics," *The National Interest* 18 (Winter 1989–90), 21–28.

4. Alexandre Kojève, *Introduction à la lecture de Hégel: Leçons sur la Phénoménologie de l'esprit professées de 1933 à 1939 à l École des Hautes Études*, ed. Raymond Queneau (Paris: Gallimard, 1947), 495; 2d ed. (Paris: Gallimard [n.d., but between 1959 and 1968], rpt. 1971), 497. All references are to the second edition unless otherwise indicated. The long footnote which distinguishes the first from the second French edition is translated in Bloom, 158–61.

5. Patrick Riley argues in "Introduction to the Reading of Alexandre Kojève" (*Political Theory* 9 [February 1981], 5–48) that the omnipresence of the master-slave dialectic should not necessarily be seen as evidence of specifically Marxist influence on Kojève's interpretation. Riley's reason for questioning this usual view

seems mainly to reflect doubt about whether there is any agreed criterion about what constitutes a Marxist interpretation of this problem, and not any special evidence about Kojève's real views. Riley argues that whatever the level of Marxist influence on Kojève's reading of Hegel, there are also distinctly existentialist and Nietzschean strands in it which are independent of Marxist influence. But this, of course, is further ground for doubt that Kojève could plausibly be treated as the last authentic Hegelian.

6. Alexandre Koyré, "Hegel à Iéna (à propos de publications récentes)," *Revue philosophique de France* 59 (1934), 274–83; also published in *Revue d'histoire et de philosophie religieuse* 15 (1935), 420–58; also collected in Alexandre Koyré, *Études d'histoire de la pensée philosophique* (Paris: Colin, 1961), 135–73; 2d ed. (Paris: Gallimard, 1971), 147–89. All references are to the 1971 edition.

7. According to Koyré the materials from the 1802 lectures, which form the *Jenenser Logik,* were published first by Hans Ehrenberg and Herbert Link under the title *Hegels erstes System: Nach den Handschriften der Bibliothek in Berlin* (Heidelberg: Winter 1915). This text was reedited by Georg Lasson as *Jenenser Logik, Metaphysik und Naturphilosophie: Aus dem Manuskript* (Leipzig: Meiner, 1923 [Koyré says 1925]; reprint, Hamburg: Meiner, 1967), vol. 18 of Hegel's *Sämtliche Werke.* The materials from the 1803–4 and 1805–6 lectures had just become available to Koyré two years earlier in Johannes Hoffmeister's edition, *Jenenser Realphilosophie* (Leipzig: Meiner, 1932), vols. 19–20 of the *Werke.*

8. The *Naturphilosophie* which Koyré, following the original editors, describes as having been written in 1802, has now been dated as Summer 1804 through Winter 1804–5 by Heinz Kimmerle, "Zur Chronologie von Hegels Jenaer Schriften," *Hegel-Studien* 4 (1967), 125–76, esp. 126–27, 142–45, 164–67. Hereafter the 1802 designation in scarequotes will signify Koyré's use of this dating.

9. Referring to the *Encyclopedia* system, and especially to the *Naturphilosophie,* Koyré asserts on 153, "Or le 'système' hégélien est mort, et bien mort." In n. 1 on that page, he further remarks, "Les efforts récents de faire revivre le hégélianisme n'ont fait, à notre avis, que démontrer, une fois de plus, la stérilité du 'système.' "

10. Koyré viewed these passages as extraordinarily important, as a description of "the constitution or the self-constitution of the concept of time" (174; all translations from Koyré are mine). He also described these passages as a "phenomenology" of time.

> It is not at all a question of . . . an analysis of the notion of time, an abstract notion of abstract time, of time such as it is presented in physics, Newtonian time, Kantian time, time in a straight line of formulas and clocks. It is a question of something else. It is a question of time "itself," of the spiritual reality of time. This time does not run in a uniform way; nor is it a homogeneous medium through which we pass; it is neither number of movement nor order of phenomena. It is enrichment, life, victory. It is—let us say it at once—itself spirit and concept. (175)

11. George L. Kline has recently drawn attention to Kojève's assertion of the primacy of the future in his interpretation of Hegel, suggesting that Kojève was influenced by Heidegger's formulations in *Being and Time*; cf. Kline's "Presidential

Address [to the Hegel Society of America, 1986]: The Use and Abuse of Hegel by Nietzsche and Marx," in *Hegel and his Critics: Philosophy in the Aftermath of Hegel*, ed. William Desmond (Albany: SUNY, 1989), 1–34, esp. 10. I hope to have established here that Kojève took this theme from Koyré's discussion of the "1802" Jena *Naturphilosophie*; but since that text had been available in the Ehrenberg and Link edition since 1915, is it not also possible that Heidegger was himself influenced by this (apparently discarded) passage from the early Hegel? If the passages on time and the future had such an electrifying effect upon Koyré and Kojève, might they not have similarly caught Heidegger's attention? It is also possible, of course, that Koyré's reaction to the passages on time was itself influenced by his reading of *Being and Time*.

12. See the discussion by H. S. Harris in his *Hegel's Development: Night Thoughts, Jena 1801–1806* (Oxford: Clarendon, 1983), 244–52.

13. Der Äther ist der absolute Geist als die Seite seiner absoluten Sichselbstgleichheit. . . .

> Der Äther ist nicht der lebendige Gott; denn er ist nur die Idee Gottes; der lebendige Gott aber ist der, der aus seiner Idee sich selbst erkennend [ist] und in dem Anders seiner selbst sich als sich selbst erkennt. Der Äther aber is absoluter Geist, der sich auf sich selbst bezieht, sich nicht als absoluten Geist erkennt. (Lasson, 197)

14. If Kimmerle's datings are accepted as correct, then the 1803–4 manuscripts were written mostly prior to what Koyré took to be the "1802" manuscript; but the remainder of his evidence and the substance of his conclusion are not affected.

15. Kojève's extraordinary emphasis on the master-slave dialectic is not taken from Koyré, however. Hence the interweaving of that theme with the end-of-history argument supplied by Koyré must be regarded as Kojève's own contribution.

16. The only hint we have that Kojève saw anything strange in this occurs in the following remark: "Or, *chose curieuse* [my emphasis], le texte décisif sur le temps se trouve dans la 'Philosophie de la *Nature*' de la 'Jenenser Realphilosophie' " (Queneau, 367).

17. Hegel's expression is *der daseiende Begriff.* As George Kline has pointed out in a personal communication, Kojève's rendering of that as "the *empirically* existing concept" (*le Concept . . . existant empiriquement* [Queneau, 365]) is quite arbitrary; there is no evident textual or contextual basis for adding "empirically." But Kojève's interpretation draws quite heavily on this questionable notion of "empirical" existence, as illustrated in this paragraph.

18. Allan Bloom, "Responses to Fukuyama," *The National Interest* 16 (Summer 1989), 19.

19. The late William Earle used to insist on a connection between the consummation of history in Hegel's sense and the Latin translation of the words spoken by Christ on the cross in John 19:30: "*Consummatum est*" (it is fulfilled). All having come to its appointed end (telos), the Scripture is fulfilled, and history

has acquired a new meaning. It is also highly instructive to consider this entire question in the light of Collingwood's *An Essay on Philosophical Method*, esp. chap. 3, par. 31, and chap. 9, par. 10.

20. G. W. F. Hegel, *Lectures on the Philosophy of World History*, trans. H. B. Nisbet with an introduction by Duncan Forbes (Cambridge: Cambridge University Press, 1975), 170–71. The same passage was indicated by Gertrude Himmelfarb in her response to Fukuyama in the same issue of *The National Interest* (26). We should note that the concluding phrase—*Der Philosoph hat es nicht mit dem Prophezeien zu tun*—appears not in the original edition, *Vorlesungen über die Philosophie der Geschichte*, vol. 11, ed. Eduard Gans (Berlin: Duncker und Humbolt, 1837), 129, but first in a later edition, *Vorlesungen über die Philosophie der Weltgeschichte: Erste Hälfte—Die Vernunft in der Geschichte*, ed. Johannes Hoffmeister (Hamburg: Felix Meiner, 1955), 210, as pointed out by George Kline in a personal communication.

21. Sunday, 27 August 1989, sec. E, 5.

22. Monday, 11 September 1989.

23. Wednesday, 1 November 1989, sec. A, 29.

24. Sunday, 22 October 1989, 38–42, 54–55.

25. 14 August 1989.

26. *The National Interest* 17 (Fall 1989), 92–100, 3–11, 11–16.

27. Sunday, 10 December 1989, sec. C, 1, 4.

28. Sunday, 10 December 1989, sec. E, 6.

29. *The National Interest* 17 (Fall 1989), 16.

30. Harvey J. Kaye, "Point of View," *Chronicle of Higher Education* (25 October 1989), A48.

31. John Gray, "The End of History—or of Liberalism," *National Review* (27 October 1989), 35.

32. Kojève's work, along with Koyré's, obviously belongs to that circle of commentators in the 1930s who were reacting in the first flush of excitement to the appearance a few years earlier of some of Hegel's early manuscripts. This episode might be compared to the similar burst of enthusiasm for "the young Marx" as his juvenilia appeared in a succession of translations into various languages through much of the twentieth century. As of 1969, anyone looking for a competent commentary on Hegel in English need have looked no farther than those of G. R. G. Mure or J. N. Findlay, to name only two.

33. The quotation is taken from Václav Havel, "Stories and Totalitarianism" (1987), originally published in the underground journal *Jednou nohu*. It was later published in English translation in the *Index on Censorship* 17, no. 3 (March 1988), and also in *Open Letters: Selected Writings 1965–1990* by Václav Havel, ed. Paul Wilson (New York: Alfred A. Knopf, 1991), 328–50.

Reinhart Klemens Maurer, Hegel and the End of History

1. The present translation is based on the text "Teleologische Aspekte der Hegelsche Philosophie: Zur Kritik des neuen Chiliasmus" from Prof. Maurer's

Hegel und das Ende der Geschichte (2d ed., Freiburg, Munich: Alber, 1980), 173–207.—*Trans.*

2. This is a reprint of the essay "Endgeschichtliche Aspekte der Hegelschen Philosophie," from the *Philosophisches Jahrbuch der Görresgesellschaft* 76 (1968), 88–122.

The essay is a self-enclosed addition to the book *Hegel und das Ende der Geschichte* (Stuttgart, 1965). Cf. also "Hegel et la fin de l'histoire," *Archives de Philosophie* 30 (1967), 483–518. Although the book begins with an interpretation of the *Phenomenology of Spirit*, the question about the end of history only comes about there in the course of the investigation. By contrast here this question stands in the foreground right from the beginning; this question is specifically directed above all toward Hegel's writings in which this issue is most expressly treated. More exactly speaking, these are not writings but rather Hegel's Berlin lectures, especially his most esoteric *Lectures on the Philosophy of History.* Along with placing emphasis on the unity of his entire work, I want at the same time to portray a Hegel here who had the most influence but in such a way that he has not yet been influential.

The transmission of the lectures is unreliable and only in the newest editions is the information given about from which of the students' manuscripts a given passage comes. Even apart from the fact that Hegel would have formulated many things differently and given more precise accounts for a publication in the form of a book, we are still on shaky ground with this text.

The following are the abbreviated works of Hegel referred to here:

Einl = Einleitung in die Geschichte der Philosophie, ed. Hoffmeister (Hamburg, 1959) (PhB 166).

Log = Wissenschaft der Logik, ed. Lasson (Leipzig, 1934) (PhB 56/57).

Phä = Phänomenologie des Geistes, ed. Hoffmeister (Hamburg, 1952) (PhB 114).

Recht = Grundlinien der Philosophie des Rechts, ed. Hoffmeister (Hamburg, 1955) (PhB 124a).

Rel = Vorlesungen über die Philosophie der Religion, ed. Lasson (Hamburg, 1966) (reprint of the edition from 1925; PhB 59).

Vern = Die Vernunft in der Geschichte, ed. Hoffmeister (1955) (PhB 171a).

WG = Sämtliche Werke, ed. Glockner (Stuttgart, 1927ff.).

3. L. Landgrebe treats this same theme chiefly with a view toward Kant in his essay "Das philosophische Problem des Endes der Geschichte," in *Kritik und Metaphysik* (Berlin, 1966), 224–43.

4. A. Gehlen, *Studien zur Anthropologie und Soziologie.* (Berlin, 1963), 344.

5. Paris, 1947.

6. With this he means the disappearance of the heretofore historical human type and explains:

> Man remains living as an animal who is in agreement with nature or the being which is given. What disappears is man, properly speaking, that is to say the negative action of the given and the error in general of the subject opposed to the object. . . .

Practically, this means the disappearance of wars and of bloody revolutions, but
also the disappearance of philosophy. Because man no longer essentially changes
in himself, there is no longer any reason to change the (true) principles which are
at the base of his knowledge of the world and of himself. But everything else can
maintain itself indefinitely: art, love, sport, etc.; in short everything which makes
man happy. (434ff., remark)

In a remark to the second otherwise unaltered edition of his book, Kojève weakens
his talk about man as a happy animal, insofar as he says that the posthistorical
people are not happy as such, but rather are "happy as a function of their artistic,
erotic and sporting behavior" (436).

    7. For the immanent, planned technical criticism of the concept of "*post-
histoire*" which lives from the rapturous ideology of a total, instead of technical,
planning, cf. H.-J. Arndt, "Die Figur des Plans als Utopie des Bewahrens," in
Säkularisation und Utopie, Ebracher Studien (Stuttgart, 1967), 119–54, esp. 135ff.

    8. K. Löwith, *Weltgeschichte und Heilsgeschehen: Die theologischen Voraussetzun-
gen der Geschichtsphilosophie* (Stuttgart, 1953). Hereafter cited as *Löw 2*.

    9. J. Taubes, *Abendländische Eschatologie* (Bern, 1947).

    10. In his earlier book, *Von Hegel zu Nietzsche* (Zurich, 1941; Stuttgart, 1958;
hereafter *Löw 1*), Löwith unambiguously attaches the end to Hegel. There we
read, "Hegel's philosophical theology was really an end" (58). The meaning of
this connection of philosophy with theology and its end is explained by Hegel's
concept of reconciliation: "But Hegel could *reconcile* himself with the empirical
contradictions in the existing world because he, as the last Christian philosopher,
was still in the world, as if he were not of this world" (111). Löwith writes later:
"while the spirit of the old Europe collapsed, its civilization rose up and conquered
the world" (*Löw 2*, 185; cf. above the first meaning of "the end of history"). This
passage can obviously be understood in this way. What for Löwith came to an end
with Hegel and his time was a specific realization and secularization of Christianity
in the sense of the Paul's recommendation "to deal with the world as if one had
no dealings with it" (1 Cor. 7:29ff.). This dialectical unity has fallen to pieces or
better should fall to pieces in a radically secularized civilization and a possible
"Christian pilgrimage *in hoc saeculo*" (cf. *Löw 1*, 415). For the question of the
end of the realization of Christianity and of the possibility of a new one, cf. also
A. Mirgeler, *Rückblick auf das abendländische Christentum* (Mainz, 1961).

    11. In *Kant-Studien* 11 (1906), 40–108.

    12. R. Haym, *Hegel und seine Zeit* (Berlin, 1857; reprint, Darmstadt, 1962),
4ff. Cf., e.g., the "Vorwort" from P. Marheineke to the first edition of Hegel's
Philosophy of Religion (*WG*, vol. 15, 6). Generally one can say that Hegel, if indeed
he discusses it at all, speaks of the end of history in the following sense, and it
was not he, but rather some Hegelians, who wanted to raise his philosophy out of
a contemporary consciousness to an ultimate and absolute one. Marx, probably
the most genial of these contemporaries, saw in the Hegelian philosophy not
the total philosophy but "a total" philosophy among others, e.g., the Aristotelian
(*Frühschriften*, ed. Landshut [Stuttgart, 1953], 12ff.) And he knew also in contrast

to most of the other Hegelians what had to be done according to a total philosophy. He deduced it historically and philosophically in his dissertation even before the misery of the working class came so decisively into his view. Philosophy should be practical. The realization of philosophy through its sublation and the sublation through realization or "the becoming philosophical of the world at the same time a becoming worldly of philosophy" (ibid., 215, 17) means the formula of transubstantiation. With this ambiguous announcement and the movement to the primacy of praxis, Marxism became a main cause of today's talk about the end of history and of the beginning of posthistory. By employing the stylistically brilliant fogginess of that formulation and by simultaneously using the theoretical problems of Hegelian philosophy and by turning to political praxis and economic theory of this praxis, Marx also became the originator of an endless theoretical back and forth debate between theory and practice. As philosopher and dialectician, he remains stuck in the category of the mutual determination, which, understood as an interaction of "being and consciousness" (ibid., 349), fostered the later scholastic ontologizing of Marxism.

13. At the end of the *Phenomenology*, he writes, "Time appears . . . as the fate and the necessity of Spirit, which is not completed in itself . . . before therefore Spirit completes itself not as in itself, not as World Spirit. It cannot reach its completion as a self-conscious Spirit" (*Phä*, 558ff.) What "in itself" and "self-conscious" mean in this context cannot be discussed in detail here, although it would be important for the sense of "completion" that Hegel discusses. But it is clear that, according to Hegel's formulation, time only *appears* as the fate of Spirit, an appearance, which it cancels retroactively when time has done its duty" (*Phä*, 558). This happens through "sacrifice" and "externalization" through which Spirit takes up or back its becoming in itself, discovering nothing foreign on the ground of time (and of space) but rather "its pure self" (*Phä*, 563).

14. We should here recall the Platonic distinction between *upothesis* and *archē* (*Politeia*, 510Bff., 533Af.) which belongs to the basic principles of Hegel's philosophy. Dialectic, which is according to Plato the most important organ of philosophy, moves between these two poles. Its critical activity exists not in making "presuppositions beginnings but rather in making them presuppositions," and that means to prove bare presuppositions as such and to clear the way for the "presuppositionless" (cf. 551B). Hegel's *Logic* is in the same sense a progressing sublation of the false positing of absolutes, and this dialectic that forms the basis of first philosophy also determines other parts of his philosophy.

15. Here used more in the sense of *archē* as the addition shows: "in itself at hand."

16. For this see G. E. Müller, "The Hegel Legend of 'Thesis-Antithesis-Synthesis,' " *Journal of the History of Ideas* 19 (1958), 411–14. W. Kaufmann, *Hegel* (New York, 1965), 167ff.

17. Cf. Maurer, *Hegel und das Ende der Geschichte*, 92ff.; and M. Riedel, "Hegels Kritik des Naturrechts," *Hegelstudien* 4 (1967), 177–204.

18. From the fact that such an end of history would not be a "kingdom of Spirit" in the sense of some reconciliation of thought with reality but rather in

\

the sense of a destroying dialectic that would produce a richer field of activity than ever before, one may induce that Hegel writes with a view to history, "No limited figure can make itself strong against thought or the concept. If there were such a thing, which the concept could not digest or undermine, this would lie there clearly as the highest disruption, unholiness. But if there were such a thing, it would be thought itself, as it understands itself. . . . This would be the final goal of the world" (*Vern*, 180ff.). Concerning this passage, H. F. Fulda explains, "The fiction of an ultimate final figure is so used that this would be the highest disruption. Then it is said that the imaginary could only be thought as it understands itself. But this does not exist as world historical reality, even if it can come up in history" (*Das Problem einer Einleitung in Hegels Wissenschaft der Logik* [Frankfurt, 1965], 214ff.). For the theme of the end of history, cf. in general his book and his review of R. K. Maurer in *Philosophische Rundschau* 14 (1967), 208–20.

19. Here the German word "*Zugrundegehen*" is a substantive from the verbal form which means both "to go to ruin" and "to return to a foundation."—*Trans.*

20. *Zum ewigen Frieden*, A/B 25.

21. *Einl*, 4.

22. Hegel in principle remained true to what he wrote in his early work "Das Leben Jesu" about Jewish messianism and its "sensible representation of the kingdom of God." In this passage we read concerning the interpretation of Luke 17:21 (*idou gar ē basileia tou theou entos umōn estin*),

> You will often wish to see the kingdom of God on earth. They will often say to you, here or there there is such a happy brotherhood of man. . . . Do not run after such delusions; do not hope to see the kingdom of God in a brilliant, external unification of mankind, for instance, in the external form of a state, in a society, or among the public laws of a church. Rather as such a peaceful, brilliant condition, the pursuit will be the lot of the true citizen of the kingdom of God and of the virtuous, often most of all of those who like for instance the Jews know themselves to be members of such a society. ("Das Leben Jesu," ed. Roques [Jena, 1906], 45ff.; cf. 48; cf. *Hegels theologische Jugendschriften*, ed. Nohl [Tübingen, 1907], 112).

For the question of the translation and meaning of *entos umōn*, see M. Theunissen, *Das Andere: Studien zur Sozialontologie der Gegenwart* (Berlin, 1965), 506ff.

23. Cf., e.g., *Vern*, 77: "The true good, the universal divine reason is also the power to bring itself to completion"; and *System der Philosophie*, §234 Addition (*WG*, vol. 8, 445):

> The unsatisfied striving disappears when we recognize that the ultimate goal of the world is now just as completed as it completes itself eternally. . . . This harmony of "is" and "ought" is yet not something frozen or lacking development; for the good is the ultimate goal of the world since it always brings itself forth, and the distinction between the spiritual and natural world still exists that while the latter constantly turns back into itself, a progress takes place in the former.

24. In *Theorie und Praxis: Sozialphilosophische Studien* (Berlin, 1963), Jürgen Habermas treats the relation of these two concepts or realities on the basis of the presupposition of Vico and Hobbes "that we only recognize an object to the degree to which we can ourselves bring it forth" (14). This position implies, as is shown in Habermas, a turning away not just from Hegel but from philosophy in general.

25. Cf. R. Dahrendorf, *Die angewandte Aufklärung: Gesellschaft und Soziologie in Amerika* (Munich, 1963).

26. Ibid., 209.

27. "Das Leben Jesu," 4.

28. *Recht* §194; passim §§189–98.

29. *WG*, vol. 11, 256. "The inactivity ceases just like the mere raw bravery. In their place come the activity of industry and of sober courage, which with the coolness to navigate the sea considers the means. . . . In industry man is himself a goal and treats nature as something subordinate to him." Cf. *WG*, vol. 11, 318: "Work is serious in relation to the need: either I or nature must be destroyed"; and *WG*, vol. 11, 483.

30. Plato, *Protagoras*, 320D–322C.

31. W. Jaeger, *Paideia*, vol. 1 (Berlin, 1959), 379.

32. Cf. W. Kamlah, *Christentum und Geschichtlichkeit* (Stuttgart, 1951); R. Niebuhr, *Glaube und Geschichte* (Munich, 1951) (English translation, *Faith and History* [New York, 1949]).

33. Under the catchword "philosophy of reflexion" [*Reflexionsphilosophie*] Hegel criticizes the epistemological and moral side of subjectivity which is partly too modest (concerning knowledge of the absolute) and partly too fixated on domination (concerning the relation with nature) (Kant, Jacobi, Fichte), above all in his works *Differenz des Fichteschen und Schellingschen Systems der Philosophie* and *Glauben und Wissen*. In a limited sector, he anticipates Heidegger's criticism of occidental metaphysics.

34. Cf. my review, in *Hegelstudien* 4 (1967), 265–67, of W.-D. Marsch, *Gegenwart Christi in der Gesellschaft: Eine Studie zu Hegels Dialektik* (Munich, 1965).

35. "Eins und Alles."

36. On the question of whether Hegel saw himself as the bearer of an absolute end-historical knowledge, cf. "Fragment eines Briefes an Hinrichs," *Briefe von und an Hegel*, vol. 2, ed. Hoffmeister (Hamburg, 1953), 215f.

37. Kojève, *Introduction à la lecture de Hegel*, 40. [In the original text, this passage is cited in French.—*Trans.*]

38. "System und Geschichte bei Hegel," in *Logos* 20 (1931), 243–58, esp. 256ff. Cf. *Löw 1*, 225ff.

39. Practically, Kant also emphasizes the presentness of the goal to be reached in itself first in an infinite progress: "We must so take our maxims as if with all of the changes from good to better running into infinity our moral condition, according to attitude . . . were not subordinate to any change of time" ("Das Ende aller Dinge," A511). For Hegel's criticism of the Kantian merely moral, mental "making-present" of the good end goal, cf., e.g., *Glauben und Wissen*, *WG*,

vol. 1, 277ff; *Phä,* 421ff.; *WG,* vol. 8, 157ff. On his criticism of the category of infinite progress, see especially *Log,* vol. 1, 222ff., 140ff.; *WG,* vol. 8, 222ff., 245ff.; *WG,* vol. 18, 569ff.

40. E. Bloch, *Philosophische Grundfragen,* vol. 1: *Zur Ontologie des Noch-Nicht-Seins* (Frankfurt, 1961).

41. Hegel apparently repeats the doctrine of eternity as *nunc stans* with such considerations.

42. "The idea pays the tribute of existence and of the past not from itself but rather with the passions of the individuals" (*Vern,* 105). Cf. *Log,* vol. 2, 398: "That the goal posits itself in the immediate relation with the object and that it inserts another object between itself, and this can be seen as the cunning of reason. . . . But thus it makes an object a means and instead of letting it slave away externally, abandons it to wearing down and maintains itself behind it against the mechanical force (cf. *WG,* vol. 6, 127). The most perverse ideas exist about the cunning of reason, as if World Spirit and not rather everyone who is ready to give himself rational ends could make use it it.

43. Also in the *Philosophie der Geschichte zur Bildung der Menschheit,* in *Sämtliche Werke,* vol. 5, ed. Suphan (Berlin, 1877; reprint Hildesheim, 1967), 558. Like Hegel later, Herder associated the concept of history, which contains a lasting foundation through all change, with the concept of progress which is seen by him even more ambivalently than Hegel.

44. From F. Brunstäd's remark 37 to his edition of Hegel's *Lectures on the Philosophy of History* (Leipzig, ca. 1907). The whole remark reads, "In the theory of the historical possibility of the absoluteness of Christianity, the question about the end of history is also answered or rather the question about the possibility of the 'absoluteness' arises purely philosophically from the problem of the end (of the object) of history."

45. The philosophy of religion treats this sooner. In this context the concept of development in general becomes problematic. Hegel writes, "Piety is outside of history and without history, for history is rather the realm of self-enpresenting Spirit in its subjective freedom as the ethical kingdom of the state" (*WG,* vol. 11, 483), and such extrahistorical things must be seen in connection with what he says about the "inner middle-point" of religiosity and ethical life, which remains taken away from "the loud sound of world history and not only from the external and temporal changes but also from those which the absolute necessity of the concept of freedom bring with itself" (*Vern,* 109). The participation in the divine through religion, of its absolute present conscious self is an unmoved mover of history. Here process arises from rest and is again "remembered" [*er-innert*] as totality, i.e., internalized.

46. For the sake of brevity Professor Maurer's section 8, in which he discusses at length Löwith's Hegel interpretation, has been omitted.—*Trans.*

47. Cf. R. Spaemann, "Natürliche Existenz und politische Existenz bei Rousseau," in *Collegium Philosophicum* (J.-Ritter-Festschrift) (Basel, 1965), 373–88.

48. Showing the way for the most modern period, L. Feuerbach said, "When man practically comes to the position of the Christian, then theoretically

human essence must also come to the position of the divine. . . . For we must become religious—politics must become our religion—but it can only do this if we have a highest thing in our intuition which turns politics into religion for us" (*Notwendigkeit einer Reform der Philosophie* [1842], in *Werke*, vol. 2, ed. Bolin [Stuttgart, 1959], 219).

49. A marginal note of Hegel to the passage cited from *Vern*, 45 reads, "This—the understanding of our time."

H. S. Harris, The End of History in Hegel

1. Except the faith in reason that is universal and compulsory, the faith that keeps Philo from walking out of the window when Cleanthes challenges him to live up to his critical skepticism. The Hegelian philosophy does not "depend" on that either. But there would be no "absolute" knowing (other than that of mathematics and formal logic) if the certainty of experience were not there for the circle of logical cognition to start from. The circle itself abolishes the presupposed—or faithlike—character of the commonsense beginning—and history is what shows that this circular sublation is necessary.

2. Compare Schelling's letter (10) of 4 February 1795. *Hegel: The Letters*, trans. Clark Butler and Christian Seiler (Bloomington: Indiana University Press, 1984), 32. Further evidence can easily be found in *Toward the Sunlight*.

3. I mean those of us who are not willing to begin from the religious belief in providence, because we want our philosophical interpretation of the world to be "autonomous." "Autonomous" means (1) "presuppositionless" in Hegel's sense; and (2) acknowledging only the "necessities" that enforce themselves in every rational consciousness indifferently, so that one ceases to be rational when one seeks to deny them (as Philo would cease to be rational if he went out by the window instead of the door). The enforcement does not have to be as immediate or as categorical as Philo's death—let us suppose—when he hits the ground. The point is that we all know that "faith" or "trust" in Providence (the religious attitude) could never enforce itself in every mind, in the way that the acceptance of "necessity" or "fate" does. That is exactly why we say that it requires an "act." Faith in reason requires only the desire to be rational (i.e., to acknowledge only what everyone must acknowledge. One can still have voluntary commitments that go beyond that minimum ("acts of faith"); but one must not pretend that there is anything philosophical about them.

4. Kant, Immanuel, *On History*, ed. Lewis White Beck, trans. Lewis White Beck, Robert E. Anchor, and Emil L. Fackenheim (Indianapolis: Bobbs-Merrill, 1963), 11n. Subsequent references will be given in the text.

5. To speak thus, of a direct interaction between Kant and Hegel, is a radical simplification of the complex story of Hegel's concept of providence. Lessing, Herder, Hölderlin, and Schelling's system of transcendental idealism were all influential in the formation of Hegel's mature theory. But the whole development is "rational" in the Kantian sense; and it is "critical" in the sense that no transcendent self-conscious power is posited or appealed to. Hegel's

providence belongs to the World Spirit, i.e., to that community of active minds living and dead upon which the human development of every one of us is dependent, and of which our human achievements become a permanent part.

6. Hegel's calm acceptance of the exclusion of the female half of the human race from active politics could lead us to say that the rational was not completely actual even in his thought. On this view, Kojève's work came at the precise moment of the "end of history"; but the view itself is a mistake. No one is excluded from the community; and everyone is equal before the law and in conscience. The womenfolk are like the peasants. They are excluded from politics for reasons of "natural necessity." The judgment of actual necessity is strictly historical. Our historical situation (and our judgments) are different from those of the European Restoration. It is not the task of the philosopher to prescribe judgments to his world, but to comprehend those that are "objective" (universally valid) for his time. He is supposed to surrender his arbitrary freedom of judgment to the *Sache selbst.*

7. "The End of History," *The National Interest* (Summer 1989), 3–18 (see 17).

8. "Responses to Fukuyama," *The National Interest* (Summer 1989), 19–21 (see 20). For Kojève, reason can only be subjectively actual in a Kantian critical way, because his own existentialist ontology makes the conception of a spiritual substance impossible. But in his diminished way Kojève is a better Hegelian than Fukuyama, precisely because he has the Marxist belief in the "brotherhood of man."

9. In the version read at the conference I claimed "that Marx was mistaken in his belief that fraternity can be politically articulated and embodied." That was a serious mistake, which I recognized as soon as someone expressed doubt that it was true, during the discussion period. Fraternity must be articulated and embodied in social institutions that are self-consciously established. But those institutions cannot embody it completely (i.e., in a reliably self-maintaining way). They articulate a free consciousness which can as readily destroy itself as it can maintain itself. Thus the maintenance of rational fraternity depends upon the free consciousness of an ideal community that is not "political," but "absolute." The sense of fraternity is the "religion" upon which "the state" is founded. It cannot be "brought into the state in bushels and baskets." But if the actual life of the state does not enlighten it into the awareness of membership in the absolutely rational community, it can easily break the modern state down into fraternal communities that are (properly speaking) prepolitical. Antigone and Creon provide the logical paradigm of this. Thus only the whole process of self-consciousness (in which the religious "subjectivity" of Absolute Spirit is concordantly equal with the objective substantiality of political institutions) can articulate and embody "fraternity" adequately.

Robert Pippin, Hegel's Metaphysics and the Problem of Contradiction

1. It remains true that many of the most detailed studies of the *Logic* are by such nineteenth-century scholars as A. Trendelenburg, *Logische Untersuchungen*

(Berlin, 1840); E. V. Hartmann, *Die dialektische Methode* (Berlin, 1868); K. Werder, *Logik* (Berlin, 1841); H. Ulrici, *Über Prinzip und Methode der Hegelschen Philosophie* (Halle, 1841); and K. Fischer, *Spekulative Charakteristik und Kritik des Hegelschen Systems* (Erlangen, 1845). See Dieter Henrich's account of these interpretations in *Hegel im Kontext* (Frankfurt: Surhkamp, 1971), 73–94.

2. *Wissenschaft der Logic* (Hamburg: Meiner, 1971), hereafter cited as *WL*; trans. A. V. Miller, *Hegel's Science of Logic* (New York: Humanities Press, 1969), hereafter cited as *SL*.

3. Some of the most prominent references to the priority of the *Logic* occur in *Lectures on the Philosophy of World History, Introduction: Reason in History*, trans. H. B. Nisbet (Cambridge: Cambridge University Press, 1975), 28, 130, 132–39; *Hegel's Philosophy of Right*, trans. T. M. Knox (Oxford: Oxford University Press, 1967), 4, 14; *Phenomenology of Mind*, trans. J. B. Baillie (New York: Harper Torchbooks, 1967) 805–8; and the claims made for logic in *WL* itself, 23–47 (*SL*, 43–64).

4. *WL*, vol. 2, 58 (*SL*, 439).

5. *WL*, vol. 2, 61 (*SL*, 442).

6. *WL*, vol. 2, 61–62 (*SL*, 442).

7. Bertrand Russell, "Logic as the Essence of Philosophy," in *Readings on Logic* ed. I. M. Copi and J. A. Gould (New York: Macmillan, 1972), 78.

8. *WL*, vol. 2, 3 (*SL*, 389).

9. *WL*, vol. 2, 9 (*SL*, 393).

10. *WL*, vol. 2, 7 (*SL*, 394).

11. *WL*, vol. 1, 387–98 (*SL*, 375–85). For a discussion of this section, and its role in making necessary what he calls a "two-tiered" category, see Charles Taylor, *Hegel* (Cambridge: Cambridge University Press, 1975), 256–57. Taylor's remarks on book 2 are often clear and helpful, but he rushes very quickly through the section we are interested in here (see 260–62). A much more detailed analysis of the general issue at stake in the transition from the *Seinslogik* to the *Wesenslogik* can be found in Dieter Henrich, "Hegels Logik der Reflexion," *Hegel im Kontext*, 95–156. Henrich argues that much of what is at stake in this transition involves a variation in meaning (a *Bedeutungsverschiebung*) in the concept of "immediacy," shifting from a relationless, independent (*"nur mit sich"*) *Unmittelbarkeit* to a determinate, but *self*-mediated, or internally determined, essence.

12. It can now be seen that Shaftesbury's views on the moral sense support my analysis of (2) in section 2. The affections generated by the moral sense are repeatedly called natural, as I noted above, although their intentional objects are sometimes actions that work to the ill of the kind or species.

13. See his remarks on Spinoza: "Absolute indifference may seem to be the fundamental determination of Spinoza's substance" (*WL*, vol. 1, 396 [*SL*, 382]). "With Spinoza, the moments of difference—attributes, thought, and extension, then the modes too, the affections, and every other determination—is introduced quite empirically: it is intellect, itself a mode, which is the source of the differentiation." Or, "Substance is not determined as self-differentiating, not as subject" (*WL*, vol. 1, 396 [*SL*, 383]).

14. Of course, this characterization hardly does full justice to Hegel's view of skepticism. A fairer account would have to deal with the entire section on *Schein* (*WL*, vol. 2, 8–23 [*SL*, 394–408]).

15. *WL*, vol. 1, 397–98 (*SL*, 384).

16. Given the terms Henrich uses, as noted earlier (n. 11), his argument establishes the identity of the two concepts of "immediacy" used in books 1 and 2, 116–17. For a detailed analysis of this case, see Henrich's section on "Setzen und Voraussetzen," 117–25. Also quite helpful are the introductory remarks made by Peter Rohs, *Form und Grund, Hegel-Studien*, Beiheft 6 (Bonn: Bouvier, 1969), 11–76.

17. This point is stated well in Stanley Rosen, *G. W. F. Hegel: An Introduction to the Science of Wisdom* (New Haven: Yale University Press, 1974), 109.

18. *WL*, vol. 2, 22 (*SL*, 407).

19. *WL*, vol. 2, 23 (*SL*, 408).

20. A fuller discussion of the issues involved here can be found in Richard E. Aquila "Predication and Hegel's Metaphysics," *Kant-Studien* 64 (1973), 231–45.

21. *WL*, vol. 2, 62 (*SL*, 443).

22. See a more extended use of this same example in Herbert Marcuse, *Hegels Ontologie* (Frankfurt: Klostermann, 1968), 78.

23. For some brief indications of the relevance of this claim to modern theories of "*Bedeutungswandel*" (especially Kuhn and Feyerabend), see Henrich, "Hegels Logik der Reflexion," 138.

24. I do not intend, of course, by such brief formulations, to indicate a full resolution of the difficulty of interpreting the relation between Hegel's *Phenomenology* and his *Logic*. At its most serious, that issue involves the proper relation between ordinary, or prescientific, consciousness and reflective, or philosophic, consciousness and is well beyond the scope of this essay. I can only point here to recent, excellent discussions of the issues: H. F. Fulda, *Das Problem einer Einleitung in Hegels Wissenschaft der Logik* (Frankfurt: Klostermann, 1975); Otto Pöggeler, *Hegels Idee einer Phänomenologie des Geistes* (Freiburg: Karl Alber, 1973); and chap. 6 of Rosen, 123–50.

25. See Henrich, "Hegels Logik der Refelxion," 135, 151ff.

26. *WL*, vol. 2, 56 (*SL*, 438).

Robert Hanna, From an Ontological Point of View

1. G. W. F. Hegel, *Science of Logic*, trans. A. V. Miller (London: Allen and Unwin, 1969); *Wissenschaft der Logik*, vols. 1, 2, in *Theorie Werkausgabe*, vols. 5, 6 (Frankfurt: Suhrkamp, 1969). All subsequent references to the *Science of Logic* within the text of the essay are taken from these editions, signified by the abbreviation *SL* and two page numbers—the first referring to the English edition, the second referring to the German edition by respective volume—enclosed in parentheses.

2. G. W. F. Hegel, *Logic: Being Part One of the Encyclopedia of the Philosophical Sciences*, trans. W. Wallace (Oxford: Clarendon Press, 1975); *Enzyklopädie der philosophischen Wissenschaften im Grundrisse; Erster Teil: Die Wissenschaft der Logik*, in

Theorie Werkausgabe, vol. 8 (Frankfurt: Suhrkamp, 1970). All subsequent references to the *Encyclopedia Logic* within the text of the essay are taken from these editions, signified by the abbreviation *EL* and two page numbers—the first referring to the English edition, the second referring to the German edition—enclosed in parentheses.

3. I. Kant, *Logic,* trans. R. S. Hartman and W. Schwarz (Indianapolis: Bobbs-Merrill Co., 1974); *Logik,* in *Theorie Werkausgabe,* vol. 6 (Frankfurt: Suhrkamp, 1958). All subsequent references within the text of the essay to Kant's *Logic* are taken from these editions, signified by the abbreviation *KL* and two page numbers—the first referring to the English edition, the second referring to the German edition—enclosed in parentheses.

4. Common logic in this Kantian sense is of course by no means identical with modern "elementary logic"—which presupposes the great technical and theoretical advances introduced by Frege, Whitehead, Russell, Tarski, and others. An excellent example of modern elementary logic is Benson Mates's *Elementary Logic,* 2d ed. (New York: Oxford University Press, 1972).

5. I. Kant, *Critique of Pure Reason,* trans. N. K. Smith (London: Macmillan, 1964), 92–95, 97–99.

6. There is a strong analogy between Kant's transformation of the common logic of his time into a transcendental logic, and the modern development of the common logic of *its* time (i.e., elementary logic) into a logic with at least implicit ontological import. Wittgensteins's *Tractatus Logico-Philosophicus,* Russell's early philosophy of "logical atomism," Carnap's *The Logical Structure of the World,* and Kripke's *Naming and Necessity* all reveal a strong tendency to transfer modern logical concepts onto a metaphysical or at least an ontological footing. Hegel's answer to this, based on his criticism of Kant, would be that such a transference is not sufficiently critical of the ontological biases and presuppositions of modern symbolic logic. I noted in n. 4 that Kant's common logic and our elementary logic differed greatly in respect of technical and theoretical advances. But advances in technique or logical theory are not necessarily advances in ontological sophistication. Thus it seems that a suitably updated version of Hegel's critique of the common logic of his day could be turned mutatis mutandis upon the common logic of our time, and thereby have a great impact upon recent uses of logical concepts for ontological purposes.

7. Heidegger's ontological account of logic may be found mainly in *Being and Time,* trans. J. Macquarrie and E. Robinson (New York: Harper and Row, 1962), 195–203; *Basic Problems of Phenomenology,* trans. A. Hofstadter (Bloomington: Indiana University Press, 1983), 177–224; *Logik: die Frage nach der Wahrheit* (Frankfurt: Klostermann, 1976); and *Metaphysical Foundations of Logic,* trans. M. Heim (Bloomington: Indiana University Press, 1984).

8. J. L. Austin, "Truth," in *Philosophical Papers* (Oxford: Clarendon Press, 1970), 119–21.

9. Hegel's awareness that every judgment in logic belongs to an actual speech situation comports well with Husserl's analysis of logical acts in *Logical Investigations,* trans. J. N. Findlay (London: Routledge and Kegan Paul, 1970).

This comparison brings forward the conspicuous absence of the human voice in modern symbolic logic. Of course we are all aware of the theoretical benefits of ridding logic of "psychologism." But what are the *ontological* consequences of this development? Does this render modern elementary logic *less* or *more* ontologically naive than Kant's common logic?

10. I. Kant, "The Mistaken Subtility of the Four Syllogistic Figures," in *Kant's Introduction to Logic*, trans. T. K. Abbott (New York: Philosophical Library, 1963), 79.

11. John Smith, "The Logic of Hegel Revisited: A Review of Errol E. Harris, *An Interpretation of the Logic of Hegel*," *British Journal for the Philosophy of Science* 36, no. 4 (Dec. 1985): 461–65.

12. This can be seen in the traditional notion of a "categorical" judgment, that is, an ordinary subject-predicate judgment. The Greek root of "category," "Kategorein," seems to have had the basic meaning of making a definite assertion or affirmative predication: most concretely, of making a legal claim against someone in public. See H. G. Lidell and R. Scott, *A Greek-English Lexicon* (Oxford: Clarendon Press, 1966), 927.

13. Kant, *Critique of Pure Reason*, 308–22.

14. B. Russell, "On Denoting," in *Essays in Analysis* (New York: George Braziller, 1973), 110.

15. See William Kneale and Martha Kneale, *The Development of Logic* (Oxford: Clarendon Press, 1962), 742.

16. J. N. Findlay, *Hegel: A Re-examination* (London: Allen and Unwin, 1958), 189–90.

17. It is obvious that Hegel's critique of the analyticity of identity has important parallels with Quine's famous attack on the analytic/synthetic distinction in "Two Dogmas of Empiricism," in *From a Logical Point of View* (Cambridge: Harvard University Press, 1964), 20–46. But Hegel's critique goes far deeper than Quine's in that it demonstrates the syntheticity of even *logical* analyticity. This raises ontological problems about logic *itself*, a line of questioning that Quine never pursues.

18. See G. W. F. Hegel, *Phenomenology of Spirit*, trans. A. V. Miller (Oxford: Oxford University Press, 1979), 36, 51.

19. For "identity" in this quotation read "sameness" in order to correspond to the terminology of this essay; unfortunately, Hegel uses the same term "identity" to refer to abstract common-logical identity and concrete ontological sameness.

20. G. R. G. Mure, *A Study of Hegel's Logic* (Oxford: Clarendon Press, 1990), 302.

21. Hegel, *Phenomenology of Spirit*, 99.

22. J. N. Findlay, "The Contemporary Relevance of Hegel," in *Language, Mind and Value* (London: Allen and Unwin, 1963), 221–22.

23. W. V. O. Quine, "The Ways of Paradox," in *The Ways of Paradox and Other Essays* (Cambridge: Harvard University Press, 1976), 1–18.

24. See B. Bosanquet, *Implication and Linear Inference* (New York: Macmillan, 1920).

25. L. Wittgenstein, *Tractatus Logico-Philosophicus*, trans. D. F. Pears and B. F. McGuinness (London: Routledge and Kegan Paul, 1961), 151. For an account of what Hegelian logic *can* say about just those things which "logical atomism" must pass over in silence, see E. Harris, *An Interpretation of the Logic of Hegel* (Lanham: University Press of America, 1983), esp. 8, 39, 62, 126, 311–19.

26. I would like to thank John E. Smith for his helpful comments on an earlier version of this essay.

Franz Grégoire, A Semi-Legend: The "Divinity" of the State in Hegel

1. *Philosophie des Rechts*, §272 (Zusatz), Glockner, 370. [Grégoire cites from Hermann Glockner's edition of the *Philosophy of Right*: *Grundlinien der Philosophie des Rechts oder Naturrecht und Staatswissenschaft im Grundrisse*, vol. 7 of *Sämtliche Werke. Jubiläumsausgabe in 20 Bänden*. Stuttgart: Friedrich Frommann Verlag, 1927–1940, which he hereafter abbreviates as *Gl.—Trans.*]

2. Ibid., §258, *Gl*, 330–31.

3. Here we see that Grégoire himself is not wholly disabused of all the Hegel myths.—*Trans.*

4. I hope to publish in a short time a volume of *Études hégéliennes* where the object of the present article will be treated in more detail. This is why we are content here, concerning references to Hegel's works, with a few examples for each case.

5. *Philosophie der Religion*, IV, *Absolute Religion*, Lasson, 102. [Grégoire cites from Georg Lasson's edition of Hegel's works: *Sämtliche Werke*, Leipzig: Meiner, 1928–1938, 21 volumes, which he abbreviates as *Las.—Trans.*]

6. Ibid., I, *Begriff*, *Las*, 43.

7. *Encyclopädie*, I, §213, *Gl*, 8, 425.

8. *Encyclopedia*, III, §381 (Zusatz), *Gl*, 10, 21.

9. *Philosophie der Weltgeschichte*, I, *Las*, 84–85.

10. *Recht*, §163, *Gl*, 7, 242.

11. Ibid., §187, *Gl*, 7, 269.

12. *Weltg*, I, *Las*, 107–8.

13. *Gesch. Philo.*, II, *Gl*, 18, 443.

In sum, the expression "divine" functions in Hegel as a flexible analogue to the word "*theion*" in the ancient Greek philosophers. The Greek usage perhaps played a role in putting Hegel at ease with this language.

Elsewhere we see Saint Thomas Aquinas, under precisely this Greek influence, write that the collective good is more divine ("*divinius*") than the individual good, "*eo quod magis pertinet ad Dei similitudinem*" (*Comment. in I Ethic.*, lect. 2).

14. Here we see Grégoire fall victim to another Hegel myth. Although to his credit, it is not clear to what degree he takes this as indicative of Hegel's conception of the dialectic.—*Trans.*

15. Cf. *Aesthetik*, I, *Gl*, 12, 193–94.

16. *Weltg*, I, *Las*, 88–89.

17. *Relig*, I, *Begriff*, *Las*, 1–4.

18. *Recht,* §270, *Gl,* 7, 353–56; Vorrede, 29–30.

19. *Relig,* I, *Begriff, Las,* 176–80.

20. *Recht,* §270, *Gl,* 7, 349–50.

21. *Weltg,* III, *Las,* 662.

22. The triad: family, civil society, state is compared to an organism expressly and in detail (*Recht* §263, Zusatz, *Gl,* 7, 347–48). We are going to examine whether Hegel draws the logical consequences of this doctrine, which is related to that of the ordering of civil society to the good of the individuals.

23. *Recht, Gl,* 7, 90–91; 182–83; *Gesch. Philo.,* I, *Gl,* 17, 79–80.

24. Concerning the right of the individual to pursue his private satisfactions, Hegel curiously unites Christianity and Romanticism in the same praise (*Recht,* §124, *Gl,* 7, 182).

25. Ibid., §209, 286.

26. Ibid., §270, 354, n. 1.

27. *Recht,* §124, *Gl,* 7, 182–83.

28. *Weltg,* I, *Las* 91; *Gesch. Philos.,* II, *Gl,* 18, 394–400.

29. *Recht,* §33, *Gl,* 7, 84–87.

30. Ibid., §324, *Gl,* 7, 433–36.

31. Ibid., §3, *Gl,* 7, 43; §212, *Gl,* 7, 290–91; §258 (Zusatz), *Gl,* 7, 336 *et alibi.*

Gustav E. Mueller, The Hegel Legend of "Thesis-Antithesis-Synthesis"

1. See the excellent study by Walter A. Kaufmann, "The Hegel Myth and Its Method," *Philosophical Review* 60 (1951), 459–86.

2. W. T. Stace, *The Philosophy of Hegel* (Dover, 1955).

3. Hermann Glockner, *Hegel Lexikon,* 4 vols. (Stuttgart, 1935).

4. The new critical edition, being published by F. Meiner in Hamburg, will contain 32 volumes.

5. Hegel, *Werke,* vol. 2 (Stuttgart, 1928), preface, 48–49.

6. Hegel, *Werke,* vol. 19, *Vorlesungen über die Geschichte der Philosophie,* 610.

7. Theodor Haering, *Hegel, Sein Wollen und Sein Werk,* 2 vols. (Teubner, 1929, 1938).

8. Iwan Iljin, *Hegel's Philosophie als kontemplative Gotteslehre* (Bern, 1946).

9. Herman Glockner, *Hegel,* 2 vols. (Stuttgart, 1929); Theodor Steinbüchel, *Das Gundproblem der Hegelschen Philosophie* (Bonn, 1933); Theodor Litt, *Hegel: Eine Kritische Erneuerung* (Heidelberg, 1953); Emerich Coreth, *Das dialektische Sein in Hegels Logik* (Wien, 1952).

10. Gustav Mueller, *Hegel über Offenbarung, Kirche und Philosophie* (Munich, 1939); *Hegel über Sittlichkeit und Geschichte* (Reinhardt, 1940).

11. *G. W. F. Hegel: Early Theological Writings* (Chicago, 1948), 32.

12. J. Flugge, *Die sittlichen Grundlagen des Denkens in Hegels Logik* (Hamburg, 1953), 17.

13. N. Hartmann, *Kleinere Schriften,* vol. 2 (Berlin, 1957), 225. Hartmann concluded: "this twaddle should gradually subside" (227).

14. See Karl Marx, *Das Elend der Philosophie* (Berlin: Dietz Verlag, 1957), summary of chap. 2, par. 1.

15. Hegel, *Werke*, vol. 12, 59.

16. R. Tsanoff, *The Great Thinkers* (New York, 1953), 487.

17. Benedetto Croce, *What Is Dead and What Is Alive in Hegel* (English trans., London, 1912).

Jon Stewart, Hegel and the Myth of Reason

1. I would like to express my sincere gratitude to Professors Henry E. Allison and S. Nicholas Jolley for their invaluable comments on an earlier draft of this essay.

2. For a list of the Hegel myths see the following: Wilhelm Seeberger, "Vorurteile gegen Hegel," in his *Hegel oder die Entwicklung des Geistes zur Freiheit* (Stuttgart: Ernst Klett, 1961), 42ff.; John Findlay, *The Philosophy of Hegel: An Introduction and Re-Examination* (New York: Collier, 1962), 15ff.

3. Cf. M. W. Jackson, "Hegel, the Real and the Rational," *International Studies in Philosophy* 19 (1987), 12.

4. Cf. Karl R. Popper, "What is Dialectic?" *Mind* 49 (1940), 413ff. Cf. also W. T. Stace, *The Philosophy of Hegel* (New York: Dover, 1955), 94, 183; Bertrand Russell, *History of Western Philosophy and Its Connection with Political and Social Circumstances from the Earliest Times to the Present Day* (London: Allen and Unwin, 1961), 703; Stanley Rosen, *G. W. F. Hegel: An Introduction to the Science of Wisdom* (New Haven: Yale University Press, 1974), 64–68; and Findlay, *The Philosophy of Hegel*, 62ff., 73ff.

5. For an example of this belief, see J. M. E. MacTaggert, *A Commentary on Hegel's Logic* (Cambridge: Cambridge University Press, 1910), §4: "The whole course of the dialectic forms one example of the dialectic rhythm, with Being as Thesis, essence as Antithesis and Notion as Synthesis. Each of these has again the same moments of Thesis, Antithesis and Synthesis." For a debunking of this myth, see Gustav E. Mueller, "The Hegel Legend of 'Thesis-Antithesis-Synthesis,' " *Journal of the History of Ideas* 19 (1958); Philipp Merlan, "Ist die 'These-Antithese-Synthese'-Formel unhegelisch?" *Archiv für die Geschichte der Philosophie* 53 (1971), 35–40; and Walter Kaufmann, *Hegel: A Reinterpretation* (Garden City: Anchor Books, 1966), 154ff., 198ff.

6. Cf. Alexandre Kojève, *Introduction à la lecture de Hégel: Leçons sur la Phénoménologie de l'esprit professées de 1933 à 1939 à l'École des Hautes Études*, ed. Raymond Queneau (Paris: Gallimard, 1947, 1971). In English as *Introduction to the Reading of Hegel*, trans. James H. Nichols, Jr. (New York: Basic Books, 1969). Alexandre Koyré, "Hégel à Iéna (à propos de publications récentes)," *Revue philosophique de la France* 59 (1934), 274–83; reprinted in *Revue d'histoire et de philosophie religieuse* 15 (1935), 420–58; L. Esposito, "Hegel, Absolute Knowledge, and the End of History," *Clio* 12 (1983), 355–65; Reinhard Klemens Maurer, *Hegel und das Ende der Geschichte: Interpretationen zur "Phänomenologie des Geistes"* (Stuttgart: Kohlhammer, 1965); Philip T. Grier, "The End of History and the

Return of History," *The Owl of Minerva* 21 (1990), 131–44; Wilhelm Seeberger, *Hegel oder die Entwicklung des Geistes zur Freiheit*, 63.

7. Cf. Bertrand Beaumont, "Hegel and the Seven Planets," *Mind* 63 (1954), 246–48; Karl Popper, *The Open Society and Its Enemies*, vol. 2 (London: Routledge and Kegan Paul, 1952), 27; Otto Neurath, "Wege der wissenschaftlichen Weltauf-fassung," *Erkenntnis* 1 (1930–31), 107; Kaufmann, *Hegel: A Reinterpretation*, 52–53.

8. Rudolf Haym, *Hegel und seine Zeit* (Berlin: Gaertner, 1857), 357ff; Bertrand Russell, *History of Western Philosophy*, 705, 709; T. M. Knox, "Hegel and Prussianism," *Philosophy* 15 (1940), 51–63, 313–14; Hans-Christian Lucas and U. Rameil, "Furcht vor der Zensur?" *Hegel-Studien* 15 (1980), 63–93; Hans-Christian Lucas, "Philosophie und Wirklichkeit: Einige Bemerkungen wider die Legende von Hegel als preußischem Staatsphilosophen," *Zeitschrift für Didaktik der Philosophie* 9 (1987), 154–61; E. F. Carritt, "Hegel and Prussianism," *Philosophy* 15 (1940), 190–96, 315–17; Henning Ottmann, "Hegel und die Politik: Zur Kritik der politischen Hegellegenden," *Zeitschrift für Politik* 26 (1979), 235–53; Sidney Hook, "Hegel Rehabilitated" and "Hegel and His Apologist," in *Hegel's Political Philosophy*, ed. Walter Kaufmann (New York: Atherton Press, 1970), 55ff., 87ff.; Shlomo Avineri, *Hegel and the Modern State* (Cambridge: Cambridge University Press, 1972).

9. The classic example of this is of course Karl Popper's account in *The Open Society and Its Enemies*. See also Gilbert Ryle, "Critical Notice," *Mind* 55 (1947), 170, 172; Jacques Maritain, *La philosophie morale* (Paris: Gallimard, 1960), 159; Bertrand Russell, *Philosophy and Politics* (London: Cambridge University Press, 1947); Bertrand Russell, *Unpopular Essays* (London: Allen and Unwin, 1950), 22; Hubert Kiesewetter, *Von Hegel zu Hitler: Eine Analyse der Hegelschen Machtstaatsideologie und der politischen Wirkungsgeschichte des Rechts-Hegelianismus* (Hamburg: Hoffmann and Campe, 1974). For a debunking of this myth see Walter A. Kaufmann, "The Hegel Myth and its Method," *Philosophical Review* 60 (1951), 246–48; and Shlomo Avineri, "Hegel and Nationalism," in *Hegel's Political Philosophy*, 109–36.

10. Cf. Karl R. Popper, "What is Dialectic?" *Mind* 49 (1940), 414ff.

11. William Barrett, *Irrational Man: A Study in Existential Philosophy* (New York: Doubleday, 1958), 155.

12. Robert Heiss, *Hegel, Kierkegaard, Marx*, trans. E. B. Garside (New York: Dell, 1963), 190–91. Originally: *Die großen Dialektiker des 19. Jahrhunderts: Hegel, Kierkegaard, Marx* (Berlin: Kiepenheuer und Witsch, 1963), 202. Also see Marcuse's discussion, *Reason and Revolution: Hegel and the Rise of Social Theory* (New York: Humanities Press, 1941), 4ff.

13. William Earle, "Hegel and Some Contemporary Philosophies," *Philosophy and Phenomenological Research* 20 (1959–60), 364.

14. Richard Kroner, *Von Kant bis Hegel*, vol. 2 (Tübingen: Mohr, 1924), 268 (my translation).

15. Russell, *History of Western Philosophy*, 706, 712: "The time-process, according to Hegel, is from the less to the more perfect, both in an ethical and in a logical sense."

16. Passages which have led to this conclusion include the following: Hegel, *Hegel's Philosophy of Right*, trans. T. M. Knox (Oxford: Oxford University Press, 1967) (hereafter *PR*), 12: "To recognize reason as the rose in the cross of the present and thereby to enjoy the present, this is the rational insight which reconciles us to the actual." Cf. also Hegel, *Hegel's Logic*, trans. William Wallace (Oxford: Oxford University Press, 1975) (hereafter *Lesser Logic*) §6: "Similarly it may be held the highest and final aim of philosophic science to bring about, through the ascertainment of this harmony, a reconcilation of the self-conscious reason with the reason which *is* in the world."

17. William Earle, "Hegel and Some Contemporary Philosophies," *Philosophy and Phenomenological Research* 20 (1959–60), 352–64; Pantschu Russew, "Hegel im Schatten des Irrationalismus," *Hegel-Jahrbuch* (1971), 300–305; Georg Lukács, *Die Zerstörung der Vernunft: Irrationalismus zwischen den Revolutionen*, vol. 1 (Darmstadt: Hermann Luchterhand, 1962, 1973), esp. chap. 2: "Die Begründung des Irrationalismus in der Periode zwischen zwei Revolutionen (1789–1848)," 84ff.

18. Cf. Robert Solomon, *In the Spirit of Hegel* (New York: Oxford University Press, 1987), 582.

19. Kaufmann attributes this to the fact that Kierkegaard, the great propagator of a number of Hegel legends, was a student of the embittered Schelling, who was jealous of the success of Hegel's philosophy and jaded at the decline of his own influence in the German academy. Kaufmann writes, "Through Kierkegaard, legions of twentieth-century readers who barely know Schelling's name have come to take for granted as historically accurate his spiteful caricature of Hegel. Many people assume that Hegel is the antipodes of existentialism" (Kaufmann, *Hegel: A Reinterpretation*, 290).

20. Hegel, *PR*, preface, 10. Cf. also *Lesser Logic*, §6, 9.

21. Haym, *Hegel und seine Zeit*, 357ff. Also cf. Popper, "What is Dialectic?" 413ff.

22. Cf. Russell, *History of Western Philosophy*, 702: "Nevertheless, the identification of the real and the rational leads unavoidably to some of the complacency inseparable from the belief that 'whatever is, is right.' "

23. Cf. Popper's analysis of this passage in *The Open Society and Its Enemies*, 113–20. Also see Russell, *History of Western Philosophy*, 711: "Such is Hegel's doctrine of the State—a doctrine which, if accepted, justifies every internal tyranny and every external aggression that can possibly be imagined."

24. Cf. Walter Kaufmann, *Nietzsche: Philosopher, Psychologist, Antichrist* (Princeton: Princeton University Press, 1950), 108: "One can oppose the shallow optimism of so many Western thinkers and yet refuse to negate life. Schopenhauer's negativistic pessimism is rejected [i.e., by Nietzsche] together with the *superficial optimism of the popular Hegelians*" (my italics).

25. Emil L. Fackenheim, "On the Actuality of the Rational and the Rationality of the Actual," *Review of Metaphysics* 23 (1969), 698.

26. Cf. Aveneri, *Hegel's Theory of the Modern State*, 115–31; M. W. Jackson, "Hegel, the Real and the Rational," *International Studies in Philosophy* 19 (1987),

11–19; Adriaan Peperzak, *Philosophy and Politics: A Commentary on the Preface to Hegel's "Philosophy of Right"* (Dordrecht: Nijhoff, 1987), 92–103; Allan W. Wood, *Hegel's Ethical Thought* (Cambridge: Cambridge University Press, 1990), 10ff.

27. Hegel, *Lesser Logic*, §6, 10.

28. Hegel, *PR*, Zusatz to §3, 17.

29. Hegel, *PR*, Zusatz to §3, 17.

30. Cf. Hegel, *PR*, 10: "For since rationality (which is synonymous with the idea) enters upon external existence simultaneously with its actualization, it emerges with an infinite wealth of forms, shapes, and appearances."

31. Cf. Hegel, *PR*, 12: "for form in its most concrete signification is reason as speculative knowing, and content is reason as the substantial essence of actuality, whether ethical or natural. The known identity of these two is the philosophical Idea."

32. Cf. Hegel, *PR*, 10: "since philosophy is the exploration of the rational, it is for that very reason the apprehension of the present and the actual, not the erection of a beyond, supposed to exist, God knows where, or rather which exists, and we can perfectly well say where, namely in the error of a one-sided, empty, ratiocination."

33. Hegel, *PR*, 4.

34. A certain kind of mysticism or irrationalism has occasionally been attributed to Hegel, which would have to be accounted for before we could begin to answer these questions fully. Cf. Kroner, *Von Kant bis Hegel*, vol. 2, 270ff.; Russew, "Hegel im Schatten des Irrationalismus," 300–5; Lukács, *Die Zerstörung der Vernunft*, vol. 1, 84ff.

35. Note that all of the passages cited from the *Phenomenology* are from the Miller translation: *Hegel's Phenomenology of Spirit*, trans. A. V. Miller (Oxford: Oxford University Press, 1977) (hereafter *PhS*). Also n.b. the references are not to page numbers but to Miller's paragraph numbers.

36. This influence has been strongly mediated by Alexandre Kojève's famous lectures at the École practique des Hautes Études (1933–39). Published as *Introduction à la lecture de Hégel*.

37. Cf. Arthur Lessing, "Hegel and Existentialism: On Unhappiness," *The Personalist* 49 (1968), 61–77.

38. On Hegel's account, the Enlightenment caricatures religion for its literal belief that God is in objects, but this is merely a straw-man criticism, since for religion God is not literally in the religious objects but rather these objects have merely symbolic value. The Enlightenment thus unjustly transfers its own emphasis on sense-certainty and the empirical to religion (cf. *PhS*, §§552–53). Moreover the Enlightenment questions the religious proselyte's grounds for belief, seeing that belief as based on dubious philological evidence of chance historical events. But in fact the true believer, for Hegel as for Kierkegaard, does not base his belief on philological or historical evidence, but rather the origin of belief is in the inwardness of the individual consciousness (cf. *PhS*, §554). Cf. Søren Kierkegaard, *Concluding Unscientific Postscript*. trans. Swenson and Lowrie (Princeton: Princeton University Press, 1941), 29ff.

39. Jean Hyppolite, "La signification de la Révolution française dans la *Phénoménologie* de Hegel," in his *Études sur Marx et Hegel* (Paris: Librairie Marcel Riviére et Cie, 1955), 45–81; Danko Grlic, "Revolution und Terror (Zum Kapitel 'Die absolute Freiheit und der Schrecken' aus Hegels *Phänomenologie des Geistes*)," *Praxis* 8 (1971), 49–61; K.-H. Nusser, "Die französische Revolution und Hegels *Phänomenologie des Geistes*," *Philosophisches Jahrbuch der Görres-Gesellschaft* 77 (1970), 276–96; Wilfred Ver Eecke, "Hegel's Dialectic Analysis of the French Revolution," *Hegel-Jahrbuch* (1975), 561–67; Joachim Ritter, *Hegel und die Französische Revolution* (Frankfurt: Suhrkamp, 1965); Jürgen Habermas, "Hegels Kritik der Französische Revolution," in *Theorie und Praxis* (Frankfurt: Suhrkamp, 1971), 126–47—in English as *Theory and Practice*, trans. J. Viertel (Boston: Beacon Press, 1973).

40. Hegel, *Lesser Logic*, §19, Zusatz.

41. Hegel, *PhS*, §545.

42. Hegel, *PhS*, §545.

43. Cf. Kierkegaard's criticism of rational theology in *Concluding Unscientific Postscript*, 39ff.

44. Hegel, *PhS*, §545.

45. Nietzsche sees science as replacing the beliefs of religion, e.g., in God, in miracles, and so on, with its own set of beliefs, e.g., in reason, in causality, and so on. Cf. *The Gay Science* trans. Walter Kaufmann (New York: Vintage, 1974), §§344, 372.

46. Fyodor Dostoevsky, *Notes from Underground and The Grand Inquisitor*, trans. Ralph E. Matlaw (New York: Meridian Books, 1960), 182.

47. The "myth of reason" in Hegel continues to persist despite the fact that this connection has been occasionally noted although not by means of the illness metaphor. Cf. Maurice Merleau-Ponty, "Hegel's Existentialism," in *Sense and Nonsense*, trans. H. L. Dreyfus and P. A. Dreyfus (Evanston: Northwestern University Press, 1964), 63: "it was he [i.e., Hegel] who started the attempt to explore the irrational and integrate it into an expanded reason which remains the task of our century." Cf. Kroner, *Von Kant bis Hegel*, vol. 2, 270: "*Der Rationalismus des Hegelschen Denkens enthält also einen Irrationalismus an ihm selbst.*"

48. Dostoevsky, *Notes from Underground*, 6.

49. For an interesting account of these similarities see Geoffrey Clive, "The Sickness unto Death in the Underworld: A Study of Nihilism," *Harvard Theological Review* 51 (1958), 135–67.

50. Søren Kierkegaard, *The Sickness unto Death: A Christian Psychological Exposition for Upbuilding and Awakening*, ed. and trans. Howard V. Hong and Edna H. Hong (Princeton: Princeton University Press, 1980), 6.

51. Cf. Clive, "The Sickness unto Death," 142: "Ultimately every form of despair . . . is tied to the sickness, although Kierkegaard focuses on those manifestations which presuppose a considerable degree of self-reflection and awareness. Hence most of the aspects under which he examines despair are particularly germane to the feverishly conscious Underground Man."

52. Kierkegaard, *The Sickness unto Death*, 29.

53. Ibid., 42.

54. For a rather different account of this metaphor in Nietzsche, see Kaufmann, *Nietzsche*, 107ff.

55. Friedrich Nietzsche, *The Birth of Tragedy and The Case of Wagner*, trans. Walter Kaufmann (New York: Vintage, 1967), 38.

56. Ibid., 45.

57. Ibid., 18 (my italics).

58. Ibid., 21.

59. Ibid., 96–97 (my italics).

60. Despite drawing a number of interesting parallels between Hegel and Nietzsche's *Birth of Tragedy*, Blasche, in a manner characteristic of many Hegel-Nietzsche studies, fails to note this similiarity. Siegfried Blasche, "Hegelianismus im Umfeld von Nietzsches *Geburt der Tragödie*," *Nietzsche-Studien* 15 (1986), 59–71.

61. Albert Camus, *The Myth of Sisyphus and Other Essays*, trans. Justin O'Brien (New York: Random House, 1975), 2.

62. Ibid., 13.

63. Albert Camus, *The Plague*, trans. Stuart Gilbert (New York: Random House, 1974), 245.

64. Ibid.

65. Ibid., 38.

66. Cf. Nietzsche, *Birth of Tragedy*, §7.

67. Jean-Paul Sartre, *Nausea*, trans. Lloyd Alexander (New York: New Directions, 1964), 4 (my italics).

68. Ibid., 96.

69. Ibid., 99 (ellipses from the original text).

70. Cf. Seeberger, *Hegel oder die Entwicklung des Geistes zur Freiheit*, 43: "Solange es in der beiläufig betriebenen Hegel-Kritik an der Tagesordnung bleibt, auf Grund von Urteilen aus zweiter und dritter Hand über Hegel Gericht zu halten, statt sich erst einmal auf Grund eines soliden Quellenstudiums ein eigenständgies Urteil zu erarbeiten, wird eine solche Kritik stets von mehr als nur zweifelhaftem Werte sein. Auch bei der Philosophie Hegels kann die via regia nur über das eigene Studium und über den eigenen Nachvollzug führen; solange man sich, wie es bei Hegel Usus geworden ist, damit begnügt, öffentlich Urteile über ihn zu fällen, ohne ihn auch nur gelesen und so die minimalsten Voraussetzungen für ein wirkliches Verständnis geschaffen zu haben, wird die Urteilsgrundlage stets nur eine vage Vorstellung von der Sache sein und das so häufig mit Aplomb verkündete Urteil sich in Wirklichkeit als ein bloßes Vorurteil erweisen."

Bibliography

1. Propagators of the Hegel Myths

Abusch, Alexander. "Die Authorität der Vernunft." *Hegel-Jahruch* (1972), 68–80. Also in *Einheit* 27 (1972), 1297–1304.

Barker, Ernest. *Nietzsche and Treitschke: The Worship of Power in Modern Germany.* Oxford: Oxford University Press, 1914.

———. *Principles of Social and Political Thought.* Oxford: Oxford University Press, 1915.

Barrett, William. *Irrational Man: A Study in Existential Philosophy.* New York: Doubleday, 1958.

Beyer, Wilhelm Raimond. "Die List der Vernunft." *Deutsche Zeitschrift für Philosophie* 18 (1970), 777–90.

Bowle, John. *Politics and Opinion in the 19th Century.* London: Cape, 1954.

Brann, Henry. "Hegel, Nietzsche and the Nazi Lesson." *Humanist* 12 (1952), 179–82.

Bullock, Alan. *Hitler.* New York: Harper and Row, 1962.

Carritt, E. F. "Hegel and Prussianism." *Philosophy* 15 (1940), 190–96, 315–17.

———. "Hegel's Sittlichkeit." *Proceedings of the Aristotelian Society* 36 (1935–36), 223–35.

———. *Morals and Politics.* Oxford: Oxford University Press, 1935.

Coker, R. "Pluralistic Theories and the Attack upon State Sovereignty." In *Principles of Social and Political Theory.* Edited by Charles Edward Merriam. Oxford: Oxford University Press, 1932. 80–119.

Cole, George Douglas Howard. *Some Relations between Political and Economic Theory.* London: Macmillan, 1934.

d'Entréves, Alexander P. *The Notion of the State.* Oxford: Oxford University Press, 1967.

Drydyk, J. J. "Who Is Fooled by the Cunning of Reason?" *History and Theory* 24 (1985), 147–69.

Ebenstein, William. *Great Political Thinkers.* New York: Rinehart, 1956.

Gordon, Scott. *Welfare, Justice and Freedom.* New York: Columbia University Press, 1980.

Hacker, Andrew. *Political Theory: Philosophy, Ideology, Science.* New York: Macmillan, 1961.

Haym, Rudolf. *Hegel und seine Zeit.* Berlin: Gaertner, 1857; reprint, Hildesheim: Georg Olms, 1962.

Heiden, Konrad. *Der Führer: Hitler's Rise to Power.* New York: Lexington Press, 1944.

Heller, Hermann. *Hegel und der nationale Machtstaatsgedanke in Deutschland.* Leipzig: B. G. Teubner, 1921.

Hook, Sidney. "Hegel Rehabilitated." *Encounter* 24 (1965), 53–58. Also in *Hegel's Political Philosophy.* Edited by Walter Kaufmann. New York: Atherton Press, 1970. 55–70.

———. "Hegel and His Apologists." *Encounter* 26 (1966), 84–91. Also in *Hegel's Political Philosophy.* Edited by Walter Kaufmann. New York: Atherton Press, 1970. 87–105.

———. *From Hegel to Marx.* New York: Reynal and Hitchcock, 1936.

Huxley, Aldous. *Ends and Means: An Enquiry into the Nature of Ideals and into the Methods Employed for Their Realization.* London: Chatto and Windus, 1937.

Joad, Cyril Edwin Mitchinson. *Guide to the Philosophy of Morals and Politics.* London: Gollancz, 1938.

Joll, James. "Prussia and the German Problem 1830–1866." In *New Cambridge Modern History.* Vol. 10. *The Zenith of European Power.* Edited by John Bury. Cambridge: Cambridge University Press, 1960. 493–522.

Kelly, Michael. *Hegel's Charlatanism Exposed.* London: Allen, 1911.

Kiesewetter, Hubert. *Von Hegel zu Hitler: Eine Analyse der Hegelschen Machtstaatsideologie und der politischen Wirkungsgeschichte des Rechts-Hegelianismus.* Hamburg: Hoffmann und Campe, 1974.

Kohn, Hans. *Prelude to Nation-State.* Princeton: Princeton University Press, 1967.

———. "Political Theory and the History of Ideas." *Journal of the History of Ideas* 25 (1964), 303–7.

Kojève, Alexandre. *Introduction à la lecture de Hegel: Leçons sur la Phénoménologie de l'esprit professées de 1933 à 1939 à l'École des Hautes Études.* Collected and edited by Raymond Queneau. Paris: Gallimard, 1947, 1971. In English as *Introduction to the Reading of Hegel.* Edited by Alan Bloom, translated by James H. Nichols, Jr. New York: Basic Books, 1969.

Kolakowski, Leszek. *Main Currents of Marxism.* Vol. 1. London: Oxford University Press, 1981.

Köstlin, Karl Reinhold von. *Hegel in philosophischer, politischer und nationaler Beziehung.* Tübingen: H. Laupp, 1870.

Koyré, Alexandre. "Hegel à Iéna (à propos de publications récentes)." *Revue philosophique de France* 59 (1934), 274–83. Also in *Revue d'histoire et de philosophie religieuse* 15 (1935), 420–58.

Lange, Maximilian. "Hegels philosophische Rechtfertigung des Krieges." *Vergangenheit und Gegenwart* 30 (1940), 264–72.

MacTaggert, J. M. E. *A Commentary on Hegel's Logic.* Cambridge: Cambridge University Press, 1911.

Maritain, Jacques. *La Philosophie Morale.* Paris: Gallimard, 1960.

McGovern, William Montgomery. *From Luther to Hitler: The History of Fascist-Nazi Political Philosophy.* Boston: Houghton Mifflin Co., 1941.

Mowrer, Edgar Ansel. *Germany Puts the Clock Back.* London: Penguin, 1938.

Neurath, Otto. "Wege der wissenschaftlichen Weltauffassung." *Erkenntnis* 1 (1930–31), 106–25.

Oiserman, T. I. "Die Hegelsche Philosophie als Lehre über die Macht der Vernunft." *Hegel-Jahrbuch* (1976), 113–21.

Pateman, C. *The Problem of Political Obligation.* New York: Wiley, 1979.

Popper, Karl. "What is Dialectic?" *Mind* 49 (1940), 403–26.

———. *The Open Society and Its Enemies.* Vol. 2. *The High Tide of Prophecy: Hegel, Marx and the Aftermath.* London: Routledge and Kegan Paul, 1944–45.

Russell, Bertrand. *History of Western Philosophy and Its Connection with Political and Social Circumstances from the Earliest Times to the Present Day.* London: George Allen & Unwin Ltd., 1961.

———. *Philosophy and Politics.* London: Cambridge University Press, 1947.

———. *Unpopular Essays.* London: Allen and Unwin, 1950.

———. "Logic as the Essence of Philosophy." In *Readings on Logic.* Edited by I. M. Copi and A. Gould. New York: Macmillan, 1972.

Ryle, Gilbert. "Critical Notice." *Mind* 55 (1947): 167–72.

Shirer, William Lawrence. *The Rise and Fall of the Third Reich.* London: Secker and Warburg, 1961.

Stace, W. T. *The Philosophy of Hegel.* New York: Dover, 1955.

Topitsch, Ernst. *Die Sozialphilosophie Hegels als Heilslehre und Herrschaftsideologie.* Neuwied: Luchterhand, 1967.

Viereck, Peter. *Meta-Politics.* New York: Capricorn, 1965.

2. Critics of the Hegel Myths

Ahrweiler, Georg. "Der Stellenwert faschistischer Hegel-Rezeption in der aktuellen Hegel-Kritik." *Hegel-Jahrbuch* (1977–78), 343–48.

Avineri, Shlomo. *Hegel and the Modern State.* Cambridge: Cambridge University Press, 1972.

Besnier, Jean-Michel. "Le droit international chez Kant et Hegel." *Archives de Philosophie du Droit* 32 (1987), 85–99.

Black, Edward. "Hegel on War." *Monist* 57 (1973), 570–83.

Breton, Stanislas. "Réel et rationnel dans la philosophie hégélienne." In *La crise de la raison dans la pensée contemporaine.* Edmond Barbotin, et al. Paris-Bruge: Desclée de Brouwer, 1960. 213–15.

Dohrmann, Ralf, and Christoph Stein. "Der Begriff des Krieges bei Hegel und Clausewitz." *Hegel-Jahrbuch* (1984–85), 341–60.

Esposito, Joseph L. "Hegel, Absolute Knowledge, and the End of History." *Clio* 12 (1983), 355–65.

Findlay, John. *The Philosophy of Hegel: An Introduction and Re-Examination.* New York: Collier, 1962.

Glockner, Hermann. "Thesis, Antithesis, Synthesis oder Ein-und-Andere, das Ganze und das Eine." In his *Beiträge zum Verständnis und zur Kritik Hegels.* *Hegel-Studien.* Vol. 2. Bonn: Bouvier, 1965. 135–41.

Grégoire, Franz. "Hegel et la primauté respective de la raison et du rationnel." *Revue néoscholastique de philosophie* 43 (1945), 252–64.

Harris, H. S. "Hegel and the French Revolution." *Clio* 7 (1977), 5–18.

Lucas, Hans-Christian. "Philosophie und Wirklichkeit: Einige Bemerkungen wider die Legende von Hegel als preußischem Staatsphilosophen." *Zeitschrift für Didaktik der Philosophie* 9 (1987) 154–61.

Lucas, Hans-Christian, and Udo Rameil. "Furcht vor der Zensur?" *Hegel-Studien* 15 (1980), 63–93.

Maurer, Reinhard Klemens. *Hegel und das Ende der Geschichte.* Stuttgart, Berlin: Kohlhammer, 1965; 2d ed., Freiburg: Karl Alber, 1980.

Merlan, Philipp. "Ist die 'These-Antithese-Synthese'-Formel unhegelisch?" *Archiv für die Geschichte der Philosophie* 53 (1971), 35–40.

Mitias, Howard P. "Hegel on International Law." *Clio* 9 (1980), 269–81. Also in *Perspektiven der Philosophie* 10 (1984), 37–51.

Mueller, Gustav E. *Hegel: The Man, His Vision and Work.* New York: Pageant Press, 1968.

Nederman, Cary J. "Sovereignty, War and the Corporation: Hegel on the Medieval Foundation of the Modern State." *Journal of Politics* 49 (1987), 500–520.

Paolucci, Henry. "Hegel and the Nation State System of International Relations." In *Hegel's Social and Political Thought.* Edited by Donald Phillip Verene. Atlantic Highlands: Humanities Press, 1980, 155–66.

Philonenko, Alexis. "Éthique et guerre dans la pensée de Hegel." *Guerres et Paix* 4 (1969), 7–18.

Reuvers, Hans-Bert. "Dialektik von Krieg und Frieden." *Annalen der Internationalen Gesellschaft für Dialektische Philosophie* 1 (1983), 182–90.

Roth, Michael S. "A Problem of Recognition: Alexandre Kojève and the End of History." *History and Theory* 24 (1985), 293–306.

Rothe, Barbara, and Andrée Törpe. "Das Wesen des Krieges bei Hegel und Clausewitz." *Deutsche Zeitschrift für Philosophie* 25 (1977), 1331–43.

Schmitz, Kenneth. "Hegel on War and Peace." In *Conceptions de la paix dans l'histoire de la philosophie.* Edited by Venant Caucy. Montreal: Éditions Montmorency, 1987. 127–40.

Seeberger, Wilhelm "Vorurteile gegen Hegel." In his *Hegel oder die Entwicklung des Geistes zur Freiheit.* Stuttgart: Ernst Klett, 1961.

Smith, Constance I. "Hegel on War." *Journal of the History of Ideas* 26 (1965), 282–85.

Smith, S. B. "Hegel's Views on War, the State and International Relations." *American Political Science Review* 77 (1982), 624–32.

Solomon, Robert C. "Teaching Hegel." *Teaching Philosophy* 2 (1977–78), 213–24.

Sönkel, Wolfgang. "Hegel und der Krieg." *Hegel-Jahrbuch* (1988), 242–50.

ten Bruggencate, H. G. "Hegel's Views on War." *Philosophical Quarterly* 1 (1950), 58–60.

Trott zu Solz, Adam von. *Hegels Staatsphilosophie und das internationale Recht.* Göttingen: Vandenhoeck und Ruprecht, 1967.

Wroblewski, Jerzy. "Racionalidad de la realidad en la filosofía del derecho de Hegel y el dualismo de ser y deber." *Diálogos* 5 (1968), 35–53.